SPIRITUAL ASTROLOGY

SPIRITUAL ASTROLOGY
A PATH TO DIVINE AWAKENING

JAN SPILLER AND KAREN McCOY

ATRIA PAPERBACK

New York   London   Toronto   Sydney   New Delhi

An Imprint of Simon & Schuster, Inc.
1230 Avenue of the Americas
New York, NY 10020

This Atria Paperback edition October 2019

ATRIA PAPERBACK and colophon are trademarks of Simon & Schuster, Inc.

For information about special discounts for bulk purchases,
please contact Simon & Schuster Special Sales at 1-866-506-1949 or
business@simonandschuster.com

The Simon & Schuster Speakers Bureau can bring authors to your live event.
For more information or to book an event, contact the Simon & Schuster
Speakers Bureau at 1-866-248-3049 or visit our website at
www.simonspeakers.com.

Designed by Lisa Stokes

Manufactured in the United States of America

17   19   20   18

Library of Congress Cataloging-in-Publication Data

ISBN 978-1-4165-9951-7
ISBN 978-1-4391-2420-8 (ebook)

My work on this book is dedicated to those spiritual forces available in the world today that gave us the insights we needed, and to the people everywhere whose inner beauty inspired our love and created the space for this book to be written.

Jan Spiller

I want to dedicate my work on part 2 of this book to my son, John McCoy, for all the nights he fixed himself soup and tuna fish, screened telephone calls, and ran interference for Jan and me while we used our time together to work on the book. Thanks, John, for all your support, encouragement, and patience. You are truly my greatest blessing. I love you.

Mom (Karen McCoy)

CONTENTS

ACKNOWLEDGMENTS

PART 1 OF this volume would have been impossible without the loving support and encouragement of my ex-husband, Steven Spiller. I would also like to acknowledge the late Kerry Tinney for his participation in the early formation of part 1. As the initial coauthor he helped to supply the traditional information regarding the planets and their effects.

My heartfelt thanks go to Ray and Debby Merriman of Seek-It Publications in Birmingham, Michigan, for believing in me and for being willing to release publication rights on part 1 so it could reach a wider public with a larger publishing company. I would also like to acknowledge Debra Burrell of the New York School of Astrology in Manhattan for inviting me to New York and prodding me to reach greater horizons.

Much appreciation to editors Alan Maislen, Judith Horton, Bill Williams, and Jack Pettey for their ability to clarify the meaning while keeping the integrity of the material intact. The difference a talented editor can make in bridging the gap between writer and reader is enormous. Thanks also to Henry Seltzer of www.astrograph.com for providing the tables used at the back of this book.

I want especially to recognize my coauthor on part 2, Karen McCoy. Her pioneering research into the effect of the eclipses on individual destiny has given an added dimension to the field of astrology.

JAN SPILLER

THERE ARE SOME very special people I want to thank whose influence and assistance have been instrumental to the success of this project.

My original astrology teacher, Suzie Carrson, taught me more than astrology; she taught me to listen to my inner voice first and *then* to investigate.

I want to acknowledge my indebtedness to one of the finest astrologers and metaphysicians I've had the pleasure to know, Mr. Robert (Buz) Myers, who introduced me to the theory of the eclipses. When I shared my research findings with Buz and thanked him for the spark, he said to pass the thanks on to the spark's originator, the late Robert Jansky.

I would also like to thank Julia Wright, Mimi Donner Levine, and Diane and Jerry Church, special friends without whose love, support, and time this book could never have been written.

Finally, a very special thanks to my partner and friend, Jan Spiller, for her faith and determination.

KAREN P. MCCOY

PART 1

THE PLANETS, SIGNS, AND HOUSES

Jan Spiller

INTRODUCTION TO PART 1

YOU ARE TOTALLY unique. Mathematically, a birth chart is not duplicated for twenty-five thousand years. This is because all the planets are traveling at different speeds around the Sun, and it takes more than twenty-five thousand years for all of them to line up the same way twice. Consequently, in terms of the astrology chart, each individual is totally unique. Astrology is not a study of general truth but rather a key to specific information that can unlock the knowledge of your unique inner self.

The common denominators all astrologers use are the mathematically calculated positions of the planets, signs, and houses. The "aspects"—depicting the energetic relationship between the planets in an individual's chart—are also used.

There are as many different approaches to interpreting the astrology chart as there are astrologers. This is because each of us is unique, and the astrologer brings the dimension of herself or himself to the science and to the interpretation of the basic symbols. The meaning of the birth chart is filtered through the astrologer's biases and basic outlook on life. For this reason, the validation of your inner self—your "sense" of what is true for you—is the ultimate judge of the accuracy and completeness of the insights offered you. This is also the case with psychiatry, psychology, and any of the other social science approaches dealing with understanding the uniqueness of a human being.

Astrologers focus on different things when they look at a birth chart. Consequently, I wish to share some basic premises I hold about life—my biases—so that you will know the filter through which this information is being presented.

FATE VERSUS FREE WILL

Many people believe that everything in astrology is predestined, that free will is precluded. In fact, quite the opposite is true. The astrology chart is simply a picture of the inner person, just as the physical body is a picture of the outer person.

Without boundaries, there is no free will or choice; there is nothing to choose between. In that sense your astrology chart, which shows a picture of your inner self, is set or predestined in the same way that your body is set or predestined at the moment of your birth. Your physical body, though it grows and matures, remains essentially the same. It is still your body, unique from all others, and the only body you have.

In the same way, the astrology chart pictures your intangible body, your inner world, unique from everyone else on Earth, and the only internal wiring you have to work with. The tangible aspects of a person, the body, can be seen physically. The intangible aspects, the individual being within the body, can be seen in the graph of the astrology chart.

It is in how you use what you have that free will, or choice, enters in. Physically, you are aware of choice. You know what actions lead inevitably to pain, and if you do not want pain, you do not do those actions. On the intangible level, the guideposts are just as inevitable, yet not as obvious, except through graphs that can display your internal wiring, such as astrology.

For example, if you were to start your automobile, accelerate to forty miles per hour, and drive into a brick wall, you know that would inevitably lead to pain. There is no way of getting around it; pain would be an unavoidable consequence of taking that action.

On the other hand, on the intangible level, each of us is continually putting into motion factors that inevitably lead to experiencing pain, emotionally, mentally, even physically. The only difference is that when it is not strictly physical pain, you are not as aware of the connection between cause and consequence. Astrology is a means of logically becoming aware of that connection on the intangible levels. Psychologically, you are doing things just as foolish as driving a car into a brick wall and then wondering what went wrong. Why isn't life supporting you? I use astrology as a means for objectively getting in touch with brick walls for myself and others.

I'd like to share with you what I'm actually doing with astrology. I'm interested in experiencing happiness while on Earth, so for me astrology is a tool, not an end in itself. It is a tool that can unlock self-knowledge and that relaxes the mind, thereby allowing your natural light and love from within to arise.

THE SOURCE OF HAPPINESS

To achieve consistent happiness, you need to discover the laws of happiness and begin to cooperate with them rather than resist them. The most important thing to notice: All the joy you have ever experienced has been felt in one place only—inside your own heart. Personal happiness is a by-product of the times when your mind is centered inside your heart, the source of happiness. When your mind is resting in your heart, you're happy because you're home.

Certain materialistic experiences, common to most of us, can *temporarily* produce an experience of happiness. One is falling in love or infatuation. Before you fall in love, your mind runs around telling you, "If only I get this, then I'll be happy"; "If only I get that, then I'll be happy"; "If only that person will go along with me, then I'll be happy." Then you fall in love. Since the mind is not programmed to handle love, as soon as you feel it, love "pops" your mind from its attachment to the world, back into your heart center (where it is naturally attached), and for a while you're happy because you're "home."

Now we all know that the happiness you experienced when you were in love had nothing to do with the other person, because if he or she stays around long enough, the mind tries to change the other person. The moment it does that, it leaves the heart center and the restlessness, the sense that something is "missing," comes back.

Other materialistic experiences can temporarily produce happiness: reaching a goal or purchasing a possession. But again your happiness is temporary. The restlessness resumes and your mind goes out to acquire more. There's always the incompleteness, the feeling that something has to happen for you to be happy again.

A moment of beauty in nature, or seeing someone do something nice for someone else, with no motive for personal gain, can temporarily produce joy as your mind is surprised and flies back into your heart. But then you walk a little farther down the street and see a neighbor kicking a dog, and your mind makes a judgment. The moment it does that, it leaves your heart center, and the unhappiness, the vague dissatisfaction, returns.

So experiencing happiness has to do with getting your mind to go into your heart center and remain there. Then you can do whatever you like—experience romantic love, make lots of money, do all the things that are happy and fun. But everything is approached from a feeling of lightness, of "play," because you already have what you need: that feeling of consistent internal well-being.

CONSISTENT HAPPINESS

There are three techniques that I used that have resulted in consciously experiencing Love on a consistent basis.

MEDITATION AND ENLIGHTENED SPIRITUAL TEACHERS

On a daily basis, meditation takes your mind out of its habit of preoccupation with the world, turns it inward to your heart, and gently says: "Here's where the happiness is; it's inside, not outside." And little by little your mind begins to get the idea.

With proper meditation, the power of contacting reality within yourself for even twenty minutes a day grows so strong that you can spend the remaining twenty-three hours and forty minutes out in the world without losing the feeling of assurance and inner joy that begins to arise within you.

Keeping company with enlightened spiritual teachers—through reading, CDs, gatherings, or retreats—was also part of my path. In my own case, I followed the teachings of Ramana Maharshi.

SONG LYRICS: THE VALUE OF RUNNING EXPERIMENTS

Learning truth without applying it in your daily life is merely an intellectual experience. In my own case, I began writing songs while on the spiritual path, and the lyrics provided a road map for how to apply the abstract truths into the daily situations I encountered. The books I have written are also filled with practical experiments for each sign to run in daily life that can break through old, self-limiting patterns of behavior.

ASTROLOGY AND SELF-EXAMINATION

Socrates said the unexamined life is not worth living. From that perspective, why does your mind go outward to begin with? When you were in love, why did your mind go out and try to change the other person? When you reached a goal, why did your mind go out and immediately try to reach another one? When you had a high meditation or when you were in a good mood, why could somebody push your buttons and send you out again?

The answers have to do with basic imbalances inside your mind itself that are karmic, stemming from past patterns and tendencies. Astrology is the fastest, most precise technique I know for getting in touch with those imbalances on an individual basis and making the corrections. Because each of us is so totally unique, working with the individual astrology chart empowers you to see the overall patterns in your own life that are seeking to be examined and corrected so you can achieve permanent happiness.

You can learn about these patterns through understanding the relationships between your planets, signs, and houses. As each of these factors are understood and purified individually, your entire inner structure becomes harmonized and resolved. When your ego is calmed it relaxes, and the natural light from within you can shine forth.

MAKING THE INTANGIBLES TANGIBLE

The astrology chart is a mathematical graph showing the inner person and where the individual needs to manifest potential outwardly in order to experience satisfaction inwardly. We all want to be happy, yet there are no magic rules that lead to happiness for everyone.

For example, a person whose Moon is in Cancer can find emotional security through establishing a deep, intimate connection with another; a person whose Moon is in Libra finds emotional security through establishing a sense of harmonious cooperation in relationships. What works for one person does not work for another. The idea is to get in touch with what works for you. It is in recognizing and respecting the differences between us that individual happiness and satisfaction can be obtained in a realistic way.

LASTING VICTORY

This book is written to clarify your internal wiring so you can achieve victory in those areas of life that are important to you. In this context, winning is defined by what works—what produces happiness, joy, an increased level of clear energy. Losing is what does not work—what produces unhappiness and a lowering of energy.

Consequently, this book is written in the context of "unconscious expression" and "conscious expression," how to lose and how to win. When I refer to victory, I do not mean at somebody's else's expense, but victory over one's own self-sabotaging patterns. When you defeat them and emerge victorious over those fears and behaviors that kept you limited and miserable, not only do you win, but your personal victory reverberates and is felt and by everyone on the planet. In clearing out your own energy, you do your part to help your fellow beings.

PAIN VERSUS SUFFERING

Pain is inevitable, suffering is a choice. For example, when I had major surgery for a liver transplant, pain was part of the experience. My body felt pain; there was no choice. But for me to say: "Woe is me! Why did this happen to me? How did I get hepatitis C? God doesn't love me. . . ." and go on and on—that is suffering. It prolongs the perceived negativity of the experience. It is a waste of time and precious life force. It also makes recovery more difficult.

Every experience life hands us—every challenge—has good behind it that outweighs the difficulty in going through it. In the above example, it changed my life and my values, and I wouldn't have avoided going through it for anything. Losing the experience means losing the gifts the experience brought.

UNCONSCIOUS EXPRESSION AND
CONSCIOUS EXPRESSION

Each of the planets is divided into the "unconscious expression" and "conscious expression" categories as they travel through each of the signs.

The unconscious expression is a picture of past-life tendencies that without awareness you will continue to enact. This section describes habitual responses that result in personal defeat and isolation from inner joy. The conscious expression suggests the purification process that can provide the antidote for the specific past-life self-defeating tendency. Unconsciousness is like a dark room. Turn the light on and the darkness is dissolved. Once the unconsciousness is exposed, the light from your inner self will dissolve it. Once clearly seen, it can be released and you can make a new choice.

As you read the unconscious expression category, the corresponding unconsciousness is stimulated and rises to the surface to be released. It's okay to feel unsettled after reading the unconscious expression condition. In fact, it is appropriate. The degree to which you allow yourself to feel totally hopeless when reading the unconscious expression condition is the depth to which the unconsciousness can be cleared out and released. It will be replaced with a sense of inner freedom and ease as you read the conscious expression description that reveals new options.

As you begin actively practicing in your daily life one or more of the approaches outlined in the conscious expression category (with the appropriate planet and sign placement in your individual birth chart), you will find yourself less affected by environmental stimuli throwing you off your center of inner joy. A side benefit is that this focal point empowers you to take charge of your life—how you spend your time—rather than being buffeted around by the whims of others.

As you determine the location of each of your planets in the signs and houses, you are ready to read the unconscious expression and conscious expression descriptions of your internal wiring. You will also be able to better understand family members and friends. You can locate which signs your planets are in in part 3. Or you can obtain a free copy of your birth chart by going to www.janspiller.com. Click on the "Free Astrology Charts" icon on the home page.

The moment of your birth, which is what your chart is based on, is perfect and very carefully chosen on the spiritual level of your own soul. Your astrology chart defines precisely the path you need to follow in order to fulfill personal potential and gain the satisfaction of wholeness. It is, in terms of individual completeness, the map back home.

The idea is to have it all on a physical level by aligning and cooperating with the direction of your own internal energies. The purpose of this book is simply to show the choices for action in planets located in specific signs. It is then possible to exercise conscious free will within that framework.

REINCARNATION: TAKING CARE OF UNFINISHED BUSINESS

A belief in reincarnation is not necessary to receive practical value from this book. Again, so that you may know my biases, I accept the idea of reincarnation, since it provides a larger context for viewing current personality complications.

The moment of your birth was not an accident. You are not a victim of your birth chart, and it is not a matter beyond your control. I view the planets, signs, houses, and aspects in the birth chart as totally perfect and appropriate for the individual involved; it is exactly what your soul needs for completion and happiness. The chart is a scientific picture of the life that your soul has chosen as a process for your own growth.

RUNNING EXPERIMENTS TO DISCOVER TRUTH

None of us break ancient patterns of unconsciousness all at once. It's a process, a game of choosing to do things a little differently, with a little more awareness of what's going on, step by step. It's gradual. Take one aspect and run the experiment of expressing that area of yourself differently in daily situations. See what happens. It's an enlivening kind of research.

The idea is to use what works, what produces increased happiness and ease in your relationship with others and with life. Your soul is the only entity with your total records, and you are the only one who knows what things are true for you. For this reason, your inner self is the ultimate judge of the completeness and accuracy of the insights offered here. With some planetary descriptions you may feel a sense of "Yes, that's exactly how I experience it," and with others there may be no immediate recognition. You are the authority. What is leading to productive and nonproductive results for you? Your practical experience is the best measurement.

HOW TO USE PART 1

THE ASTROLOGY CHART is a mathematical graph depicting the exact location of each of the planets at the moment of your birth. Although systems for interpreting the astrology chart vary, all astrologers work with the four basic components: planets, signs, houses, and aspects.

THE PLANETS: THE TEN BASIC INTERNAL URGES

Astrology uses ten planets (Pluto is still included as a planet by astrologers), and we all have these same ten planets in our birth chart. The sign and house in which each planet is located is what varies with the individual.

The planets represent ten basic, distinct human urges we all experience on an internal level. An urge refers to the desire to express and/or experience a specific, unique energy (love, security, self-expression, vitality, etc.). Even though we all feel these urges, the path to fulfilling them is different for each of us, as indicated by the signs and houses where our planets are located. It's as if we all have these ten different domains inside us, and each planet rules its own realm of experience.

For example, you and I both have the planet Mars located somewhere in our birth charts. Regardless of the sign or the house it falls in, Mars always represents the urge to initiate action and move toward a goal. However, the path we take to fulfill this urge and the area of life where we take action will vary depending on the sign and the house where Mars is found.

For a more detailed description of these ten basic urges the planets represent, please read the planet descriptions at the beginning of each chapter.

Each of the ten planets is represented in astrology by a symbol, or glyph. If you have a copy of your birth chart, you will notice that there are ten glyphs drawn inside the circle of the chart (or see the sample chart on page 14). The following is a list of the glyphs for each of the ten planets.

PLANET		SYMBOL OR GLYPH
Sun	=	☉
Moon	=	☽
Mercury	=	☿
Venus	=	♀
Mars	=	♂
Jupiter	=	♃
Saturn	=	♄
Uranus	=	♅
Neptune	=	♆
Pluto	=	♇

THE SIGNS: SHADINGS OF THE BASIC URGES

There are twelve signs in astrology, corresponding to twelve of the major constellations of the zodiac. As the planets travel around the Sun, each planet moves at a different speed through the constellations. Astronomy calculates the mathematical location of the planets in the heavens, relative to time and space. Astrology interprets those mathematical calculations as they affect life on Earth.

Although we all share the same ten basic human urges, the way we experience them—and the path we take to fulfill them—is different for each of us. This is determined by the specific sign in which each planet is located. The signs modify the planets, filtering the basic energy through their own "mood" or "tone" that will characterize your experience of the planet or urge in question.

The sign shows the specific way that you, individually, need to express *and* fulfill the urge of each planet. And it is *only* by expressing the urge in question through the filter of the sign where the planet is located that natural fulfillment and completion are possible in that particular aspect of yourself.

For example, Venus represents the urge within each of us to experience a sense of our own individual worth. Yet if your Venus is located in the sign of Taurus, the process that leads to self-worth is very different than if Venus is in the sign of Gemini at the moment of your birth. In Taurus, a sense of self-worth is established through a material and sensual process. In Gemini, self-worth is experienced and strengthened through a social communication process. Part 1 discusses this specific process for fulfillment of each planet's urges in each of the signs.

To determine the sign in which each of your planets was located at the moment of your birth, consult the tables in part 3, or go to www.janspiller .com. Click on "Free Astrology Charts" on the home page, follow the steps, and a chart will be provided for you free of charge. Once you find the sign in which each planet falls, you can consult part 1 to gain information on the significance of each planet when located in each specific sign.

The following is a list of the twelve signs of the heavenly constellations and the equivalent astrological symbol, or glyph, for each sign:

SIGN		SYMBOL OR GLYPH
Aries	=	♈
Taurus	=	♉
Gemini	=	♊
Cancer	=	♋
Leo	=	♌
Virgo	=	♍
Libra	=	♎
Scorpio	=	♏
Sagittarius	=	♐
Capricorn	=	♑
Aquarius	=	♒
Pisces	=	♓

THE HOUSES: WHERE THE DRAMA IS PLAYED OUT

The astrology chart has twelve houses, and each of your planets is located in one of them. The houses are mathematically calculated according to your individual time, date, and place of birth. If you have a complete birth chart that includes your planets in the houses, locate the house for each of your planets by using the list of planets and their symbols found earlier in this section.

Look for the Sun and its corresponding symbol in your birth chart, and notice in which of the twelve houses it resides. Once you have located the house for each of your planets, read the description located at the end of each planet's section in part 1. (See the house descriptions list, page 13.)

The houses denote the areas of life in which you tangibly experience the energy of each planet in its specific sign. For example, if Venus is located in the 3rd house of your birth chart, you can most directly notice the issue of self-worth (Venus) during the process of communication (3rd house). If Venus is located in your 6th house, you feel the issue of self-worth (Venus) when interacting with your coworkers or on the job (6th house). Each house shows the area of your life in the external world in which you will most vividly experience the urge indicated by the planet(s) located there.

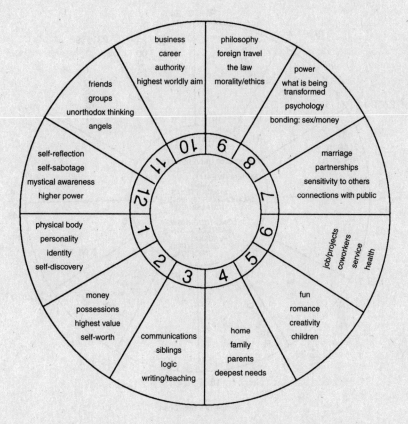

THE ASPECTS: PREDISPOSITION TO EASE OR DIFFICULTY IN SOME AREAS OF LIFE

The aspects show the energetic relationship within you between the basic human urges—as represented by the planets—that we all share. For example, if the planet Venus (self-worth/love) is in square aspect (ninety degrees apart) to the planet Mars (assertiveness/sex) in your birth chart, you will feel a conflict between love and sex.

For instance, the people you are attracted to in terms of affection may not be the same people you are attracted to sexually. However, if the same two planetary urges are in a trine aspect (120 degrees apart) in your birth chart, inwardly you are at ease with the idea of having both love and sex in the same relationship. For more information on the aspects, see page 192.

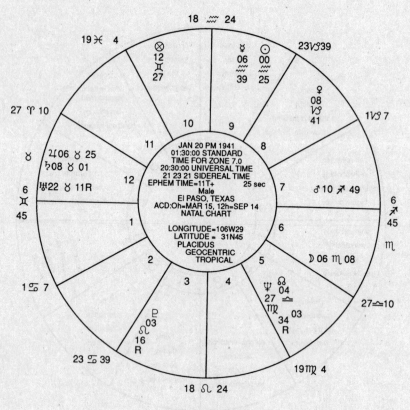

Sample of a Birth Chart

THE PLANETS IN
THE SIGNS AND HOUSES

SUN: KEY TO FULL SELF-EXPRESSION

THE SUN IN the birth chart:*

- Signifies power and talent; shows your individual, creative style of self-expression and leadership.
- Defines the key for manifesting personal power and talent in ways that inspire others to express their creativity. Unites your leadership abilities with theirs, promoting feelings of fellowship and love for all.
- Reveals how you may unconsciously express personal power in a way that sparks resentment from others.
- Conveys self-expression by divine right, showing that area of life where your talents can be spontaneously expressed.
- Denotes how you can increase your vitality through the instinctive expression of the warmth and strength of your nature.
- Indicates in what area you need to express yourself spontaneously in order to attain and maintain personal liveliness.
- Discloses the area of radiance, creativity, and greatest childlike joy where your talents for the contributing to the well-being of others reflects your natural ability for benevolent expression.

UNCONSCIOUS EXPRESSION VERSUS CONSCIOUS EXPRESSION

Choices, Not Absolutes

The unconscious expression and conscious expression descriptions are not intended to denote absolute states. When you are in the *unconscious expression*

---

*To discover the sign and house your SUN is located in, go to www.janspiller.com and a free chart will be calculated for you.

state, you are encountering resistance, lacking new movement, and feeling nonproductive. When you are in the *conscious expression* state, you feel powerful, confident, and productive.

None of us is in the conscious expression mode all the time. This state describes a means of experimentation, making different choices in expression that can lead to a more satisfying result. The degree to which you can accept the unconscious expression description in a nonjudgmental way is the degree to which you are open to receive conscious expression energies as a transforming agent.

The Sun signs have received by far the most attention by modern astrology writers. Many fine, in-depth studies of Sun behavior are already available, so this discussion of the Sun is purposely kept brief. What is dealt with is the primary choice that the Sun offers, regardless of sign: to use your vital energies to demand center stage and attention from others; or to use those gifts to give others center stage, empowering them by radiating your own Sun power, according to the nature of the sign.

SUN IN ARIES

You feel you have the right:
- To do as you please;
- To display independent action and thought;
- To act upon a whim without regard for protocol, timing, or the wishes or opinions of others.

UNCONSCIOUS EXPRESSION

Asleep focus: Gaining recognition for your independence from others.

Risk: You may unknowingly act in ways that result in disruption and alienation in relationships.

Result: Wanting to be recognized as your own person, you can resist cooperating in team efforts. When you behave with rashness and lack of consideration, you experience other people blocking your path of action.

Thus, using your natural independence to dominate by insisting that others put you first can result in lack of confidence when they fail to respond.

CONSCIOUS EXPRESSION

With a new focus: Sharing your talents and courageous nature.

Result: You notice how your independent action can be an inspiration to others. Being aware of this natural leadership, you can encourage them to express their independence. Thus, you eliminate the need for constant battle.

Recognizing your gift for contributing a quick, courageous assertion of your positive spirit empowers you to inspire others. You are now free to exit on the desired positive note. Awareness of this impact allows you to express your exuberance in ways that endear you to others. Then you will find they respond with love and appreciation for your dynamic energy.

SUN IN TAURUS

You feel you have the right:
- To actualize your material and sensual values and never change them;
- To accumulate a comfortable level of material security;
- To establish rigid, fixed, *nonmaterialistic* values;
- To opt for a stubborn passivity in including the talents of others.

UNCONSCIOUS EXPRESSION

Asleep focus: Gaining agreement from others on the validity of your tangible, material values.
Risk: You may appear stubborn and intractable.
Result: By giving in to a tendency to want to be recognized as worthwhile and important, you can resist the efforts of others to expand your position by adding their input.

You can be totally dedicated to establishing your merit by accumulating money and goods. When this happens and you fail to consider the values of others, you cheat yourself of the opportunity to expand your material security and comfort.

CONSCIOUS EXPRESSION

With a new focus: Uplifting others with your talents and abilities.
Result: Others can respond by sharing their own values. By giving them center stage and encouraging them in establishing their own worth, you give yourself the opportunity to become more objective about your values. From this objectivity, you can create an even deeper sense of security in relationships.

You revitalize your worth as you recognize the worth of others. Being conscious of their values expands your material security in the world.

SUN IN GEMINI

You feel you have the right:
- To experience the superficial variety in life;
- To change your mind frequently;
- To dance over the surface of existence.

UNCONSCIOUS EXPRESSION

Asleep focus: Gaining a quick, superficial interaction with others through stimulating conversation.

Risk: You may appear unable to maintain deep friendships.

Result: Indulging in a tendency toward superficiality can create a shallow life experience without your realizing it. If you want to be recognized as quick-witted and congenial, you may tend to talk in a manner others don't trust. You may become a gadfly, refusing to discuss personal feelings or matters of depth, impatient with profound thinking and looking for fast, logical insights.

This style of expression can cause loved ones to mistrust your spontaneity and yearn to impose restrictions on you.

CONSCIOUS EXPRESSION

With a new focus: Uplifting others with your ability to think quickly.

Result: Now you show your knack for expressing a lighthearted, friendly approach. You have a gift for creating a feeling of ease in tense or serious circumstances. By giving others the opportunity to communicate, you let them share the depths of their feelings, knowledge, and goals.

Then you can respond in an open-minded way that enhances the congeniality of the moment. By listening, you expand your viewpoints and opportunities to connect with others on a broader range of ideas.

When you become conscious of others' ideas, you inspire them to enjoy and see value in a variety of experiences. This leads to mutual love and appreciation. Accepting other people's points of view—encouraging a two-way flow of ideas—increases your vitality.

SUN IN CANCER

You feel you have the right:
- To be emotionally self-centered;
- To be pampered by others;

- To be motherly to a fault;
- To demand that others respect your sensitivity.

UNCONSCIOUS EXPRESSION

Asleep focus: You focus your attention on yourself.
Risk: You may expect others to react so that they never injure your sensitivities.
Result: You can appear hypersensitive, moody, and self-protective. When you yearn to be recognized for your sensitivity, you may demand that others constantly stay aware of your every mood. You may require any intimacy to center around your feelings. This makes others feel alienated, since they cannot share themselves without fear of your defensive reaction.

You might be so dedicated to protecting your vulnerability, the slightest input can make you withdraw into your shell.

CONSCIOUS EXPRESSION

With a new focus: Sharing your talent for emotional perception with others.
Result: Now you can care for and about them. Simultaneously, you become more objective and content with your feelings. The idea is to use your natural sensitivity to recognize the emotional pain of others. This recognition empowers you to inspire them, and yourself, through your sympathetic understanding of their distress.

By giving others center stage to express their feelings and vulnerabilities, you empathize with their suffering and your vitality increases. Others appreciate your intuitive, loving nature.

By expressing your gifts for emotional perception in a way that serves others, you realize that your best security rests in caring for those *outside* yourself.

SUN IN LEO

You feel you have the right:
- To express yourself gloriously;
- To be noticed and admired just for being yourself;
- To be treated as someone special.

UNCONSCIOUS EXPRESSION

Asleep focus: Yourself, and gaining the admiration and attention of others.
Risk: You may expect others to react so that they never show disapproval.

Result: You may act in needlessly dramatic or understated or overstated ways. In the desire to be admired, you may subdue true emotional expression. This leads to empty displays of drama. You may fall into Leo traps: demanding attention, whether earned or not; being hypersensitive, taking criticism as a personal affront; and refusing input from others that could actually lead to a more powerful expression of your creative gifts.

Trying to obtain the attention and approval of others leads to compromising your own identity. This defeats the natural and healthy expression of your spontaneous, childlike ego.

CONSCIOUS EXPRESSION

With a new focus: Putting others on center stage and encouraging them.
Result: Now you can create warmth and sunshine. You experience your vitality and power as you recognize and uplift those around you. Your natural enthusiasm inspires the life in others by drawing them onto the stage. This dramatic ability can motivate them to become excited about themselves. When you consider yourself part of the team and truly seek to enrich and enhance those around you, you experience not only their magnificence but your own as well.

By acknowledging others' uniqueness, you let them occupy center stage. This gives you the objectivity needed for confidence to express yourself. Exemplifying childlike innocence and spontaneous vitality, your gift inspires others to express the radiance within themselves.

SUN IN VIRGO

You feel you have the right:
- To be right;
- To discriminate; to analyze and criticize yourself and others;
- To be acknowledged for your righteousness.

UNCONSCIOUS EXPRESSION

Asleep focus: Wanting others to recognize your righteousness and purity.
Risk: You may unconsciously behave in stuffy, prudish, puritanical, compulsively ordered, haughty ways. To be acknowledged, you may elicit judgment on right and wrong, using your analytical ability to appear important and set apart from others.
Result: In proving your ultimate rightness, you may use your finely honed

critical talents to point out your own flaws. This backfires, resulting in a lack of confidence in your own spontaneity. You may also point out the flaws in others, according to a value system of rigid rules for perfect behavior. When others don't appreciate or understand your good intentions, you are surprised.

Indulging in a tendency toward compulsive self-righteousness can scatter and deplete your energy, disrupting the focus and self-confidence you need to act.

CONSCIOUS EXPRESSION

With a new focus: Uplifting others through your talent for creating order and healing.
Result: Now you notice how you can truly serve others without having to feel right about it. Recognizing the inherent worth of others gives you trust in your vision of their perfection. This frees you to contribute in a way that effectively supports them. When you expose others to your perception of their inherent value, they appreciate your desire to serve. This reinforces mutual self-worth.

By being aware of others' personal plans, you can motivate them to achieve what they want. This success increases their vitality and sense of well-being. When you place serving others above your judgment of whether or not it's the right thing to do, you can abandon rules and regulations. This results in self-trust, allowing you to act spontaneously in a way that automatically works to facilitate any situation.

If you are aware that your intentions are truly pure, your motivation for acting rightly is fulfilled.

SUN IN LIBRA

You feel you have the right:
- To develop harmonious relationships;
- To know what others want;
- To be treated fairly.

UNCONSCIOUS EXPRESSION

Asleep focus: Wanting others to recognize you as fair and harmonious.
Risk: Temptation to behave in ways that are compromising and manipulative. You may act like "Mr. or Ms. Nice Person" and naively expect others

to respond the same way. When you use good manners to get your way, your manipulations create only an artificial harmony.

Result: If your attention is on achieving a positive image of yourself, it leads to indulging in a tendency to play tit-for-tat games. This puts you in situations where others can manipulate your integrity just by convincing you that you're being treated fairly and getting an equal portion.

When you let yourself become lost in the realm of cooperatively sharing ideas, you may not realize that whatever you do to control others, others can also do to you.

CONSCIOUS EXPRESSION

With a new focus: Uplifting others through sharing talents.

Result: Now you can enliven social situations by contributing to the inherent harmony. You add the missing ingredient: your independent point of view. By trusting the overall picture, you intuitively perceive your ability to interject your ideas of justice and fair play into situations. This occurs in a spontaneous way that brings about a higher level of cooperation but does not offend.

By recognizing your ability to bring a larger truth into a situation, you are able to contribute your ideas of justice, fairness, and harmony. This sharing increases your vitality and well-being.

You can create true harmony in relationships through willingness to communicate the full truth of what you're experiencing. This integrity establishes a higher harmony.

Instead of trying to manipulate others into a state of false harmony, you use your gifts to establish good relationships by facing the existing harmonies and disharmonies with acceptance and objectivity. This frees you to share your intuitive sense of fair play with others.

SUN IN SCORPIO

You feel you have the right:
- To possess, investigate, and control;
- To search out the secret desires and needs of others.

UNCONSCIOUS EXPRESSION

Asleep focus: Getting a reaction from others that reflects your power.

Risk: You may instigate conflicts, merely as a cheap thrill and test of your dominance.

Result: This alienates those closest to you. If you covertly insist that others recognize your ultimate strength, you may become impatient and insecure when they don't offer you the deference you expect. When your potency is not acknowledged, you can become angry and demand attention through an inappropriate provocation.

Scorpio's unpredictable, sharp responses may be emotional and destructive. Indulging in agitating others leads to their mistrust and wariness in including you on the core levels you want most.

There is a tendency to rely on inciting others as a means of validating and measuring your power and control by their responses. This can lead to a type of self-expression that defeats your independence.

CONSCIOUS EXPRESSION

With a new focus: Uplifting others by putting them in touch with their own power.
Result: Now you can express your power in a constructive way, vital for both parties. Revealing your perceptions of another person's inner thoughts and emotions allows you to feel significant participation and a fresh sense of being alive.

You inspire others when you validate your self-control by exposing those factors that can enable them to achieve the same self-mastery.

Be aware of the goals and ambitions of others. You can then contribute your perceptions effectively, in a way they can accept. This results in increased vitality and well-being. You give others the power to know you and to appreciate the power of your discernment, as you reveal the psychological insights that further their aims.

Seeing the foibles and hidden motivations in others can inspire you to help them become aware of their own deepest desires. You can then experience the satisfaction of your power to transform the lives of others constructively.

SUN IN SAGITTARIUS

You feel you have the right:
- To be free;
- To be the intellectual authority;
- To be acknowledged and appreciated as noble and deserving.

UNCONSCIOUS EXPRESSION

Asleep focus: Continually wanting others to acknowledge your intellectual superiority.

Risk: Your intellect may appear pompous and self-serving.

Result: Your communication may become directed toward proving your moral righteousness. Indulging in the need to be recognized for a broad mental perspective may make you focus on one area of perception. Then you might demand to be the focus of attention, whether you deserve it or not, spouting off your ideas. Thus you unknowingly alienate others by insisting that they agree with you. Consequently, when you refuse to add the factual input from others to your calculations, you lose the base you could expand upon.

When others don't agree with your conclusions, your vitality diminishes. This leads to losing contact with your ideals and sense of humanity. If you need others to acknowledge you as noble and deserving, you may only talk about action—distracting you from putting energy into accomplishing the action itself.

CONSCIOUS EXPRESSION

With a new focus: Inspiring others with your confidence in positive outcomes.

Result: Now you can effectively listen when others ask you questions. Then you're able to share relevant insights that others can appreciate. The idea is to take the gallant approach: Use your intellect to help others by showing your capacity to see their lives from a broader, more optimistic viewpoint. When you share beliefs that enhance other people's levels of self-trust, you effectively expand their faith in themselves, which leads to their acknowledging and appreciating your intellect.

Awareness of yourself as part of a larger community can empower you to express your perceptions in a spontaneous, loving way. This enhances the situation for all and increases your vitality and well-being. Consequently, when you use enthusiasm to recognize the significance of others and bring out *their* importance, you experience pride and a sense of responsibility as your reward.

SUN IN CAPRICORN

You feel you have the right:
- To authority;
- To govern and control others to establish order;
- To be respected for your achievements and position.

UNCONSCIOUS EXPRESSION

Asleep focus: Wanting others to recognize and respect your being in control.

Risk: You may use your authority to dominate those around you.

Result: If you become totally dedicated to appearing authoritative and earning approval for your achievements, you may neglect to use your talents to get the job done. Being in control and getting respect have become more important that actually accomplishing the task. You may also expect others to be *sensitive* to your ambitions, even as you are *insensitive* to theirs; when they don't offer the deference you expect, you turn defensive and critical.

If you want your coworkers to sanction your behavior as perfect, tensions may arise. There is a tendency to not use your organizational talents to benefit others, but solely to manipulate them into improving your social image.

Thus, your self-interest may require you to manage them constantly, in order to keep control. This can limit success and put a tremendous drain on your energy and vitality. You'll be left in a state of tense watchfulness.

CONSCIOUS EXPRESSION

With a new focus: Using your organizational abilities to encourage others.

Result: Now you can expand your sensitivity into areas where others are disorganized and could use your natural sense of order. As you effectively assist them, with an awareness of their feelings, you automatically get their respect without having to justify it. Recognizing the intangible order and perfection of things empowers you to plan on a material level with less tension.

Awareness of your emotional connection to the whole allows you to organize coworkers successfully. You can do this in a way that improves the situation and increases your vitality and well-being. In managing others more effectively to produce results that are in their best interests, you automatically gain their admiration for your executive abilities. This eliminates the need for further supervision. As you organize and delegate authority to get the job done most productively for all, your self-respect increases.

When your integrity comes to the fore, you stop looking for the regard of others to justify your position. A better bet is to forcefully channel your energy into accomplishing the task at hand—producing results that earn you lasting respect.

SUN IN AQUARIUS

You feel you have the right:
• To be different and unique;
• To be impersonal and objective in your search for individuality;
• To intellectualize the sensitivities of others.

UNCONSCIOUS EXPRESSION

Asleep focus: Public acknowledgment from others of your uniqueness.
Risk: You may enhance your ego but fail to contribute to the group or to individuals.
Result: You might want to be recognized as cooperative and fair, yet feel defensive about losing your identity in relationships. This can lead to responding erratically, disrupting and alienating others.

If, under the pretense of objectivity, you try to impress others with the certainty of your knowledge, you may become detached and insensitive to individuals or the group. If you become uncertain of your own wisdom in interplay with others, you lose vitality.

CONSCIOUS EXPRESSION

With a new focus: Inspiring others with relatively inventive insights.
Result: Now you realize that your knowledge is less important than the individuality of others. By letting them express their point of view, you can expand facets of your intelligence. Then you can share appropriate knowledge that contributes to mutual inspiration. When you use your objectivity in the framework of other people's sensitivities, your unique talents are enhanced.

Awareness of the power of your identity and natural independence allows you to share insights with balance. This revitalizes both you and the relationship. The idea is to recognize the power and willfulness of the free child within you. This gives you the clarity to handle relationships with a sense of humor and the perspective to relate peacefully to others.

You have the gift of viewing any situation objectively. Thus, you can inspire, enhance, and lead group activities without appearing dominating. This automatically leads to cooperation, since others feel included in the governing of the group.

SUN IN PISCES

You feel you have the right:
- To live in a dream world of ideals;
- To express your artistic or otherworldly talents;
- To disregard having a worldly ambition.

UNCONSCIOUS EXPRESSION

Asleep focus: Seeking an indulgent, sympathetic ear for your ideals.
Risk: You may appear impractical, untested, and irresponsible.
Result: If you want others to recognize your inherent goodness and compassion, you might unconsciously try to live up to their expectations. This causes a loss of values and a self-defeating process.

You might appear indecisive, hesitant, ambivalent, and lacking commitment to a particular goal or direction. This leads to experiencing the role of the destitute victim. Instead of pursuing your ideals, your sensitivity may respond to the psychological pull of others: You may try to be all things to all people, thereby sabotaging your self-worth and vitality.

You may not be aware of the difference between grandiose desires and realistic aspirations. If so, you may experience lack of fulfillment of your ideals.

CONSCIOUS EXPRESSION

With a new focus: Uplifting others with your sensitivity.
Result: Now you can become the mystic, the artist, the poet, the voice of humankind's spiritual and emotional ideals. By recognizing the need for practical, step-by-step methods to enact your ideals, you are empowered to commit yourself to express compassion for humanity in a tangible way. You do this through realistic channels that will beneficially inspire others.

By being aware of your resources for systematic implementation, you can express your visions in a solid or artistic form. Then you can assist, soothe, and heal others. This results in a feeling of universal belonging for all

The idea is to commit yourself to establishing with others the standards and values that you consider worthwhile. Then you can use your sensitivity to reveal their hidden desires and motivations, to combine with them ideals that can heal.

Your awareness of your own values enables you to relate compassionately to others' desires without losing integrity. This can increase your vitality and well-being, as well as your worth to both yourself and others.

SUN IN THE HOUSES

HOW TO SPARK YOUR VITALITY

1st house: If the Sun is located in the 1st house of your birth chart, you feel you have the right to be acknowledged as a leader. Your vitality is increased when you follow your own instincts and display your self-sufficiency. You bring about your position as a leader when you assert your independence.

2nd house: If the Sun is located in the 2nd house of your birth chart, you gain vitality when you are involved in making money or in an activity that increases your self-worth. You feel you have the right to establish your personal values and the ability to attract monetary success.

3rd house: If the Sun is located in the 3rd house of your birth chart, you gain vitality from reading, taking classes, writing, or exchanging information with others. You feel you have the right to communicate at your will and the talent to create circumstances for sharing information.

4th house: If the Sun is located in the 4th house of your birth chart, you feel you have the right to be accepted on a personal level. Your vitality is increased when you spend time in your home and with members of the family circle. You have the talent and the desire to dominate the immediate (domestic) environment.

5th house: If the Sun is located in the 5th house of your birth chart, you gain vitality when you are involved in recreational, playful activities, immersed in a creative pursuit, or spending time with children. You feel you have the right to enjoy pleasure, to be a child forever, and the ability to share pleasure with others.

6th house: If the Sun is located in the 6th house of your birth chart, you gain vitality from your job, being with coworkers, or working on projects. You feel you have the right to enjoy your daily work and the ability to express a sense of duty effectively.

7th house: If the Sun is located in the 7th house of your birth chart, you gain vitality when involved in a partnership. You feel you have the right to be acknowledged by others as an equal, and the talent to bring about that circumstance.

8th house: If the Sun is located in the 8th house of your birth chart, you gain vitality when you are in a close, bonded relationship with another and mutually dedicated to a common goal. You feel you have the right to use other people's resources and the ability to do this in ways that increase mutual power.

9th house: If the Sun is located in the 9th house of your birth chart, you gain vitality when you are exploring new horizons: either through foreign travel or expanding your educational, philosophical, or spiritual perspectives. You feel you have the right to be the perpetual teacher and the ability to intuitively contact all the answers.

10th house: If the Sun is located in the 10th house of your birth chart, you gain vitality when you are out in the world involved in your profession or taking charge of a situation. The process of reaching a goal revitalizes you. You feel you have the right to social achievement and public recognition, and the ability to create it.

11th house: If the Sun is located in the 11th house of your birth chart, you gain vitality by spending time with your friends. You feel you have the right and the ability to lead through the expression of your unique individuality in group situations (the "no leader" leader).

12th house: If the Sun is located in the 12th house of your birth chart, you recharge and gain vitality by spending time alone. You feel you have the right and the ability to express your divinity, intangible identity, or private dream.

MOON: KEY TO EMOTIONAL SATISFACTION

The Moon in the birth chart:*

- Shows what you need for emotional satisfaction.
- The process through which you may separate yourself emotionally from other people, depriving yourself of the closeness and intimacy you need for personal security.
- The unconscious process by which you attempt to manipulate people through dependencies and sensitivities, and by expressing emotional needs in a way that repels others.
- Shows the path to gaining inner fulfillment and illuminates your ability to integrate change without being disrupted.
- Where the lessons of emotional dependency and personal insecurity arise. These feelings need to be made conscious and be purified in order for you to pass through the changing situations of life with a stable emotional foundation.
- Reveals that area of life in which you need to nourish others and to be nourished in a way that produces intimacy, acceptance, and nonverbal caring.

---

* To discover the sign and house your MOON is located in, go to www.janspiller.com and a free chart will be calculated for you.

- Your ability to adjust emotionally to the changing situations of life.
- Habits of survival dependency from childhood that result in insecurity and a perpetual lack of true inner satisfaction when carried into adult life.
- Shows where the need for emotional nurturing and deep personal caring can be met in a way that satisfies your yearning for emotional completion.

MOON IN ARIES

UNCONSCIOUS EXPRESSION

When you habitually seek to be in control of situations relating to personal independence, you can be competitive to the point of "winning" by withdrawing from interaction with others. You may avoid asserting your needs and then working it out with the other person, not wanting to risk the Aries independence. This nonassertion leads to repressing your independent impulses and creating situations where others dominate you.

Key: Powerlessness and Alienation

Needing others' permission before taking the lead results in insecurity and loss of personal power. This leads to a resentment of others because you feel they are responsible for your inability to act. You may react to their outbursts by withdrawing and feeling violated when they are insensitive to your repressed emotions. Withdrawal adds to your own state of angry, unexpressed, and tightly controlled feelings.

In addition, there is a tendency to hide your emotional needs in order to maintain distance and control the circumstances. But this leads to losing touch with the power of your own independent inner core. If you are unwilling to assert your needs and feelings and work it out with others, you may find you are not able to work it out at all. The result is withdrawing from participation. Such an action leads to the frustration and anger of feeling unable to express and accept recognition for your natural executive abilities.

CONSCIOUS EXPRESSION

Your challenge is to take responsibility for creating the independence you need. This empowers you to notice that repressing your feelings and letting others have their way does not lead to your feeling in control. The truth is that others cannot provide sensitivity to your emotional states. *You* are the one with the gift of sensitivity to underlying instinctive feelings.

Your lesson is to acknowledge your need to feel close by initiating a mutual awareness of basic human feelings and needs. You can accomplish this by moving your attention away from yourself and toward perceiving the human insecurities and feelings of others. First, verbally acknowledging how the other person may feel relaxes any resistance he or she may feel toward you. Then you can express your own needs, and closeness is created.

Key: Opening Sensitivity

Avoiding judgmental thoughts about another's lack of sensitivity opens you to recognize the true nature of arising feelings. This knowledge leads to sensitivity to others as individuals rather than taking their expression personally. Thus, the basic insecurities of others can put you in touch with your own underlying feelings in an objective, balanced way. You then possess the clarity you need to work constructively in relationships.

You win when you show your sensitivity and vulnerability to others' insecurities. By revealing your feelings and needs, your innate power is acknowledged, and others respond with emotional support. You can then express feelings successfully since you are sharing yourself with diplomacy born of awareness of another's sensitivities. Consequently, you are able to *feel* close by having your true feelings accepted and shared. From there, it's easier to work through situations with others.

This process empowers you with the security of independence and courage in relating to others. When you support the ability of other people to handle situations, you reinforce their self-confidence. Thus, your own independence and initiative are spontaneously recognized, respected, and appreciated.

IN PAST LIVES

Unconscious past-life memories of battlegrounds, direct physical combat, and competition for the attainment of your personal needs have made issues of personal survival strong in this lifetime. You are always on the alert but camouflaged so that you can spot the enemy without showing your own strength. To maintain this disguise you may feel you must suppress your strength, which actually invites provocations and attacks from the outside. By suppressing your spirit you invite others to walk all over you.

Due to these past-life experiences and the tendency to view everything in terms of personal survival, you may interpret any opposition in this lifetime as a direct threat to your own goals. Thus, you could respond with either vehement resistance or by "cutting off" the other person entirely and going your own, independent way.

The lesson you are learning is to incorporate the resistance of others into your plan, to see it as a means of actualizing your goals more efficiently. You are learning to be objective enough to welcome the input of others. By taking into consideration their objections, needs, and feelings relative to your own plans, you can expand your objectives to ensure genuine partnership and harmony in working together toward a mutual goal.

Key: Inclusiveness Yields Fulfillment

As you learn to stop projecting your identity (either positive or negative) on to other people, you begin to see them objectively and take them into account. Then you can "be first" in a way that allows the other person's needs to be met as well. Many past lifetimes have been spent developing your own identity, and you are not accustomed to easy cooperation with others in joint projects and team efforts. Rather than feeling you need to compete with others to get your own way, you are learning to include their desires and fears in working out solutions that are fair to all.

Past lives spent in high-speed activity, without time for tact and diplomacy, have led to a certain naiveté and directness in fulfilling your personal needs. This makes your intentions clear for all to see; thus, those who feel threatened by your goals may try to block or manipulate you in some way. When this happens, you feel you have to fight to survive and get what you want. The only other alternative you see is allowing the other person to be the conqueror and to totally suppress your own needs. You don't realize that your impatience and carelessness are creating the very opposition you fear.

The less naïve and direct in your speech you become, as well as being more diplomatic in communicating your wants and needs, the less others will feel threatened—and will have no need to oppose you. Your new tactfulness will encourage others to feel that they too are winning by going along with your plan. You are learning to enlist the support of others in going toward the goals that fulfill your own needs.

MOON IN TAURUS

UNCONSCIOUS EXPRESSION

You might habitually seek others to provide attention, pampering, and love by supplying material and sensual comforts. This dependency can create an impression of personal inadequacy in order to induce others to give you their resources. By projecting a helplessness in obtaining material goods, you encourage them to furnish you with comforts. Then you feel loved, secure, and worthwhile. But in displaying an image of helplessness to others, you also begin to believe it.

Your self-worth can be undermined when others respond by contributing to your sustenance. Their aid reinforces the belief that you lack the energy or abilities to provide your support. When your security depends upon the material aid of others, you cannot be creative or capable, for fear that these comforts may be taken away. So you feel helpless and unable to actively establish your material sense of worth.

CONSCIOUS EXPRESSION

Notice that relying on others to create your self-worth has not worked. Others cannot provide this sense if you possess a supply of personal resources that is not being used. The lesson is to contribute your resources to the world, thus earning your comforts and establishing self-esteem. You can accomplish this by recognizing other people's emotions coming into expression. This recognition can inspire you to get in touch with your creativity.

You gain a deeper sense of inner stability and self-worth by supporting and contributing to the material stability of the environment. Choosing to sacrifice the role of pampered child empowers you to create goals and objectives that motivate you to establish a set of values. When you notice that the people who feel good about themselves are those who are contributing their talents and resources in a tangible way, you are inspired to manifest and establish your creativity. When you appreciate your ideals enough to manifest them, you find the confirmation of self-worth that you need.

IN PAST LIVES

Past lives spent in positions of affluence, material security, and comfort have caused you to come into this lifetime seeking material security above all else. You associate having a strong financial base with emotional stability and ease. Because you are accustomed to accumulation, you can have a difficult time letting go of anything, even things that are holding you back. This can impede the flow of money coming into your life.

The first thing to let go of is counterproductive ideas: the idea that you have a difficult time with money; the idea that you have to earn every penny on your own and that it's going to be a tough process; and the idea that you have to do everything yourself, in exactly your way, for your needs to be met.

Key: Money and Going with the Flow

You can have such a strong fear of losing your material security that you actually create a poverty consciousness in your life, feeling that resources are limited and that you must be very careful how you spend every penny.

Your lesson is to learn to trust the universe and be open to the flow of money coming in and out of your life. You can do this by not focusing so intensely on your financial restrictions (that is, exactly how much this month's bills are) and by simply being open to the universe blessing you with prosperity! The idea is to focus your creative mind less on financial worry and more on visualizing the universe pouring money on you, and your joyful appreciation. In this way you can open yourself at last to the abundance you seek.

You are also learning to accept the gift of money by allowing the resources of others to enrich your life without feeling you have to pay back every penny. The challenge is to be open to the joy of freely accepting money from other people and releasing the ego identification, not feeling that you have to do something in return.

Due to past lives of physical sensitivity and indulgence, you have strong physical desires for sensuality, touching, and physical contact in this incarnation. Once again you are learning to accept the natural healthiness of your needs and be open to having them fulfilled by others. Here, as in finances, you are learning to focus less on your needs and to be more aware of the enrichment that the universe is offering you through other people. You are also learning to accept the idea of bargaining and discounts, and to not assume that you have to pay the full dollar amount for everything you want. By being aware of others' motives to sell, you enhance your capacity to buy what you want at discount.

MOON IN GEMINI

UNCONSCIOUS EXPRESSION

When you seek others to provide an emotional escape from the isolation of your mental gymnastics, you embark on a search for the perfect person. This leads to the frustration of never finding a single relationship that can satisfy and provide release from idealistic mental visions.

If you lack confidence in your instincts, you may fear losing one option by choosing another. Such behavior does not bring stability in relationships. Constant disillusionment can result in an endless series of relationships, a scattering of energies, and loss of identity. It can be difficult to see inspiring influences that you can trust and aim toward. This results in a loss of confidence in your ability to be spontaneous. You may hold back in communicating due to fearing that others will judge you; thus, you lose the benefit of others' abilities to put your ideas in a practical perspective. You may deprive yourself of the very solutions you seek by withholding the truth.

CONSCIOUS EXPRESSION

You can create an atmosphere in which you get your point across by noticing that logical methods have not worked. The truth is that others cannot accept ideas that are not relevant to the practical solutions they seek.

The lesson is to allow the needs of others to direct your mental talents so that you can share ideas they can accept. This is accomplished by focusing beyond the threat of others' motives. Then you can see the disorder in their lives and their attempts to organize themselves.

The challenge is to sacrifice the assumption that you know what is right in the long run. This enables you to accept the needs of others, allowing their goals to guide your intuitive talents. Now you can arrive at mutually beneficial and practical results. When you realize that, to achieve happiness, you must give it to others, you experience what you are giving in the process. This interaction brings about wholehearted participation in assisting others to find their answers.

By paying attention to problems others are having in their daily lives, you can make a commitment to teach on a practical level. Thus, you discover the very solutions that are next on your own path. You gain the spontaneous faith you need by encouraging others to believe in themselves. You finally realize that the power to direct your life is a by-product of inspiring others, exercising your own role as a mentor appropriately. The moment you realize that your excitement comes from teaching and inspiring others, you develop unshakable self-confidence and a sense of variety in all relationships.

IN PAST LIVES

Past lifetimes spent as gatherers and dispensers of information—as travelers, teachers, wandering bards and minstrels—have left you with a feeling of incessant restlessness. You feel the urge to move on, thinking that there is always something new and exciting over the next hill. What actually lures you on is the past-life memory that the next piece of information to be gained and shared with others is to be found in the next town. Thus, the urge for continual movement from person to person continues into this lifetime—the "grass is greener" syndrome.

In past lives you were not accustomed to having a family; you were accustomed to being a traveler. Therefore, you are constantly seeking new mental stimulation and may have a difficult time settling down with one person in a family relationship. An internal restlessness drives you on with the lure: The best relationship is just over the next hill. This idea served you well in past lives, but in this one it can lead to a feeling of dissatisfaction in whatever relationship you are in, no matter how idyllic or healthy it may be for you.

Key: The Satisfaction of Connecting More Deeply

You are learning to relax, to deepen your mental connection with those in your immediate environment so that the stimulation you seek can be nurtured at more profound levels. You are learning to exchange a *quantity* of ideas for the *quality* of a deep rapport by integrating the dimension of feeling into your arena of mental exchange. In this way your desires for constant communication take on a new dimension of satisfaction and fulfillment.

To develop deep mental connections with others, you are learning first to develop a connection with your own spiritual, intuitive processes. Once in touch with your intuition you will have access to the information you need, when you need it, without the restless sense that you continually need more information from the outside in order to feel secure. Then you can share ideas with others with a feeling of ease based on the joy of exchanging those energies that release both people into truth.

MOON IN CANCER

UNCONSCIOUS EXPRESSION

You may have an impulsive tendency to trample on or ignore the feelings of others if you habitually seek to fill your emotional needs first. Indulging in a world of self-centered emotion, it may be difficult to see beyond your own needs to the solutions offered by others for emotional balance. Wanting others to pay attention to you can lead to feeling crushed if you are rebuffed. This can result in a negative self-image, of feeling unable to create positive and nourishing emotional situations in your life.

CONSCIOUS EXPRESSION

When you take responsibility for creating the emotional closeness you need, it becomes apparent that past methods have not been working to satisfy your longing. The truth is, others cannot provide your fulfillment because you already have a surplus of emotional fullness.

Your lesson is to empty your own cup first so that it can be refilled. You can do this by discovering afresh the other people who exist in your universe. Temporarily suspending your own emotional demands empowers you to fill the cups of others by discerning their needs for self-confidence and by encouraging them to reveal their feelings. When you give your attention to others and fill their needs for personal closeness and empathy—by entering into *their* world—you find yourself experiencing the tender intimacy and security you have been seeking.

IN PAST LIVES

Past lives spent in situations of enforced dependency on family members have resulted in a basic insecurity that you might need to be taken care of by others. You fear needing someone else's sympathy to survive. There are active subconscious past-life memories of having sustained a physical injury or handicap that prevented you from being able to take care of yourself (for example, a coal mine accident); or the fear of becoming too old to take care of yourself or having to rely on family members to do things for you.

Such memories lend urgency to your need for an emotional "parent" figure to rely on for protection and care. Thus, family is extremely important in this incarnation and is subconsciously related to basic survival. This insecurity results in unhealthy patterns of manipulation through dependencies, clinging, and controlling family members by being overprotective.

Key: Security by Releasing Dependencies

The lesson here is to enjoy the nourishment of intimacy and empathy without accompanying debilitating bondage. To do this, the challenge is learning to rely on the authority within yourself. Redirect those past tendencies to hold on to family, and cling to goals and ideals that are larger than your personal life. Then the sense of dependency will shift to depending on yourself to hold true to your goals and ideals.

Since you are learning that there is a higher authority you can rely on to take care of your needs, you are able to release family members from these debilitating dependencies. In this way you open yourself to experiencing true intimacy and loving closeness because the clinging attachment has been replaced by an atmosphere of freedom, support, and confidence in your family members' ability to achieve great heights and to take care of themselves.

MOON IN LEO

UNCONSCIOUS EXPRESSION

If you subconsciously seek to confirm your worth by superiority, you may expect others to come to you, like the ruler waiting to receive his or her audience. Sometimes you use the pretense of objectivity to ensure that others will admire you on your pedestal. There can be a tendency to select associates on the basis of their ability to increase your material status. This leads to the experiencing the discomfort of relating without inner affinity. Thus, in needing others as tools to further your *own* values and goals, you close the door to receiving rewards that are beyond your expectations or defined objectives.

Due to needing to be entertained, you can go on automatic and unconsciously use your charm to increase your material position. This is born of an inner attitude of "what can *you* do for *me*?" and costs you your self-confidence in expressing truly spontaneous feelings. You may hoard resources, begrudgingly sharing them with those who are close. Concealing assets causes you to lose status in others' eyes and consequently in your own. You erode confidence in others when you seek to enhance your material position and feel superior in comparison.

CONSCIOUS EXPRESSION

You can create the self-worth you need by noticing that old methods for achieving admiration from others do not result in success. The values projected may not be what others want or need. Your key is to first relinquish the position of director, producer, and main character in your life drama. This empowers you to get in touch with the audience and find out which of your many talents and resources are appropriate to the situation.

By approaching relationships thinking, "It's not what you can do for me, it's what *I* can do for *you*," you experience an unshakable sense of your own worth. When you open yourself to the desires and needs of others, you gain insight into the role you can play. By inspiring others you are not only entertained but gain a sense of self-worth in the process.

Key: Having Fun

When you focus on others' needs it frees you to express your flamboyant, generous nature in a way that supports what they need. In the process your worth is validated. By uplifting others, *you* find enjoyment and happiness. You earn the loyalty and love of your family when you support their values and needs to establish their worth. Stepping out of your drama and realizing how much fun you're having in your dramatics lightens your whole outlook on life.

IN PAST LIVES

You were celebrated royalty in other lives: actors, actresses, musicians, kings, queens, and stars in one form or another. Consequently, you came into this lifetime with a need for recognition, approval, and praise. You are accustomed to applause, and insecurity results when you feel ignored or not treated as someone special.

This insecurity can result in feeling that you must perform according to other people's standards and to further other people's goals in order to gain applause. You can be almost childlike in your need for approval, totally dependent on being with people who will flatter you and pamper your ego. The need for constant reassurance can tax the energies of those who love you, and rob you of your freedom and self-confidence.

Key: Security as a By-Product of Having Higher Goals

During this lifetime you are learning to dedicate yourself to more universal causes that allow you to do your part in furthering the evolution of humankind. When you focus on the larger drama and allow yourself to be a vehicle for an energy that promotes the goals of humanity, your powerful ego assumes a lovely, balanced role. Seeing yourself as a channel for helping your brothers and sisters allows you to accept your childlike qualities and be more tolerant of your mistakes, because you know you had the highest motive.

When you regard those you are close to as friends rather than as subjects or your private audience, you begin supporting their special life force, which will naturally result in their freely acknowledging you. Clarity about the ideals of humanity that you support empowers you to offer approval and vital support to others without expectations of loyalty. This opens the gateway to a flood of unexpected appreciation of your generosity of spirit when you least expect it.

MOON IN VIRGO

UNCONSCIOUS EXPRESSION

Following the urge to appear perfect in the eyes of others leads to using your analytical powers to defend your behavior when others question you. When others do not behave according to your expectations, you may feel affronted and react with sarcasm or cold silence. Indulging in a fear of criticism can lead to withholding your helpful opinions and valuable perceptions.

Often you may refuse to share your internal reactions with a loved one and unwittingly create a secret barrier. As a result you sacrifice integrity in order to be accepted, at least momentarily. This leads to feeling guilty and not knowing why. Relating superficially deprives others of the value your astute perceptions and deprives you of the opportunity to feel useful. In violating your code, you undergo severe self-criticism, which in turn takes away the security you need.

CONSCIOUS EXPRESSION

You can communicate your high standards in a way that confirms your goodness and perfection. When you let go of your expectations of what perfect behavior ought to look like (yours or the other person's), you rid yourself of ideas that prevent closeness.

As you empty your mind of the judgments that cause separation, you experience the joy and closeness in communication you want. You can do this by casting aside the need to have others think of you as perfect. This frees you to have faith in your intuition. Then you can tell what, for you, is the truth, expressed as your own point of view.

Key: Transcending Superficiality

In releasing scattered pictures of what you think service to others ought to look like, you are able to transcend superficiality. The first step is to speak with integrity and sacrifice judgments of your "rightness" and others' "wrongness." Then you discover that what you formerly judged as imperfect behavior in others was only their lack of the information needed to put their lives in order. You have the ability to satisfy your own need to feel useful in relationships by looking beyond fears of personal rejection and sharing what you see.

When you use your practical ability for analysis to share your reactions and assist others in dealing with their emotional systems, you experience a sense of your true ability to serve. This gives you the self-acceptance you need to feel close.

IN PAST LIVES

Past lives spent in positions of ministering to others, healing them, taking care of their needs, and helping to put them back together have resulted in a gentle humility and the desire to serve. From lifetimes spent as artisans, craftspeople, and physical healers, you have become concerned with the details of perfection in your work. Thus, in this life you have a tendency to feel that all aspects of your behavior and performance must be perfect before they can be allowed expression. This attitude can interfere with the flow of your charitable deeds in the world.

You are learning to express whatever helpful detail you have at the moment, without having to see the whole picture. When your piece of the puzzle has been added, the larger vision becomes clearer for all concerned. Then others can cooperate more easily with you in attaining mutually beneficial results.

Key: Releasing Past-Life Rigidities

Lifetimes spent as doctors, nurses, and nuns have left you feeling that your behavior has to be exemplary—an example of perfection above the standards of the rest of humankind. This leads to feeling separate from others through an inflated sense of rightness that is actually part of a past-life egotism. Yet deeper than this, there is a natural purity of intent at the core of your nature.

In this life you are learning to relax, to dissolve past-life rigidities, to trust that universal events unfold perfectly, and to be responsible for simply doing your part. By freely adding your piece of the puzzle—whether it be a feeling, thought, perception, or momentary desire—without needing it to be perfect before expression, you are cooperating with the people and events that flow through your life. And you become an example of perfection to others by operating from the integrity of expressing yourself fully and innocently, piece by piece, along the way.

MOON IN LIBRA

UNCONSCIOUS EXPRESSION

When you habitually expect others to notice your sensitivity to discord and aggression, you respond with emotional touchiness if confronted in any way. You may compromise your own direction and sense of fairness in order to appease others, expecting them to reciprocate by meeting your needs for stability. If your manipulations don't work, you may revert to an abrasive attitude of independence and carelessness, or give vent to wounded feelings to gain their attention.

If you depend on others to be compatible with you, you are easily thrown off the center of harmony when unpleasantness occurs. In this case, you swallow your own feelings and appease everyone for fear that otherwise you may offend them or they may consider you unfair.

Your lack of directness may invite others to take the advantage until finally all unacknowledged previous difficulties burst forth from you in a disastrous tirade. Such frantic emotional smoke screens may repel others who do not know how to penetrate your defenses. The result is that you don't understand when these actions keep others from trusting you.

If you are afraid of creating scenes, you may withhold sharing your internal reactions to others' emotional demands. Then later you wonder why they are not more considerate. As a result you may lose confidence in their trustworthiness and your own ability to discriminate. Indulging in a tendency to internalize and identify with the disharmony from others may also result in sudden emotional outbursts.

CONSCIOUS EXPRESSION

When you take responsibility for creating the internal balance that you need to feel close in relationships, you begin to notice that compromising and expecting others to create peacefulness and fairness simply has not worked. You will be unable to experience harmony if you are waiting for others to initiate it.

Those who are not attuned to your sense of fair play may be unable to treat you fairly until you state the injustices you perceive (that is, "I don't feel good about this . . ."). This gives you strength and completeness in your own direction.

Your best bet is to pledge yourself to a goal outside the relationship. It can supply confidence to state your need for support to meet that goal in a direct, objective, and organized way. This gives others the opportunity to cooperate with you in attaining the goal. You can commit yourself to the integrity of your own direction in relationships by trusting that the outcome will be for your highest good. The result brings you the self-respect you need to put yourself forward and declare the truth of your feelings regardless of the consequences. When you thus assert yourself, the situations around you automatically come into balance according to their higher plan, regardless of outer appearance.

Key: Discovering a World of Kindred Spirits

When you realize that the supply of people is absolutely unlimited, it encourages you to express your own identity and display who you authentically are. This acts as an automatic means of attracting people who are akin to you.

If you give voice to your real, independent point of view, you will attract appreciation and love for the person you truly are. Thus, in surrounding yourself with people of true affinity, you experience the joy of knowing that you are valued simply for being there in the present moment with them. When you trust your own perceptions and act accordingly to create an inner equilibrium, you add the peacefulness of your presence to the situation.

By going to your deep self and then expressing from the balance and stability that is there, you silently invite others to go to that place within themselves. The power of your harmony impels others to go to their depths also if they wish to relate to you; in this way, through claiming your center, you create harmony.

IN PAST LIVES

Past lives have been spent in positions of support, as mediators, diplomats, concubines, or traditional female supportive roles. These lives have resulted in an identity based on sharing; your survival has depended on a sense of inner emotional accord with your partner. In this lifetime you may find yourself compromising your true identity in order to maintain the feeling of internal accord with your mate or partner.

Your lesson now is to learn to express yourself—to *be* yourself—in the context of a relationship. To do this you must become aware of your own needs, realizing that if they aren't met, the relationship as a whole will suffer.

You are learning to put yourself back into the picture so that a fair exchange can take place. This requires that you let your partner know verbally what you would like to have occur in the relationship, in a way that invites a response about what your partner would like. Once both persons' needs are out in the open, you are naturally able to suggest a mutually satisfactory solution.

Key: Learning Effective Assertiveness

One of the lessons is learning equilibrium: not to overassert for fear of not getting your way. You have a defensiveness based on resentment from past lives and a present-life assumption that others are going to object to your having your own way. Thus, when you do assert your needs there's a tendency to do it in a rather harsh and defensive way that cuts off the honest response of your partner.

Thus, through fear of compromising your own needs, you sometimes overcompensate with unnecessary forcefulness. Unknown to you, this actually provokes the other person's resistance to cooperating with you. It reinforces the sense of separation in the relationship, the feeling that you can't relax and be yourself but have to be always on the alert to either resist or accommodate the nonverbal needs of your partner.

You can be so afraid of losing the relationship altogether by not keeping the other person's emotional state harmonized at all times that you subvert your own identity in order to keep the partner pleased and content. The self-suppression that was necessary in past lives to support and flatter the person in power can harden into a resentment that erupts in the future with violent consequences.

Key: Sharing as an Equal

This lifetime you can learn to share your needs with others as an equal, with the confident expectation that they will also want to please and accommodate *you*. The idea is to realize that others *want* your harmonious, pleasant, happy disposition around them, and to keep you, they will go out of their way to make you happy.

You are also learning to assume the role of manager in relationships by objectively equalizing the injustices that are the cause of social discontent. You do this best only after your own needs and goals are verbally expressed and asking for the other person's corresponding needs. In this way a fair and balanced plan that fills the needs of both partners can be realized.

MOON IN SCORPIO

UNCONSCIOUS EXPRESSION

When you habitually require others to give you their unconditional loyalty and allegiance, you may become crushed, insecure, and angered when they don't. You may respond with defiance, exercising the instinctive power you have over others, and subtly attempt to enforce loyalty and control. Therefore, in your eyes, they lose power. In this process you lose your capacity to feel the joys of equal interaction. The consequence is that you create emotional stagnation for yourself.

Feeling insecure about losing control can lead to attempting to have all the answers for everyone in a way that creates a dependency in them and assures you of one-upmanship. However, diminishing another's power lessens the potency of the relationship. Then it cannot provide you with the emotional intensity, change, and new levels of depth that you need for personal fulfillment. When you sense another's vulnerabilities and provoke that person's response, you get to be powerful momentarily, but may feel isolated. There is a basic tendency to feel insecure in financial and sexual relationships. If unchecked, this can lead to a need to manipulate everyone to prove potency.

CONSCIOUS EXPRESSION

You need deep feelings of joy, vitality, and intensity in relationships. When you take responsibility for creating situations in which you can experience those emotions, you begin to notice that relying on others to recognize your worth does not work. The truth is that others cannot renew you. You are the one withholding the depths of perception that would bring this about.

For emotional fulfillment, the idea is to first release manipulative control of others. Then you can experience the combining of resources that regenerates your own energy and creativity. You accomplish this renewal by pledging your loyalties to those ideals and areas of growth potential that make you feel good about yourself. By releasing your vision of being in command, you are able to find out what others are really made of.

As you enter uncharted ground and are willing to take risks by letting go of exclusive power, you can interact with another in a manner that is exhilarating for you. When you choose the stimulation of change over a stagnant status quo, you are able to go forward. Then you gain knowledge of what enhances self-worth through an exciting process of risk and the unpredictable mystery you need for fulfillment.

Key: Sharing Power

You can gain more knowledge and strength only by first releasing what you already have. This decision encourages you to contribute your inspiring insights generously, exposing perceptions that awaken others to their hidden resources. As you communicate your recognition of others' hidden abilities, it empowers them to reach their own objectives. This creates deeper, more satisfying camaraderie.

You can then allow yourself to go spontaneously in the direction others want, rather than resisting the current. This opens the way for you to interact with them on deeper, previously unknown levels.

By being committed to freedom through renewal, you begin to realize that the way to win the most is to share the power. Thus, you reach deeper levels by releasing the tendency to control. Finally, in the process of expressing loyalty to your ideals, you contribute potency by exposing your hidden perceptions to others. You can then experience your inner worth and the satisfaction of your transformation coming into expression.

IN PAST LIVES

Past lifetimes have carried extremes of emotional intensity and battles for power. You have been severely wounded, which has resulted in an overdevelopment of the survival instinct in this lifetime. Past lives filled with crisis and betrayal have resulted in an attitude of distrust, and you are attuned to the possibility of others having evil motives. This is so strong that the power of your belief (and resulting unconscious provocations) can actually bring out the worst in other people, which only heightens your feelings of emotional isolation.

To compensate for severe loneliness, you seek that one other person you can trust, your soul mate, sensing that this will somehow bring you peace. But because of past-life experiences, your approach to relationships is so obsessive and demanding that it often becomes mutually destructive. Instead of finding the peace you seek, you again experience being wounded.

Key: Positive Bonding

The challenge is balancing these intense past-life experiences with a feeling of peacefulness and serenity in this incarnation. To do this, you need to discover what you want to build with another person. Then you can bond with someone trustworthy who is interested in the same kind of solid, mutually nourishing relationship. With the focus on what you want to create, in terms of a spiritual goal, you can use the power and intensity gained in past lives to build the life that will bring you peace.

For successful fulfillment of the long-sought soul-mate relationship, you must build step by step and not skip any stages in laying the foundation. And by taking the other person's desires into account, the foundation will benefit from both people's creative energies. Since past lives were spent in destruction, remember that it may take only three days to demolish a skyscraper but three years to build one. By going slowly and keeping your mind on the goal, you can enjoy the process of mutually creating a solid relationship.

MOON IN SAGITTARIUS

UNCONSCIOUS EXPRESSION

Acting out the urge to strive perpetually to confirm your intellectual superiority leads to becoming obsessed with feeling you have to obtain a tangible result. You may seek the ultimate grand vision that will empower you to put your physical universe in order. Or you might believe that when you demonstrate perfection in all aspects of your life, others will bow to your moral knowledge and bestow the faith that you need.

You may unconsciously search for the elusive ideal of the perfect solution that gives you proof of your righteousness. In the absence of an ultimate ideal, you may feel unable to act and can become lost and confused, lacking confidence in your perspective.

CONSCIOUS EXPRESSION

When you take responsibility for creating closeness with others, you find that spreading your theoretical conclusions does not result in effective communication. You can become so preoccupied with imperfection that you fail to see your perfect image in the eyes of others. The truth is that others already see the nobility of your striving. The idea is to free yourself of judgments and evaluations so that you can accept your own perfection. You accomplish this by concentrating on the deeper messages of others, thus experiencing their perfection, which puts you in touch with your own.

Key: Listening Leads to Security

By sacrificing the impulse to prove superior knowledge, you can hear what others are asking. Responding with spontaneous intuitive answers enables them to find the truth and source of their own perfection. In this way you also find security and the closeness with others that you want. By putting others in touch with their completeness, you experience your own.

You can communicate innocently by sharing your vision and allowing others to apply it in their own lives. This technique lets you contribute to them in a way they can accept; this acceptance is the acknowledgment you need. When you discover that you are able to communicate truth, you experience your own security along with the idealistic closeness with others that you desire.

IN PAST LIVES

Past-life experiences have been spent gaining—and being an example of—spiritual truth, as philosophers, spiritual leaders, and naturalists. In some cases, misuse of spiritual authority in past lives (putting oneself above the law) has caused a blind spot regarding social mores in this lifetime. Until this is understood, there may be blundering in this life, accompanied by seemingly unfair social punishment and retribution. If this is the case, you are learning not to put yourself above social laws and ethics of appropriate conduct. Once you decide to cooperate with prevailing social mores, the blind spot is removed and you will no longer experience society as unexpectedly inhibiting your desire for freedom.

You have a long history of going your own way, unfettered by the demands of society—a law unto yourself. Consequently, you have been socially isolated from others and come into this lifetime with a sense of loneliness and wanting to be understood and *accepted* by others. You long to be able to share the truth and inspiration gained in past lives with others, hoping that the vitality of this exchange will reconnect you with your own source.

Key: Understanding, to Be Understood

When you come off your philosophical mountaintop and learn to relate, you will realize that to be understood, you must first seek to understand others.

You are learning to drop isolating self-righteous attitudes and to use your mind to discover the unspoken rules of personality interactions—rules that others take for granted. When you accept these boundaries of socially accepted behavior, you will be able to share your philosophical awareness with others in a way they can accept and appreciate.

MOON IN CAPRICORN

UNCONSCIOUS EXPRESSION

When you unconsciously need others' reassurance that you are the most important part of their interpersonal relationships, you may unknowingly manipulate them emotionally to gain respect. This can lead you to express needless dramas of personal suffering that force them to acknowledge and admire your ability to survive. You may instinctively guard your image and try to appease others by becoming, for that moment, what they respect.

In sacrificing your self for the respect of another, you lose your own identity. Indulging in the tendency to control the relationship can rob others of their authority and ability to give you the admiration you want. Simultaneously, in order to feel loved you may need constant reassurance. This tendency gives your power to others and can leave you insecure and bewildered.

CONSCIOUS EXPRESSION

Capricorn Moon people feel drawn to establish control in relationships. However, methods of having others validate your identity do not lead to self-respect. The truth is that others cannot give respect when you are so busy cloaking yourself with their personalities. This process leaves you with no identity available to receive recognition!

The lesson is to relinquish control over others in order to see to whom you are relating. You can achieve this by acknowledging the uniqueness of the person with whom you are dealing. This in turn gives you insight into your own unique being and appreciation of yourself as different from others.

When you give others confidence in developing their ability to take charge of their lives, you become aware of your power. Your sensitivity can nurture others and reflect back to them your assurance of their ability to succeed and get on top of their emotions. Their self-esteem enables them to rise to the occasion. This technique of support empowers you to experience your ability to organize others to reach a goal.

Key: The Security of Respect

When you encourage authority and leadership abilities in others, you recognize those qualities in yourself. Respecting the needs of others to establish their identity frees you to honor your own impulses. This gives you a sense of self. As you pursue the personal needs of your identity, you can choose independent action. When you make a commitment to your direction and follow through on it, you gain confidence in your authority as well as the respect of others.

IN PAST LIVES

Past lives spent in positions of control and authority have left you feeling that you must have absolute control in order to be emotionally secure. Your experiences have included being a figurehead, a political leader, and in positions of social prestige. These roles you've played in past lives have accustomed you to receiving respect, deference, and automatic cooperation from those around you. When this isn't forthcoming in your present incarnation, you feel that something is missing. You experience insecurity in your relationships. You seek to plug up the hole in order to feel that the foundation is firm and so you can enter relationships confidently, knowing you can handle any situation.

Unconscious past-life tendencies to close down emotionally and be invulnerable by virtue of *noninvolvement* will not bring the emotional satisfaction you want in this lifetime. You are seeking emotional control, but the first step in gaining control is to be open to experiencing and expressing your feelings in the moment. Even though you don't have all the pieces under control at the onset, success lies in being willing to walk through the process of experiencing and integrating the male and female parts of yourself (control and emotions). The idea is to be willing to walk the path to obtain the desired result of emotional involvement in relationships balanced with a calm sense of self-authority.

Key: Including Feelings as a Pathway to the Goal

As you learn not to judge or invalidate your feelings, you can simply express them to others in the spirit of sharing self-identity. This allows the other person to share his or her feelings, leading to a positive, alchemical change in the relationship. Then you can identify one another's desires, which gives you a sense of clarity and lets you view the relationship from an entirely new perspective.

Once you gain this new view you can see a vision of yourself in the future—a new sense of self that is emerging through the relationship. This is the important thing. Through expressing your feelings you come into a new sense of balance and adjustment between yourself and your circumstances. You also gain the confidence of knowing that no matter what comes to you, you will know where each particle belongs in the overall scheme of things. From this you will derive a solid sense of your own authority in relating to the world.

MOON IN AQUARIUS

UNCONSCIOUS EXPRESSION

When you habitually seek the feedback of others to supply your need for feelings of self-worth, you simultaneously relinquish power and self-control. You are attuned to the hidden motives and desires of other people. If you use this knowledge to manipulate your value in their eyes, you may find yourself unable to maintain your integrity and identity. Consequently, your self-worth can be at the precarious mercy of the outside world and how successful a manipulator you are.

Additionally, looking to others for feedback leaves you feeling uncertain about what action to take. Indulging in a need for validation leads to uneasiness about your material and sexual connections. Thus, you may feel afraid that any intimate relationship might put you in a vulnerable position for an unexpected emotional rejection. To avoid this you may create emotional drama that ensures others will stay at a distance. This game results in a negative self-image and emotional isolation.

CONSCIOUS EXPRESSION

The idea is to take responsibility for creating loving relationships that nurture you. Past methods have not brought about a consistent feeling of being worthwhile to others. Others cannot provide you with idealism in relationships; in seeking their approval, you miss awareness of what they actually offer to bring about your ideal.

Your lesson is to release the need for others' approval in order to determine what is valuable to you in other people. Having a sense of your own worth puts you in touch with your values. At the same time, doing what *you* feel is worthwhile and needs to be done automatically enhances self-worth. Then you have something to offer others, and your relationships automatically begin to meet the idealism you want. As a by-product, others give unexpected approval without your consciously seeking it.

Getting in touch with the spontaneity of your own inner child empowers you to express yourself in ways that invite others to play with you and be your friend. Doing things that keep you feeling a sense of fun about life keeps you in touch with your inner vitality and worth.

As you inspire confidence in others and encourage them to express their talents, they begin furthering your ideals of community whether or not they are aware of it. In this process you create the many loving friendships you want, and experience the fulfillment of seeing your own humanitarian ideals and values being actualized.

IN PAST LIVES

Past lives spent in communal living situations (harems, monasteries, orphanages, etc.) have given you self-awareness in the context of group situations. Thus, in this life your emotional stability tends to be dependent upon maintaining mental accord and harmony with those around you. There's a tendency to compromise your own individuality in order to keep the peace with others, since you fear you may need to count on these friendships later for survival. Past-life group involvement has made you too dependent on your peers for support, to the extent that you may concentrate on friendships to the exclusion of more intimate involvements.

One lesson you are learning in this incarnation is to make *yourself* strong.

By becoming more aware of what you want and then exercising your creative power to fulfill it, you revitalize your past-life attachment to disassociation and get reinvolved with life in a healthy way.

Key: The Common Good

You are learning to enjoy the creative process by using its tools—excitement, romance, and playfulness—to enlist others to follow your lead in creating goals for the common good. Since there has been a lack of experience in wholehearted personal love and a sense of impersonalness from past incarnations, you naturally feel insecure about entering into a deeply personal attachment. You are learning to infuse your more personal, intense relationships with humane treatment of the other person, to create closeness while working for the common good.

From your past-life experiences you have an inborn sense of what serves the good of the whole and a natural predisposition for doing what is best for others. Yours can be the highest form of friendship. You are learning to combine this awareness with a realization of what *you* want to create in the relationship, and then joyously to go about creating a structure that encompasses the needs of you both.

Key: The Safety of Humor

You are learning to create what you want by giving attention to those relationships that are important to you and carefully monitoring the situation to see that it is still headed toward your goals. Having a goal in your relationships is important; its creation and attainment validates your effective participation.

Part of your process is noticing that giving attention to a relationship makes it thrive, while withdrawing attention allows it to wither. Then the other person will go somewhere else, looking for involvement that is more constant.

Your natural humor allows you to take the more selfish foibles and perspectives of others in stride, and this serves as a safety valve in the event that your experimentation with close personal involvement may occasionally go awry.

MOON IN PISCES

UNCONSCIOUS EXPRESSION

Habitually expecting others to automatically validate your concept of universal perfection leads to refusing to see life as it exists. Living in your vision, you may lose yourself in ivory-tower beliefs. These beliefs prevent you from *listening* to people and seeing them in a realistic and predictable way.

When others fail to live up to your vision of perfection, you might feel personally betrayed. Seeking others to live up to your higher standards creates self-isolation. This constant disappointment brought on by others violating your expectations results in self-invalidation, confusion, and a feeling of help-lessness in coping with relationships.

CONSCIOUS EXPRESSION

When you take responsibility for sharing your vision of other people's perfection, you begin to notice that theoretical communications have simply not worked. The truth is that others cannot provide the perfection you seek. They are preoccupied with thinking about their own imperfection.

Your lesson is to heal the negative thoughts of others so that there is room for the positive solutions within them to come forth. Then they are able to alter their behavior and align themselves with their inner perfection.

You can help heal negative beliefs by acknowledging the *reality* of other points of view. The idea is to recognize that a person's perspective in a given situation automatically dictates behavior. When you stop expecting others to spontaneously accept your answers, you are able to truly listen to their logic about their problems and reasons for lack of perfection.

Recognizing that individuals want only to share their pain with you so that they can be healed encourages you to listen to what they are saying. You can heal others instantly when you listen to their opinions and negativity from a silent perspective of "Yes, now you are telling me what makes you suffer."

Key: The Value in Understanding Another's Behavior

Misunderstandings are cleared up when you question the other person and compassionately seek to understand that person's point of view. You can relate on an equal and sharing level when you embrace the person's point of view and understand the thoughts behind his or her action. By opening this door you experience the unconditional love you seek.

As you create a positive atmosphere, you reassure individuals with your trust in the perfection of things as they are. You have the ability to supply a larger picture of their growth. When you use your perceptive powers to dis-cern where another is feeling a lack of self-perfection, you can contribute the communication that promotes faith and self-acceptance in them. In this pro-cess you validate your vision and are also healed.

IN PAST LIVES

Past lives spent in monasteries or convents, or otherwise shut away from society, have left you with an idealistic and naïve approach to life. You seem to float through the harsh realities of daily routine, seeing life from an idealistic point of view. Deep disappointments can result when the world does not live up to your standards of humane behavior, but before too long you pick yourself up and put on your rose-colored glasses again.

These past-life monastic experiences have led to certain material dependencies that you feel are necessary to maintain your healing spiritual consciousness. You are accustomed to having others take care of you, cook for you, and set your daily routine. In the monastery, for example, someone rang the gong, signaling when you should get up, when you should go to church or temple, when you should eat, and so forth. Consequently, you have never developed self-discipline, which is a task for this lifetime; you are learning to accept these responsibilities and to "ring your own gong."

You are accustomed to living in a timeless reality, but in this lifetime you are learning the practical value of infusing celestial reality into daily life by sticking to a routine and by paying attention to being on time. These factors make your life strong and give you confidence in relating your spiritual consciousness effectively to daily living.

Key: Serve or Suffer

Confidence comes when you pay attention to diet and health. In other lifetimes you were not responsible for your own nutritional well-being. In this life you are learning to discriminate and to ingest those foods that give your body a feeling of balanced strength, which allows your spiritual consciousness to flow without interruption.

In past lives you were discouraged from reaching material goals because you were learning to trust the universe completely and to merge yourself with total reliance on its flow. This patterning was overdone, however, and has led to a certain stagnation in your current incarnation. It is only by learning to apply your sense of faith and unconditional love in daily life that your bliss feelings can be regenerated. Again, focusing on your clearly defined goals and applying the necessary surrender to routine are necessary.

In this incarnation you will be paying society back for the many lifetimes where its institutions have supported your enlightenment by taking care of your material needs. It is time for you to use the fruits of your spiritual practices—unconditional love, the ability to heal, your vision of loveliness—to freely and effectively work for the good of those in your circle of influence.

This is a serve-or-suffer lifetime. You can choose either to actively and constructively serve society or to suffer behind the private walls of feeling misunderstood and walked on by the world. When you have taken responsibility for setting up the necessary structures and routines in your life, this will act as a support system through which universal emotional energies can flow in a balanced way. Then you will be on the path to emotional fulfillment in this lifetime.

MOON IN THE HOUSES

HOW TO GAIN EMOTIONAL SECURITY

1st house: If the Moon is located in the 1st house of your birth chart, the nurturing you need to feel emotionally satisfied comes through putting the focus on yourself. You gain emotional security by the honest, forthright expression of feelings and by the willingness to express your emotions on the surface.

2nd house: If the Moon is located in the 2nd house of your birth chart, the nurturing you need to feel emotionally satisfied comes by enjoying the sensual side of life. You gain emotional security by establishing concrete material values and through acquiring and building a secure material structure.

3rd house: If the Moon is located in the 3rd house of your birth chart, the nurturing you need to feel emotionally satisfied comes by attending social gatherings where you can exchange information with others. You gain security by communicating your changing thoughts and then listening to the ideas of others. You also feel emotionally satisfied through teaching and writing.

4th house: If the Moon is located in the 4th house of your birth chart, the nurturing you need to feel emotionally satisfied comes through spending time in your home and with family members. You gain security by nourishing others with your sensitive, personal feelings and through a secure family environment.

5th house: If the Moon is located in the 5th house of your birth chart, the nurturing you need to feel emotionally satisfied comes through following your heart, in terms of activities you become involved in. Children evoke your nurturing energy. You gain emotional security by using your dramatic expression of personal feelings in ways that inspire others, and by being able to dramatize yourself through creative efforts.

6th house: If the Moon is located in the 6th house of your birth chart, the nurturing you need to feel emotionally satisfied comes through setting healthy routines and involving yourself in productive work activities. You gain emotional security by serving others in practical ways that express your sense of obligation and duty, and by being of service to others on a material, practical level.

7th house: If the Moon is located in the 7th house of your birth chart, the nurturing you need to feel satisfied comes through spending time with a partner. You need people you can connect with emotionally, involved in the process of giving and receiving caring and support with one other person. You gain emotional security by uniting with another in a partnership (including marriage), and through involving yourself in social interactions and establishing partnerships out of those situations.

8th house: If the Moon is located in the 8th house of your birth chart, the nurturing you need to feel satisfied comes through totally blending your energies with another person. You gain emotional security by establishing a psychological, material, or emotional bond with someone else, and by experiencing others on deep emotional levels that lead to positive psychological realignment of your self-image.

9th house: If the Moon is located in the 9th house of your birth chart, the nurturing you need to feel satisfied comes through participating in spiritual or religious activities. You gain emotional security by sharing lofty, philosophical thoughts with others and through teaching, traveling, and involving yourself in experiences that expand yourself to new horizons.

10th house: If the Moon is located in the 10th house of your birth chart, the nurturing you need to feel satisfied comes through taking charge and reaching goals. You gain emotional security by involving yourself in public activity that will bring personal recognition and a position of authority, and by acquiring positions of authority where you can organize others.

11th house: If the Moon is located in the 11th house of your birth chart, the nurturing you need to feel emotionally satisfied comes through spending time with your peers. Regardless of work and family tasks, to feel satisfied you will need to allot time with your friends or in a group activity. You gain emotional security by involving yourself in friendships that allow for the expression of personal feelings and ideals, and through participating in a wide range of impersonal interactions and group activities that are geared toward humanitarian goals.

12th house: If the Moon is located in the 12th house of your birth chart, the nurturing you need to feel satisfied comes through spending time alone. You gain emotional security by identifying with ideals and esoteric visions that are beyond the realm of material existence, and through being of spiritual service to others through universal compassion and a healing vision.

☿

MERCURY: KEY TO REWARDING COMMUNICATION

Mercury in the birth chart:*
- Signifies your talent for verbal communication with others.
- Indicates the fear that may unconsciously keep you from being yourself and telling the truth.
- Illuminates the motives that cause you to withhold yourself verbally, which inevitably causes misunderstandings with others.
- Displays the process by which you may create endless mental worries and negative expectations that lead to isolating and withholding yourself from true contact with others out of fear.
- Shows the way to communicate in a manner that inspires a sense of affinity and mutual sharing with other people.
- Reveals the type of mental connection with others that can bring about a true sharing of information resulting in mutual, expanding understanding.
- Defines the nature of your mental talents and intellectual approach.
- The subjects you think about.
- Signifies the area upon which you can focus mental attention, then communication becomes a vehicle leading to the satisfaction of being understood by others.

MERCURY IN ARIES

UNCONSCIOUS EXPRESSION

Asleep fear: Losing the visible impact of direct and authoritative communication.

Result: You cease to communicate successfully with others. You may tend to speak in ways that appear aggressive, overbearing, and almost militant. This challenging, intimidating attitude toward the audience can result in alienation and misunderstanding.

---

* To discover the sign and house your MERCURY is located in, go to www.janspiller.com and a free chart will be calculated for you.

CONSCIOUS EXPRESSION

When your attention is on communicating in a way that inspires others to act, your natural sense of combat is turned into a creative, stimulating interaction. By focusing on inspiring others, you are able to express yourself in ways that awaken them to new perceptions of their immediate circumstances. By becoming aware of their reactions, you can know in advance the impact your communication will have. This awareness of the other person leads to successfully gaining the Aries sense of freedom for assertive expression.

MERCURY IN TAURUS

UNCONSCIOUS EXPRESSION

Asleep fear: Losing tangible support.
Result: From a rational point of view, this may lead you to repeat ideas and plans. This leads to an overstructured mind that gets tied up in a material or literal level of thought and stifles your creativity. Indulging in the tendency to resist ideas that are not your own can result in excluding others from assisting you in achieving what you value.

CONSCIOUS EXPRESSION

When you are willing to communicate openly and to acknowledge that the ideas of others can be as valuable as yours, you discover that these ideas may actually transform and enhance your own. By using other people's ideas as resources, your own concepts gain acceptance through the resultant transformation. By listening to others first and then communicating your perceptions—how *their* ideas can produce tangible results—your sense of self-worth is increased.

MERCURY IN GEMINI

UNCONSCIOUS EXPRESSION

Asleep fear: Losing the ability to connect on a surface level with a variety of people and ideas.
Result: Your rational mind can become submerged in superficial thinking. The master of trivia within can collect bits and pieces of information that may or may not be of any practical value. Indulging in the Gemini tendency to flit from thought to thought results in a great deal of talking and no true communication.

CONSCIOUS EXPRESSION

When you concentrate on any *one* of your many interests, your quick mind, adaptability, and pure logic can bring about clear communication with diverse people. By focusing, communicating clearly, and reaching a conclusion before moving on, you cease to be the perpetual student and are able to teach and direct others to sources of knowledge.

MERCURY IN CANCER

UNCONSCIOUS EXPRESSION

Asleep fear: Losing your emotional connections with others.
Result: Your rational mind can become dominated almost entirely by moods, feelings, and emotions. This inadvertently forces others to respond with either sympathetic indulgence or overt rebuff. Indulging in communications that demand the sympathy of others may expose you to unnecessary rejection.

CONSCIOUS EXPRESSION

When you focus on being aware of the sensitivities of others as well as your own, your ability to communicate goes beyond words. You can then reach out emotionally, sensitively, and empathetically in ways that are a true reflection of your caring for others.

MERCURY IN LEO

UNCONSCIOUS EXPRESSION

Asleep fear: Losing your dramatic impact and the loyalty of others.
Result: Expressing yourself in ways that appear dictatorial, arrogant, and egotistical. This can produce one-sided communication, inadvertently implying that everything you have to say is more important than what anyone else has to say. This unbalanced communication can unintentionally alienate those closest to you.

CONSCIOUS EXPRESSION

Being open to noticing the effects you have on others shows you that the Leo dramatic ability to communicate can enhance or destroy what you are saying. This talent for communicating with a theatrical impact leaves a lasting impression, for good or ill. When the focus is on conversing with an awareness of shared humanity, you are able to inspire the ideas of others with creativity. By being aware of your love for others, you can instinctively express yourself in a way that inspires loyalty.

MERCURY IN VIRGO

UNCONSCIOUS EXPRESSION

Asleep fear: Indulging in the Virgo tendency to analyze and judge what is right and wrong in yourself and others creates endless categories in your mind. This makes it difficult to communicate in an orderly and confident way.
Result: This compartmental analysis of right and wrong might appear harsh, inadvertently alienating those close to you. Concurrently, in judging others you can pave the way for heavy self-criticism if you distort perfectionism in any way.

CONSCIOUS EXPRESSION

When you trust the universal, unseen order of things, you stop feeling defensive about how actions reflect imperfection. Through developing self-tolerance you can accomplish a job with a sense of perfection but without applying the same high standards of performance to your personal life. By detaching from expecting perfection in your relationships and communications with others, you can be transformed to a new level. You will not have to be defensive with others since you no longer need to justify your humanness to yourself.

MERCURY IN LIBRA

UNCONSCIOUS EXPRESSION

Asleep fear: Not saying the right thing.
Result: By looking to others for a reflection of immediate acceptance, communications can stop. Withholding honest interchange for fear of rejection leads to your mind being stuck in a swamp of considerations that brings indecision. If you withhold disclosing what is actually on your mind, you may lose your perspective, integrity, and perceptual balance.

CONSCIOUS EXPRESSION

When you focus attention on your point of view and sharing your independent opinion, you can discover the spontaneous awareness of your impact when communicating with others. Concentrating on what needs to be said rather than on what you think other people want to hear can contribute the justice, truth, and balance required. You then may discover that you have a natural talent for diplomacy and communication that spontaneously restores harmony without compromising any sense of personal integrity.

MERCURY IN SCORPIO

UNCONSCIOUS EXPRESSION

Asleep fear: Losing power over others by exposing your motives and desires.
Result: Your communication can become defensive, secretive, and vindictive. Thus, if you withhold your thoughts, you may have constant inner turmoil, fearing that hidden emotions will be exposed and you might become vulnerable. As a consequence, anger, impatience, and intimidation can be brought forth or all communication may be withheld, alienating others and isolating yourself.

CONSCIOUS EXPRESSION

When you focus on showing others what is valuable to you, your keen perception can penetrate and reveal deeper meaning in their communication. You unveil those powerful secrets that can transform all concerned. By sharing the Scorpio incisive ability to perceive the heart behind the words, you expose hidden motivations within their communications. This awareness can make a positive contribution to others and actually increase your insight and sense of self-possession.

MERCURY IN SAGITTARIUS

UNCONSCIOUS EXPRESSION

Asleep fear: Losing the appearance of intellectual superiority.
Result: You may jump to hasty conclusions. The rational mind can become lost in empty theories with no logic or facts for a foundation. These theories may then be unwittingly presented to others in a moralizing manner, from a platform of inflated expressions of pompous self-righteousness.

CONSCIOUS EXPRESSION

When your attention is on clearly distinguishing emotionally biased thoughts from factual and logically based thoughts, you can relinquish the

Sagittarius tendency of self-righteous mental isolation. Then you can communicate your inspired perceptions without any need to prove intellectual superiority. Your ability to uplift others is through opening *two-way* sharing and communication.

MERCURY IN CAPRICORN

UNCONSCIOUS EXPRESSION

Asleep fear: Losing status by not knowing the answers to everything.
Result: You can develop a pretense of being the final intellectual authority in all fields. There's a tendency to use every opportunity to gather knowledge and impress others, always assuming an authoritarian attitude. This can produce alienation and a breakdown of your credibility with other people. A pretentious speaking manner may disenchant others, provoking them to withhold information. This can lead to a constant disruption of any attempted communication.

CONSCIOUS EXPRESSION

By focusing on the informational needs of others, you can effortlessly share relevant ideas. When your motive in giving information is to support others, you automatically communicate true knowledge and eliminate pretense. Relinquishing the Capricorn need to maintain authority allows others to share the information necessary for further mutual advancement.

You can stop taking yourself so seriously by paying attention to the sensitivities of others. Then you can organize the situation effectively and share authority. This opens the door for others to show appreciation and respect for your abilities.

MERCURY IN AQUARIUS

UNCONSCIOUS EXPRESSION

Asleep fear: Losing mental objectivity.
Result: The Aquarius rational mind can become cold and detached from feeling or empathetic intuition. This leads to losing sensitivity to others in communication. By immersing yourself in nonjudgmental objectivity, you can inadvertently alienate others with a brittle manner. Fear of losing a detached concept of universal love can bring on abstract and thoughtless retorts to the personal communications of others. This may keep people at a distance.

CONSCIOUS EXPRESSION

By focusing on making a personal connection with others, you become aware of their sensitivities. Recognizing the individuality in others enables you to apply the ideal of universal love. You are able to establish a connection for communication that then allows you to share your unique ways of perceiving life. This is done by opening yourself to experience mental empathy with others. You experience ease in getting your point across when your ability for objective communication is tempered by both an awareness of the point of view of others and their emotional sensitivities.

MERCURY IN PISCES

UNCONSCIOUS EXPRESSION

Asleep fear: Losing a vision of how perfect the ideal could be.
Result: You may sacrifice reality for a private world of fantasy. This can lead to withholding intuitive perceptions for fear of being invalidated by others. Then the ability to communicate clearly becomes muddled and lost in the distractions of your emotional world. When you retreat into your private reality and exclude interaction with others, you may lose those relevant perceptions that can help to make your thoughts manifest.

CONSCIOUS EXPRESSION

You can focus your attention on the reality of the spiritual poverty and confusion that you see in daily life. This vision inspires you to rise above fears and make a real contribution to others. Communicating your creative and intuitive abilities allows others to enter through into your psychic perceptions. Your ideals can become a healing reality in the world when you make a tangible contribution by communicating your intuitive vision.

MERCURY IN THE HOUSES

REVEALS YOUR SPECIAL INTELLECTUAL ABILITY

1st house: If Mercury is located in the 1st house of your birth chart, your thinking becomes clear when you focus on yourself and your own needs for independent action. You have a special ability for verbal expression and a tendency toward flexibility or, in the extreme, to superficiality.
2nd house: If Mercury is located in the 2nd house of your birth chart, your thinking becomes clear when you focus on your own needs to feel

comfortable. You have a natural sense of practical perception and the special ability to communicate in ways that bring about tangible results.

3rd house: If Mercury is located in the 3rd house of your birth chart, your thinking becomes clear when you focus on a logical approach to situations facing you. You have the special ability to perceive the thought processes of others and to manipulate their thinking for good or ill.

4th house: If Mercury is located in the 4th house of your birth chart, your thinking becomes clear when you focus on what will make you feel secure in the situation facing you. You have the special ability to perceive the deepest sensitivities of others and to communicate in a way that acknowledges those sensitivities.

5th house: If Mercury is located in the 5th house of your birth chart, your thinking becomes clear when you focus on following your heart. You have the special ability to perceive the opportunity to dramatically enhance communication.

6th house: If Mercury is located in the 6th house of your birth chart, your thinking becomes clear when you focus on planning a routine that will bring order into situations facing you. You have the special ability to analyze separate facts and weave them into a cohesive whole and communicate your perceptions— either through insensitive petty criticism or through objective analysis.

7th house: If Mercury is located in the 7th house of your birth chart, your thinking becomes clear when you focus on the identity of the other person. You have the special ability to perceive the positions of other people and then communicate in a way that reaches them. The choice must be made between communicating the truth about what you are experiencing or telling others what they want to hear.

8th house: If Mercury is located in the 8th house of your birth chart, your thinking becomes clear when you focus on what others need in situations facing you. You have the special ability to perceive the motives of others that are hidden in their communication and to speak in ways that transform other people, for good or ill.

9th house: If Mercury is located in the 9th house of your birth chart, your thinking becomes clear when you focus on finding a positive resolution in situations facing you that is in alignment with the most ethical behavior. You have the special ability to perceive and speak from your philosophical, intuitive mind. The choice here is between intimidating others through judging them as intellectually inferior or using your intuition to teach and communicate to others in a way they can learn.

10th house: If Mercury is located in the 10th house of your birth chart, your thinking becomes clear when you focus on what your goal is in the situation facing you. You have the special ability to perceive those things that will lead to control for good or ill, and to communicate with authority before a public audience.

11th house: If Mercury is located in the 11th house of your birth chart, your thinking becomes clear when you focus on what is for the greatest good of all in the situation facing you. You have the special gift of objective perception and communicating in a friendly, impersonal manner that does not alienate or put others on the defensive.

12th house: If Mercury is located in the 12th house of your birth chart, your thoughts become clear when you spend time alone. Often your ideas and perceptions seem to come out of nowhere. You are actually quite psychic and receptive to both an intuitive awareness of truth and mystical insights. You have the special ability to perceive the intangible truth behind physical occurrences and to successfully communicate that truth to others.

♀

VENUS: KEY TO LOVE AND SELF-WORTH

Venus in the birth chart:*

- Points out the way for social harmony entering into your personal life.
- Indicates the process by which you may lose confidence and self-esteem in social situations.
- Reveals the area in which withholding yourself socially results in feelings of personal inadequacy, while sharing your personal social gifts results in feelings of satisfaction and self-worth.
- Reveals where you may relinquish inner pleasure in order to live up to the values of others.
- Shows your natural talent for experiencing and expressing pleasure that can be shared with others in the spirit of harmonious interaction.
- Unveils your natural gift for putting other people at ease in social situations, resulting in an atmosphere of open sharing through contributing your own brand of warmth.
- Defines the specific key to building personal self-worth and establishing a firm sense of your value to others and to social situations.

---

* To discover the sign and house your VENUS is located in go to www.janspiller.com and a free chart will be calculated for you.

- Expresses the receiving, rather than initiating, sexual principle and reveals those personal values that give you pleasure.

VENUS IN ARIES

UNCONSCIOUS EXPRESSION

Self-defeating habit: Aggressive independence in relationships.
Result: Without realizing it, you might relate to others thoughtlessly and forcefully. This leads to experiencing an endless series of temporary alliances. In attempting to prove your self-worth by disregarding the values of others, you may ultimately win the conquest yet end up alone.

Consequently, a reluctance to sustain closeness often results in a lack of confidence in your worth and ability to relate to others. When you withhold your gift for positive leadership in social situations, it leads to a competitive viewpoint that is destructive for all concerned.

CONSCIOUS EXPRESSION

You have the ability to take the initiative in social situations. You can be a spontaneous leader. With the natural gifts of enthusiasm and courage you can inspire others to contribute to the group.

You realize your inherent value when you share your independence in a way that helps others to help themselves. This encourages others to actualize their potential for self-sufficiency. Becoming aware that others feel insecure about their self-reliance empowers you to motivate them to believe in themselves and assert their individuality. As you help others to build their own independence, you simultaneously come to a realization of your true worth.

Combining your talent for seizing leadership with the recognition of other people's feelings leads to confidence in your ability to stimulate others to interact socially. Using your gifts for taking the initiative in this way maintains your independence while simultaneously validating the worth of all concerned.

VENUS IN TAURUS

UNCONSCIOUS EXPRESSION

Self-defeating habit: Overconcern with comfort in social situations.
Result: You may withhold possessions from others. This deprives you both of sharing your talents for accumulating material things. Repressing the obligation to share your belongings actually leads to a lack of confidence in your ability to acquire more material goods for yourself.

At certain times you might hold back your special sensitivities to the tactile sensual part of life due to feeling unable to share them. This withholding results in a lack of enjoyment in your relationships.

CONSCIOUS EXPRESSION

The idea is to take the initiative in sharing both your material possessions and your ability for the organization and accumulation of goods. Initiative well taken leads to the stabilizing effect of reflected merit in the eyes of others. Additionally, you gain a feeling of social worth and material security in your life by verbally sharing value systems that have brought you stability.

Becoming aware of other people's psychological insecurities about their own importance empowers you to validate them. Consequently, the realization of your true benefit to others begins to emerge.

When you share your gift of sensual sensitivity to life through a form of sensual contact with others, you experience the pleasure and satisfaction of physically extending yourself to add comfort to the social environment.

VENUS IN GEMINI

UNCONSCIOUS EXPRESSION

Self-defeating habit: Preoccupation with a quick wit in social situations.
Result: You may unknowingly withhold from others your special ability for adding lightness and open communication. Neglecting to listen to others' ideas leads to feeling a distinct lack of confidence in communicating with them at all. Indulging in flightiness in social relationships results in experiencing a lack of worth in yourself and others.

When you use your talent for communication to manipulate, to deceive, or to create a superficial excitement with glib wit, you are left without an experience of your own value. In trying to look good to others, it's easy for you to get caught up in superficiality. This type of communication leads to feelings of insecurity and to being at the mercy of how others see you.

CONSCIOUS EXPRESSION

When you are willing to share your natural gift of lightheartedness, you cheer others. Your ability to listen to other points of view strengthens your capacity to contribute an appropriate optimistic insight to any social situation. Your talent for stimulating, elevating conversation can result in your experiencing a deep sense of your social self-worth.

When you see the larger picture of others' viewpoints, you have the gift of communicating in such a way that their burdens are lightened. This leads to feeling a reaction of zest and satisfaction. You establish a firm sense of self-worth and confidence in social situations by cheerfully uplifting others.

VENUS IN CANCER

UNCONSCIOUS EXPRESSION

Self-defeating habit: Oversensitivity and self-protection in social situations.
Result: Indulging in self-protection exaggerates your feelings of isolation. Self-absorption leads to withholding your ability to empathize with others on deep, personal levels for fear that such caring may be rejected. Feelings of inadequacy and withdrawal in relationships can then result.

You have a tendency to cling to private ideals of how people should respond so your feelings won't be hurt and you'll feel worthwhile. This expectation inevitably leads to experiencing others as being abrasive and unsympathetic to your subjective personal needs.

If you seek to manipulate others' emotions to gain attention and caring, you may hold back your ability to care for and nourish others. This behavior results in social isolation and deep feelings of inadequacy.

CONSCIOUS EXPRESSION

By being willing to share your gift of sensitivity, you'll develop a sense of other people's situations. Then you can assist them by sharing the wealth of your loving emotional nature. In extending empathy to help others overcome their emotional hurt, you simultaneously realize a deep sense of social worth.

When this ability to put people in touch with their sensitivities is brought forth, you are appreciated for your value. You experience an unshakable sense of self-worth when you encourage others to communicate their feelings and respond with your unusual sensitivity.

When you give others confidence in their capabilities to achieve what they want, you confirm your usefulness and value. Emotional nourishment and security in all social relations become yours when love and nurturing is freely given to others and nothing is expected in return.

VENUS IN LEO

UNCONSCIOUS EXPRESSION

Self-defeating habit: Seeking the approval of others in social situations.
Result: The fear of disapproval holds back your ability to spread sunshine and

light. You become trapped in self-absorption when you withhold your ability to inspire others with your warm and gregarious nature.

There's a tendency to censor yourself by expressing a type of spontaneity you feel will be approved of. If you indulge in the fear that others may hold back their love, ignore you, or judge you harshly, you experience a lack of social ease.

Inadvertently, you might manipulate others by moderating your expressiveness in order to gain recognition. Social isolation and powerlessness ensue when you interpret others' reactions as a personal rejection.

CONSCIOUS EXPRESSION

Being willing to share your natural gift for drama with others leads to the empowerment of paying attention to *their* needs for acceptance and supporting them with your warmth. In taking the initiative to include others, you are automatically included as part of the group. The idea is to use your charismatic dramatic flair to *share* the center of the stage. By recognizing others' individuality, you are uniquely gifted in proving emotional encouragement, empowering them to overcome disabling emotions and the monotony of daily life.

You are sensitive to the inner reactions of others, and by using this knowledge objectively you lift the audience to new heights of inspired experience. You can bring about ease of communication through your inclusive open-arms policy in which each person is able to relate comfortably with others.

When you use your generosity and sensitivity to help others reach positive emotional states, you can experience without fear your own social worth. You have a dramatic talent for inspiring others and an inbred confidence, warmth, and enthusiasm that bring about self-worth. Security with others comes from knowing that you have acted according to your humanitarian ideals.

VENUS IN VIRGO

UNCONSCIOUS EXPRESSION

Self-defeating habit: Being right in social interactions.
Result: You may unknowingly use relationships in a self-serving way rather than serving others. This leads to the frustration of having relationships fall short of your high standards. Engaging in the tendency to discriminate against and criticize others leads to trying to hide your biases in order to prevent alienation. This indulgence results in feelings of isolation that come from silent, separative judgments.

If you give into fears that your service may not be accepted by others, that you are unworthy to serve others, or that you might be criticized, the result is a disintegration of your ability to make practical use of relationships. You may withhold your gift for unselfish service and instead seek to serve in a way that you think will elicit a particular response. This withholding results in feelings of inadequacy and lack of self-worth.

CONSCIOUS EXPRESSION

You have a natural gift for serving others in practical ways that are compatible with your ideals. When you do, you experience the satisfaction of relating in a way that is consistent with your integrity. By sharing your understanding of order and discrimination, adjusting relationships in such a way that the whole is served, you can experience a heightened sense of self-worth.

Rising above the fear that your service to others may not be accepted empowers you to trust your inner feelings and the higher order that you see. Then you can experience the perfection inherent in being and sharing yourself. In knowing that you have been useful to others, you feel a deep sense of enduring personal value. Recognizing that your outreach has truly stemmed from a *motive* of wanting to serve and be helpful frees you from attachment to others' response and gives you an unshakable sense of self-worth.

VENUS IN LIBRA

UNCONSCIOUS EXPRESSION

Self-defeating habit: Harmony in social situations, regardless of the cost.
Result: There is a tendency to withhold your opinions and sense of justice. You may gain a false sense of harmony with others when in effect you are constantly at the mercy of their approval. When you withhold your ability for creating harmony and instead seek to appease others by telling them what you think they want to hear (according to *their* sense of fair play), your manipulations inadvertently create chaos. Inevitably, such chaos leads to feelings of self-doubt and worthlessness.

In situations of conflict, if you fear that your solution may not be accepted, then you may withhold an honest sharing of yourself for the sake of harmony. This can lead to confusion and helplessness in your relationships.

CONSCIOUS EXPRESSION

Being willing to risk losing your role of Mr. or Ms. Nice Person in social situations empowers you to share the injustices that you feel as well as the fair solution that you see. In so doing, your courage can pave the way for a higher, fairer order to take place. By asserting integrity and openly sharing your insights, you appreciate and value yourself in your relationships.

When you state your independent value system, your sense of balance and harmony is acknowledged. This leads to a feeling of self-worth. Declaring your innate perception of fair play to others (and risking the threat of possible disharmony in order to reach a greater harmony) results in inner satisfaction from sharing your fine gifts of social organization. The invitation is to take the initiative to create harmony that is in alignment with the integrity of your inner sense of fair play. The result is a firm, consistent sense of self-worth.

VENUS IN SCORPIO

UNCONSCIOUS EXPRESSION

Self-defeating habit: Controlling your power in social situations.
Result: The tendency is to withhold sharing your abilities to perceive the hidden talents and resources of others. You may tend to use others as a means of fulfilling your desires. The result is experiencing tension from constantly trying to maintain secret control of those around you. Thus you become the one who is actually controlled—by your fear that others may withdraw their resources. When you ignore bringing others to an awareness of their talents, stagnation and rigidity may result from your incomplete interaction.

Forming rigid personal values results in lost opportunities for interacting with others. In neglecting to stimulate self-worth in other people, you lose your own feeling of worth.

CONSCIOUS EXPRESSION

You have the aptitude and awareness to perceive and encourage the undiscovered abilities of others. You can inspire them to use their potential. When you bring out other people's talents in such a way that you both benefit, you experience a transformation of your values and material opportunities.

You have the opportunity to experience a continual transformation of your feelings of self-worth. This comes from taking the initiative to help others awaken their latent talents, thus showing them their hidden worth. The more you arouse and enhance the power of others, the more valuable you become to them and the more worthwhile you feel about yourself.

VENUS IN SAGITTARIUS

UNCONSCIOUS EXPRESSION

Self-defeating habit: The personal freedom you gain from the power of your philosophical perspectives in relationships.

Result: This can lead to withholding your special ability for providing inspiration to other people. When you indulge in the fear of being limited by relating to others on deep, personal levels, you become the person who's always unavailable—never really there for anybody, including yourself.

If you allow tension and fear of commitment to block you from any relationship, you experience a haunting sense of rootlessness. This results in a curiously empty feeling when you are thrust into unexpected situations. If you are content with fickle infatuations and careless involvements, you may eventually sink into low self-esteem. Your sense of values can be eroded if you neglect to establish worthwhile goals in partnerships.

CONSCIOUS EXPRESSION

You have a special gift for being able to teach others true freedom in relationships. You can do this by allowing the relationship to guide itself to its own goals. Imparting your trust and optimism to others allows you to share with them a larger perspective. Thus, you can experience a constant expansion and excitement in your alliances.

Conveying trust empowers you to focus on a few deeper yet more rewarding partnerships. When you are in touch with the psychological processes of other people, you experience a continual sense of self-worth by inspiring and encouraging them to lofty goals that free them from the limitation of old beliefs.

VENUS IN CAPRICORN

UNCONSCIOUS EXPRESSION

Self-defeating habit: Projecting to others that you are absolutely on top of everything.

Result: This attitude stifles your special ability to exemplify and share awareness of social appropriateness. If you neglect demonstrating such knowledge, you may feel self-doubt and lack of control when others reflect your ineptitude. When relationships are used to ensure your social position, people can become mere objects on the way toward your prestigious or sensual ends. Thus, the spirit of true relationships can be lost in pursuit of materialism that eventually leaves you alone with only your tangible assets for company.

You might deny your special ability to achieve material success in every area of your life, giving in to fears of social rejection if you fail. This path leads to feeling sorry for yourself. Another self-sabotaging fear can be losing your sense of self-worth if your values are not accepted and praised by others and are not reflected through material success.

CONSCIOUS EXPRESSION

You possess the ability to demonstrate social appropriateness as a means toward attaining a desired social position. The goal is to express your unique gifts by sharing your perception and encouraging others to execute their intentions in a practical way. This produces a result that brings you a solid sense of your own worth.

You have a gift for using the social and material values of others for your own goals. Thus, in attaining material success you set an example and demonstrate your awareness of social values. This assists others in tangibly expressing their talents and intentions at the highest level of public acceptance.

You are able to establish a firm, reliable sense of self-worth when you share with others your understanding of how to manipulate the material world toward one's ends. Above all, you become an inspirational example when you demonstrate your natural knowledge of social suitability, using those standards in a creative way to produce the desired results.

VENUS IN AQUARIUS

UNCONSCIOUS EXPRESSION

Self-defeating habit: A desire to create more excitement.
Result: There is a tendency to withhold your gift of objective understanding and loving acceptance. If indulged in, you may experience a series of shallow, chaotic, and scattered encounters. You might use the pretext of universal love for humankind as an excuse for neglecting to establish personal relationships. Eventually, this path leads to the haunting realization that the detachment is simply feeling an inability and unwillingness to relate to anyone on a personal level.

CONSCIOUS EXPRESSION

You experience the joy and exhilaration of coming into contact with others when you are willing to share openly your unique gift of loving in an impartial way. No matter how intimate or personal a relationship may be, you have the ability to retain your sense of individual freedom.

If you do not abuse your freedom through eccentric behavior in an attempt to guarantee your independence, you can attract people who are willing to be your equal. In doing so you eliminate the possibility of your dependency through their independence. A firm sense of your self-worth can be established when you allow a deep personal pledge to develop within your intimate relationship.

VENUS IN PISCES

UNCONSCIOUS EXPRESSION

Self-defeating habit: Not exposing your psychic sensitivity.
Result: Fears of inadequacy may suppress potential psychic healing ability. The results in a feeling of helplessness to alleviate the discomforts that affect others.

When you allow other people to take advantage of your gentle, sympathetic manner and you absorb their ills, you might experience a depletion of energy. Indiscriminately indulging in your romantic ideal of serving and helping others can diminish your self-worth.

CONSCIOUS EXPRESSION

You have a natural gift for relating to others on the level of unconditional love. Your compassion can overcome any social disharmony that arises.

When you see beyond the rules and regulations to the spiritual *purpose* of relationships, your compassionate understanding and willingness to fully participate can automatically heal the situation. You establish a firm sense of self-worth through sharing with others your ability to respond with compassion to both the seen and unseen sources of disharmony.

VENUS IN THE HOUSES

HOW TO INCREASE SELF-WORTH

1st house: If Venus is located in the 1st house of your birth chart, you experience the pleasure of feeling loved when you are aware of your own body and the love that you inherently feel. You feel love in your physical body, simply by tuning in to it. You can increase your self-worth by using your personality as a vehicle for expressing love to others. This position indicates a need to be liked by all or the special ability to express love to others.
2nd house: If Venus is located in the 2nd House of your birth chart, you experience the pleasure of feeling loved when you allow yourself to indulge

in sensual pleasures. You can increase your self-worth by using your personal resources in the world; by using your ability to organize the material world in such a way that optimum comfort, with an awareness of artistic value, is created.

3rd house: If Venus is located in the 3rd house of your birth chart, you experience the pleasure of feeling loved when you attend social events and exchange information with a variety of people. Reading, writing, and going to classes are activities you enjoy. You can increase your self-worth by communicating, learning, and teaching diverse people in ways that add lightness to all, and by using your ability for diplomatic communication with an awareness of opposing views.

4th house: If Venus is located in the 4th house of your birth chart, you experience the pleasure of feeling loved when you host social activities in your home. You can increase your self-worth by using personal resources to build a firm foundation for those closest to you and by integrating your social life with the home environment.

5th house: If Venus is located in the 5th house of your birth chart, you experience the pleasure of feeling loved when you indulge yourself in activities that open your heart. Children are also a source of loving exchange for you. You can increase your self-worth by using your creative talents as a vehicle for self-expression and through initiating and using your special ability to enjoy and enhance any social situation.

6th house: If Venus is located in the 6th house of your birth chart, you experience the pleasure of feeling loved when you involve yourself in processes that bring order out of confusion. You can increase your self-worth by being of practical service to others and through enjoying your duties and facilitating a harmonious working environment.

7th house: If Venus is located in the 7th house of your birth chart, you experience the pleasure of feeling loved when you involve yourself in partnership situations. You can increase your self-worth by the generous sharing of your personal resources and affections with a partner and through exercising your ability to be tolerant and tactful with people, always giving them the benefit of the doubt.

8th house: If Venus is located in the 8th house of your birth chart, you experience the pleasure of feeling loved when you involve yourself in deeply passionate and transformative activities. You can increase your self-worth by merging resources with other people on deep sexual or material levels and through using your ability to connect harmoniously with others on psychic levels.

9th house: If Venus is located in the 9th house of your birth chart, you experience the pleasure of feeling loved when you involve yourself in having adventures. You enjoy activities in which you can expand your horizons. You can increase your self-worth by inspiring others through exchanging philosophical insights and through exercising your ability to teach others, helping them understand philosophical or theoretical ideas.

10th house: If Venus is located in the 10th house of your birth chart, you experience the pleasure of feeling loved when you put yourself in a public arena. Setting and reaching a goal makes you feel self-love. You can increase your self-worth by using personal resources to achieve public goals to produce a result and by using your ability to move toward goals while maintaining a sensitivity to social circumstances and social values.

11th house: If Venus is located in the 11th house of your birth chart, you experience the pleasure of feeling loved when you involve yourself in spending time with your friends. You can increase your self-worth by sharing personal resources in group situations and through exercising your ability to initiate and bring harmony into your friendships and group activities.

12th house: If Venus is located in the 12th house of your birth chart, you often feel the most love when you are alone. For this reason, you may create long-distance relationships; you need to sometimes be apart from loved ones to appreciate them. Due to your sensitivity, there is a shyness in your nature until you learn to use your gift of sharing love to help others. You can increase your self-worth by sharing the experience of spiritual love and order. The gift of tolerance allows people to be where they are. This position reveals the *need* to be understood by all or the *ability* to be understanding of the actions of others.

MARS: KEY TO PERSONAL ASSERTIVENESS

Mars in the birth chart:★
- Depicts your unique skill in taking the initiative; shows the key to successful and effective personal assertion and leadership.
- Reveals the process by which you may unintentionally separate yourself and alienate others.
- Shows how to assert yourself in a way that can be accepted by others and encourages a creative and satisfying interaction with them.

★ To discover the sign and house your MARS is located in, go to www.janspiller.com and a free chart will be calculated for you.

- Shows where you can make an individual commitment that will inspire and give you boldness in productive self-assertion.
- Indicates the initiating, rather than receiving, sexual principle and reveals the desire that motivates you to act.
- Denotes the area in which self-assertion leads to joyous independence and renewed physical energy.

MARS IN ARIES

UNCONSCIOUS EXPRESSION

Asleep tendency: Alienating others by aggressively refusing to accept demands placed upon you.

Result: By acting on the premise that everyone looks out for himself, your behavior may appear rash, abrasive in exaggerated independence, and inconsiderate to others. You lose energy and acceptance when you fiercely maintain your right to absolute independence.

CONSCIOUS EXPRESSION

Awake leadership: Using independence in ways that inspire others to take the initiative. Viewing your impact on them objectively empowers you to assert your courage and initiative in ways that lead to freedom for all concerned. You gain physical energy when you consider the other person and give that person confidence in his or her ability to follow destiny.

MARS IN TAURUS

UNCONSCIOUS EXPRESSION

Asleep tendency: Alienating others by judging or ignoring their values in order to confirm your own sense of self-worth.

Result: This mental competitiveness brings about defeat by cutting off others on a material or sensual level. You lose the energy needed to establish your worth if you refuse to allow the experience of others to be incorporated into a rigid value system.

CONSCIOUS EXPRESSION

Awake leadership: allowing others to contribute their ideas and values in a way that supports getting material results.

When you commit yourself to participating actively in the world, you can establish a solid foundation for material security and comfort. Your values can be transformed and translated into greater material and sensual results by viewing others as *your* resources.

MARS IN GEMINI

UNCONSCIOUS EXPRESSION

Asleep tendency: Alienating others by aggressively using sharp logic to prove that you have the fastest mind.

Result: This is often done in a competitive manner at the expense of others. If you confront and provoke in a verbal, combative way, you create shallow and meaningless mental skirmishes. You lose energy when you inflict incisive, passionate logic, proving personal points that win the battle but lose the war.

CONSCIOUS EXPRESSION

Awake leadership: Directing mental energies to a wider perspective than yourself.

As you accept the larger outlook of others' views, you are able to brilliantly translate information intuitively received. Your communication then becomes a sharing experience rather than a pointless battle of wits when you welcome and include the knowledge of others. Your energy increases in direct proportion to responsible communication.

MARS IN CANCER

UNCONSCIOUS EXPRESSION

Asleep tendency: Alienating others by competing with them for fulfillment of emotional needs.

Result: Aggressively demanding attention and assuming that the needs of others are a threat to your security. When others don't give you the support and attention you think you need, you lose energy by using your emotional touchiness to reject them.

CONSCIOUS EXPRESSION

Awake leadership: Using sensitivity to become aware of others' needs.

Your challenge is to set aside self-centeredness, become aware of the other person's need, and adopt a position of responsibility. Then you can acknowledge the feelings of others as well as express your own needs positively. You gain energy when you commit yourself to initiating closeness and objectively organizing situations that meet everyone's needs.

MARS IN LEO

UNCONSCIOUS EXPRESSION

Asleep tendency: Alienating others by asserting in ways that make you appear larger than life.
Result: If you compete for center stage to ensure that you will be acknowledged, you may sacrifice leadership. You lose energy by indulging in dramatic demonstrations of authority over others and by pressing to get your way regardless of their feelings.

CONSCIOUS EXPRESSION

Awake leadership: Using the power of dramatic emotional expression to inspire and encourage others in their self-expression.

Acting on a commitment to inspire others through your enthusiasm reinforces your sense of independence. Your energies increase in direct proportion to your willingness to unite with others.

MARS IN VIRGO

UNCONSCIOUS EXPRESSION

Asleep tendency: Alienating others by taking what they do or say too personally and then aggressively demanding to be acknowledged as right all the time.
Result: You may seek to prove your rightness by making others wrong. When your own or the actions of others fall short of your standards, you can be quick to criticize and judge. By focusing on errors you lose your momentum.

CONSCIOUS EXPRESSION

Awake leadership: Taking the initiative in assisting others to straighten out their lives.

Acting on your commitment to serve effectively empowers you to share responsibility and overcome the need to be right about everything. Then you can release the feeling that you have to do others' work for them. Your gift is in developing practical methods that aid others in achieving *their* ideals of perfection.

When you humanely apply your passionate sense of order to chaotic situations in a tolerant way, you experience satisfaction and a new sense of system. Your energy is increased in the process of initiating these changes.

MARS IN LIBRA

UNCONSCIOUS EXPRESSION

Asleep tendency: Alienating others by manipulating their responses in an aggressive way that produces false harmony.

Result: You may demand your version of harmony by behaving as you think others want you to and expecting them to act as you want in exchange. You may subtly compete with others to see who can be the most harmonious person and thus victimize yourself by continually demanding that others act fairly. You lose energy when you hold others responsible for creating justice and cooperation in your world, and when disruption occurs, blaming them for the disharmony.

CONSCIOUS EXPRESSION

Awake leadership: Actively, responsibly, and directly initiating social interaction on the basis of personal integrity.

When you ask others what it is they want from the relationship and honestly share what you want, you are then able to create harmony based on truth. Thus, you gain energy by experiencing yourself as the source of harmony or disharmony in your interactions.

MARS IN SCORPIO

UNCONSCIOUS EXPRESSION

Asleep tendency: Alienating others by competing for power over your environment.

Result: You can lose energy if you suppress your desires and motives in order to maintain control. Your secretiveness in taking action may cause others to mistrust you and thus set the stage for explosive confrontations.

CONSCIOUS EXPRESSION

Awake leadership: Committing yourself to responsible expression of motives and intentions. When you reveal your desires, others will know and trust your leadership and ability to use existing circumstances to transform a stagnant situation. You gain energy when you reveal your motives to others and simultaneously free yourself to act.

MARS IN SAGITTARIUS

UNCONSCIOUS EXPRESSION

Asleep tendency: Alienating others by competitively pitting your philosophical understanding against another's intelligence.

Result: You can inadvertently imply that the beliefs of others are based on inferior understanding and intellectual ability. You lose energy for expanded insights when you use the power of your intellect to intimidate others with demonstrations of self-righteousness.

CONSCIOUS EXPRESSION

Awake leadership: Inspiring others to attain their intellectual heights. When you are willing to learn as well as teach, you can accept the views of others and incorporate their ideas with yours. Taking the time to understand another's point of view first allows you to establish a line of communication. You gain energy by acknowledging the intellectual contributions of others and actively inspiring them to reach out and expand their goals and ideals.

MARS IN CAPRICORN

UNCONSCIOUS EXPRESSION

Asleep tendency: Alienating others by competitively pitting your need for maintaining a social image against the well-being of others.

Result: When you regard social prestige as a means of self-justification, you can treat yourself and others as objects to be used in fulfilling your ambitions. In adopting austerity to achieve your aims, you may lose energy by cutting off your feelings and emotions.

CONSCIOUS EXPRESSION

Awake leadership: Sharing a sense of organization and social protocol. By encouraging others to accomplish their ambitions you relieve the tension brought on by the need to justify yourself. When you share your natural ability for organizational leadership, you experience the more personal rewards of career accomplishment. Your energy increases when you establish social prestige for an organization that is bigger than yourself.

MARS IN AQUARIUS

UNCONSCIOUS EXPRESSION

Asleep tendency: Alienating others by asserting your ability to express and achieve humanitarian ideals is exclusive.

Result: You may think you need to become coldly dispassionate toward others in order to act freely on these ideals. Thus, you estrange yourself from those who might participate in group efforts. You lose energy by cutting yourself off from the conscious expressions of the group consciousness.

CONSCIOUS EXPRESSION

Awake leadership: Asserting for the group ideals rather than using the group to support personal plans. When you are able to identify yourself as part of the group rather than separate, you can implement your humanitarian ideals. You gain energy by inspiring yourself and others to grow toward and manifest these ideals.

MARS IN PISCES

UNCONSCIOUS EXPRESSION

Asleep tendency: Alienating others by assuming that you are the only one who sees the true spiritual vision.

Result: By operating from a belief in your spiritual superiority, you can camouflage your motives and desires and negate the input of others. If you withhold yourself from direct involvement, you lose the vitality of your direction and become confused. This may result in a scattering of your personal energies.

CONSCIOUS EXPRESSION

Awake leadership: Communicating openly about problems that exist in your personal life. As you share spiritual solutions to practical problems and allow others to share their insights also, everyone benefits from an expanded spiritual awareness. You gain energy from practical service and a revitalizing sense of faith in your vision when you allow open and direct interaction with others.

MARS IN THE HOUSES

YOUR ABILITY FOR ASSERTION AND ACCOMPLISHMENT

1st house: If Mars is located in the 1st house of your birth chart, you regain strength and energize yourself by focusing on your body and taking action on your independent impulses. Your ability for assertion and accomplishment is connected to an expressive and impulsive personality.

2nd house: If Mars is located in the 2nd house of your birth chart, you regain strength and energize yourself by becoming involved in moneymaking activities. You are also reenergized by sensual enjoyments that bring your body comfort. Your ability for assertion and accomplishment is connected to a need for material things and the ability to attain them.

3rd house: If Mars is located in the 3rd house of your birth chart, you regain strength and energize yourself by going out and about to social gatherings and connecting with a variety of people. Reading, learning, and exchanging information recharges your battery. Your ability for assertion and accomplishment is connected to logic and the talent for clear communication.

4th house: If Mars is located in the 4th house of your birth chart, you regain strength and energize yourself by spending time in your home and with close family members. Your ability for assertion and accomplishment is connected to sensitivity and the ability to express personal feelings.

5th house: If Mars is located in the 5th house of your birth chart, you regain strength and energize yourself by becoming involved in a creative project that opens your heart. Having fun energizes you. Your ability for assertion and accomplishment is connected to your ability for artistic, dramatic, and creative expression.

6th house: If Mars is located in the 6th house of your birth chart, you regain strength and energize yourself by planning routines that add healthy organization to your life. Your ability for assertion and accomplishment is connected to a sense of duty and self-perfection. You have the ability to attain a sense of self-perfection by taking the initiative in actively serving others.

7th house: If Mars is located in the 7th house of your birth chart, you regain strength and energize yourself by spending time with a partner. Your ability for assertion and accomplishment is connected to the reactions of others. You have the ability to initiate activity with other people.

8th house: If Mars is located in the 8th house of your birth chart, you regain strength and energize yourself by involving yourself in intense transformational processes. Your ability for assertion and accomplishment is connected to your material connections with others in sex, money, and shared resources.

9th house: If Mars is located in the 9th house of your birth chart, you regain strength and energize yourself by going on an adventure. Your energy soars when you are in an activity that expands your horizons, either physically or mentally. Your ability for assertion and accomplishment is connected to your theoretical mind, and intellectual accomplishments as recognized by society.

10th house: If Mars is located in the 10th house of your birth chart, you regain strength and energize yourself by going into the public arena and organizing the different factions to successfully reach a goal. Your ability for assertion and accomplishment is connected to positions of authority and how those positions enhance your personal position.

11th house: If Mars is located in the 11th house of your birth chart, you regain strength and energize yourself by spending time with friends and involving yourself in unconventional activities that are in alignment with listening to your inner wisdom. Your ability for assertion and accomplishment is connected to humanitarian goals or ideals, as well as to impersonal or group relationships.

12th house: If Mars is located in the 12th house of your birth chart, you regain strength and energize yourself by spending time alone. When you are by yourself your best path of action becomes apparent. Your ability for assertion and accomplishment is connected to your private dream and to manifesting universal urges and visions.

♃

JUPITER: KEY TO SOCIAL OPPORTUNITY AND REWARD

Jupiter in the birth chart:*
- Shows how to build trust and faith in yourself and consequently in others.
- Represents that key of understanding by which you can independently create value and personal growth out of any circumstances that life presents.
- Reveals where you naturally see the larger perspective, which leads to faith in life and confidence in yourself.
- Shows how trust can be cultivated—faith in yourself and in your ability to handle any unfamiliar or unexpected circumstance that may occur—by taking a more philosophical view of life.
- Pinpoints the perspective that can free you to act in a way that automatically leads to joy through using social opportunity for personal expansion.
- Denotes an area of natural good fortune that when activated overcomes feelings of limitation and fear.

---

* To discover the sign and house your JUPITER is located in, go to www.janspiller.com and a free chart will be calculated for you.

- Illuminates that area of life where your perspective teaches faith in an ordered universe behind chaotic appearances and locates the source of trust that can be tapped and developed within each individual.

JUPITER IN ARIES

UNCONSCIOUS EXPRESSION

Habitual hesitation: To take the initiative to go your own way.
Result: Fears of inadequacy arise that may block your actions. If you succumb to a lack of faith in your independence, you may neglect the social opportunity for leadership and feel a deep sense of frustration. By indulging in distrust and not following your sense of immediate and personal expression, you may fail to reach beyond the state of survival and into creativity.

CONSCIOUS EXPRESSION

Accepted leap of faith: When you wholeheartedly express confidence, vision, and a sense of opportunity, you feel the joy of uncompromised self-expression. You build trust in others by relying on your instincts and taking the initiative to pioneer activities that naturally attract and enlist other people. By trusting yourself, you can appreciate the value of independence and thus expand your field of leadership and opportunity for initiating new enterprises.

JUPITER IN TAURUS

UNCONSCIOUS EXPRESSION

Habitual hesitation: Failure to use current and nearby resources to their greatest potential.
Result: A lack of confidence in your ability to ensure a stable financial base. Such rigid values may bring about the disappointment of achieving less materially than what you knew were potentially able to achieve.

CONSCIOUS EXPRESSION

Accepted leap of faith: When you invest yourself in the potential of what you consider materially valuable, you increase your opportunities to satisfy those values and desires. In trusting yourself to actualize material ideals that make you comfortable, you are supported by many opportunities to accomplish your ends and to fulfill yourself in practical ways.

JUPITER IN GEMINI

UNCONSCIOUS EXPRESSION

Habitual hesitation: Postponing communicating insights to others.
Result: You may experience an endless accumulation of trivial information. When you use your buoyant expressions carelessly as a defense mechanism against other people's unfamiliar points of view, you may experience a transitory trust in yourself. But this leads to shallow conversations and a frivolous attitude, lessening your chances to better yourself in the world.

CONSCIOUS EXPRESSION

Accepted leap of faith: Seek information from others and yourself, trusting that there is an answer and listening for that resolution. When you actively expand your curiosity into dealing with information creatively, you find answers instead of being stuck in a perpetual question machine. You experience truly meaningful communication with others and inner faith by sincerely listening for the right answers to your questions.

JUPITER IN CANCER

UNCONSCIOUS EXPRESSION

Habitual hesitation: Postponing sharing personal feelings and emotions with others, fearing that they may not empathize with you.
Result: You may lose the opportunity to relate deeply with others. You may unknowingly use your emotionally subjective beliefs as a defense mechanism against unfamiliar situations, in such a way that the result is self-righteous alienation and a loss of your faith in others as well as in yourself.

CONSCIOUS EXPRESSION

Accepted leap of faith: When you expand your ability to make other people feel that they belong in a given social situation, your skills help build a feeling of family in any circumstance. That process creates faith in your basic security instincts. By actively using your talent to help others realize their belonging and acceptance, you build faith and confidence in yourself and everyone around you.

JUPITER IN LEO

UNCONSCIOUS EXPRESSION

Habitual hesitation: Not participating joyfully with others because you fear that they might not be loyal to your leadership.

Result: You may experience frustration over your eventual failure to obtain this desired position. You can have so much faith in your ego that you may unknowingly act in ways that discount the value of others. As a result you can become bewildered by others' lack of allegiance to your guidance. In the end you may alienate others by your dramatic demonstrations of belief in yourself.

CONSCIOUS EXPRESSION

Accepted leap of faith: When you trust your ability to give to others, you can actively initiate situations in which you attract those social rewards you most value. You may find that others welcome your generosity when your aim is to be morally or intellectually equal. Acting in the best interests of the situation, you can concentrate on producing beneficial results for all and gain the opportunity for natural leadership.

JUPITER IN VIRGO

UNCONSCIOUS EXPRESSION

Habitual hesitation: Fear of never being perfect enough to serve.

Result: You may postpone and thus lose the opportunity to serve others. This can create a general lack of self-trust in your abilities. Using analytical talents to find fault with your service can leave you lacking confidence and afraid to contribute.

If you withhold actual assistance and substitute righteous beliefs about service, it submerges you in unnecessary details. An exaggerated self-critical attitude can lead to feelings of insufficiency. You feel a constant need to prepare that is never complete enough to contribute.

CONSCIOUS EXPRESSION

Accepted leap of faith: Consciously put your desire to assist before your personal concept of how you think you should serve. If you trust the purity of your motives and are willing to make some mistakes in your desire to serve other people, you can experience the freedom of finding social situations in which you serve and develop yourself. Then you can expand your arena and attract many vocational and social opportunities. Self-trust increases as you use your finely honed analytical abilities to actively support others.

JUPITER IN LIBRA

UNCONSCIOUS EXPRESSION

Habitual hesitation: Postponing dealing with others on a one-to-one level.
Result: Fearing inability to maintain harmony in your relationships, you may experience many shallow, unsatisfying associations throughout life. If you avoid a deep, intimate alliance and instead adopt an insensitive attitude of expectation toward your friends and partners, you may inadvertently create isolation from others.

CONSCIOUS EXPRESSION

Accepted leap of faith: Put yourself in situations where you will experience intimate contacts with people. Then you undergo a sense of expansion and joy. As you accept and trust deep relationships and get close to people on more than superficial levels, you gain a continuous inspiration to self-growth. Self-trust increases as you use your natural abilities for creating ease in social situations to unite others into a harmonic whole.

JUPITER IN SCORPIO

UNCONSCIOUS EXPRESSION

Habitual hesitation: Postponing participation with others on business, sexual, and deep psychological levels, fearing the loss of personal control.
Result: You may create deadlocked situations in which no one is able to use mutual resources. When you avoid transformational connections with others, you can experience a frustrating sense of losing power while being obsessed with the need to control others.

CONSCIOUS EXPRESSION

Accepted leap of faith: Risk exposing your hidden motivations by sharing intimately with another. This leads to expansion, opportunities, and trust emerging from allowing yourself to become a part of another's life. Then it is no longer necessary to control or be controlled by them. By trusting the occult vision of the transforming energy of relationships to manifest in mutually beneficial ways, you can surrender to its power. You may then discover that you possess intuitive perception to use these resources so that each person benefits. Through this process you can expand your own power and opportunity on all levels of close relationships.

JUPITER IN SAGITTARIUS

UNCONSCIOUS EXPRESSION

Habitual hesitation: Postponing joining with others in deep philosophical pursuits.

Result: You may instead fritter away the time as a perpetual traveler, both in mind and in body. If you are content to be motivated by superficial reasons and internal reflections, you can inadvertently create a situation of intellectual isolation by presuming you know the answers to everything.

CONSCIOUS EXPRESSION

Accepted leap of faith: Let yourself share new ideas rather than using knowledge to establish intellectual authority. You can then truly become a teacher. When you decide to involve yourself seriously with deep philosophical study and communication, trusting your knowledge to flow spontaneously, you experience the joy and personal expansion of learning and teaching. Self-trust increases as you take the initiative in sharing your positive outlook and philosophical insights with others.

JUPITER IN CAPRICORN

UNCONSCIOUS EXPRESSION

Habitual hesitation: Postponing the use of your natural talents to fulfill your desires, formulate plans, or manipulate business dealings.

Result: You may experience insecurity about your integrity that is aimed toward achievement. Thus, you can be at a loss to manifest the talents within you. If you give in to righteous ideas about controlling others or repress your fine managerial abilities, you experience frustration and doubts about yourself.

CONSCIOUS EXPRESSION

Accepted leap of faith: Put yourself in situations where you can delegate authority and manage resources, so you can experience an expansion of faith in yourself to use your talents with integrity. When you trust your uprightness and utilize your natural managerial talents to organize what you truly believe in, you discover that your abilities to manage others brings joy to everyone as well as yourself.

JUPITER IN AQUARIUS

UNCONSCIOUS EXPRESSION

Habitual hesitation: Postponing the open expression of knowledge, fearing you may not have enough to share or that the information you have is not important. Result: This leads to repressing communication of your learning. Personal frustration can follow. You may allow righteous judgments about the unimportance of all knowledge, including your own, to prevent you from sharing with others. The result is likely to be intense internal frustration.

CONSCIOUS EXPRESSION

Accepted leap of faith: Allow your knowledge to flow freely into group situations, so you can experience the joy and expansion that comes as a natural result of your generous sharing. By not trying to prove uniqueness or superiority and instead seeking to share knowledge in a way that actually contributes to situations at hand, you begin to experience the joy and freedom of speaking from higher levels of intuitive knowing in a way that expands the circumstances for everyone. Self-trust increases as you use your innate connectedness with groups to promote a natural sharing of objective knowledge.

JUPITER IN PISCES

UNCONSCIOUS EXPRESSION

Habitual hesitation: Postponing using your visionary abilities to see through and beyond the limiting, insensitive social, intellectual, and moralistic values of society.
Result: A widespread state of perpetual confusion. You may inadvertently allow righteous ideas about how circumstances should be—but are not—to alienate you from trusting yourself and from life. The lack of faith that ensues can create a state of helpless stagnation and confusion about how to improve your present circumstances.

CONSCIOUS EXPRESSION

Accepted leap of faith: Greet the many facets of life with a basic trust in the universe so you can experience the joy of having your vision fulfilled at every moment. When you accept circumstances as they are, with your vision on the perfection behind the appearance, you undergo the joy and personal expansion of being able to assist people in realizing their potential. Self-trust is increased as you use your natural trust in the unseen workings behind the appearances of life as a personal foundation.

JUPITER IN THE HOUSES

HOW TO ATTRACT SOCIAL OPPORTUNITIES AND REWARDS

1st house: If Jupiter is located in the 1st house of your birth chart, you inherently trust in your impulses to lead you in the right direction. You trust yourself, your own strength and independence. You attract social opportunities and rewards when you concentrate on expanding your self-expression and the impact of your personality.

2nd house: If Jupiter is located in the 2nd house of your birth chart, you inherently trust in your good luck in always having money flow into your life. You attract social opportunities and rewards when you actively expand your material values and act on your ability to earn money.

3rd house: If Jupiter is located in the 3rd house of your birth chart, you inherently trust your logic and ability to gain information to see your options, safely guiding your way in life. You attract social opportunities and rewards when you expand your intellect by following your thirst for information and sharing that knowledge with others. The arena of formal education brings many rewards.

4th house: If Jupiter is located in the 4th house of your birth chart, you inherently trust in your own family and belief system to take care of you. You attract social opportunities and rewards when you expand your understanding of the past to include the whole world as your home. This increases your security and gives rise to latent talents in business, finance, and real estate.

5th house: If Jupiter is located in the 5th house of your birth chart, you inherently trust in your ability to gamble and take risks in life in creating success. You attract social opportunities and rewards when you work with children, theater, and the arts, and expand your opportunities to express your creative talents.

6th house: If Jupiter is located in the 6th house of your birth chart, you inherently trust in your ability to create order out of chaos. You attract social opportunities and rewards when you expand your ability to serve in the world. The areas of health and helping professions bring social rewards.

7th house: If Jupiter is located in the 7th house of your birth chart, you inherently trust in your partners sharing with you in a mutually supportive way. You attract social opportunities and rewards when you align yourself with a partner. The establishment of a primary relationship can lead to personal rewards.

8th house: If Jupiter is located in the 8th house of your birth chart, you inherently trust in deep, bonded partnerships to ensure your survival and help you to thrive. You attract social opportunities and rewards when you expand through a deep psychological or sexual involvement, or business partnerships.

9th house: If Jupiter is located in the 9th house of your birth chart, you inherently trust in taking risks and having adventures in life. You feel that there are spiritual powers protecting you and you believe in your own good luck. You attract social opportunities and rewards when you involve yourself in publishing, philosophy, higher consciousness, education, and foreign travel.

10th house: If Jupiter is located in the 10th house of your birth chart, you inherently trust in your desire to do something good in the world. You have confidence in your ability to manage others in situations in a way that all of you are going toward the same goal. You attract social opportunities and rewards when you expand your public expression in the world. Positions of management and authority bring social rewards.

11th house: If Jupiter is located in the 11th house of your birth chart, you inherently trust in your abilities for creating friendships to help you expand and glide through life successfully. You attract social opportunities and rewards when you align yourself in group activities with scientific or humanitarian aims.

12th house: If Jupiter is located in the 12th house of your birth chart, you inherently trust in a higher power to take care of you. You have an innocent, trusting, well-intended nature that sometimes puts you in perilous situations into which your angels intercede to get you out safely. You attract social opportunities and rewards when you become aware of the most spiritual and esoteric part of yourself. By expanding your understanding of your role in the universe and allowing the universal mind to flow through you in poetry, music, acting, or other spiritual or artistic forms of self-expression, you can attract social rewards.

ħ

SATURN: KEY TO PUBLIC ACHIEVEMENT

Saturn in the birth chart:*

- Shows the process of fulfilling your social obligation in a public way that results in a sense of personal achievement.
- Indicates the process by which fears deflect you from fulfilling your ambitions.
- Pinpoints the area of your greatest desire and greatest fear.
- Illuminates self-discipline and physical responsibility; your endurance and where you have the ability to see things through.
- The purpose, direction, and social responsibility in your life, showing those factors that can lead to a life direction that evokes the self-esteem and respect of others for your natural authority in the world.
- Where the power of personal commitment to contribute to society gives you the courage to rise above inhibition and fear, making those personal corrections that are necessary to contribute in a way that is supported and respected by the rest of the world.
- Pinpoints where you do not yet have it straight, that area where you must apply repeated effort to gain mastery on a nonego level. Only through accepting and meeting the tests of Saturn can the bliss and freedom of states of consciousness (represented by Uranus, Neptune, and Pluto) be secured on a permanent basis.

SATURN IN ARIES

UNCONSCIOUS EXPRESSION

You may try: To stand out as a leader by ignoring established protocol and being impatient.
Result: This form of assertion leads the material world to exercise harsh discipline over your energies by severe limitations. When you endeavor to lead for self-serving motivations only, you can become restless and narrow. This alienates others and results in frustration of your productive efforts.

---

* To discover the sign and house your SATURN is located in, go to www.janspiller.com and a free chart will be calculated for you.

CONSCIOUS EXPRESSION

Your skills and social responsibility: The ability to be a leader. Acknowledge yourself as creator of your sense of independence and of situations in which you lead or follow. This self-recognition empowers you to feel secure enough to act independently. As you use your leadership capacity, more and more you become aware of others' wishes. Fostering new ideals and ideas into a form that answers a collective need, your innovative ambitions have the potential for reaching and affecting society at large.

IN PAST LIVES

Karmically, your destiny is to formulate a new identity. An entire cycle of ego expression through an old sense of self has ended, and that ego has dissolved. This is why you feel so vulnerable in this lifetime: You have no instinctive ego to serve as a buffer against environmental stimuli. Thus, there is a tendency either to overreact or to underreact when asserting yourself because you don't yet have a solid sense of self to assert from.

Your task: To rise above the limitations of past life personality expressions; to discover and formulate a new, more powerful sense of identity.

SATURN IN TAURUS

UNCONSCIOUS EXPRESSION

You may try: To accumulate money or possessions to stand out as a separate identity, seeking to justify your worth to others.
Result: Poverty consciousness and a feeling of being victimized by the material world in relation to your personal security and self-esteem. The upshot is feeling continually thwarted from accumulating the money, comfort, and status you seek. If you struggle to avoid pursuing practical monetary ambitions, frustration with material status ensues.

CONSCIOUS EXPRESSION

Your skills and social responsibility: To manifest material abundance, comfort, and security in the world. The idea is to recognize yourself as creating limitations stemming from your values, which brings about circumstances that render you unable to regenerate your financial situation. Then your self-worth can be expanded to include new methods for making money.

Once you are willing to use your abilities to build tangible resources in a way that also helps others build their tangible resources, you can experience the worldly abundance and sensual satisfaction that you seek.

IN PAST LIVES

Material resources can be scanty in this lifetime until you gain a clear sense of what is really important, what has meaning and value in your life. You are discovering the principles that when manifested will give you an internal sense of stability, comfort, and self-worth. Then material resources are unlimited and you can become wealthy through your own efforts. When you act in generous ways that help others feel comfortable in your presence, you create the experience of abundance within yourself on a moment-to-moment basis.

You have formulated a new sense of self in recent past lifetimes and now must build a foundation that will give strength, stability, and support to the fresh identity that has emerged.

Your task: To become more aware of helping others to feel comfortable when they are with you.

SATURN IN GEMINI

UNCONSCIOUS EXPRESSION

You may try: To build barriers against intimate relationships in order to ensure the option to mingle with many people and to pursue goals and friendships in a superficial, social way.
Result: This form of relating to life leads to the jack-of-all-trades, master-of-none syndrome. The result is frustration due to a failure to complete long-range goals because of your need to detach from everything. You may experience defeat by always creating an option and by refusing to commit yourself.

CONSCIOUS EXPRESSION

Your skills and social responsibility: To bring many ideas into reality. When you acknowledge your need for a variety of ambitious outlets, you begin to notice that a flitting-about, social frame of reference does not encourage a consistent, conscious center from which you can handle your divergent ambitions.

Dedicating yourself to building an inner focus point empowers you to complete your ideas one at a time or give them to someone who can bring them to completion. Following a consistent philosophical identity within yourself allows you to use your many talents and abilities to communicate information that organizes and supports others in a solid way. Thus, you will attract a variety of people and experiences. The result will be the positive stimulus and the variety of challenges needed for fulfillment.

IN PAST LIVES

Recent past lives have yielded a strong internal sense of self, and you are now recognizing your own strength through connecting and communicating with others. This lifetime you are learning how to be open to a clear and mutually beneficial exchange of information through eliminating a tendency to self-censorship. Your job is to live in the moment and to verbalize clearly the ideas that come into consciousness as they arise.

Through cultivating this innocent, spontaneous honesty with others you find that the people around you take their rightful positions in your life without any need for conscious manipulation on your part.

Your task: Learning to communicate clearly, honestly, and openly.

SATURN IN CANCER

UNCONSCIOUS EXPRESSION

You may try: To make other people respect your feelings because you are a sensitive person.
Result: This invites rejection. The resulting self-protection leads to creating emotional limitations in your life that appear to be vulnerable to your security. When you are afraid of dealing directly and objectively with others about your sensitivities, you experience a severe limitation and repression of your emotional nature. This eventually cuts off your ability to experience feeling anything at all.

CONSCIOUS EXPRESSION

Your skills and social responsibility: To experience your subjective feelings deeply and then to bring those feelings into manifestation in a way that benefits others as well as yourself. Acknowledging yourself as the creator of your feelings empowers you to delve into your sensitivities.

Once in touch with your true feelings, you have the ability to bring those feelings to the surface in an objective way that clears the air and benefits everyone. You possess the ability and the responsibility in the world for creating an environment in which everyone, including yourself, is nurtured and secure.

IN PAST LIVES

You have reached a stage in your evolutionary path where it is necessary to bring past-life sensitivities and caring into an organized format for public expression. This process emerges from subconscious levels—suddenly you may find yourself excited and involved in activities that have the potential to lead to a profession or career. As you begin to use and express these instinctive past-life talents, you gain a sense of the career that can be truly fulfilling to your basic inner needs. You are learning to take responsibility for the expression of past-life identities, desires, and talents in the context of the current lifetime environment.

There is insecurity about really belonging in the home and family environment of origin. This leads to feeling needy and overly dependent on others for emotional support. Karmically, you are bringing in new ideas that are not yet familiar to society or understood by your family. It is as though you are from another planet and do not find affinity with the consciousness of your family structure.

Your task: To find a sense of belonging and comfort within yourself, and to make new families based on an inner connection with others.

SATURN IN LEO

UNCONSCIOUS EXPRESSION

You may try: To impose your right for self-expression by creating situations that are larger than life.
Result: If you dramatize your ups and downs in order to gain respect and awe, your experiences might resemble those of the heroes in Shakespeare's tragedies. The dramas produced may be self-destructive and unfulfilling. You will find the outer world unsympathetic and limiting to your dramatic behavior.

CONSCIOUS EXPRESSION

Your skills and social responsibility: To bring your capacity for moving dramatic expression into manifestation. Acknowledging yourself as the originator of the melodramas in your life empowers you to be responsible for the intense scenes you attract. You gain confidence in your skill to handle emotional display when you are in touch with the love center within yourself. Then the potential to align your dramatic sense with the knowledge that you can serve a larger community comes forth.

You contribute to others by giving expression to your *true* inner feelings,

inspiring them through your own courageous example in dramatically revealing your innermost sentiments. The idea is to commit yourself to your ability
to use drama as a means of consciously inspiring constructive goals in the
world. Then you experience the excitement and security of designing ex-
travaganzas that you know will not undermine your most profound creative
abilities.

IN PAST LIVES

You have reached a stage of needing to be responsible for creating what
you really want. To do this you must first have a vision of the goal or ideal you
want to manifest. From this dream your energies can begin to flow in a constructive, consistent direction that supports your childlike spirit.

Past lives spent as entertainers or kings have left you feeling that you have
to perform within a rigid structure that keeps you on top and in control of the
audience.

Your task: To let dissolve all the feelings of having to play an approved role,
so that your childlike spirit of excitement and fun can begin to emerge and
lead you home, into the happiness and fulfillment of your dreams.

SATURN IN VIRGO

UNCONSCIOUS EXPRESSION

You may try: To fit spontaneous expression into structures that block it, fearing
imperfection in expressing yourself or in your ability to be of service.
Result: This form of perfectionism leads to the painful self-imposed restriction
of failing to live up to your own standards. Your power to perform is undermined when you indulge in painful, abrasive self-criticism. This can result in
health or work imbalances. Feeling unable to use your strong sense of duty can
lead to withdrawal from participation on almost every level of life.

CONSCIOUS EXPRESSION

Your skills and social responsibility: To manifest your talents for creating
order in the world. Acknowledging yourself as the creator of any debilitating thoughts used against yourself and others empowers you to cease taking
yourself so seriously. This gives you more security in actualizing yourself in
ways that serve other people. You can then offer your precise analytical talents
to give aid to the community; by seeing its imperfections, you can use your
power of discrimination to bring about order where there is chaos.

When you are able to see yourself as the servant of life, a form of non-judgmental perfectionism can enter into your affairs. Then you can offer in a balanced, sharing, spontaneous way your vision of helping others. You experience the confidence to be of practical service to other people by creating appropriate outlets for your strong sense of duty.

IN PAST LIVES

Your challenge is to be responsible for an effective integration between your body and mind. When any aspect within becomes too extreme or out of balance, the result is a breakdown in health or work. You are learning to allow health to be a barometer of the degree of balance in your life. In this incarnation you want to work on yourself, to perfect yourself, so that you can manifest your spirituality and visionary ideals in a practical, tangible way.

Past lives have been spent in service to others on a menial level that resulted in your ego being attached to a sense of perfection about how you did your job and carried through your duties. The idea this lifetime is to relinquish a sense of superiority about being perfect, above the rest of society, and allow your vision to manifest in a flowing way through your work. You are learning to release the tension of preplanning and to focus on the abstract vision you want to manifest.

Your task: Handling the details of your life spontaneously as they arise; to do your part and fulfill your role as a disciple of life.

SATURN IN LIBRA

UNCONSCIOUS EXPRESSION

You may try: To maintain the harmony of emotional security by clinging to certain social ideals and always being pleasant.
Result: Difficulty with being yourself, since it cuts off personal expression with others. When you place a limit on your actions with expectations of how others should respond, severe limitations may be felt. All of your relationships may become burdensome and disappointing.

CONSCIOUS EXPRESSION

Your skills and social responsibility: To create relationships that actually work by bringing into manifestation their natural inherent harmony. Acknowledging yourself as creator of the harmony and disharmony that you experience gives you security in your ability to experience what is created. Once you are willing to undergo the possibility of disharmony in relationships, you have the capacity to actualize yourself by sharing your honest, individual point of view. A natural, authentic balance can manifest in response.

The idea is to commit yourself to your integrity, sharing your independent point of view honestly, and then objectively notice how others respond. This process allows you to use your diplomatic abilities on an impersonal level that serve a collective need. The result can bring about the necessary structure to produce an alliance that answers both your needs and the needs of the other person, with no limiting justifications of how you think the relationship should appear.

IN PAST LIVES

You have come into this incarnation to manifest a marriage or partnership in the truest sense. You have reached a point in your evolution where your own sense of separate identity has been completed and perfected as an effective, self-integrated entity.

In past lives you were a counselor, advisor, and diplomat, playing the role of the supportive other to the exclusion of involving your own identity in creating a partnership.

Your task: This lifetime you are looking for another person with whom to share. Recognizing your own independence will empower you to recognize a partnership with another who is also a fully self-integrated, independent being.

SATURN IN SCORPIO

UNCONSCIOUS EXPRESSION

You may think: You are all-powerful and must take responsibility for everybody else's physical or material situation.
Result: Compulsion for control and dominance limits your power. Needing to create roles of control and dependency blocks your energies from others. This form of using power leads to giving your partner and yourself the experience of frustrating isolation. Due to a paralyzing fear of losing command, you may deny yourself and others the deep, powerful connection with the very intimacy and energy you seek.

CONSCIOUS EXPRESSION

Your skills and social responsibility: To potently manifest the latent forces of mutual transformation and regeneration of values in your intimate relationships.

Acknowledging yourself as the creator of drives for power and control that you experience with others empowers you to undergo the challenges created. You can gain even more personal security from realizing that the power you release is strong enough to allow you to easily experience an intimate contact with another.

Your challenge is to accept and work with the responsibility of dependence on others or having others depend on you, or both simultaneously. Then you can realize that past secretive, selfish values served only to undermine and rob yourself and others. Risking your role of control empowers you to relate to another on a truly intimate, equal, trusting level where you both can experience the sensual enjoyment of deep emotional transformation and regeneration.

Through using and sharing the power to release yourself to higher levels of worth and value, you can experience increased power and vitality.

IN PAST LIVES

In this stage of your evolutionary pattern it's time to deal with your fear of bonding with another on a psychic level. You are learning that you will not be dissolved by the power released in the process of achieving oneness with another if you take responsibility for making the process conscious.

Not getting stuck in your awareness of the desires of others empowers you to hold to your own value system and build what you consider important into the context of merging with another. You are learning to use power consciously, to validate your worth, and to bond with another on levels that are mutually constructive.

Past lives have been spent in the military and on battlegrounds of power where survival depended on playing a role of absolute and invulnerable control.

Your task: This lifetime you are learning to discard your psychic defenses against oneness with another, allowing yourself to build the ideals you value into the power of the relationship. In this way the relationship becomes a source of energy that works to the mutual, lasting benefit of both parties involved.

SATURN IN SAGITTARIUS

UNCONSCIOUS EXPRESSION

You may try: To justify your superiority or inferiority by exhibiting your beliefs in a way that makes you right through the established reputation and credibility of others (for example: "I'm smarter than you or superior to you

because I have a degree" or "I'm not smart because I don't have a degree").
Result: This leads to the tension of thinking that you never have enough justi-
fication for the righteousness of your knowledge or lack of knowledge.

CONSCIOUS EXPRESSION

Your skills and social responsibility: To manifest the inspiring energies of
philosophy and higher thought in the world. Your challenge is to acknowledge yourself as the creator of the responsibility of being—or wanting to be—
intellectually superior. This empowers you to feel more secure in your ability
to learn as well as to teach.

Committing yourself to increasing your knowledge in order to serve
a larger community more effectively empowers you to use your abilities to
organize inspiring, expansive thoughts. This process also frees you to employ
knowledge in a way that fosters your social identity without threatening your
intellectual ambitions.

IN PAST LIVES

You are in a stage of evolution where you are learning to release and surrender old, outworn belief structures regarding the nature of right conduct and
truth based on outer authority.

Past lifetimes have been spent as a religious figure and authority of spiritual truth, accepting church doctrines and holding to the letter of dogmatic
law. There is a fear of disobeying a higher spiritual authority that accompanies
this pattern, and this lifetime you are learning to release a sense of punitive
subservience to the fear of breaking spiritual law. Getting in touch with your
own ideas and opinions empowers you to integrate your values into the constructs of society's righteous beliefs.

Your task: To accept the responsibility of connecting directly with spiritual
truth yourself rather than being subservient to any outer spiritual or religious
dogma. This allows the universal energy of spiritual truth to flow through you
into the constructs of society.

SATURN IN CAPRICORN

UNCONSCIOUS EXPRESSION

You may try: To justify your current actions on the basis of the false authority
of time, ambition, material accomplishment, or some other highly structured
or traditional reason that you think justifies your actions.

Result: The experience of accomplishment without fulfillment. You may also experience others resenting your position of authority, which is the price of always having to be in control.

CONSCIOUS EXPRESSION

Your skills and social responsibility: To manifest your authority in the world. Acknowledging yourself as the creator of the authority or lack of authority and respect that you have in the world empowers you to climb above self-imposed limitations. By committing yourself to use your natural abilities to organize, manage, and systematize—without crushing the spirit of those involved—you gain respect for your natural authority and executive leadership.

IN PAST LIVES

This is the lifetime of fruition and accomplishment. Past lifetimes have gone along a path of steady preparation for the accomplishment that is destined to manifest in this incarnation. There is a feeling of having a public destiny, something that you are supposed to accomplish for the good of all. Frustration arises when you hold back from assuming an active role in the affairs of the world.

This is a leadership lifetime in the sense of your being willing to act as a figurehead in guiding others along a particular path. It is time to stand up and be counted.

Your task: When you accept the responsibility and authority for manifesting the goals that you determine to be for the public good, you are fulfilling your destiny.

SATURN IN AQUARIUS

UNCONSCIOUS EXPRESSION

You may try: To accentuate your behavior by being commonplace, thus contradicting yourself.

Result: This leads to social limitations because of a compulsive need always to be the all-around ordinary person. You may secretly seek to separate from others by being what you picture an ordinary person is. This separation results in repression and frustration from continually trying to justify that image to others.

CONSCIOUS EXPRESSION

Your skills and social responsibility: To manifest your individuality and the principles of social progress, brother/sisterhood, and humanitarian ideals. Acknowledging yourself as the creator of your uniqueness—or lack of it— empowers you to bring forth your personality in ways that serve others. By being committed to expressing nonconformity in humanitarian or political roles, you experience a new security in your social identity.

IN PAST LIVES

This is a lifetime pledged to breaking away from old conventions and turning to innovative ways of serving others that extend beyond the boundaries of what is usually considered to be publicly acceptable. In recent past lives, conventional ways of behaving led to public acclaim, prestige, and the attainment of positions of authority and respect. It is no longer necessary, however, for you to receive public approval in order to thrive.

Your task: It is time to look within to find values that extend beyond what is currently acceptable and that can lead humankind to new levels of freedom and universal love. Frustration arises from trying to behave appropriately and do things in the old ways that led to social acclaim. Instead, your challenge is to turn your attention to formulating new goals and ideals for humankind that extend beyond current social structures. You see the next step for humanity, and when you begin to manifest this in your own life, your destiny is fulfilled.

SATURN IN PISCES

UNCONSCIOUS EXPRESSION

You may try: To justify your lack of alignment with any worldly purpose because nothing measures up to your ideals of service.
Result: Frustration from failing to undertake action that contributes to bringing your ideals into manifestation. When you feel helpless in bringing about your visions and ideals, you lose a sense of having a constructive purpose in society.

CONSCIOUS EXPRESSION

Your skills and social responsibility: To bring your private dream and ideals into the world. Acknowledging yourself as creator of your private visions and dreams empowers you to manifest what has already been created in your imagination.

You have the gift of demonstrating your dreams. Your challenge is to commit yourself unconditionally to manifesting those dreams that serve humankind. This empowers you to accept the opportunities that are currently available. Through consistent, daily demonstration of your spiritual ideals, no matter how seemingly insignificant, you gain a sense of achievement. This leaves you with the knowledge that you have contributed to the manifestation of society's ideals in a realistic way.

IN PAST LIVES

In this lifetime it's time to dissolve ego identification with all past accomplishments. You can become immersed in feelings of vague frustration and helplessness that keep you from manifesting your dreams. This is because the vision is changing: The old cycle of identity is dissolving, and the new is not yet on the threshold. But visions of a new identity and what the new cycle of manifestation will be like do occur.

Your task: To release internal blocks to implementing the new vision, even though it can be frustrating. Your destiny is to allow the vision of the new to give you enough confidence to release old forms of ego expression that are not working in the current incarnation. In this way you can become identified with the source, rather than activity, and your destiny is fulfilled.

SATURN IN THE HOUSES

THE NEED TO ACKNOWLEDGE A DESIRE

1st house: If Saturn is located in the 1st house of your birth chart, you gain healthy control of your life when you are willing to take charge of the way in which you express your personality and present yourself to others. There is a need to acknowledge your desire to appear in control and to be committed to developing those attitudes of personal responsibility that lead to control without domination.

2nd house: If Saturn is located in the 2nd house of your birth chart, you gain healthy control of your life when you are willing to take charge of successfully managing your finances. There is a need to acknowledge your desire to find security in your values and material possessions. Saturn offers the responsibility and rewards of changing your fixed value systems to include the potentials inherent in your current circumstances.

3rd house: If Saturn is located in the 3rd house of your birth chart, you gain healthy control of your life when you are willing to take charge of successfully establishing a clear channel of communication between you and others. There is a need to acknowledge your desire to have your communication taken seriously. Saturn offers the responsibility and rewards of gaining the education and the learning that others will respect.

4th house: If Saturn is located in the 4th house of your birth chart, you gain healthy control of your life when you are willing to take charge of successfully creating a home-base foundation that gives you security. There is a need to acknowledge your desire to feel strong emotional bonds with others. Saturn offers the responsibility and rewards of establishing your personal security through open, honest communication of your real feelings.

5th house: If Saturn is located in the 5th house of your birth chart, you gain healthy control of your life when you are willing to take charge of following your heart in a way that creates a happy experience for everyone, including yourself. There is a need to acknowledge your desire to feel secure by playing a leading role in life. Saturn offers the responsibility and reward of expressing your creative talents in constructive ways that bring closeness to loved ones rather than isolation.

6th house: If Saturn is located in the 6th house of your birth chart, you gain healthy control of your life when you are willing to take charge of successfully setting healthy routines in your life. There is a need to acknowledge your desire to express a strong sense of duty. Saturn offers the responsibility and reward of doing a good job without disrupting your life through overwork.

7th house: If Saturn is located in the 7th house of your birth chart, you gain healthy control of your life when you are willing to take charge of discovering the identity of the other person and creating a happy, successful partnership. There is a need to acknowledge your desire for a partner you can lean on to gain social balance. Saturn offers the responsibility and reward of using your talent for creating a partnership that will support you and the other person constructively.

8th house: If Saturn is located in the 8th house of your birth chart, you gain healthy control of your life when you are willing to take charge of consciously creating successful outcomes in relationships involving a bonding through sex, money, or passion. There is a need to acknowledge your desire to have power over others. Saturn offers the responsibility and reward of control by expressing a level of integrity that will constructively transform you as well as those closest to you.

9th house: If Saturn is located in the 9th house of your birth chart, you gain healthy control of your life when you are willing to take charge of allowing your mind to reach new plateaus of understanding. There is a need to acknowledge your desire to inspire others through your knowledge. Saturn offers the responsibility and reward of having faith in your philosophical belief system, allowing it to expand to include the information that comes from new ideas and experiences.

10th house: If Saturn is located in the 10th house of your birth chart, you gain healthy control of your life when you are willing to take charge and be the CEO, organizing the skills of others to reach a common goal. There is a need to acknowledge your desire to be taken seriously as an authority in the world. Saturn offers the responsibility and reward of expressing yourself on a public level in the area of your expertise.

11th house: If Saturn is located in the 11th house of your birth chart, you gain healthy control of your life when you are willing to take charge of successfully guiding yourself and others to reaching larger life dreams. There is a need to acknowledge your desire to distinguish yourself among your peers. Saturn offers the responsibility and reward of gaining the knowledge that will make you an authority among equals.

12th house: If Saturn is located in the 12th house of your birth chart, you gain healthy control of your life when you are willing to take charge of bringing your vision into the world. There is a need to acknowledge your desire to manifest your private dream. Saturn offers the responsibility and reward of continuing to manifest your spiritual ideal with a commitment to what goes beyond the visible and tangible.

URANUS: KEY TO ALIVENESS

Uranus in the birth chart:*
- Illuminates the circumstances in which an intuitive perception of life can be received, empowering you to rise above the confusion of interfering ideas.
- Indicates the process by which your unpredictable behavior may lead others to feel that you are too untrustworthy, disruptive, and eccentric to be taken seriously.
- Shows that area of life where you must experience a sense of personal independence and assume responsibility to safeguard and express your need for freedom in a way that does not alienate others.

---

* To discover the sign and house your URANUS is located in, go to www.janspiller.com and a free chart will be calculated for you.

- Pinpoints that area in which you need to experience, in a responsible, conscious way, the excitement of independence and personal freedom in order to maintain clear perceptions.
- Reveals the manner in which your unconscious expression of careless, eccentric indifference to other people can lead to unexpected situations of emotional disruption, separation, and alienation.
- Denotes where you have the potential to express innovative ideas that can alter antiquated situations that no longer meet people's needs.

DEFINING A WHOLE GENERATION

Uranus spends approximately seven years in each sign before moving on. It is one of the three outer planets, along with Neptune and Pluto, that depict the nature of a *generation* in addition to defining personal qualities. As such, the sign containing Uranus shows the need for change and progress within an entire peer group, as well as being an indicator of the need for personal change and progress. In many ways the personal and generational effect is the same. As the individual makes necessary intuitive connections, the entire generation is elevated, and the influence of that generation in turn introduces that element of change and progress into the world.

On a strictly personal level, the influence of Uranus is felt and worked within the house location of your chart. The term "planetary mind," as used in the following descriptions of Uranus, refers to the mind of God. It is omniscience—the place where creative ideas originate, where problems are solved, and from which all inventions come. When you tap into Uranus you tap into a higher frequency of mental energy.

URANUS IN ARIES

Your ability: To intuitively receive from the planetary mind a fresh direction for humankind. You will have individualistic ideas about how to pioneer new ways. Disruption occurs: Only when a path of leadership is sought that is not in accord with the good of society as a whole.

URANUS IN TAURUS

Your ability: To receive intuitively ideas for materially implementing the fresh directions that are being taken on the planet. You will receive insights about ways to structure the new directions, to establish innovative energies in a practical, essential way.

Disruption occurs: Only through holding on to old value systems that are not in harmony with the new direction of society as a whole.

URANUS IN GEMINI

Your ability: To perceive innovative forms of communication for reaching people with the message of the times. You have fresh insights into how to verbalize and promote the new directions that have been established.

Disruption occurs: Only when attempts are made to stay on a logical, rational level with your messages instead of expanding the mind to a more intuitive form of communication.

URANUS IN CANCER

Your ability: To receive intuitively from the planetary mind new emotional states that cause trauma or transformation on a very personal level. The insights received about the potential of these new emotional states can be upsetting to the home life and traditional roots of personal security.

Disruption occurs: Through being attached to, or relying upon, the traditional forms of security, such as home and family on a private, noncollective level.

URANUS IN LEO

Your ability: To intuitively perceive new ways of creatively expressing your emotions and talents. The ego can experience intense disruption by taking your creativity too personally.

Disruption occurs: Through demanding personal recognition for creative or artistic expression.

URANUS IN VIRGO

Your ability: To perceive innovative ways of cleaning up the social environment on both physical and mental levels.

Disruption occurs: When new ways of serving society are misunderstood and taken too literally.

URANUS IN LIBRA

Your ability: To intuitively perceive innovative ways of relating to people and handling the area of personal relationships from a new level of understanding.

Disruption occurs: From outmoded ideals about the marriage relationship, and in the arena of partnership agreements in general.

URANUS IN SCORPIO

Your ability: To intuitively perceive new ways to substantially transform the society as it is presently operating, especially on a worldly and sexual level.
Disruption occurs: By holding on to outworn sexual standards and outmoded ideas about material partnerships.

URANUS IN SAGITTARIUS

Your ability: To intuitively perceive new philosophical directions and innovative horizons for society's moral behavior.
Disruption occurs: In hanging on to belief systems and moral attitudes that justify old social behaviors.

URANUS IN CAPRICORN

Your ability: To intuitively perceive fresh ways to plan and establish a new social order. Experiences include insights of innovative ways to organize society in a collective whole.
Disruption occurs: By hanging on to old forms of society's governmental structures.

URANUS IN AQUARIUS

Your ability: To intuitively perceive new ideas to link humankind beyond the level of traditional social order into an integrated whole, aligned with humanitarian ideals and relationship standards. A creative form of disorder occurs when Uranus in Aquarius operates on its highest, most inventive and original level.
Disruption occurs: Through the awareness of obsolete social systems.

URANUS IN PISCES

Your ability: To intuitively perceive new pinnacles of understanding that have the effect of dissolving all previous knowledge. The way will be cleared for change and revolution, to make way for renewed ideals for humankind.
Disruption occurs: By holding on to old belief systems and outdated perceptions of reality.

URANUS IN THE HOUSES

URANUS IN THE 1ST HOUSE

UNCONSCIOUS EXPRESSION

Habitual tendency: Demanding independence in such a way that your freedom becomes a limitation or a burden to others.
Result: Constant personal disruption, a scattering of your energy, and a loss of independence. This occurs when you react with eccentric behavior that is more destructive than creative.

CONSCIOUS EXPRESSION

You know how to uniquely express your individuality through being an example of responsible independence. As a result of your ability to see everyone, including yourself, as an equal, you can be respected as an innovative leader of your group or community. By knowing no class boundaries you become the people's choice.

URANUS IN THE 2ND HOUSE

UNCONSCIOUS EXPRESSION

Habitual tendency: Demanding independence in a way that results in a scattering of personal talents and resources.
Result: If you seek to impose an unusual and eccentric sense of material values on others, they will resist you. If you have no regard for practical responsibility, the result may be dependence on others for support and well-being.

CONSCIOUS EXPRESSION

You know how to uniquely express your individuality through implementing your unusual ideas on a practical, material level. Your innovative vision can develop into operative structures through which a unique means for accumulating money can be established.

URANUS IN THE 3RD HOUSE

UNCONSCIOUS EXPRESSION

Habitual tendency: Demanding independence through carelessly using your communication in a way that is disruptive.

Result: If you choose to be so erratic and abstract that you purposely confuse others, the result is a scattering of mental energies, misunderstanding, and a loss of any true communication.

CONSCIOUS EXPRESSION

You know how to uniquely express your individuality through using your mind to innovate new ways for more clearly and effectively communicating with others. The result can be a sensation of excitement through stimulation from true mind-to-mind connections.

URANUS IN THE 4TH HOUSE

UNCONSCIOUS EXPRESSION

Habitual tendency: Demanding independence by rebelling against close relationships.
Result: You may rebel for the sake of asserting a false sense of emotional freedom and self-centered independence. This results in feeling instability about your roots and constant disruption from loved ones.

CONSCIOUS EXPRESSION

You know how to uniquely express your individuality through your talent to be sensitive to people's needs. You can be *impersonally* loving enough to allow those who are emotionally close to be free from any debilitating dependency. If you choose this road, the result is a sense of personal emotional freedom that allows you to be truly yourself, even in close relationships.

URANUS IN THE 5TH HOUSE

UNCONSCIOUS EXPRESSION

Habitual tendency: To be demanding by carelessly using your own expression to disrupt the expression of other people. There is a temptation to dramatize and flaunt your independence for the purpose of drawing attention to yourself.
Result: When you choose this road, you may get a reputation as an eccentric rebel and a person whom others do not trust.

CONSCIOUS EXPRESSION

You know how to uniquely express your individuality through asserting your independence in ways that are constructively creative. When you use your innovative abilities to allow for and enhance the free expression of those close by, you experience a feeling of loyalty that supports your uniqueness.

URANUS IN THE 6TH HOUSE

UNCONSCIOUS EXPRESSION

Habitual tendency: Demanding independence by distorting your sense of duty to justify the refusal to assist others in a practical way.
Result: A constant change of jobs and dissatisfaction with your pragmatic ability to serve.

CONSCIOUS EXPRESSION

You know how to uniquely express your individuality through your ability to serve others by disclosing to them the knowledge of freedom. When you follow a personal sense of duty to serve by imparting your universal knowledge, you can attract and successfully fill unusual job opportunities.

URANUS IN THE 7TH HOUSE

UNCONSCIOUS EXPRESSION

Habitual tendency: Demanding independence by dealing with others on the basis of how much stimulation and excitement they can provide.
Result: By indulging in such behavior you attract sporadic, disruptive relationships that scatter and deplete your energy. You may also experience boredom in close involvements, expecting too much from too few.

CONSCIOUS EXPRESSION

You know how to uniquely put across your individuality through creatively expressing variety and exciting stimulation in your responses to others. Recognize this need and enlarge your sphere to include impersonal alliances as well as a primary personal one.

When you understand that having many deep, intimate relationships scatters and depletes your energy, you can expand to a natural interaction of impersonal connections. This results in having all the associations you need for stimulus without a disruption of your energy.

URANUS IN THE 8TH HOUSE

UNCONSCIOUS EXPRESSION

Habitual tendency: To be demanding by bringing eccentric, bizarre, independent attitudes into a sexual relationship with no regard for the other person's needs.
Result: Sexual encounters that are intense, explosive, erratic, energy-draining, and transitory.

CONSCIOUS EXPRESSION

You know how to uniquely express your individuality through connecting deeply with another on sexual levels with the intention of creating freedom for them as well as for yourself.

By bringing out the uniqueness in your partner you may discover an expansion in your sexuality. This approach can also increase your power to break through archaic beliefs and inhibitions surrounding your sexuality.

URANUS IN THE 9TH HOUSE

UNCONSCIOUS EXPRESSION

Habitual tendency: To be demanding by thoughtlessly destroying the belief systems of others without taking the responsibility of replacing them with appropriate knowledge.
Result: This can disrupt and divide the group. There is also a temptation to make erratic, theoretical statements simply for shock effect or to try to prove that you possess superior knowledge that invalidates all perspectives, even yours. When you yield to this temptation, the result is that no one listens or takes you seriously.

CONSCIOUS EXPRESSION

You know how to uniquely express your individuality through expressing perceptive, philosophical talents by expanding the beliefs of others with factual knowledge. This connection inspires others to go beyond believing in you, to knowing for themselves.

By becoming an example of an individual's quest for objective, workable knowledge, you inspire others to tap into their abilities to attune to intuitive, impersonal learning. Thus, you experience a truly stimulating meeting with the minds of others.

URANUS IN THE 10TH HOUSE

UNCONSCIOUS EXPRESSION

Habitual tendency: To be demanding by believing that you can alter things in the world through careless, rash behavior.

Result: You may attain worldly positions that are made in your image without being aware of the social responsibilities of what you seek to accomplish in the world. There is a temptation to destroy for destruction's sake, which results in disrupting instead of freeing the status quo, a revolution with no social purpose.

CONSCIOUS EXPRESSION

You know how to uniquely express your individuality through responsibly taking on the role of world reformer. When you act with awareness of the social structure of which you are a part and with awareness of how much can be creatively changed for the good of all, the result is executive or political genius.

URANUS IN THE 11TH HOUSE

UNCONSCIOUS EXPRESSION

Habitual tendency: To demand your independence by assuming that you know everything.

Result: You may unwittingly use a permanently impersonal position to justify avoiding responsibility for using knowledge in a creative and constructive way. This position results in attracting disruptive circumstances through groups and peers, and experiencing limited freedom to be yourself.

CONSCIOUS EXPRESSION

You know how to uniquely express your individuality through using ideas so those around you are encouraged to express their original insights and individuality without judging themselves or others. The result can be an expanded sense of freedom and personal independence in situations that involve groups and peers.

URANUS IN THE 12TH HOUSE

UNCONSCIOUS EXPRESSION

Habitual tendency: To demand independence by pretending to others that you are not a unique and free individual with dreams and ideas of your own.

Result: Disruption through inner pressure building until you express your eccentric tendencies in ways that are unconsciously self-destructive.

CONSCIOUS EXPRESSION

You know how to uniquely express your individuality through using your own intuitive vision and impulses by creatively conveying them to other people. When you choose to follow your unusual insights constructively, the result is public acknowledgment of that ideal and a perception of the inner knowledge that will sustain the spirit.

♆

NEPTUNE: KEY TO EMOTIONAL ECSTASY

Neptune in the birth chart:*
- Removes the illusion and reveals the truth, thereby showing how to actualize your ideals in a way that works and produces rewards in the material world.
- Depicts the self-defeating and confusing patterns where your expectations are the highest and disappointments are the most intense.
- Defines how your preconceived notions of how the ideal would manifest must be sacrificed in order for the reality of the ideal to appear.
- Shows those patterns perpetuating the self-deception and emotional illusions that prevent you from experiencing the ecstasy inherent in the true ideal.
- Indicates the arena in which you can begin the process of trusting the universe in order to fulfill an idealistic desire; or where you allow the universe to manifest, according to its standards of perfection, by releasing your preconceived notions, standards, and ideals.
- Signifies that area of life offering the strength, serenity, and ecstasy of a divine contact, and a vision and trust in the workings of the universe.

---

* To discover the sign and house your NEPTUNE is located in, go to www.janspiller.com and a free chart will be calculated for you.

A GENERATION EXPRESSES ITS IDEALS

Since Neptune spends approximately fourteen years in each sign, in many ways the sign containing Neptune is an earmark of a generation. As such, Neptune shows the idealistic desires of an entire group of people, as well as being an indicator of personal idealism.

Thus, the personal and generational effects of Neptune are the same. As the energies of the planet are purified on a personal level, the entire generation is uplifted, and the influence of that generation in turn raises the ideals of the world. On a strictly personal level, Neptune's influences are felt and worked with in the house location of your chart.

NEPTUNE IN ARIES

Your generation's potential: To achieve higher states of personal integrity and authenticity—being true to yourself.

Your gift: The recognition that the key to having right relationships is the honest expression of individual identity.

The innate vision: Pure self-expression, unpolluted by hidden motives or desires that might make you pretend to be who you are not.

The Neptune-in-Aries dilemma: How to be yourself while cooperating with others so you achieve successful partnerships. Your generation believes that the keys to spiritual bliss are the power and beauty within the self. That highly idealized expectation will be challenged until you gain awareness that others also have the right to express their real identity.

This generation has the opportunity to express their true selves while taking into account the needs of others, with the diplomacy necessary for cooperative relationships.

NEPTUNE IN TAURUS

Your generation's potential: To realize higher states of sharing, exchanging material goods to increase the comfort level for all.

Your gift: Your appreciation of the beauty of planet Earth and the value of enjoying the sensual delights of being alive.

The innate vision: Understanding the importance of taking care of needs for personal comfort, for yourself and for the peoples of the world.

The Neptune-in-Taurus dilemma: How to build a comfortable life that does not result in stagnation, or feeling as if your possessions are taking over your life. Your highly idealized expectation—that material well-being is the key to spiritual bliss—will be challenged until you create a lifestyle that shows aware-ness of others' needs for physical and material security.

This generation has the opportunity to learn to take care of their own needs while understanding that they can't be secure until everyone's needs are met. Only then can they ensure the positive changes with others that lead to vitality and personal growth.

NEPTUNE IN GEMINI

Your generation's potential: To realize higher states of constructive thought and communication.
Your gift: The recognition that an undisciplined mind, filled with random thoughts, can lead to unhappiness and unnecessary feelings of alienation.
The innate vision: Forms of communication that enable each person to feel connected with everyone else, in terms of understanding, acceptance, and the open, positive exchange of ideas and information.
The Neptune-in-Gemini dilemma: Believing that your thoughts should meet with universal acceptance. Your generation sees proper communication and positive mental connections as the tools to consistent spiritual bliss. That highly idealized expectation will be challenged until you embrace a larger awareness of truth—beyond the way you perceive it.

This generation has the challenge to make a commitment to base their thoughts and communication on intuitive truth.

NEPTUNE IN CANCER

Your generation's potential: Realizing the higher levels of personal and family security on a planetary basis.
The innate vision: Initiating an awareness of the world family. The League of Nations was formed naturally from the efforts of those born in this age.
The Neptune-in-Cancer dilemma: Dealing with idealistic expectations of an automatic emotional fulfillment coming out of your position in a family. It offers the choice of accepting or denying the responsibility to develop the personal security necessary to experience the realization of your highest family ideals.

NEPTUNE IN LEO

Your generation's potential: Realizing the higher aspects of sharing art and act-ing that inspires others on a planetary level.

The innate vision: Performing in a way that inspires and uplifts others to their creative potential. The motion picture industry in Hollywood emerged from the efforts of those born in this age. Countless numbers were affected through motion pictures, the stage, and on television.

The Neptune-in-Leo dilemma: Dealing with the idealistic expectations of automatic joyous emotional states coming through the experience of parenthood, the expression of creative and artistic talents, or of romantic affairs. It offers the choice of accepting or denying the responsibility to appreciate the inherent perfection that already exists in your children, creative expression, and romantic involvements. It is the opportunity to manifest your creative ideals, seeing the perfection in things as they are.

NEPTUNE IN VIRGO

Your generation's potential: Realizing the higher aspects of health and service on a planetary level.

The innate vision: Plans that make perfect health available to everyone. Growing world concern over the effects of pollution, environmental hazards, and devitalized foods has increased through the efforts of this generation.

The Neptune-in-Virgo dilemma: Dealing with idealistic expectations of automatic emotional fulfillment coming from your job in life. If offers the choice of accepting or denying the responsibility of serving your fellow human beings in whatever capacity you may find yourself. A sense of true inner joy is possible through the conscious dedication of manifesting your ideals of service in your line of work.

NEPTUNE IN LIBRA

Your generation's potential: Realizing the higher aspects of relating to people on the level of planetary awareness.

The innate vision: Creating lasting peace and the abolition of war on this planet. It is also the generation following an ideal of spiritual union and oneness among people. They initiated new ethics of living together that replaced old forms of marriage.

The Neptune-in-Libra dilemma: Dealing with idealistic expectations in relationships. It offers the choice of accepting or denying the commitment to personal integrity that is necessary to realize your highest ideals in relationships.

NEPTUNE IN SCORPIO

Your generation's potential: Realizing the higher levels of shared material ownership on a planetary level.

The innate vision: Spiritual responsibility for Earth's resources as a whole. You are aware of the current human material values and the potential for transformation of those values that will lead humankind to a higher level of relating to the physical world.

The Neptune-in-Scorpio dilemma: Dealing with establishing your value with other people. It is the choice between idealistically expecting the automatic support of other people's resources or responsibly defining material values with them. It also deals with the choice between expecting automatic emotional fulfillment through sex or committing yourself to the self-purification that will actually bring about the realization of those ideals.

NEPTUNE IN SAGITTARIUS

Your generation's potential: Realizing the higher levels of communicating in the areas of intellect, philosophy, and religion on a planetary basis.

The innate vision: The rise of enlightenment in the realms of religion and philosophy, and the struggle to find a worldwide medium for positive communication.

The Neptune-in-Sagittarius dilemma: Expecting automatic emotional fulfillment to come from following a philosophy. It offers the choice of accepting or denying the commitment to rise above blind philosophical belief and reliance on others. Your opportunity for fulfillment lies in allowing personal experience in the material world to transform and expand your philosophical ideals.

NEPTUNE IN CAPRICORN

Your generation's potential: To make an impact on the higher levels of government.

Your gift: To manage people and resources.

The innate vision: A one-world government, where everyone can work efficiently toward idealistic goals.

The Neptune-in-Capricorn dilemma: Recognizing true responsibility. You believe that the government will automatically take responsibility for the well-being of its people. Your challenge is to take personal responsibility for governing your life, according to your own vision.

You have the opportunity to take charge of situations with a compassionate awareness of the feelings and needs of those being governed.

NEPTUNE IN AQUARIUS

Your generation's potential: To realize higher states of true humanitarianism and altruism.

Your gift: To help others recognize we are all brothers and sisters on this Earth; that we either work together for the common good or destroy ourselves through disunity and conflict.

The innate vision: You are infused with a sense of spiritual responsibility for the well-being of all the peoples of the Earth. You are aware of the world's current inequities and have a global vision for fairness and equality.

The Neptune-in-Aquarius dilemma: How to create equality while still honoring the differences in individual talents and abilities. Your generation has highly idealistic expectations of fairness: in friendship, in groups, and in universal brother- and sisterhood. Those beliefs will be challenged until people recognize, accept, and embrace individual differences. Your challenge is to take personal responsibility for walking the walk you're advocating in your own life.

This generation can use personal creativity to make their ideals and visions a reality.

NEPTUNE IN PISCES

Your generation's potential: To make possible higher states of love, compassion, forgiveness, and understanding.

Your gift: The recognition that we are all essentially one, and that what we do to one another, we do to ourselves.

The innate vision: To spread healing and compassion on the Earth in a way that creates acceptance, unity, and peace.

The Neptune-in-Pisces dilemma: To accept and go with the spiritual flow of life while still actively working to make your vision tangible. Your generation has a highly idealistic expectation—that a lofty spiritual ideal is the cure for all the world's ills. This belief will be challenged until you balance it with greater practical application and personal organization.

This generation has the opportunity to play an active part in manifesting their spiritual vision so it bears fruit.

NEPTUNE IN THE HOUSES

NEPTUNE IN THE 1ST HOUSE

UNCONSCIOUS EXPRESSION

When you try to express yourself based on a preconceived ideal of personal behavior, you unwittingly deceive yourself and others. This leads to feeling confused and misunderstood when others do not understand your good intentions and react with mistrust. The result is feeling frustrated that you have never expressed yourself perfectly enough or lived up to your ideal of being a positive influence in the world.

CONSCIOUS EXPRESSION

Letting go of ideals of being a perfect person leads to simply telling the truth about your feelings at the time. This example inspires others to be more in touch with their immediate feelings. As you look to the universe for support, you can purify yourself by objectively exposing that inner core that is not yet the ideal. Thus, you heal those close by with truth.

This leads to experiencing the spiritual energy within you. By turning inward, you have the gift of being able to feel bliss in your physical body. Emotional purity naturally shines forth by being an inspiring example of personal integrity, expressing your real feelings and perceptions, and being unconcerned about others' reaction.

NEPTUNE IN THE 2ND HOUSE

UNCONSCIOUS EXPRESSION

When you try to create a show of self-value, it causes you to lose contact with your inner sense of self-esteem. Desiring to prove your individual worth by making money (or not making money) leads to disillusionment when others do not accept your worth as you think they should. This can also result in frustration when you are unable to buy the feeling of self-esteem that is sought.

CONSCIOUS EXPRESSION

The key is to let go of ideals of how you should establish your worth. This empowers you to use your assets for building something of worthwhile emotional and spiritual service. Allowing the universe to support you gives you confidence to trust and look to life for material rewards. These will come to you when your goal performs a true service to others. When you realize that money or lack of it is not the way to acquire self-esteem, you can pledge yourself to establishing universal values.

This leads to experiencing the ecstasy of knowing that the universe always supports you and gives you its material possessions when you use these resources to heal others. This in turn provides the realization of your worth to the universe, and results in personal happiness and self-esteem in the process.

NEPTUNE IN THE 3RD HOUSE

UNCONSCIOUS EXPRESSION

There is confusion around what to say in order to appear a certain way to others. This shuts down true communication. The motive may be fearing that others will take your words in the wrong way. Yet in failing to verbalize your spontaneous perceptions, you lose touch with your ideas.

Thus, if you project the illusion of well-being when it is not really there, and communicate from that state, you experience the isolation of feeling that no one understands you. The result is frustration and disappointment because you feel unable to communicate in a way that lives up to your ideals.

CONSCIOUS EXPRESSION

When you let go of those ideals, you can allow the universe to communicate through you. The key is to focus your attention on verbalizing what your intuition is showing you, rather than on the impression you want to make.

This leads to experiencing the ecstasy resulting from true communication. As you learn to trust the universe to offer you appropriate words to communicate the truth of your feelings, your speech automatically heals the exchange. You experience the emotional satisfaction of serving yourself and others by allowing the truth to be spoken through you, with a lack of attachment to the results.

NEPTUNE IN THE 4TH HOUSE

UNCONSCIOUS EXPRESSION

Your tendency is to envision your immediate family as the one that you always wanted and never had. Getting lost in your ideals results in your feeling dissatisfied and disappointed with them.

In addition, the family group around you will likely take your feelings of dissatisfaction personally. This causes them to lose confidence in their ability to meet their own ideals, and they may feel increasingly unable to relate to you.

CONSCIOUS EXPRESSION

The key is letting go of your fantasy of your family as the perfect kin. When you realize that they are not here to live up to your personal ideals, you can experience true, unconditional, emotional communion with them.

This leads to experiencing the ecstasy of emotional satisfaction and safety, as you trust the universe to provide you with perfection in your own kindred as they are. From there you can come to realize that all humankind is your family. The key is in letting go of your expectations and trusting the universe.

NEPTUNE IN THE 5TH HOUSE

UNCONSCIOUS EXPRESSION

If you try to create a dramatic love life based on preconceived expectations, the result is no lasting satisfaction from your sexual relationships. Playing the role of the ideal lover rather than yourself causes you to lose touch with the joy and spontaneity of your inner child.

Projecting and playing out your romantic ideals results in continuous frustration when these fantasies unexpectedly turn into tragic disillusionments.

CONSCIOUS EXPRESSION

The key is in letting go of your ideals of glamour. The challenge is to choose to play your true self, acknowledging and expressing your feelings and needs for loyalty. In this process, you become the lover that you actually are, creating mutual trust. You inspire enthusiasm in others and release creative healing energy when you innocently display the exuberance and joy of your childlike nature. By being yourself, spontaneously expressing your playful and creative side, you attract the right person.

Relinquishing your fantasies is the key to gaining confidence in trusting the universe to provide the satisfaction you seek. Then you can attract that one person who can lead you toward experiencing the inner emotional ecstasy of your ideal.

NEPTUNE IN THE 6TH HOUSE

UNCONSCIOUS EXPRESSION

Your tendency is to sacrifice on the altar of duty. If you seek to measure up to some perfected ideal in your work, you will fail to be recognized as the willing servant that you aim to be.

Striving to be acknowledged as a self-sacrificing, spiritual person can lead to severe health conditions, tensions with coworkers, and a tremendous sense of frustration and paranoia in the job.

CONSCIOUS EXPRESSION

They key is in letting go of ideals of how you should look as the worker. Then you can focus on serving others rather than on your image. You are empowered to serve others in a positive way by releasing a need for reflected perfection. In this process you free yourself to experience joy and union with coworkers in getting the job done together.

Happiness results when you relax and trust that the universe is supporting you in your work. This process leads to experiencing the ecstasy of consciously participating in being of service in your workplace.

NEPTUNE IN THE 7TH HOUSE

UNCONSCIOUS EXPRESSION

There's a tendency to try, through the power of your expectations, to have partners live up to your ideals of perfection. This leads to experiencing harsh disappointment in people as human beings. The continuous disenchantment in relationships and disappointment—when people do not behave as stock characters in your projected fantasies—causes feelings of inadequacy in others.

Also, in a close relationship you may find the other person falling constantly short of your ideal. This leaves you feeling unable to relate without fearing disappointment. An unwillingness to experience the way the other person really is, not how you may want that person to be, leads to the isolation and unfulfiliment of relating to a fantasy that never quite comes true.

CONSCIOUS EXPRESSION

The key is in letting go of your ideals of the perfect partner. Your challenge is to cease relating to your partner as a fantasy and trust that life will be fulfilling if you experience others as they are. This leads to the empowerment

of being able to inspire the best in them. You are able to dismiss petty standards by accepting your partner as human. This leads to discovering the ecstasy
in truly relating to another person the way he or she is.

As you share in the idealistic goals of others, encouraging them to follow
their highest ideals, you are freed. This process leads to experiencing the ecstasy
of participating in their natural unfoldment.

NEPTUNE IN THE 8TH HOUSE

UNCONSCIOUS EXPRESSION

Your tendency is to try to relate intimately to others on the basis of a preconceived ideal of personal power in the relationship. This leads to experiencing the surprise and disappointment of their constantly acting in opposition to
your ideals.

You create an obsession with material ideals and erotic fantasies when
you allow your imagination to combine with your sexual power. This process
leaves you unfulfilled and alienated from the sexual bonding that you seek to
experience.

CONSCIOUS EXPRESSION

The key is in letting go of your ideals of how you should be powerful in
order to manifest the ideal of sexual fulfillment. This enables you to open up
to the experience of relating on an intimate level with another human being.
Eliminating your stance of personal strength allows you to perceive the potential force in the relationship itself.

This process leads to experiencing the ecstasy of fulfillment in both sexual
and financial contacts with others. When you trust the universe to bring forth
mutual power through relationships, you see the true inherent potency unfold
before you.

NEPTUNE IN THE 9TH HOUSE

UNCONSCIOUS EXPRESSION

Your tendency to try to create an illusion of appearing intelligent leads to
acting on the basis of how you think intellectual superiority should be manifested. In displaying an attitude of intellectual superiority over other people,
you invite the disappointment of being unable to substantiate your authority.

You might be concerned with projecting the image that you exclusively
possess spiritual knowledge. This leads to making false assumptions and giving

too much importance to those things not yet checked for validity. The result is confusion and disappointment when others become alienated and suspicious of your perceptions.

CONSCIOUS EXPRESSION

The key is in letting go of your ideals of being the spiritual teacher. Your challenge is to relax pretensions and open to receive new, higher ideas. You gain the base on which you may philosophize and expand when you are willing to work with the new perceptions and acquaint yourself with the facts relevant to your subject matter.

Once acquainted with relevant facts, you can spontaneously communicate the spiritual ideals shown you through your intuition. This leads to experiencing the ecstasy of inspiring others as well as yourself to reach new intellectual heights and spiritual insights.

NEPTUNE IN THE 10TH HOUSE

UNCONSCIOUS EXPRESSION

There is a tendency to try to create the impression of being the greatest authority according to your pictures of how you should appear to others. This leads to experiencing the disappointment and isolation that result from never being able to abandon your role.

If your ego identifies with the feeling of having a destiny ordained by the gods, you will seek to act it out according to your nearsighted, limited ideals. This cuts you off from the true sense of inspiration. This process leads to feeling like the abandoned victim or puppet of the gods when people contest or contradict your authority. You are left feeling confused, helpless, and unable to live up to your idealized potential.

CONSCIOUS EXPRESSION

The key is in letting go of your ideals of being a spiritual authority and role model in the world. This frees you to commit yourself to participating in the world as it really is, according to its own ideals, and gives you a feeling of confidence. Not demanding that a personal ideal be met before you commit yourself empowers you to actively join in within the framework of the world's established standards and models of success, honor, respect, and credibility. Then you can enact the best of those traditions.

Confidence comes from releasing your vision of what it looks like to be on top and instead trusting that the universe is manifesting its authority in the world through you, without your involvement with the results.

The greatest satisfaction comes when you make a solid contribution in the world by channeling spontaneous participation and overlooking any acknowledgment. This process leads to experiencing the ecstasy of your inner sense of accomplishment.

NEPTUNE IN THE 11TH HOUSE

UNCONSCIOUS EXPRESSION

When you try to relate in groups according to your ideal of what this interaction ought to be, you experience an endless search for the perfect group. This leads to the disappointment of failing to find friends with whom you can accomplish humanitarian visions and goals.

You may actually contribute to the dissension and confusion existing in the group situation when you project your ideals of perfection onto them. The result is deep personal feelings of being misunderstood and isolated from your peers.

CONSCIOUS EXPRESSION

The key is in letting go of your expectations of the ideal group. Then you can open yourself to honestly relating your experience in the closed circle as it currently exists. This process sets the stage for a new perfection to occur. As you allow fresh visions to present themselves among your peers, the inspiration that comes from your ideals can inspire them to attain new heights beyond your vision.

This process leads to your experiencing the ecstasy of openly trusting the universe to flow through you in situations involving friends and groups.

NEPTUNE IN THE 12TH HOUSE

UNCONSCIOUS EXPRESSION

There is a tendency to try to commune with the universe on the basis of preconceived ideas of how the universe ought to be treating you. The result is experiencing the frustration that God is not living up to your ideals.

Indulging in the belief that you are above the material world leads to idealizing universal reality according to your expectations of what that source should be. Inevitably, this process results in the confusion and disappointment of being unable to depend on or trust either the tangible or intangible realms of existence.

CONSCIOUS EXPRESSION

The key is in letting go of projecting your ideals of perfection onto the universe. Your challenge is to appreciate the perfection of things as they already are. This unlocks the key to understanding why things happen the way they do. Releasing personal expectations of how things ought to be gives you the confidence to trust that the universe is unfolding according to its own truly perfect nature. This process opens you to inspiring new revelations of the universal purpose behind specific material situations.

In the process of accepting the premise that people and events are perfect the way they are, you access a higher meaning resulting from an all-encompassing view of the universe. This process leads to experiencing the ecstasy of trusting in the intangible perfection, and being in constant communion and harmony with the unseen forces of life.

♇

PLUTO: KEY TO FEARLESSNESS AND EMPOWERMENT

Pluto in the birth chart:*
- Reveals where you most covertly resist change; where a willingness to change will have the biggest impact on your life and will result in fearlessness.
- Depicts the part of yourself that is the most difficult to face and to expose to others.
- Shows the way to release the area of greatest internal repression and in the process experience a new sense of personal empowerment and self-mastery.
- Represents the area where you are constantly challenged to use your power to alter stagnant situations drastically.
- Illuminates that area of life in which you can obtain the rewards of true self-mastery if you are willing to risk it all, exposing personal perceptions and values on the deepest levels.
- Exposes the temptation to use divine power as a tool of the personal ego and self-will, which can have explosive repercussions that lead to self-suppression.

---

* To discover the sign and house your PLUTO is located in, go to www.janspiller.com and a free chart will be calculated for you.

- Indicates the area in which you need to be willing to die *psychologically* in order to be reborn into an experience of life on a whole new level.
- Signifies where you can claim the high consciousness of clear right action and alignment with the self. It is also the area where you fear that embracing your connection with the high consciousness might make you different from everyone else; aloneness.

Pluto takes approximately 248 years to orbit one time around the zodiac and remains in one sign for up to thirty years. The influences of the sign bearing Pluto mark an entire generation, in addition to having an individual impact. Thus, Pluto signifies the transformation of an entire group of people as well as being an indicator of personal challenge for transformation and mastery.

In many ways the personal and generational effects are the same. As the challenge is accepted and the necessary risks are dealt with on an individual basis, the entire generation is activated and its energy in turn is released to transform the world. On a strictly personal level, Pluto's most intense emotional influences are felt and worked with in the house location of your chart.

THE PATH OF PLUTO

Pluto shows where you have the opportunity to rise above personal fears, into a state of charismatic fearlessness. The house containing Pluto in your birth chart shows the environment that will either provoke your feelings of powerlessness or be a stimulus for your transformation into fearlessness.

Pluto shows where you have the opportunity to walk the path of terror. It is the chance to take a risky action—based on a sense of moral or ethical integrity—as you walk your life path. It's choosing right action over desired results. It is the dark night of the soul—the test of worthiness to play a larger role in life than the one dictated by your past.

PLUTO IN ARIES

Your generation's calling: To transform the world with a new definition of self-interest: What's best for the good of all is ultimately what is best for the self. To challenge traditional ideas about survival on Earth.

Personal fear: Losing autonomy by revealing who you really are.

The Pluto-in-Aries challenge: To let go of your own illusions about what constitutes independence. To express spontaneously your innate desires and natural responses within the context of creating relationships based on a true sense of integrity and authenticity.

PLUTO IN TAURUS

Your generation's calling: To transform the world with new ways to distribute goods and material wealth to the nations. To transform traditional ideas about ownership and sharing the wealth of Earth.

Personal fear: Losing personal comfort by openly revealing your needs and encouraging others to do the same.

The Pluto-in-Taurus challenge: To let go of your own illusions about stability and to openly reveal what is important to you, in order to create greater comfort and mutual empowerment for all.

PLUTO IN GEMINI

Your generation's calling: To participate in world transformation through a greater sense of global contact. As a generation you are handed the challenge of transforming the existing methods of communication and transportation to a position that puts you in contact with the rest of the world.

Personal fear: Openly communicating your thoughts and ideas with other people.

The Pluto-in-Gemini challenge: To risk the honest expression of your perceptions and ideas and to accept the responses of others.

PLUTO IN CANCER

Your generation's calling: To participate in world transformation by creating a new security based on cooperation with other nations. During the Great Depression, this generation's sense of family isolation as a key to their basic survival was transformed.

Personal fear: Maintaining control over your personal safety.

The Pluto-in-Cancer challenge: To risk your self-protective instincts for a larger security in cooperation with others.

PLUTO IN LEO

Your generation's calling: To participate in world transformation by altering your creative self-expression and communicating with other nations on the level of art, music, and the new consciousness. You are also handed the challenge of dealing with each nation asserting itself as a power in the world.

Personal fear: Expressing your emotions honestly through your sense of drama and creative talents.

The Pluto-in-Leo challenge: To risk the disapproval of others for a larger sense of self-approval through open and powerful self-expression.

PLUTO IN VIRGO

Your generation's calling: To participate in world transformation on the levels of health and service to those less fortunate. You are also given the challenge of transforming the ecology of Earth.

Personal fear: Risking the criticism of others through a commitment to your sense of duty.

The Pluto-in-Virgo challenge: To serve others on practical levels even though you may not have attained the perception of self-perfection you seek.

PLUTO IN LIBRA

Your generation's calling: To participate in world transformation by introducing new forms of cooperation between nations. You are also given the challenge of transforming traditional ideas of partnership relationships on Earth.

Personal fear: Risking disharmony through disclosure of what you feel is unjust.

The Pluto-in-Libra Challenge: To be willing to discard personal illusions of balance and objectively express your power in relationships so a new and greater harmony can be established.

PLUTO IN SCORPIO

Your generation's calling: To transform the world with new forms of monetary exchange and handling debt and the sharing of resources between nations. To transform ideas surrounding commitment in bonded relationships, primarily those involving sex and/or money.

Personal fear: Losing individual power by exposing your awareness of the needs and desires of others.

The Pluto-in-Scorpio challenge: To be willing to let go of personal illusions about the power of secrecy. To openly express your desires to your partner in a bonded relationship, for greater mutual empowerment.

PLUTO IN SAGITTARIUS

Your generation's calling: To introduce new standards of morality, ethics, and integrity among nations, transforming traditional ideas about spiritual truth and freedom on Earth.

Personal fear: Losing spontaneity. When you encounter what you feel to be unethical or spiritually incorrect behavior, you must disclose it.

The Pluto-in-Sagittarius challenge: To let go of your own illusions about what constitutes truth and freedom. To sense intuitively what is actually occurring around you and to express it verbally. In this way, you pave the way for a higher order of ethics to emerge.

PLUTO IN CAPRICORN

Your generation's calling: To transform the world with new forms of government. To challenge traditional ideas of management. To achieve global acceptance of a concept of personal responsibility.

Personal fear: Losing control by disclosing your true aims and goals.

The Pluto-in-Capricorn challenge: To let go of your own illusions about what constitutes responsibility and commitment and to openly take charge, creating a higher form of government that appreciates people's need for security. To behave responsibly, in a way that results in a deep sense of self-respect.

PLUTO IN AQUARIUS

Your generation's calling: To transform the world with new forms of science and technology that can link the peoples of the planet; to push the traditional limits of science and technology.

Personal fear: Losing freedom by openly committing yourself to a cause, a scientific principle, or to spreading knowledge that will benefit humankind.

The Pluto-in-Aquarius challenge: To let go of your own illusions about fairness equaling the will of the majority and not go with the flow. To express the power of objective knowledge while respecting individual differences.

PLUTO IN PISCES

Your generation's calling: To transform the world with new spiritual awareness that can unite the nations of the Earth at the heart. To transform spiritual traditions that rely on discrediting other faiths to establish their own credibility.

Personal fear: Losing privacy by openly disclosing your visions and dreams.

The Pluto-in-Pisces challenge: To let go of the security of solitude and openly express and live your ideal of oneness, in order to make your vision a reality in the material world.

PLUTO IN THE HOUSES

PLUTO IN THE 1ST HOUSE

UNCONSCIOUS EXPRESSION

Fear-based withholding: You might withhold your ability to stimulate others toward deeper awareness because you fear their violent response.

Result: If you hide under the pretense of being harmless, you attract people who are basically incompatible. Withholding honest responses robs you and others of the opportunity to transform the situation to a higher level.

Conversely, you might be tempted to express your perceptions with an ego motive of wanting to intimidate or manipulate others to live up to your expectations. If you try to force others to change their self-expression, you will find yourself entangled in intense resistance from them. This impasse results in personal stagnation and a frustrating repression of involvement in your relationships.

CONSCIOUS EXPRESSION

Fearlessness and charisma result when you are willing to go beyond your greatest fear and surrender to the empowerment of your personality. By asserting yourself fully and honestly—even though it may provoke others—you are likely to experience a momentary disruption in your environment. This leads to a process of purification, eliminating those factors that inhibit self-expression.

By taking the risk of expressing your deep perceptions as they arise, you rise above stagnant levels of unspoken conflicts. When your motive is a commitment to your integrity, you are able to graciously reveal your perceptions of others' expressions. This allows them to accept or reject your insights as they choose. Others may temporarily invalidate your discernment because they feel deeply exposed and publicly unmasked. If you can allow their quick denials of your truth to pass by and move on to other areas of interaction, you leave them free to consider what you have said.

PATH TO SELF-MASTERY

Accepting the gift of having influence in your personality empowers you to be willing to go through the risks of declaring yourself regardless of the consequences. When you become committed to independent self-assertion, you are led past your greatest fears and into self-mastery.

The environment in which you meet the challenge for personal transformation: The expression of your personality.

PLUTO IN THE 2ND HOUSE

UNCONSCIOUS EXPRESSION

Fear-based withholding: You might deny your power to use personal resources to transform your financial situation.

Result: This withholding defeats all opportunity for an expansion of material security. If you neglect to take your ideas and talents out into the world for fear of being victimized, your values are not given a chance to produce material results for anyone.

Seeking to maintain total control over your personal resources perpetuates a pattern of repressed and stagnant values. The result is frustrated mediocrity.

CONSCIOUS EXPRESSION

Fearlessness and charisma result when you go beyond your greatest fears and surrender to the will of being useful. If you take the risk of using the empowerment of high consciousness, you transform your assets. This leads to greater alignment with yourself. Committing yourself to working with those resources that are available leads to a temporary disruption of your old value systems. This process opens to a new, unanticipated freedom and ease in accepting the inflowing bounty of life.

Opening to expand your resources into the world empowers you with the will that brings about results. Appreciating life makes you willing to go through the suffering to obtain the values of life, and hence its worth.

PATH TO SELF-MASTERY

By revealing your values, you establish what you feel is tangibly important. The key is to sacrifice the desire to enforce your values on others. This frees you to accept temporary invalidation for what you consider important, understanding that people may need time to align with their own empowerment.

Commitment to manifesting what *you* feel in life has value and gives you the confidence to use the empowerment of your will leads you past your greatest fears and into self-mastery.

The environment in which you meet the challenge for personal transformation: Your money and possessions.

PLUTO IN THE 3RD HOUSE

UNCONSCIOUS EXPRESSION

Fear-based withholding: Denying communicating your penetrating perceptions to others suppresses your gift of asking questions that arouse them to a deeper awareness of themselves.

Result: Defeating all opportunity for bringing new insights to yourself and others. Seeking to control others by not revealing information due to fear of rejection leads to not trusting your perceptions. As a result you might resent them, feeling unable to communicate in a powerful way.

If you use your mind for the purpose of forcing your perceptions on others, expecting them to agree with your ideas through mental intimidation, they will resist you.

CONSCIOUS EXPRESSION

Fearlessness and charisma result when you go beyond your greatest fears and surrender to the empowerment of your communicative ability. The fear that you may be misunderstood can cause a momentary disruption in your thought processes when you expose your perceptions of daily events and how others are responding to them.

When you continue to communicate, this disruption is followed by a purification of your ability to divulge insights without personally identifying with the ideas. You can overcome conflict and attain self-mastery by sharing your spontaneous perceptions, insights, and honest reactions.

PATH TO SELF-MASTERY

Sacrificing the desire to *control* or invalidate the thought processes, ideas, or statements of another frees you to offer your own points of view. By realizing that your perceptions can occasionally shake others to their core, you can give them room to invalidate ideas temporarily until they have had a chance to review your teaching and make their own choice.

The environment in which you meet the challenge for personal transformation: Your communication with others.

PLUTO IN THE 4TH HOUSE

UNCONSCIOUS EXPRESSION

Fear-based withholding: Using your sensitivities to people's feelings in ways that provoke them into confronting a deeper awareness of themselves.
Result: This repression robs them of the opportunity to experience new feelings, and also robs you. Giving in to fears of being rejected leads to withholding your deepest responses to your family. This repression of openness leads to a resentment of others' insensitivities. The result is overcontrol and emotional stagnation.

CONSCIOUS EXPRESSION

Fearlessness and charisma result when you go beyond your greatest fears, surrendering to your sensitivity. In revealing what you are feeling—in spite of fearing the consequences—you undergo a transformation of feelings. This allows for a truer alignment with your deepest sensitivities.

In sharing your responses and deep perceptions of others' feelings, you may experience a temporary invalidation from those who are closest. A purge of both your insecurities and theirs can follow.

PATH TO SELF-MASTERY

Ceasing trying to control others' feelings to protect your vulnerability frees you to operate from a stable position. This vantage empowers you to express and share from the integrity of your deepest sensitivities. Selfless commitment to recognizing and exposing your awareness of the realm of feelings leads you past your greatest fears and into self-mastery.
The environment in which you meet the challenge for personal transformation: Your home and family.

PLUTO IN THE 5TH HOUSE

UNCONSCIOUS EXPRESSION

Fear-based withholding: Using your talents in ways that arouse a creative, spontaneous reaction in others.
Result: Failing to tune others into a deeper awareness of their emotional and sexual expression robs you and them of being in touch with truly creative energies.

There's a tendency to repress responding dramatically and spontaneously to situations because you fear awakening energies that you or others might not be able to handle. And yet avoiding this process leads to emotional stagnation. When you use ego to repress natural creativity, it leads to resenting others for the loss of your spontaneity of self-expression.

CONSCIOUS EXPRESSION

Fearlessness and charisma result when you go beyond your greatest fears and use the empowerment of dramatic expression. You can provoke others into a deeper awareness of their inhibitions about expressing themselves completely.

Giving voice to your inner child tunes you in to a deeper meaning of loyalty. You can commit to fully expressing spontaneity when you realize that the creative power that flows through you is not from your ego. As a consequence you may encounter at first a temporary disruption and invalidation in your relationship with others, followed by emotional purification.

PATH TO SELF-MASTERY

When you sacrifice the unconscious motive of wanting to control others' opinions through your ego power, you are able to operate from a clear motive. Then you can express yourself with a buoyant sense of drama for the purpose of contributing inspiration. Taking the risk of recognizing and exposing your sense of creative spontaneity leads you past your greatest fears and into self-mastery.

The environment in which you meet the challenge for personal transformation: Your children, creative projects, and romance.

PLUTO IN THE 6TH HOUSE

UNCONSCIOUS EXPRESSION

Fear-based withholding: Using your intense perception of order to provoke others into a deeper awareness of their abilities to organize their lives effectively. Result: This repression can invoke the frustration of feeling powerless to create precision in your world. It can also lead to resenting others for failing to do their part.

Giving in to fears of being criticized and thought petty leads to not communicating your awareness of environmental inefficiencies. This robs you and others of the opportunity to discover a higher order. The result is a stagnant situation in which you are unable to clean up the disorder on the most personal and impersonal levels.

CONSCIOUS EXPRESSION

Fearlessness and charisma result when you go beyond your greatest fears and surrender to the empowerment of your sense of order. By divulging perceptions of disorder you may experience a temporary disruption and invalidation of your internal ordering. This disruption is followed by an emotional purging and the emergence of a new sense of duty. You can provoke others into a deeper experience of their perfection as you express your concept of the imperfection you see around you.

PATH TO SELF-MASTERY

The challenge is to sacrifice the motive of wanting others to change their behavior and become nearer to perfection according to your standards. This frees you to reveal perceptions of disorder from a clear, stable motive: simply wanting to express service by sharing your awareness of life.

Revealing these observations—not defending them or taking them personally—opens the way for a clearer sense of organization to occur in your relationships. Thus, recognizing and offering your concept of order regardless of the consequences leads you past your greatest fears and into self-mastery.

The environment in which you meet the challenge for personal transformation: Your job.

PLUTO IN THE 7TH HOUSE

UNCONSCIOUS EXPRESSION

Fear-based withholding: Using your awareness of others, especially your mate, in a way that provokes them into deeper self-awareness.

Result: Suppressing this insight of others robs you and them of the chance to reach new levels of intimacy and depth in the relationship. If you fear disrupting the interaction with your mate or losing control of the relationship, you may not share your perceptions and true reactions. This withholding leads to frustration and feeling powerless to have the kind of relationship you really want.

In order to control and hold on to the alliance, you might repress yourself and secretly resent your mate for your own reluctance to risk sharing yourself fully. This pattern results in being in control of stagnant relationships that you do not want.

CONSCIOUS EXPRESSION

Fearlessness and charisma result when you overcome your greatest fears by surrendering to the empowerment of the relationship. Then you can allow your partner to be potent by sharing your perceptions and reactions with him or her.

As a consequence, you may experience a momentary disruption and invalidation in the confrontation that leads to a process of purification. This process eliminates those factors that block a mutual sense of empowerment in the alliance.

PATH TO SELF-MASTERY

The challenge is to allow the high consciousness to emerge through a relationship. Revealing your deepest experiences and perceptions of the other person and the relationship itself, regardless of the consequences, maintains the integrity of the alliance. This leads to the unfolding of mutual empowerment. By sharing your perceptions with the other person, you empower yourself.

The idea is to sacrifice the desire to control your partner or deceive your partner into thinking he or she is in control. This frees you to operate from a clear and stable motive, expressing a desire for a complete sharing and enhancement of mutual empowerment. By revealing the perceptions you really see, you are led past your greatest fears and into self-mastery.

The environment in which you meet the challenge for personal transformation: Your marriage and partnerships.

PLUTO IN THE 8TH HOUSE

UNCONSCIOUS EXPRESSION

Fear-based withholding: Your perceptions of other people's motives; not provoking them into a deeper self-awareness.

Result: This suppression robs you and them of the opportunity to experience the potency of mutual impact. Failing to reveal your awareness of the desires and deeper yearnings of others—because you fear losing control or becoming vulnerable by exposing yourself—leaves you unaffected by your most intimate connections with them. It also brings about stagnation in close relationships.

Anticipating an intensity in close relationships can result in frustration. This only occurs when you neglect sharing the depth of your perceptions and when you don't allow yourself to become too involved. This leads to experiencing dissatisfaction as well as the resentment of others from needing many relationships because you allow none of your unions to go deeply enough to find satisfaction.

CONSCIOUS EXPRESSION

Fearlessness and charisma result when you go beyond your greatest fears by surrendering to the empowerment of yielding. This frees you to enter into deep psychic and material commitments with others and thus experience personal transformation.

Through surrendering your individual force and merging it fully into the strength of the relationship, you may experience a momentary disruption and invalidation in your sense of power. This leads to a process of purification. It eliminates those unconscious values that have blocked you from experiencing the deepest meaning of potency in your life.

PATH TO SELF-MASTERY

The call is to experience the real strength emerging from the bond of your deep psychic and material commitment to another. When you sacrifice the desire for exclusive control, you begin operating from a clear motive of wanting to increase the potency of the mutual bond.

By being committed to being powerful enough to risk giving up your self-control, you can wholly combine with another. This leads past your greatest fears and into self-mastery.

The environment in which you meet the challenge for personal transformation: Close, bonded relationships—usually involving sex or money.

PLUTO IN THE 9TH HOUSE

UNCONSCIOUS EXPRESSION

Fear-based withholding: Revealing spontaneous intuitions, thus not provoking other people into a deeper awareness of their truths and intellectual values in life.

Result: This holding back robs others and you of the chance to see newer, even higher knowledge. You may not communicate your awareness due to not wanting others to see your intellectual independence. Also, you may fear losing control of possessing superior knowledge by sharing it.

Repressing the sharing of your current understanding with others results in the frustration of failing to reach new levels of perception. Additionally, because of your belief in personal and intellectual superiority, you may resent others' levels of insight. This resentment limits your own awareness and leads to stagnation in the breadth of your intellectual ideals.

CONSCIOUS EXPRESSION

Fearlessness and charisma result when you go beyond your greatest fears by surrendering to the true power of insights. You do this by sharing your spontaneous perceptions with others in spite of fears of provoking or being misunderstood. You may then experience a momentary disruption and invalidation of your sense of intellectual pride.

This leads to a process of purification and eliminates those factors of misunderstanding that caused you to be aloof. By not identifying with the power of the intuitive insights you receive, you can commit yourself to sharing spontaneous perceptions without judgment. This allows others' ideas to combine with your thought processes. Thus, you open up to an empowering expansion of your intellectual values.

PATH TO SELF-MASTERY

Operating from the clear motive of simply expressing yourself by sharing the answers you see with others releases you from the burden of feeling you have to prove you have superior knowledge. Empowerment results when you sacrifice the temptation to use your intellect to force others' alignment with your beliefs. By being selflessly committed to taking the risk and exposing your spontaneous perceptions, you are led past your greatest fears and into self-mastery.

The environment in which you meet the challenge for personal transformation: Higher education; religious settings; foreign travel—of mind or body.

PLUTO IN THE 10TH HOUSE

UNCONSCIOUS EXPRESSION

Fear-based withholding: You may avoid using your perceptive abilities to establish true authority in the world.

Result: This withholding leads to inviting others to victimize you. By being afraid to risk your public image, you might repress yourself and fail to attempt the ultimate goal. If you shun the risk of public failure, you may pretend to be successful while suppressing desires to attain specific objectives.

Settling for mediocrity gives you a sense of control that you may fear losing if you become powerful in the world. However, by withholding your empowerment, you rob yourself and others of the consequence of your impact.

If you do not risk using all your power and perceptive resources to attain what you seek professionally, you deny your own destiny. Thus, you may experience the frustrating powerlessness that comes from being unwilling to venture the use of your authority on a public level.

CONSCIOUS EXPRESSION

Fearlessness and charisma result when you are willing to go beyond your greatest fears and surrender to the true power of your ambitions. The idea is to recognize and fully establish your authority with integrity in a public arena. Taking this risk leads to experiencing a positive alteration in your sense of empowerment. In the process of going forth to reach goals, your highest aims for achievement combine with the power of your will. This results in experiencing a momentary disruption and invalidation of control over your public image.

A process of purification follows, eliminating those feelings of inadequacy that kept you from a sense of destiny and expression of authority. Self-mastery can be attained by exposing your potency on a public level. Allowing the integrity of your perceptions to provoke the public into transforming expands your authority into appropriate leadership.

PATH TO SELF-MASTERY

You experience the emergence of your true mastery as you cease to identify with the power and the authority that is released through you into the world. The idea is to sacrifice the motive of wanting to force ego control over the direction of others. This frees you to operate from a clear and stable motive of simply wanting to express a sense of destiny.

By being committed to recognizing and publicly establishing the potency and authority within yourself, regardless of the consequences, you are led past your greatest fears and into self-mastery.

The enviroment in which you meet the challenge for personal transformation: Your profession and goals.

PLUTO IN THE 11TH HOUSE

UNCONSCIOUS EXPRESSION

Fear-based withholding: Not exposing factors in group situations that are out of alignment with the universal goals you see.

Result: Fearing the loss of acceptance if you express unconventional ideas leads to robbing yourself and others of a chance to actualize the potential of a collective ideal. You may fail to share your knowledge and then resent your peers for not being of higher intent.

Separating your ideals from those of your peers leads to repressing insights that, if revealed, would contribute to a higher sense of group unity. If you indulge in egotistical motives—such as forcing on others the certainty of your knowledge or desiring to be accepted and validated by the group—you will experience resistance.

If you fail to expose the knowledge you see, the result is losing the opportunity of allowing the power of the group (or your friends) to combine with you and effect a mutual change. By not risking personal power, you stay in total control of a stagnant sense of collective ideals and values. As a result you may feel intimidated, powerless, and isolated.

CONSCIOUS EXPRESSION

Fearlessness and charisma result when you go beyond your greatest fears, being an example of your ideals by revealing unconventional knowledge. By sharing objective perceptions during interactions with peers, regardless of the consequences, you experience a transformation into greater empowerment. When you risk exposing those hidden factors that you perceive do not support the ideal—and point to the big picture of what all of you are trying to achieve together—you may experience a temporary disruption and invalidation of your knowledge.

This leads to a process of purification, eliminating factors that blocked you and your peers from experiencing combined and expanded powers. Self-mastery can be attained through the objective sharing of information, increasing the potency of the group as an entity unto itself. Thus, you experience your own mastery emerging through your impersonal commitment to increasing the power of the ideal. You access the high consciousness as you cease to identify with the power that is released through you when you express knowledge. This allows you to reveal with integrity your most threatening insights.

In exposing unusual awareness, you may release an intense power that stuns others. Realizing this empowers you to accept the fact that they may temporarily invalidate the revelations until they have had a chance to reevaluate and accept them on their own. Only when you *sacrifice* enforcing ideals through maintaining power over group ideals—wanting to prove the power of your information through peer validation—are you free to operate from a clear and stable motive, simply wanting to contribute your insights.

PATH TO SELF-MASTERY

For you, the key to self-mastery lies in accepting the commitment to establish the ideal by participating in groups and with friends. In those arenas you can expose the truth of your desires and the ideals you see, allowing your peers to transform and support or not support you. Thus, you are led past your greatest fears and into the dimension of self-mastery.

The environment in which you meet the challenge for personal transformation: Friends and group situations; pursuing your dreams.

PLUTO IN THE 12TH HOUSE

UNCONSCIOUS EXPRESSION

Fear-based withholding: Repressing the power to use your contact with larger, unseen spiritual forces of life in ways that provoke you and others into deeper awareness of the spiritual dimension of self.
Result: This holding back robs everyone of the chance to experience life by personally contacting the deepest source of empowerment and identity. The temptation is to deny the empowerment of your ideals and fail to express your vision.

Fearing the loss of control or the disruption of the rest of your life results in not responding to circumstances on the basis of a vision you see. This leads to frustration, a feeling of being misunderstood by the world, and a resentment of others for their lack of vision and understanding.

Fearing you may lose your spiritual security by sharing it may lead to not exposing the power of intangible causes to others. This leaves you with only a stagnant sense of the power of the real self.

CONSCIOUS EXPRESSION

Fearlessness and charisma result when: You go beyond your greatest fears by surrendering to the power of your vision. Taking the risk of trusting life to support you—knowing you are acting in accord with right action—empowers you to express your spiritual vision. This can result in a temporary disruption and invalidation of your private sense of security. It leads to the purging of repressive unconscious fears and the purification of a new connection with the unseen forces of life.

You claim high consciousness when you reveal the perceptions of hidden causes and profound inner meanings of others' lives. The challenge is to expose the truth of the visions that you see regardless of the consequences. Taking the risk of fully expressing your vision releases empowerment. This allows you to both experience and perceive a deeper relationship with self.

Exposing your discernment releases an intense potency that can stun others. This allows you to understand with compassion that others may temporarily invalidate the insight until they have had a chance to accept and incorporate it. Your challenge is to sacrifice the motive of wanting your observations validated by others or forcing them to align with their real self as you envision it. This frees you to operate from a clear motive of accepting and sharing the private insights you receive from a motive of helpfulness.

PATH TO SELF-MASTERY

As you cease to identify with the power of the intangible insights that flow through you, you experience true spiritual security. This allows you to share your perceptions without taking the reactions of others personally. By being selflessly committed to taking the risk and revealing the spiritual visions you receive, you are led past your greatest fears and into self-mastery.

The environment in which you meet the challenge for personal transformation: Spending time by yourself; the challenge of self-purification.

A^{SC}

ASCENDANT: KEY TO SELF-CONFIDENCE

Mathematically, the ascendant, or rising, is the sign that was rising over the horizon when you were born.* If you view your astrology chart as a clock, it is that sign located at nine o'clock.

In concrete terms, the ascendant rules your physical body and your direct physical experience of the world. It acts is the filter through which everything you are internally is projected into the external world, and through which everything in your outer environment is personally experienced and interpreted by you. On a more intangible level, it's the filter through which your personality is displayed to the world—what others see when they see you—and your sense of personal identity.

Naturally, who you are is constantly growing and changing as you interact with others and the world around you. In order for this process to unfold smoothly and happily, the way you express your personality also needs to adapt in order to reflect these changes in a positive way. You can easily see where such

---

* To discover the sign of your ASCENDANT (or Rising Sign) go to www.janspiller.com, follow prompts, and a free chart will be calculated for you.

adjustments are needed through your interactions with others. In fact, the feedback you receive from other people provides exactly the information you need to discover how to best express your authentic self through your personality.

For example, say that a person with Leo ascendant has a new idea and is bubbling over with enthusiasm for his or her project. Someone may be critical: "That won't work—people don't need that and they won't buy it!" In reality, this is just feedback from the environment telling the native that it's necessary to take other people's needs into account when presenting their ideas. This information will allow them to fine-tune their presentation so that they can express themselves more effectively and create the results they want.

However, too often we interpret the reactions of others as negative. Then, rather than just looking to see where we could make an adjustment in the way we present ourselves and our ideas, we feel not okay and end up suppressing that part of ourselves altogether.

We may even become so focused on our concerns about how others see us that we totally lose touch with our own innate strength and beauty. If we allow this to happen, then over time our experience of the world—and the world's experience of us—will grow more limited and less interesting. And this, in turn, will restrict the flow of vital energy in our life.

The information found in the sections on each ascendant sign will provide specific tools to help you avoid these unconscious reactions that can lead to shutting down parts of yourself and your life-affirming energy, as well as assist you in making choices that increase your happiness and vitality. The material on each sign is presented in the following six categories:

Your Window to the World discusses how you can express yourself in ways that make it easier for others to be receptive and supportive of you and your ideas. If you experience any social awkwardness in relating with other people, simply begin to consciously develop the qualities of your ascendant sign. Strengthening these innate abilities will automatically create an approach that allows you to more easily connect with others, and in the process you will gain self-confidence in this area of your life.

Your Achilles' Heel describes what closing down looks like for each ascendant sign. With this information you can recognize the symptoms and take steps to reverse this destructive process.

Self-Actualization suggests experiments with changes in behavior that can reopen the full expression of your personality in ways that allow others to respond by valuing you and appreciating your innate gifts.

Relationships provides information that can help you enhance your connections with others, both on a daily basis and in your intimate and primary relationships. In fact, the ascendant is the axis of personal satisfaction in relationships.

Entering into a significant relationship requires shifting your perspective to incorporate the concept of "we" as well as "me." The process of combining with another in partnership forms a kind of mutual identity. The knowledge presented in this section can help guide you through this tricky process of linking with another in this way to create a successful team effort, while simultaneously affirming the gifts and strength of your own individual identity.

Specific information is also included for each ascendant sign to help you incorporate the idea that success in the area of relationships requires focusing on the means rather than the end. In other words, a mutually satisfying relationship cannot be created by striving toward a predetermined picture of what you think it should look like. Rather, it is the natural outgrowth of authentically expressing who you are while maintaining a balanced awareness of the other person's individuality.

Since there is nothing to "achieve," a lasting positive result can only be created through sincerity, not strategy (which is the opposite of sincerity). Success comes through the process of being candid, open, genuine, and truthful about your honest reactions to outer circumstances as they occur, regardless of any imagined outcome. In this way a mutually satisfying relationship is the result of your inner authenticity, since those who inherently resonate with your true nature will grow closer, while those who don't will move on.

Past-Life Gifts describes a powerful legacy that can be available to you by expanding your awareness of its presence in your life. The sign on the ascendant shows those innate qualities that have been the most fully developed and mastered through numerous past-life experiences. Once you recognize these gifts you have so beautifully fine-tuned in past incarnations, whether or not you consciously use them is up to you.

Confidence in Social Situations provides a valuable resource for each ascendant sign when you're in a challenging social situation. We all encounter situations where we feel totally lost in terms of what to say or how to act. This can be an unsettling experience, and one in which we may not put our best foot forward. Fears of not knowing how to handle the situation may prevent us from even going forward at all. Some classic examples might include:

"Oh gosh, this is a really important job interview. What's the best way for me to handle it?"

"Wow, I'm meeting my girlfriend's/boyfriend's parents for the first time—how can I make a good impression?"

"Yikes! This is a really big party and I don't know anyone—how can I fit in?"

Over the years, I have learned from personal experience that what works best on these occasions is to approach others with a genuine interest in *them,* with the underlying motive inherent in your ascendant sign. By consciously putting your attention on the *other* person and intending to benefit him or her—keeping the tips offered in this section in mind—you will have a natural persona you can count on for feeling comfortable in relating to others. As you do this, your popularity will increase and you will feel more secure and confident in social interactions.

ARIES RISING

Your Window to the World

You interact with the external world from a position of independence, expressing your inner being with an aura of self-sufficiency. When looking outside yourself, you evaluate the situations that present themselves in your life as to whether or not your independent spirit will be valued and opportunities for self-discovery exist.

You view other people in terms of whether or not they are self-reliant—people who recognize and appreciate their own individuality. You *interpret* the behavior of others toward you in terms of how well they acknowledge you as a unique and separate person and support your independent nature.

Your personality and demeanor reflect those traits that you feel demonstrate bravery, self-reliance, and openness to self-discovery. Your attitude and behavior show that you are very appreciative of others and encourage them to pursue their dreams—and you expect others to appreciate and encourage you in return.

Your Achilles' Heel

Your natural approach to life is to express your innate leadership abilities through your courage and your assertive impulses. This can result in your seeing those who *don't* approach life in this way as being compromising and/or indecisive. Because you sometimes view *others* this way, it's easy for you to assume that they could possibly view *you* this way—and it is your fear of this potential disapproval that creates your Achilles' heel.

If you don't stay in touch with your own natural instincts and instead allow this fear of how others might see you to distract you from your own independent point of view, you end up suppressing your assertive impulses and giving away your power. Then you lose confidence in your innate sense of courage and your ability to lead.

For instance, you may refuse to take the initiative and extend yourself to others—fearing they might think you are weak or needy. However, if you allow this to happen, then instead of using the power of your inborn assertive abilities constructively, you turn it inward against yourself where it becomes a stubborn impediment. When all that power is not outwardly expressed, it implodes and blocks the flow of your own vital energy.

Then others may in fact see you as indecisive, or as Mr. or Ms. Nice, which can lead them to overstep their bounds with you. If this happens, you may unexpectedly erupt into anger, which can create an ongoing sense of animosity between you. Then you may unconsciously use your sense of independence in a brusque manner to keep others away. And this in turn can lead to feelings of isolation.

Self-Actualization

Expressing your lively courage reinforces a sense of personal independence and gives you self-confidence. You have an special gift for motivating and inspiring others by being willing to act on the impulsiveness of your own bold spirit—exploring innovative ideas and emboldening other people to take a chance on something new!

While being an example of courage and independence is the only healthy way for you to experience ongoing vitality in your life, it can be difficult to get past the fear of how other people will see you, and the potential of their disapproval. But the highest path is when you use your innate boldness to overcome this obstacle and fully express your true nature, inspiring others through your leadership by being the one to take the initiative in your own life.

Then your greatest challenge becomes using the feedback you receive from your environment—both positive *and* negative—to shift and fine-tune the ways in which you express your gifts. It is only through this process that your ability to consistently create positive results can be refined and perfected.

This process can be painful, but only to the extent that you take any negative feedback personally. The feedback of others is actually a gift that allows you to see the *exact* changes that are needed in order for you to create the happy outcomes and rapport with others that you long for. By using the feedback of others to fine-tune the way you express yourself, you gain a new sense of personal independence and trust in your ability to take action, as well as the confidence and joy that come from freely expressing your authentic self. Once you are no longer living in fear of others' perceptions, the feeling of being caught between two opposing needs—to fight or keep the peace at any price—will cease.

The best outcomes will result from actively using your pioneering energies and independent spirit to inspire yourself and others with the prospect of new challenges. Then you will truly begin to experience yourself as a powerful cause in your own life.

Relationships

In the beginning of an intimate relationship, it's easy for you to think too quickly in terms of marriage or partnership—how you can support the other person and work things out—and miss seeing who that person actually is and what *he* wants for himself. Then, once involved on a close level, you may reverse yourself and tend to be a bit abrasive in trying to get him to live up to your standards.

In choosing a suitable mate, partner, or friend, your challenge is to intentionally step back and see the other person as an individual. Notice how independent the person really is. Can he carry his own weight and relate to you as an equal?

On his own, what is *his* desire for his own life? Apart from his connection with you, what stimulates his energy and gets him excited? What is his history? What are his dreams? Is this a person who has values that you want to support? Once you see him clearly, you can decide whether or not it's in your best interests to partner with him.

You have an incredible ability to create fairness and reciprocity in your relationships, and when the other person is not playing fairly, you are capable of taking a leadership role that can restore balance in the partnership. However, because you are a natural team player in your significant relationships, you may tend to lose your own sense of self in your desire to be fair to your partner. You think that if you play fairly with others that they will automatically reciprocate. And, depending upon their natural inclinations, this path can lead to disappointment. Since you naturally interact with diplomacy and grace, you are surprised if, instead, the other person responds roughly or in a crude manner.

You can't change another from following his inherent path. In the end, he will be true to his own sense of who he is. See what he wants as an individual, and support him in pursing his vision for *his* life without losing your own independence and identity. If he is not good partnership material for you, your best bet is to recognize that early on and simply leave him free to be himself.

Past-Life Gifts

You have had many past lives where your survival depended solely on your own instincts and actions. Many of these past incarnations were spent as a warrior—embracing courage and self-reliance as the most important values. This has lead to your innate sense of bravery and independence in approaching the battlefield of life with the confidence to overcome any obstacle through your courage and willingness to fight for what you feel is right.

In these past incarnations you mastered the art of taking the initiative, and you are gifted in your ability for positive self-assertion. Your motives have been purified so that you no longer engage your energies for the sake of fighting, but to serve a higher cause that you believe in.

You have learned the value of being direct and authentic in your presentation. In this regard, the example of your innate innocence can teach others the value of being straightforward and inspire them to become more authentic in their own lives.

Confidence in Social Situations

Step into the role of "the independent one."

Hold the intention of "How can I give you the confidence to make a new beginning?"

TAURUS RISING

Your Window to the World

With Taurus rising, you interact with the external world from a position of remaining comfortable in your physical body, which includes feeling good about yourself. You express your inner being in a slow, deliberate, consistent manner that radiates solid strength and dependability.

When looking outside yourself, you see the people and situations around you in terms of whether or not you feel comfortable. Are their values compatible with yours? Do they contribute positively to your sense of self-esteem? And you interpret the behavior of others in terms of how clearly they perceive your inner worth and how much they value and appreciate you.

You express your personality and demeanor in ways that you feel reflect your values of stability, practicality, and persistence. Your attitude and behavior demonstrate that you are dependable, loyal, and authentic—and you expect the allegiance of others in return.

Your Achilles' Heel

You approach life from a position of innate strength and stability, and have a natural ability for creating success in the external world. However, more than any other rising sign, you tend to equate others' acceptance and approval of you, your ideas, and your values with whether or not they agree with you and do things your way. As a result, allowing yourself to become overly concerned with how other people see you can lead to suppressing your gifts—and this creates your Achilles' heel.

So it is especially important for you to stay in touch with the strength of your own identity and your innate ability to build a concrete foundation that supports your sense of personal value in the material world. When you *don't* do this, you can become overly insistent on others doing things your way, because internally you believe that if they don't, it means there is something wrong with your ideas or values—that you're not good enough.

However, when you keep pushing the issue, the other person's natural reaction is to become quiet and distance herself from you. Then you interpret her behavior as proof of your belief that she doesn't value *you*. This further undermines your sense of self-worth and may cause you to become even *more* insistent and dependent on the other person's validation in order to feel okay about yourself.

In situations where someone voices actual disagreement with you, internally it feels to you that she has literally *taken your power*. To prevent this from happening, you either become more stubborn and push harder on the other person, or refuse to risk taking any action in terms of what you were trying to create. For instance, you may refuse to take action in the external world that you know would make you feel good about yourself and help you to establish your own sense of personal self-worth, out of fear that someone will disagree with you.

However, if you allow this to happen, then instead of using the power of your natural ability to create success in the world for yourself and others, you turn it inward against yourself where it implodes, becoming a stubborn impediment. You may even insist on holding on to your position as a defense against the possible intrusion of others on your sense of personal power and the way you view yourself—and this pushes people away. Until you gain awareness of this issue, you can become stuck in a vicious cycle that blocks the flow of your vital energy and pervade all areas of your life.

Self-Actualization

You have a natural gift for expressing yourself and building things in the external world in ways that truly communicate those things that you value, from the mundane to the spiritual. While sharing this gift to benefit others is the healthy way to experience ongoing vitality in your life, it can be difficult to get past the fear of how other people will see you, and the potential of their disapproval. But the highest path is to be courageous enough to overcome this obstacle, fully expressing your true nature by building those things in your life that embody your true values.

Then your greatest challenge becomes using the feedback you receive from your environment—both positive and negative—to shift and fine-tune the ways in which you express your gifts. It is only through this process that your ability to consistently create positive results can be refined and perfected.

This process can be painful, but only to the extent that you take any negative feedback personally. Instead, feedback from your environment is actually a gift that allows you to see the exact changes that are needed in order for you to create the results and rapport with others you long for. By being willing to listen and shift in your delivery, you experience a new sense of personal independence. Taking charge in presenting yourself in a way others can more easily go along with leads to a greater trust in your ability to take action—as well as the confidence and joy that come from freely expressing your authentic self.

By actively using your natural gifts—openly sharing what you consider valuable with others without expecting them to adopt your values—you will establish your sense of self-worth in a concrete way, as well as creating stability in the material world. Then you will truly begin to experience yourself as a powerful cause in your own life, instead of suppressing yourself due to fearing others' perceptions.

Relationships

In the beginning of an intimate relationship, it's easy for you to become so involved with your own needs that you bond and commit too soon. When you allow this to happen, you may overlook the other person's values and merge with him without any boundaries. Then, once involved on a close level, you can become quite determined to change his values to match your own, wanting him to go along with what makes *you* feel comfortable. This can lead to a power struggle on both sides, with your partner feeling invaded and you becoming overly invested in the outcome.

To avoid this scenario, when choosing a suitable mate, partner, or friend, your challenge is to stay inside your own comfort zone. It's important that you step back during times you aren't together and see what the other person's values actually are, and what gives *him* a sense of comfort. If you bond with him, will both of you feel energized by working toward common goals? Are his values truly compatible with your own? As you become aware of what is important to him, you can make a decision from a position that will allow you to create a much healthier relationship.

Because of your natural understanding of psychology—the needs and motives of the other person—you have a special ability to nurture your partner in terms of power and support. And when you see where he is behaving in a self-destructive way, you have a gift for giving him practical advice that can help him achieve his goals. In this way, you naturally increase the other person's sense of personal empowerment.

However, because you have the notion that if you support him enough he will link with you as one, your sense of independent strength can become diluted and confused. Your motive of wanting to empower the other person is correct, but this can only happen in a constructive way if you recognize early in the relationship that his values are separate from yours, and may be quite different. This awareness gives you the opportunity to relate without the negative results of bonding with him in an unconsciousness way.

When you accept another person's value system as true for him, you can form a relationship without the hindrance of an unhealthy enmeshment. Then you are able to listen to his ideas, share your ideas, and see how you can contribute to each other in ways that truly meet each other's needs. When this happens, the high energy of mutual empowerment and heartfelt spontaneous support emerges in the relationship.

Past-Life Gifts

You have had many past lifetimes where your survival depended on your own physical strength. Many of these incarnations were spent as a farmer or builder, or in other roles in which you relied on your own physical prowess and practical thinking to take care of yourself and your loved ones. These experiences have resulted in an innate confidence in being able to handle material circumstances wisely and sensibly.

During these lifetimes you mastered the art of accumulation and learned how to establish security in the material world. Thus in this life you reach your goals in a practical way, one step at a time. Because of this, you radiate solid strength, dependability, and sturdiness.

Handling money and resources effectively is another one of your gifts.

You are neither greedy nor extravagant, but remain focused on your own—and others'—needs for physical comfort, rather than engaging in far-flung speculation.

You have learned the value of material stability, realistic expectations, persistence, and loyalty to those you consider family. Your appreciation of the physical realm, enjoyment of the five senses, and natural forthright dependability can teach all of us the value of slowing down and being grateful for the abundance and comforts to be found in our own life.

Confidence in Social Situations

Step into the role of "the dependable one."
Hold the intention of "What do you need to feel comfortable?"

GEMINI RISING

Your Window to the World

You interact with the external world from an innate excitement about sharing ideas and keeping the energy in motion. This stems from your belief that through gaining a lot of information about people and events you will feel accepted and understood, and can avoid boredom. You express your inner being through the medium of your ideas, within the context of what you are currently learning.

When looking outside yourself, you see other people and situations in terms of whether or not they are mentally stimulating and can provide new avenues for social interaction. You *interpret* the behavior of others toward you in terms of how well they accept your thoughts and ideas. Are they willing to go along with you and to listen and grow, as you are?

Your personality and demeanor reflect those traits that to you demonstrate logic, open-mindedness and intelligence. Your attitude and behavior demonstrate that you are very understanding of how others think, and you expect acceptance of your ideas in return.

Your Achilles' Heel

Your innate approach to life is to enjoy your natural enthusiasm for social interaction and sharing what you have learned with others. This can result in your seeing those who *don't* react the same way to the intelligent sharing of ideas as being self-righteous and moralistic. Because you sometimes think *others* are that way, it's easy for you to assume that they could possibly view *you* that way as well—and it is your fear of this potential disapproval that creates your Achilles' heel.

If you don't stay in touch with the natural intellectual excitement of your own identity and instead give in to your fears of how other people might see you, you may end up constantly blocking the expression of your own point of view. This would suppress any meaningful communication *and* your innate way of being in the world. Then you can lose confidence in your ability to share your multidimensional personality with others.

For instance, you may stop discussing your ideas and the new pieces of information that come your way out of fear that others will think you're too philosophical or trying to be a know-it-all. However, if you allow this to happen, then instead of using the power of your inborn gift for sharing ideas with others, you turn it inward against yourself where it becomes an impediment. When all that mental energy is not expressed, it implodes and blocks the flow of your own vital energy.

Self-Actualization

You have an instinctive ability for knowing how to teach *and* how to learn, and by sharing your thought processes and exchanging your information with other people, you inspire mutual excitement. You automatically demonstrate your innate gift for teaching in a way that reaches each individual personally. Your unique approach not only allows them to absorb the subject at hand but enables them to learn your ability to ask questions that put others in touch with their *own* perspective on whatever is being discussed.

While sharing your talents with others is the only healthy way for you to experience ongoing vitality in your life, it can be difficult to get past your fear of how other people will see you and the potential of their not accepting you. But the highest path is to be courageous enough to overcome this obstacle and fully express your true nature, using your gift for instinctively understanding the mental processes of others for the benefit of all concerned.

Then your greatest challenge becomes using the feedback you receive from your environment—both positive *and* negative—to shift and fine-tune the ways in which you express your gifts. It is only through this process that your ability to consistently create positive results can be refined and perfected, and your presentation consistently accepted by others.

This process can be painful, but only to the extent that you take any negative feedback personally. Instead, it is actually a gift that allows you to see the *exact* changes that are needed in order for you to create the happy outcomes and mental rapport with others that you long for. Then you will experience a renewed confidence in your ability to communicate, as well as the joy and freedom that comes from authentically expressing your inner self.

When you actively express your natural gifts by extending yourself in ways that stimulate the excitement of exchanging information and increasing social interaction, you will truly begin to experience yourself as a powerful cause in your own life instead of living in fear of others' perceptions.

Relationships

In the beginning of an intimate relationship, your natural optimism takes over and you tend to want to bond and go on an adventure with the other person immediately. It's easy for you to only see his good points and the possibility the spiritual path will transform him into the vision you see.

However, once involved on a close level, you can reverse yourself and use your intelligence to battle with him—trying to get him to become the person you assumed he was. This results in your partner feeling the need to distance himself from you, and he may decide to go his own way.

To avoid this scenario, your challenge in choosing a suitable mate, partner, or friend is to see the reality of the situation. While your motive of wanting to inspire the other person to live a more expansive life is correct, early in the relationship it is important for you to step back and be honest with yourself in terms of what you know about the other person on a factual level. Is he intelligent? How does he think? Is he open to risk and adventure? What is *his* thinking about taking chances in life, acting on his inspiration, and moving from a comfortable situation to take a leap of faith and have an expansive adventure? As you become more aware of who he *really* is, you can better decide if he is the right partner for you.

You have an incredible ability to teach and to supply information that can help another see a more positive view of life. You are uniquely able to inspire others to see how higher law operates in their life. You are also aware when they are lacking faith, and can uplift their spirits so they believe in a brighter tomorrow.

Seeing the other person's level of faith in the universe and positive outcomes as separate from you own—and possibly quite different—gives you the opportunity to relate to him without trying to get him to constantly agree with you, or be motivated by the same things that inspire you.

When you accept that what your partner says is true for him, you can realistically see what inspires him in terms of his own life and relate to him without enmeshment. Then you can tune in to the solutions he is trying to find for himself, and use your gift of logic to help him succeed. In this way, supporting each other's hopes and dreams can become the adventure you share.

Past-Life Gifts

You have had many past lifetimes of surviving by virtue of your wits and intelligence, and your ability to use words to sell others on your ideas. Many of these incarnations were spent as a teacher, translator, storyteller, or messenger, and you are gifted in your ability to get information circulating in society.

During past lives you mastered the art of communication, and you instinctively listen to the words the other person is saying. This allows you to understand how he thinks and creates an easy mental rapport. In fact, listening to the viewpoints of others and taking them into account is one of your strongest abilities, and gives you excellent skills in sales and marketing, since you can translate a concept into words that will appeal to the other person.

You are gifted at creating ease in social situations simply by being genuinely interested and curious about what others have to say. Your motive—just to enhance your understanding of the other person—stems from your innate curiosity, and you are also happy to supply any information that may be helpful to their situation. Your ability to deeply listen without judgment, and to keep the conversation going, keeps the mood light and happy. You can help others learn the value of deeply listening to another in order to create a sense of sharing and a happy exchange of ideas.

Confidence in Social Situations

Step into the role of "the communicator."
Hold the intention of "What information will be helpful to you?"

CANCER RISING

Your Window to the World

You interact with the external world from a position of sensitivity to personal feelings, which you experience on a gut level, and are most strongly motivated by a desire to protect those you care about. You express your inner being through using your gifts to emotionally nurture other people on a personal level.

When looking outside yourself, you see the people and situations around you in terms of whether or not they provide a secure base that will be sensitive to your needs. And you interpret the behavior of others toward you in terms of how well they demonstrate that they are aware of—and care about—your feelings.

Your personality and demeanor reflect those traits that you feel demonstrate your sensitivity to others' feelings. And your attitude and behavior show that you are attentive, caring, and protective toward others, and you expect sensitive attention shown to you in return.

Your Achilles' Heel

Your innate approach to life is one of emotional sensitivity and using your gifts to nourish other people on a feeling level. This can result in your seeing those who do not share this connection to the emotional realm as cold and/or controlling. Because you sometimes think that *others* are that way, it's easy for you to assume that they could possibly view *you* that way as well—and it is your fear of this potential disapproval that creates your Achilles' heel.

If you don't stay in touch with the strength of your own identity and instead give in to this fear of how others might see you, you may end up suppressing the emotional richness and expression of your innate way of being in the world. Then you can lose confidence in your ability to care for and emotionally nurture others.

For instance, you may stop extending yourself in terms of emotionally supporting other people out of fear that your intentions will be misunderstood; that you might be rejected or seen as being manipulative. However, this is effectively turning your back on yourself. If you allow this to happen, then instead of using the power of your innate emotional sensitivity correctly through nurturing others, you turn it inward and end up using your potent personal feelings against yourself. Then your own sensitivities and fears of rejection can keep you isolated.

Self-Actualization

You have a gift for sensing what other people need in order to feel safe, and responding in a way that brings them a sense of being protected and cared for. While sharing this gift is the healthy way for you to experience ongoing vitality in your life, it can be difficult to get past your fears of how other people will see you and the potential of their disapproval. But the highest path is to be courageous enough to overcome this obstacle and fully express your true nature by caring for others in a sensitive, personal way.

Then your greatest challenge becomes using the feedback you receive from your environment—both positive *and* negative—to shift and fine-tune the ways in which you express your gifts. It is only through this process that your ability to consistently create positive results can be refined and perfected.

This process can be painful, but only to the extent that you take any negative feedback personally. Feedback from the environment is actually a gift that allows you to see the *exact* changes that are needed in order for you to express yourself in a way that creates the happy outcomes and rapport with others that you long for. Then you will experience a new sense of trust in your ability to take action, as well as the confidence and joy that come from freely expressing your authentic self.

When you actively use your unique talents for giving nurturing emotional support to others, you will truly begin to experience yourself as a powerful cause in your own life instead of living in fear of other people's perceptions.

Relationships

You have an innate ability to understand other people's goals, and an intuitive awareness of the next challenge on their personal path. As a result, you instinctively feel drawn to join them in creating a successful outcome.

However, in the beginning of an intimate relationship this makes it easy for you to become enmeshed in the idea of joint goals. You may not really notice if the other person's ideas for what she wants for her own life are different from your own. Then once you become deeply involved, you can begin to unconsciously project *your* agenda for achieving goals onto your partner—and goal enmeshment is what creates the greatest struggle for you in close relationships.

When this occurs, you may begin to fight with your partner—in the name of "support"—to get her to achieve her goals *your* way. However, this is not true support. In fact, when she resists you, you may even shift your position and want *her* to help *you* reach *your* goals, which you then refer to as "our joint goals." And if she continues in her own direction, you may become moody or emotional. This process results in you feeling powerless to help your partner and sorry for yourself.

In order to prevent this scenario, your challenge in choosing a suitable mate, partner, or friend is to maintain your own identity and stay inside the boundaries of what makes *you* feel secure in your own right. Otherwise, your sense of security becomes dependent on your partner, which creates the *opposite* of security.

It is especially important for you to take time early in the relationship to step back and focus on who the other person really is. Notice whether she has the same values and goals—or the same style for reaching her goals—as you. What makes her feel like she is in control of her life? Apart from the mountains *you* want to climb, what are her goals for her *own* life?

One of your unique talents is that you are especially good at helping others to reach goals by supporting their priorities and encouraging them to adopt a take-charge attitude. Also, when you see they are behaving in a way that is counterproductive to creating success, you have the ability to add just the support they need to stay on track.

However, it is only by acknowledging and respecting your partner as a competent, separate person—*before* you team up with her—that you will be able to relate with her in a respectful way that allows your support to be truly helpful, and gives her the freedom to voice her own needs. This also makes it possible for you to take responsibility for your own needs for personal security without trying to force your partner to manifest your goals with you.

It is by establishing and maintaining this position of respect and separateness that you open the way for mutual caring to flow in the relationship. This in turn opens the possibility of creating a family that can truly provide the safe and secure life that you seek.

Past-Life Gifts

You have had many past lives where your survival hinged on the interdependence of a close family group. As a result, you developed a keen awareness of the personal feelings of others, coupled with emotional sensitivity and a caring empathy when relating to other people.

With those in your inner circle, you are sympathetic, supportive, caring, and fiercely protective. On a deep level you still feel that survival of the family ensures your own safety, and you easily become attached to those who are close.

During past incarnations you mastered the art of blending empathy with emotional honesty—sharing how you feel in a way that the other person does not hear as rejection. You emit an energy of perceptive caring and awareness, and your natural sensitivity in communicating your needs in a way that does not put the other person in an uncomfortable position—or injure her feelings—is a gift we can all learn from.

Confidence in Social Situations

Step into the role of "the empathic one."
Hold the intention of "How can I help you feel better?"

LEO RISING

Your Window to the World

You interact with the external world from the position of wanting to play, have fun, and spread happiness and joy to all. You express your inner being through the filter of your natural sense of drama and enthusiasm. You believe that in order to live a passionate and creative life, the people and events around you need to be vital.

When looking outside yourself, you see people and situations in terms of whether or not they are enlivening, willing to play, and offer the opportunity for having a good time. And you interpret the behavior of others toward you in terms of whether they are giving you vital energy and are willing to cheer you up as well.

You express your personality and demeanor in ways that you feel demonstrate strength, enthusiasm, and a willingness to create a good mood for those around you. Your attitude and behavior show that you are willing to defer to others and are very approving of them—and you expect approval shown to you in return.

Your Achilles' Heel

Your innate approach to life is to enjoy your natural enthusiasm for having fun and your finely tuned sense of drama. This can result in your seeing those who don't share the same outlook as being cold and detached by comparison to your more exuberant nature. Because you sometimes think *others* are that way, it's easy for you to assume that they could possibly view *you* that way— and it is your huge fear of this potential disapproval that creates your Achilles' heel.

If you don't stay in touch with the natural exuberance of your own identity and instead give in to this fear of how others might see you, you can end up constantly suppressing the innate joy and drama of your own way of being in the world. Then you lose confidence in your ability to spontaneously express yourself as a sensitive leader.

For instance, you may refuse to support others with your unique leadership abilities out of fear that they will not accept you as a peer if you distinguish yourself. However, if you allow this to happen, then instead of using the power of you inborn sense of dignity correctly through supporting others, you turn it inward against yourself where it becomes a stubborn impediment. When all that power is not expressed, it implodes and blocks the flow of your own vital energy.

Self-Actualization

You have a unique talent for being a creative and sensitive leader, sharing your spontaneity and enthusiasm in ways that uplift—and encourage the self-expression of—everyone around you.

While allowing the full expression of these gifts is the healthy way for you to experience ongoing vitality in your life, it can be difficult to get past your intense fear of how other people will see you and the potential of their disapproval. But the highest path is to be courageous enough to overcome this obstacle and fully express your true nature, assuming leadership for the benefit of all concerned.

Then your greatest challenge becomes using the feedback you receive from your environment—both positive and negative—to shift and fine-tune the ways in which you express your gifts. It is only through this process that your ability to consistently create positive results can be refined and perfected, and your presentation consistently accepted by others.

This process can be painful, but only to the extent that you take any negative feedback personally. Instead, the feedback of others is actually a gift that allows you to see the *exact* modifications that are needed in your personality in order for you to create the happy outcomes and rapport with others that you long for. Then you will experience a new sense of personal independence and trust in your ability to take action, as well as the confidence and joy that come from freely expressing your authentic self.

When you actively use your natural gifts by extending yourself in ways that uplift and inspire others, you will truly begin to experience yourself as a powerful cause in your own life, instead of living in fear of others' perceptions.

Relationships

In the beginning of an intimate relationship, it's easy for you to bond too quickly and become enmeshed in the other person's goals and way of being in the world. At this point, your feeling of friendship and genuine curiosity about the other person make you open to hearing about his dreams and aspirations, and creates a sense of natural equality between you.

This can lead you to assume that if you pour your creative power into the relationship and helping your partner's dreams to come true, the other person will value your special qualities and automatically provide the type of acknowledgment you want from him. Once involved on a close level, you can reverse yourself and become demanding if your partner doesn't give you the recognition and appreciation you need to feel equally loved and supported.

Naturally this creates resistance on his part and mutual distancing in the relationship.

In choosing a suitable mate, partner, or friend, your challenge is to maintain an awareness of your own individuality and your needs for personal creative expression. While your motive of wanting to relate with the other person in a spirit of equality, friendship, and helpfulness is correct, early in the relationship it is important for you to take the time between meetings to step back and see what *his* goals are for his *own* life.

Pay special attention to how his dreams and the activities that bring him pleasure are different from your own. As you become more aware of *his* path, you can realistically decide if you have enough in common that linking with him as a life partner will truly make you happy in the long run. If not, you can continue to support and encourage him as a friend. If his values *do* resonate with your own and you reach a *mutual* decision that you will participate in building his dream, then you can add your own creative power to his and experience the joy of giving your support to something you truly believe in.

One of your gifts is a profound ability to invent confident, positive solutions. So when you see the other person getting distracted, you can offer creative ideas that can get him back on track toward his goals again! Another special talent is in helping others gain an objective awareness of the other people involved in their life situations. This aids them in navigating their path in ways that also accommodate the needs and wishes of the other people involved.

Being aware of your partner's path as separate—and possibly quite different—from your own eliminates the pressure of your needing him to acknowledge you in specific ways in order for you to feel equal and appreciated. It also makes it possible for you to relate with him without becoming enmeshed. Maintaining your separate identity allows you to support and encourage the other person in pursuing the activities that make him happy without your needing to become directly involved in all of them. And it frees you from the expectation that he will join you in everything that is important to you.

In this way, you can both expand your creative passion into projects that bring you true pleasure because the relationship supports your freedom to do so. You have a best friend who supports you in bringing forth and expressing those talents that make you happy. And in return, your enthusiasm and confidence support your partner in realizing his goals.

Past-Life Gifts

You have had many past lifetimes where your survival depended on your ability to entertain others. Many of these incarnations were spent as a performer, musician, or salesperson. As a result you developed a lot of bravado and learned how be the life of the party. You can easily add happiness and enthusiasm to any situation.

You enter a room with strength and stature, and are readily noticed regardless of your physical size. Your naturally gregarious nature cheers others, and your easy openness inspires them to relax, thus putting everyone at ease.

During your past-life experiences you mastered the art of knowing how to confidently become the center of attention—on stages both large and small—and use that position in ways that benefit and uplifts your audience. We can all learn from you how to properly use the limelight—to take center stage in a way that also allows others to shine.

Confidence in Social Situations

Step into the role of "the entertainer."
Hold the intention of "How can I cheer you up?"

VIRGO RISING

Your Window to the World

You interact with the external world in terms of how you can be helpful in the situations around you. You express your inner being through your heightened awareness of others and consideration for them—truly desiring to be of service to them and instinctively avoiding behaviors that might seem abrasive or inconvenience them in any way.

When looking outside yourself, you see other people and situations in terms of whether or not they offer the opportunity for being supportive and helpful, and for using your analytical abilities to assist them in reaching their goals. You love projects! You *interpret* the behavior of others toward you in terms of whether or not they are reciprocally considerate of your foibles and idiosyncrasies.

You express your personality and demeanor in ways that you feel demonstrate your willingness to help others. Your attitude and behavior show that you are aware of others and want to help them, and you expect others to be aware of and helpful towards you as well.

Your Achilles' Heel

Your innate approach to life is to enthusiastically engage your compassionate nature and your unique analytical talents to be of service to other people.

This can result in your seeing those who don't automatically reach out to help others as taking a wrong approach to life. Because you sometimes see *others* this way, it is easy for you to assume that they could possibly view *you* this way as well. This creates your greatest internal fear—that other people will discover your lack of perfection—and this worrisome fear becomes your Achilles' heel.

If you don't stay in touch with the helpful nature of your own identity and instead give in to this fear of how others might see you, you can end up suppressing your urge to use your gifts to be of service—and your own natural way of being in the world. Then you lose confidence in the purity of your own motives *and* the power to act on your ability to assist others on a practical level.

For instance, you may suppress your natural analytical talents in order to avoid being wrong or making a mistake that someone else might correct. However, not contributing your gifts can lead to your being seen by others as dreamy, Pollyannaish, and idealistic. Then you end up feeling vulnerable and helpless, possibly even going along with situations that you instinctively know are out of balance—which is not healthy for you since it invites being victimized by others.

If you allow this to happen, then instead of acting on your analytical abilities purely, to support others, you turn them inward against yourself where it becomes a self-critical impediment. When all those analytical talents are not expressed, they implode and block the flow of your own vital energy. The result is your becoming so preoccupied with needing to appear perfect that you never express your real self at all.

Self-Actualization

You have innate scientific abilities that can restore the natural order to the chaos you find in life's situations, and an intuitive understanding of the authentic, deeper meaning of service. Your special gift is being of true service to other people on a practical level.

While sharing your gifts with others is the only healthy way for you to experience ongoing vitality in your life, it can be difficult to get past your intense fear of how others will see you, and the potential of critical disapproval. But the highest path is to be courageous enough to overcome this obstacle and fully express your true nature by focusing on helping others become stronger and more confident.

Then your greatest challenge becomes using the feedback—both positive *and* negative—to shift and fine-tune the ways in which you express your gifts. It is only through this process that your ability to consistently create positive results can be refined and perfected, and your presentation consistently accepted by others.

This process can be painful, but only to the extent that you take any negative feedback personally. Instead, the reflection of others is actually a gift that allows you to see the *exact* changes in your personality that are needed in order for you to effectively create the happy outcomes and rapport with others that you long for. Then you will experience a new sense of independence, self-confidence, renewed faith in your gifts, and trust in your ability to take action.

When you actively express your natural inclinations by extending yourself to others in ways that help them see how to systematically reach their goals in a realistic and practical way, you will truly begin to experience yourself as a powerful cause in your own life, instead of living in fear of others' perceptions.

Relationships

In the beginning of an intimate relationship, it's easy for you to overlook the other person's flaws and only be aware of the qualities in her that you like. However, once involved on a close level you can reverse yourself and tend to focus more on her flaws. This can lead to criticism, disappointment, and distancing in your closest relationships.

In choosing a suitable mate, partner, or friend, your challenge is to be discriminating. While your motive to help her see herself in a positive light by focusing on her best qualities is correct, early in the relationship it is important to step back and intentionally notice *all* aspects of the other person.

A good exercise is to draw a line down the middle of a piece of paper, listing all the qualities that you enjoy about the person on the left side, and the behaviors that seem abrasive or hurtful on the right. Your innate power of analysis will give you a more realistic picture of the person you are becoming involved with, and can help you to avoid the disappointment that could otherwise arise later on. You may realize that she is not a good relationship choice for you or, if you do decide to bond with her, you can do so from a healthier, more realistic position.

One of your relationship gifs is an innate sense of compassion for others, so you are instinctively drawn to help your partner become stronger and more confident in her own life. Your specialty is in connecting her with a sense of faith—that she *can* make her dreams come true. You are also aware of how she sabotages herself from fully realizing her potential. Because of your strong ability to bring order out of chaos, when you see where the other person is tripping herself up you are able to offer the right technique, plan, or point of view that can help her heal any dysfunctional traits so she can stay on track and reach her goals.

Maintaining an objective outlook by remembering that the other person's dreams for her own life are separate from—and often quite different from—your own will allow you to stay involved in the relationship with an open heart. Only in this way can you accurately see her private dreams. Then you can use your analytical abilities to create a plan and contribute your idea of how she can best reach her goals in a realistic and efficient manner.

With a practical plan in place, your partner will be thankful for your help and better able to relax. This, in turn, will allow her to become more open-hearted with you. And by remaining objective, you can more easily maintain your own individual identity in the relationship.

Past-Life Gifts

You have had many past lifetimes when your survival depended on your heightened sensitivity to ways in which you could be helpful to others. Many of these incarnations were spent in the capacity of a healer. These experiences as a doctor, herbalist, and practitioner of other healing modalities have resulted in your being naturally attuned to the distress of others.

Your personality is unassuming, reserved, devotional, and open to seeing any way you can be of service to those you are involved with. Instinctively, your first response is a desire to help. You are also practical, and when you hear about a problem someone is having, you automatically think of a realistic plan to get that person from point A to point B or, if appropriate, you jump in to lend a helping hand.

Because of your analytical problem-solving response to their problems and the purity of your intent, you can often see what will truly be of practical assistance to the other person. You have gained a true understanding of what service is all about at the highest level, without thought of personal reward, and have the ability to assist others in mastering this art. You expect nothing in return for helping others, but find joy in figuring out how to do your job in supporting the well-being of another.

Confidence in Social Situations

Step into the role of "the helper."
Hold the intention of "How can I help you?"

LIBRA RISING

Your Window to the World

You interact with the external world from a position of feeling happiest when sharing experiences with others. Your heightened awareness of beauty causes you to be repelled by actions or circumstances that are rough, abrasive, or rude. You express your inner being through the filter this awareness and your innate sense of fairness. Your desire is to always express yourself with tact and kindness to ensure a pleasant interaction.

You tend to believe that people and situations need to be handled with fairness and diplomacy in order to create a life of balance and harmony. As a result, when looking outside yourself you see the people and situations around you in terms of whether or not they offer the potential of creating an equitable partnership or positive team effort, and if their nature is refined. You *interpret* the behavior of others toward you in terms of whether they are playing fair with you, according to *your* values of equality and balance.

You express your personality and demeanor in ways that you feel demonstrate an awareness of social appropriateness and your desire to get along well with others. And your attitude and behavior show that you are willing to compromise in order to create happiness and harmony—and you expect an attitude of nonabrasive diplomacy in return.

Your Achilles' Heel

Your natural approach to life is to use your gifts of objectivity, diplomacy, and sensitivity to create or restore harmony in the situations around you. This can result in your seeing those who don't share the same outlook as abrasive or inconsiderate. Because you sometimes think *others* are that way, it's easy for you to assume that they could possible view *you* that way. And it is your fear of this potential disapproval that creates your Achilles' heel.

If you don't stay in touch with the positive energy of your own identity and instead give in to this fear of how others might see you, it can lead to suppressing your own point of view, your natural flow of self-expression, and your innate way of being in the world. Then you tend to lose confidence in your ability to get along with others through the honest expression of your true nature.

For instance, you may refuse to share the solutions that you see could lead to fairness in the situations of disharmony that arise around you out of fear that those involved might see you as being too aggressive or not like you. However, if you allow this to happen, then instead of using the power of your inborn sense of objectivity and fairness to create a better relationship with others, you turn it inward against yourself. When all that power is not expressed, it implodes and blocks the flow of your own vital energy. Then you may use your talents for diplomacy to make yourself appear to others as "Mr. or Ms. Nice," and end up never expressing your real self at all.

Self-Actualization

You have the natural gifts of diplomacy, objectivity and sensitivity to the feelings of others. If you use these gifts correctly (not to manipulate others into having a good opinion of you), you have the ability to stimulate others' latent talents and help them become more forthright in their willingness to express themselves.

While acknowledging the inharmonies that you see exist is the healthy way for you to experience ongoing vitality in your life, it can be difficult to get past the fear of how other people will see you, and the potential of their rebuffing you. But the highest path is to be courageous enough to overcome this obstacle and fully express your true insights, objectively helping to create lasting harmony in social situations based on acknowledging the other person's position as well as your own. Then your greatest challenge becomes using the feedback you receive from your environment—both positive and negative—to shift and fine-tune the ways in which you express your personality. It is only through this process that your ability to consistently create positive results can be refined and perfected.

This process can be painful, but only to the extent that you take any negative feedback personally. Feedback from the environment is actually a gift that allows you to see the *exact* changes in your presentation that are needed in order for you to create the happy outcomes and rapport with others that you long for. Then you will experience a new sense of independence and trust in your ability to take action, as well as the confidence and joy that come from freely expressing your authentic self.

You benefit others by using your natural gifts to acknowledge the disharmony that you can sense in a situation, and help to balance the energies through openly sharing your objective point of view with those involved—when you take action and express your talents as a peacemaker. In this way, you will truly begin to experience yourself as a powerful cause in your own life, instead of living in fear of others' perceptions.

Relationships

In the beginning of an intimate relationship, you may become so enamored with the other person's identity that you too easily start seeing yourself as part of her world. Your innate instinct for partnering tempts you to immediately bond with her in order to become a team. Adapting to her comes naturally for you—accepting her idiosyncrasies and seeing how you think the two of you can work things out together.

However, you can get hurt when you bond with someone without an objective awareness of the kind of partnership the other person is looking for with you. In fact, once involved on a close level, you may begin to judge her in terms of her degree of fairness with you. This can lead to resentment and distancing in your closest relationships.

In order to prevent this scenario, your challenge in choosing a suitable mate, partner, or friend is to remain aware of your own identity and sense of personal balance. While your supportive nature and your ability to be a team player are a plus in any relationship, it is important that during the bonding process you periodically take time to step back and see the situation clearly. Is your own inner equilibrium still intact? Do you feel that things are working out in a way that is fair to you? Is the other person giving back to you in a reciprocal way that supports your sense of self?

You are attracted to independent people who have a life of their own. Remaining aware of their separate identity—and that they may have needs and values that are different from yours—frees you from expecting them to play by the same rules you do. You and your partner may have different ideas about what constitutes fairness in a relationship. The key is for you to stay in touch with your own inner harmony, and if you need more support from her, use your talent for diplomacy and tact to reveal that to your partner. How she responds, combined with your innate sense of harmony and fairness, will let you know how close you can be to this person and still maintain your own integrity.

You have a natural understanding of the personal identity of the other person and see her uniqueness. You are instinctively drawn to support her courage and her desire to make new beginnings in her life. You are also aware of when her lack of confidence, independence, or courage may be sabotaging her success. With your ability to be tactful and diplomatic, you can say the right words to embolden the other person to become more courageous in terms of her self-expression. In this way, you can stimulate her latent talents and abilities, giving her the motivation to take risks, move forward, and succeed.

Staying in touch with your own inner balance is the key to relationship success for you. If you feel out of sorts, ask your partner directly what *she* needs and wants in the situation. Then you can view your partner more objectively and see how to join in a team effort and support her without losing sight of your own needs for support. This allows you both to have the independence you need to thrive and keep things exciting.

Past-Life Gifts

You have had many past lifetimes where your survival depended on your accurate awareness of the other person and developing the art of diplomacy and tact. Most of these past incarnations were spent in partnerships, marriages, diplomatic positions, and other scenarios that involved making the team strong in order to ensure your individual survival.

You are instinctively aware of the importance of one-to-one relationships, and are willing to make those personal compromises necessary for a successful union. You enter a room full of people with a bit of initial reticence, due to a strong desire to be liked and feeling vulnerable to how others may react to you. Your awareness of others is actually your key to being liked; by being interested and showing approval of the other person, she is most likely to respond with approval in kind.

During your past lives you mastered the art of personifying beauty and grace. Generally, you have a pleasing physical appearance and are attractive to others. Your talents also include diplomacy, fairness, and the ability to compromise, and you have an innate sense of what is just and balanced in your relationships. You have learned the value and strength of team efforts and can be an example to all of us of how to be a fair and effective partner.

Confidence in Social Situations

Step into the role of "the partner."

Hold the intention of "How can I help you feel a greater sense of internal balance?"

SCORPIO RISING

Your Window to the World

You interact with the external world according to your intuitive perceptions of how to gain and blend power, and your belief that you need to understand the motivations of others in order to maintain your own power. You

express your inner being through instinctively recognizing—and acting on—
the sometimes hidden potential for change and transformation that you have
the ability to find in almost any circumstances. And this provides you with the
excitement of living on the edge that you thrive on.

When looking outside yourself, you view the people and situations
around you in terms of whether or not they make you feel powerful and can
offer an equal—or at least a similar—depth of perception. You *interpret* the
behavior of others toward you in terms of whether they properly acknowledge
your inherent depth and potency.

You express your attitude and personality in ways that you feel demonstrate your degree of self-containment and personal power. When you are attracted to a potential partner, it is most often someone who can increase your
power through bonding—usually sexual or financial—and your demeanor and
behavior show that you have a lot to offer as a worthy partner.

Your Achilles' Heel

Your innate approach to life is to share, and act on, your deep perceptions
that hold transformative power for yourself and others. This can result in your
seeing those who don't pursue life in this manner as opinionated or materialistic. Because you sometimes think *others* are that way, it's easy for you to assume
that they could possibly view *you* that way—and it is your fear of this potential
misperception that creates your Achilles' heel.

If you don't stay in touch with the natural perceptive power of your own
identity and instead give in to this fear of how other people might see you,
you can end up suppressing your innate potency and focus on attempting to
straighten out others' perceptions of you. This slows down your presentation,
and you may become so repetitive that others experience you as heavy and
plodding. The result is that you can lose confidence in your ability to affect
people on a deep level while still maintaining your sense of managing the situation.

For instance, you may withhold your ability to reveal your deep perceptions of another that could empower him to change his life—out of fear of
yourself being transformed in the process in some way you had not anticipated
and could not control. However, if you allow this to happen, then instead of
using the power of your perceptive abilities correctly to benefit others, you
turn it inward against yourself in a ruthless, personal way where it becomes a
stubborn impediment. This blocks the flow of your vital energy and can result
in a morbid preoccupation with your feelings of insecurity about not having
absolute control over your environment.

Self-Actualization

You instinctively know what another person values and what makes him feel worthwhile. On a deeper level, you have a unique ability for penetrating into the truth of things that are hidden, and then bringing your perceptions to the consciousness of others in ways that have a powerful, releasing impact on all concerned.

While sharing these gifts to benefit others is the healthy way for you to experience ongoing vitality in your life, it can be difficult to get past intense fears of how others will respond to you, and the potential of their acting against you. But the highest path is to be courageous enough to overcome this obstacle and fully express your deep perceptions that can empower people to change their lives.

Then your greatest challenge becomes using the feedback you receive from your environment—both positive *and* negative—to shift and fine-tune the ways in which you express yourself. It is only through this process of modifying and adapting your presentation that your ability to consistently create positive results can be refined and perfected.

This process can be painful, but only to the extent that you take any negative feedback personally. Feedback from the environment is actually a gift that allows you to see the *exact* changes that are needed in order for you to create the happy outcome and rapport with others that your long for. Then you will experience a new sense of independence and trust in your ability to take action that others will be receptive to, as well as the confidence and joy that come from freely expressing your authentic self.

You can actively use your innate gifts and talents by extending yourself in ways that alter the lives of others through the power of your deep perceptions. Then you truly begin to experience yourself as a powerful cause in your own life, instead of living in fear of others' perceptions.

Relationships

In the beginning of an intimate relationship, it's easy for you to just jump into bonding 100 percent with the other person without giving thought to whether his values really match your own. Then, once involved on a close level, you can decide that you need your partner's values to be more like your own and try to manipulate him to change. When this doesn't work, you tend to withdraw your power from the relationship, become secretive, and intentionally withhold intimacy as a form of punishment. Naturally this creates distance with those who are most important to you.

In order to prevent this scenario, your challenge in choosing a suitable mate, partner, or friend is to maintain your own base of power within yourself. While your motive of wanting to empower the other person is correct, first it is important that you step back and intentionally become aware of his core values. What is important to him? What is he looking for in a relationship?

These are things the two of you need to discuss because comfort, on all levels, is a definite requirement in order for your relationships to be successful. If the other person's values and what gives him a sense of self-worth are *too* different from your own, you will both feel increasingly uncomfortable as time goes on. By engaging in this process early in the relationship, you will know whom to bond with and how close you can be with him and still remain in your comfort zone in the relationship.

As the relationship unfolds, continuing to be clear about where your partner's values are different from your own gives you the distance you need to feel powerful in your own right, without trying to coerce him to passionately believe in the same things you do. By maintaining an awareness of what's truly important to *the other person,* you can support him in furthering his goals without becoming enmeshed and losing track of your own direction. You can see where he is stuck in his thinking and/or behavior, and when he lacks confidence, and can provide the input that allows him to get beyond these obstacles.

In fact, when you remain objective and stay connected to a sense of your own identity, you have a great ability to empower your partner. You can offer ideas that stem from the context of your own belief system and your knowledge of how society works. And with your natural understanding of the psychology of others, you know just what to say to empower your partner to reach his goals.

Past-Life Gifts

You have had many past lifetimes where your survival depended on your ability to link with a powerful partner who valued your support and who, in return, could ensure your financial and material well-being. Many of these incarnations were spent in the arenas of politics, business, or marriage to a powerful person. Experiences with unscrupulous partners have resulted in an instinctive fear of betrayal and your somewhat secretive, self-possessed nature.

Past-life scenarios involving power struggles have honed your intuitive understanding of the psychology of others. This has allowed you to master the art of bonding; you have the ability to accurately see others' resources and choose whether or not to unite with them for a common purpose.

You emanate power, even when you try to downplay your presentation.

Innately, you understand the potency of transformation and have no qualms about entering uncharted territory to gain new power—or mutual rejuvenation—by merging with another. Your deep perception of others, and the resulting depth of forgiveness of which you are capable, can teach us all the value of viewing others with more understanding and mercy.

Confidence in Social Situations

Step into the role of "the change agent."
Hold the intention of "How can I empower you?"

SAGITTARIUS RISING

Your Window to the World

You interact with the external world from an innate sense of freedom and inspiration. You like to travel and expand your horizons—both physically and mentally. You express your inner being through your natural optimism and your desire to inspire others to be the best that they can be.

When looking outside yourself, you see other people and situations in terms of whether or not you are inspired by them, and if there's a possibility that they can lead you to adventure and expansion. You interpret the behavior of others toward you in terms of whether they have faith in you and your intrinsic goodness of heart and your good intentions.

You personality and attitude reflect those traits that you feel demonstrate your faith and your strong sense of ethics. Your demeanor and behavior demonstrate your belief that living an optimistic and trusting life will attract good luck and positive outcomes, and that you expect to have your spiritual strength and intuitive gift of finding creative solutions acknowledged by others.

Your Achilles' Heel

Your innate approach to life is to trust your optimistic outlook and your sense of surety in the promise of tomorrow. This can result in you seeing those who don't share this perspective as fickle and superficial—as compared with your deep abiding faith in positive outcomes. Because you sometimes think *others* are this way, it's easy for you to assume that they could possibly view *you* this way—and it is your fear of this potential disapproval that creates your Achilles' heel.

If you don't stay in touch with the natural optimism of your own identity and instead give in to this fear of how other people might see you, you can end up constantly blocking the expression of your philosophical insights. Then your gallant, positive, and adventuresome spirit becomes restrained, and you can lose confidence in your ability to inspire freedom of thought and action in others.

For instance, fear that others may think you aren't seeing things from a deep enough perspective can lead to blocking yourself from imparting your natural sense of optimism and faith to others. However, if you allow this to happen, then instead of using the power of your faith correctly through supporting others, you turn it inward against yourself, where it implodes and obstructs the flow of your own vital energy.

Blocking this healthy energy can lead to an unhealthy sense of insolent faith in yourself, causing you to assume that others are too inferior to understand your own superior moral perspective and philosophical insights. This can result in your inadvertently cloaking your abilities behind an air of self-righteousness that repels other people and becomes a stubborn impediment to creating positive outcomes in your life.

Self-Actualization

You have a special ability for sensing where other people are in their lives, and for using your talent of perception to help them gain a more philosophical overview of their situations. You inspire them to believe that there is a higher reason behind what is happening and that tomorrow will be better. It empowers them to see their problems with an expanded understanding, and allows them to have more faith in themselves.

While sharing your special gift of extending yourself in a way that gives others a sense of faith in themselves is the healthy way for you to experience ongoing vitality in your life, it can be difficult to get past a fear of how other people will see you, and the potential of their disapproval. But the highest path is to be courageous enough to overcome this obstacle and fully express your true nature, helping others to feel more optimistic, and encouraging them through your confidence in their ability to gain a sense of victory over their daily situations.

Then your greatest challenge becomes using the feedback you receive from your environment—both positive *and* negative—to shift and fine-tune the ways in which you express your gifts. It is only through this process that your ability to consistently create positive results can be refined and perfected, and your presentation consistently accepted by others.

This process can be painful, but only to the extent that you take any negative feedback personally. Feedback from the environment is actually a gift that allows you to see the *exact* changes that are needed in order for you to create the happy outcomes and rapport with others that you long for. Then you will experience greater success, and a new sense of independence and trust in your ability to take action, as well as the confidence and joy that come from freely expressing your authentic self.

When you actively use your abilities to share with others in ways that teach them the deepest meaning of freedom, you will truly begin to experience yourself as a powerful cause in your own life—instead of living in fear of others' perceptions.

Relationships

In the beginning of an intimate relationship, it's easy for you to discount your own inner voice and instead believe what the other person is saying. Without realizing it, you can become enmeshed in her point of view and distracted by her logic, rather than remembering your own deeper truth. Once involved on a close level, you can reverse yourself and may become righteous or make your partner wrong when she is not as optimistic or as ethical as you are.

In choosing a suitable mate, partner, or friend, your challenge is to maintain awareness of your own intuition. While your motive of wanting to foster optimism in the other person is correct, as the relationship is developing it is important for you to step back periodically and reconnect with your own values and inner guidance. Intuitively, what do this person's words and actions tell you about her? How do you feel about being with someone who has that mind-set?

Also, take the time to sense whether or not she is being honest with you and, behind her words, what she is telling you about her ethics. Your Pollyannaish, risk-taking spirit is not the best approach when choosing a partner for a serious relationship. If you listen to your intuition, you will know which relationships to pursue and foster.

You have a natural understanding of the views of other people—and their unique thought processes—and are instinctively drawn to exchanging information with them to create mental rapport. You are also aware of any negative thoughts that are blocking them from reaching their goals. Your specialty is showing them an alternative way of looking at the situation that will help them feel more optimistic.

However, it is essential that you stay in touch with your own positive view of life, regardless of what your partner's thoughts are at the moment. You don't have to change her so she can see the world as you do. There are many ways to view life, and everyone has the right to his or her own unique outlook.

Also, giving her the space to think as she likes frees *you* from endless debates. Intuitively, you will see when the timing is right and you may be able to share a thought that can help her to view the situation in a more positive way. Approaching as a messenger—rather than as a truth bearer—gives you the freedom you need to avoid resistance and keep your relationship open and vital.

Past-Life Gifts

You have had many past lives where your survival depended on your ability to inspire others to believe in positive outcomes. Some of these incarnations were spent as a traveler or a gypsy, or an explorer seeking new horizons, which has resulted in your natural, healthy sense of adventure.

You have also had cause-driven lifetimes where the ideal was more important than life itself. As a consequence, you have a generous nature that is instinctively helpful toward those less fortunate, and your willingness to help others springs solely from the nobleness of your intent.

In yet other lifetimes you have been an instrument of the law. This could have been social law—such as an attorney fighting for the rights of someone weaker—or spiritual law, with time spent in meditation or in other spiritual or religious settings. Thus ethics and morality are extremely important to you. Your intuitive sense is also extremely well developed, and you instinctively rely on a higher power to help guide your way.

During these many lifetimes you have mastered the art of optimism and inspiring faith in others. You are innately spontaneous, and can offer spur-of-the-moment suggestions that work for everyone involved. Your joyful approach to life includes easily taking leaps of faith, and your confidence in positive outcomes can teach us all the value of trusting.

Confidence in Social Situations

Step into the role of "the optimist."
Hold the intention of "How can I help you feel more hopeful?"

CAPRICORN RISING

Your Window to the World

You interact with the external world in terms of the things you want to accomplish and your belief that respect and protocol need to be upheld in order for you to maintain your sense of status and self-respect. You express your inner being through your approach of quiet integrity, common sense, and willingness to take responsibility.

When looking outside yourself, you see the people and situations around you in terms of whether or not you respect their character and behavior, and offer you an opportunity to advance toward your goals. You *interpret* the behavior of others toward you in terms of whether the person is showing appropriate respect for you.

You express your personality and attitude in ways that you feel demonstrate prestige and authority. Your behavior and demeanor show that you are very respectful toward others, and that you expect them to show you respect in return.

Your Achilles' Heel

You approach life from a position of wanting to achieve results in the external world, and you have an innate executive ability to organize and direct other people, and yourself, in ways that allow goals to be achieved. This can result in your seeing those who don't share this primary value as too emotional or weak. Because you sometimes think *others* are this way, it's easy for you to assume that they could possibly view *you* this way as well—and it is your fear of this potential disapproval that creates your Achilles' heel.

If you don't stay in touch with your innate sense of authority and faith in your ability to achieve results, and instead give in to this fear of how others might see you, you may end up constantly suppressing the expression of your own natural executive talents and point of view. This leads to losing confidence in your ability to directly organize situations in ways that can achieve results.

For instance, you may refuse to use your executive abilities out of fear that others might not think you have the proper authority to do so. However, if you hold yourself back, then instead of using the power of your inborn ability to help others gain control of their lives, you can turn it inward where it becomes a frustrating impediment.

When all that power is not expressed, it implodes and blocks the flow of your own vital energy. This can result in your becoming preoccupied with your social image in an unhealthy way that keeps you isolated, and prevents you from establishing a sense of emotional security with other people.

Self-Actualization

You have special inborn abilities to achieve results in the external world through your awareness of the structure that is required in order to attain personal status and prestige. Using these gifts increases your self-confidence socially and opens the way to your experiencing ongoing vitality in your life. And yet it can be difficult to get past your reticence and fear of how other people will see you and the potential of their disapproval. But the highest path is to be courageous enough to overcome this obstacle and fully express your true nature, allowing your willingness to take personal responsibility for creating success to inspire others to do the same.

Then your greatest challenge becomes using the feedback you receive from your environment—both positive *and* negative—to shift and fine-tune the ways in which you express your gifts. It is only through this process that your ability to consistently create positive results with your personality can be refined and perfected.

This process can be painful, but only to the extent that you take any negative feedback personally. Instead, feedback from the environment is actually a gift that allows you to see the *exact* changes that are needed in order for you to express yourself in a way that creates the happy outcomes and rapport with others that you long for. Then you will experience a new level of trust in your ability to take action, as well as the confidence and joy that come from freely expressing your authentic self.

When you actively use your natural gifts for establishing authority and organizing on a level that appeals to the public, then you will experience yourself as a powerful cause in your own life, rather than living in fear of others' perceptions.

Relationships

In the beginning of an intimate relationship, it's easy for you to become enmeshed in your emotional connection to the other person and lose touch with your own innate practicality and sense of caution. You tend to relate empathetically to your new partner's problems, and give in to your urge to mother him.

However, once involved on a close level, you can reverse yourself and become overly focused on his need to take personal responsibility for achieving his full potential—whether he wants to or not! If he doesn't meet your expectations, it can lead you to lose respect for your partner and coldly withdraw from the relationship. Without conscious awareness on your part, this tendency continues to create distance in your closest relationships.

In order to prevent this scenario, your challenge in choosing a suitable mate, partner, or friend is to stay connected to your innate ability to make sensible choices. While your motive of wanting to be caring and supportive of the other person's problems is correct, it is important that as you are getting to know him you periodically step back and intentionally focus on the reality of the situation. Is this a person who strives to take charge of his circumstances and create success? Do you respect his character and values? Does he have a level of personal integrity—and emotional sensitivity to you—that would keep you invested in the relationship over time? Taking the time to honestly consider these questions will allow you to decide if becoming closer with this person is a choice that is *sensible* in terms of your individual values and goals.

You have a natural empathy for the situations of others, and when they look up to you, it brings out your caring, protective nature. You are instinctively drawn to give them the emotional support they need in order to go out in the word and be successful.

Another gift is your ability to restore clearheaded, practical thinking in the midst of strong emotion. You are also conscious of areas in which others are not taking responsibility, and know just how to motivate them to take charge.

By maintaining a conscious connection to your own individual identity, you will be able to remain aware of your partner's separate identity and not become enmeshed. Then when you offer to use your innate talents to support him he will welcome it, because you will be acting in alignment with the goals that are important to *him*.

Taking time to support him in this way, and also allowing time to pursue *your own* individual goals, leads to a true team effort that is based on mutual respect and support. Then, if you have chosen wisely, your partner can provide the emotional closeness you need to stay balanced within yourself—the caring and empathy that keeps life emotionally vital and worthwhile.

Past-Life Gifts

You have had many past lifetimes where your survival depended on your status, prestige, unquestionable integrity, and ability to make sensible decisions. Many of these past incarnations were spent in situations where you were in charge of others as a political, business, or social leader. As a result, you are innately aware of the importance of reputation and taking responsibility for making sensible decisions that lead to successful outcomes.

Lifetimes of having to postpone immediate pleasure in order to reach long-term goals have given you a somewhat austere, reserved, and serious demeanor, and a great sense of self-discipline. You do not begrudge your situation, and look to see how to use current circumstances to better your position from a position of cautious pragmatism.

During these past lives you have mastered the art of taking charge of any situation in which you are involved, and will make the personal sacrifices that are necessary to reach your goals. Your talent for recognizing the opportunities that present themselves, and your willingness to take responsibility for using those opportunities wisely, can teach us all the value of stepping up to the plate and owning our ability to create success in our own lives.

Confidence in Social Situations

Step into the role of "the achiever."
Hold the intention of "How can I help you reach your goals?"

AQUARIUS RISING

Your Window to the World

You interact with the external world from a position of equality and friendship, and you express your inner being through your perspective of non-attachment, interacting with other people with fairness, impartiality, and openness to their ideas. You allow others to be themselves and support them when they reveal their private dreams and ideals, and you expect the same consideration and support from them.

When looking outside yourself, you see the people and situations around you objectively, in terms of whether or not they provide a path that can lead to the fulfillment of your dreams. You *interpret* the behavior of others toward you in terms of whether they approach you with the same spirit of equality, camaraderie, understanding, and supportiveness you show to them.

Your personality and attitude demonstrate a genuine curiosity and an open-minded interest in what is going on around you. Your behavior and demeanor show that you have mastered the art of being a "no leader" leader, able to act as a unifying force without the use of threats or intimidation, and showing your fair-mindedness by asking others for their vote. In return, you expect that others show you the same consideration.

Your Achilles' Heel

Your innate approach to life is to objectively encourage the individualism and creative expression of all your brothers and sisters with your nonthreatening, team-oriented support. You are not interested in separative demonstrations of ego. This can result in your seeing those who have a different worldview as too emotional, bossy, or egotistical. Because you sometimes think *others* are that way, it's easy for you to assume that others could possibly view *you* that way—and it is your fear of this potential disapproval that creates your Achilles' heel.

If you don't stay in touch with your own identity as an impartial, unifying team player and instead give in to this fear of how others might see you, you may end up suppressing your own point of view and creative self-expression. This leads to losing confidence in the power of your ability to support others by sharing your knowledge with detachment.

For instance, you may hold back from supporting others through your capacity to see things with objective impartiality out of fear that you will be misunderstood and seen as a show-off or too dramatic, or somehow be forced into an emotional situation that could cause you to lose your position of nonattachment. However, if you allow this fear to stop you, then instead of using the power of your innate sense of detached objectivity correctly to encourage others, you turn it inward against yourself where it implodes and blocks the flow of your own vital energy. This may cause you to exhibit an eccentric brand of individualism that prevents you from truly expressing yourself and keeps you isolated.

Self-Actualization

You have a unique ability to share your objective point of view with others in a nonattached, supportive way that adds perspective to their lives and promotes their own sense of power and independence.

While sharing your innovative ideas is the healthy way for you to experience ongoing vitality in your life, it can be difficult to get past your fear of how other people will see you and the potential of their disapproval. But the highest path is to be courageous enough to overcome this obstacle and fully express your true nature, sharing your knowledge and often unconventional point of view with others in order to support and empower them.

Then your greatest challenge becomes using the feedback you receive from your environment—both positive *and* negative—to shift and fine-tune the ways in which you express your personality. It is only through this process that your ability to consistently create positive results can be refined and perfected.

This process can be painful, but only to the extent that you take any negative feedback personally. Feedback from the environment is actually a gift that allows you to see the *exact* changes that are needed in order for you to create the happy outcomes and rapport with others that you long for. Then you will experience a new sense of independence and trust in your ability to act, as well as the confidence and joy that come from freely expressing your authentic self in a way that others are most receptive to.

When you actively use your natural gifts to promote the advancement of other people by contributing innovative solutions for their problems, then you will truly begin to experience yourself as a powerful cause in your own life, instead of living in fear of others' perceptions.

Relationships

In the beginning of an intimate relationship, it's easy for you to get lost enjoying the other person's love of life and participating in her activities—especially since one-on-one interactions tend to inspire your sense of playfulness. You instinctively give to others in ways that make them feel important and loved, connecting them with a greater sense of how special they are. However, once involved on a close level, you can decide that the other person is too egotistical to give back to you in a fair way. Then you may detach from the relationship and begin to criticize your partner's dreams or outlook on life, which leads to increasing the distance between you.

To prevent this scenario, your challenge in choosing a suitable mate, partner, or friend is to stay connected to the innate objectivity of your own identity. While your motive of wanting to do fun things with your partner and make her feel special is correct, it is important to step back periodically and intentionally reconnect with your natural ability to see the big picture.

What are the other person's life goals? Does she play fair with others? Is she willing to be your lover *and* your best friend? The power of your detached objectivity will give you the full picture of the person you are becoming involved with. Then if you decide to pursue the relationship, you can do so with realistic expectations and create a more positive result.

One of your gifts is the natural enthusiasm you feel toward other people and your ability to see their creativity, generosity, and zest for life! Because of this, you naturally evoke happiness, vitality, and a positive view of the future in others. Your inherent objectivity allows you to see where another's lack of self-confidence is undermining her ability to make the most of her talents. Then, from your overview of the big picture, you can give her new ideas for how to use her creativity to reach her goals and make her dreams come true.

Using your innate detachment is the best way to employ your gifts in creating successful relationships. Take time to see the other person objectively so you can understand her situation from *her* point of view. Remaining conscious of her values—and the goals she has for her *own* life—will keep your heart open and give you the space you need in order to support her while maintaining your individual path.

By staying in touch with your own identity and not losing yourself in the other person, you can treat your partner as a friend as well as a person close to your heart. In this way you ensure a loving bond between you.

Past-Life Gifts

You have had many past lifetimes where your survival depended on linking with peers who had a common vision that allowed you to act as a cooperative unit. These past incarnations were spent as a revolutionary, scientist, inventor, and in other unconventional roles that benefited society. As a result, you are a big-picture person. Altruist by nature, you are not interested in any form of class or group prejudice.

These past-life experiences have also created your heightened capacity for detached observation. To others you can sometimes seem aloof, when really you are just standing back from the situation in order to see objectively what is going on, so that your involvement will be exactly what is needed and truly helpful.

During your past incarnations, you mastered the art of seeing people and situations objectively, without projecting your own ego or personal agenda onto the situation. Your ability to view the big picture and take the wants and needs of others into account allows you to know what actions are truly in the best interests of everyone involved. You also have a natural curiosity and interest in others that can teach us all the value of being more willing to accept the unique individuality of the people who come into our lives.

Confidence in Social Situations

Step into the role of "the friend."

Hold the intention of "What insight do you need in order to see the big picture?"

PISCES RISING

Your Window to the World

You interact with the external world from a position of sensitivity and a desire to heal. One of your gifts is an awareness of the subtle realms, and you express your inner being in ways that reflect this, as well as your need to do no harm. You have a deep awareness of others' feelings and you don't want to hurt anyone. As a result, you consciously share your thoughts and feelings with other people in ways that will not jar them.

When looking outside yourself, you view the people and situations around you in terms of whether or not they will be give you the privacy and support you need in order to regenerate. You *interpret* the behavior of others toward you as to whether they appreciate your unusual degree of sensitivity and take that aspect of your personality into account when relating to you.

Your personality and behavior demonstrate your basically quiet, gentle, accommodating, and trusting nature, while your attitude and demeanor reflect your subtle sensitivity. This may cause you to appear confused at times—or a bit otherworldly—but this is part of your charm.

Your Achilles' Heel

Your innate approach to life is one of psychic and emotional sensitivity to others and to the subtle realms. This can result in your seeing those people who do not share this kind of awareness as being too analytical or as having no vision. Because you sometimes think *others* are that way, it's easy for you to assume that they could possibly view *you* that way as well—and it is your fear of this potential disapproval that creates your Achilles' heel.

If you don't stay in touch with the deep sensitivity of your own identity, and instead give in to this fear of how others might see you, you may end up suppressing your own natural point of view and connection to the subtle realms. Then you lose confidence in your ability to be helpful and inspire others—both personally and spiritually.

For instance, you may refuse to use your psychic sensitivity to take on and dissolve another's ills—or to respond to his upsets with your deep sense of compassion that can heal him—out of fear that you will be seen as being not perfect enough. But if you suppress your gifts in order to avoid exposing yourself to criticism or the possibility of being misunderstood, the focus of your emotional sensitivity will turn inward against yourself.

However, when all the power of your innate gifts is not flowing outward toward others, it implodes and blocks the flow of your own vital energy. If you allow this to happen, you can end up using your sensitivity to become preoccupied with creating a victim role in the world in order to justify to yourself not participating in being a healing influence with others.

Self-Actualization

You have a gift for sharing your healing talents and emotional sensitivity with other people by bringing love and compassion into dysfunctional moments and cheer into gloomy situations. If others are being critical of themselves, you know just what to say to give them confidence that a higher power—or life itself—is looking out for them.

While using this gift to benefit others is the healthy way for you to experience ongoing vitality in your life, it can be difficult to get past a fear of how others will see you and the potential of their disapproval. But the highest path is to be courageous enough to overcome this obstacle and fully express your true nature, using your instinctive psychic sensitivity to respond to others' distress with a compassionate understanding that subtly inspires them.

Then your greatest challenge becomes using the feedback you receive from your environment—both positive *and* negative—to shift and fine-tune the ways in that you express your personality. It is only through this process that your ability to consistently create positive results can be refined and perfected.

This process can be painful, but only to the extent that you take any negative feedback personally. Instead, input from the environment is actually a gift that allows you to see the *exact* changes that are needed in the ways you express yourself in order for you to create the happy outcomes and rapport with others that you long for. Once you are willing to modify your presentation, you will experience a new sense of independence and trust in your ability to act, as well as the confidence and joy that come from freely expressing your authentic self.

When you actively use your natural abilities to understand the human condition and dissolve others' upsets through the power of your perception and receptivity to unconditional love, you will truly begin to experience yourself as a powerful cause in your own life, rather than living in fear of others' perceptions.

Relationships

In the beginning of an intimate relationship, it's easy for you to begin making plans for how the other person will fit into your life. You tend to become enmeshed in his issues and put all your energy into what he can do to improve himself—and then go about trying to help him change his behavior. However, once involved on a close level, you gradually become aware of the discrepancy between your ideal and the person you are actually dealing with.

Then you may reverse yourself, detaching from the relationship and daydreaming about other potential partners.

In order to prevent this scenario, your challenge in choosing a suitable mate, partner, or friend is to approach the other person with an attitude of unconditional love. While your motive of wanting to be of practical help to him is correct, before making plans for the future with him it is important for you to step back in between meetings and—without judging the other person or yourself—realistically evaluate whether he is truly a good match for you in terms of a primary relationship.

While by yourself, tune in to your *true* feelings for the other person and your level of serenity when you are with him. In his company, do you still feel the joy of your personal connection with a higher power? Does he support you in reaching the dreams that are important to you? Does he fulfill your ideal in terms of having similar spiritual values? Taking the time to consciously reevaluate the situation as the relationship develops will keep you in touch with your own values and identity, so that you don't let the other person, or yourself, down by not being able to fulfill the commitments you make to him.

Once you make the decision to become involved in a relationship, it is vital that you stay in touch with your own unconditionally loving nature. Releasing any flaws you see in your partner into the hands of a higher power will allow you to relate to him with an open heart.

You have a natural desire to be of service to your partner, and have a special ability to help him come up with a practical plan that will empower him to create more order in his life. Through your unique sensitivity, you are also aware of his self-criticism and the negative thought patterns and behaviors that are keeping him from feeling truly joyful about life.

By staying in touch with your own identity and consciously avoiding enmeshment with your partner, you will be able to present this information in a way that is loving and nonjudgmental, and share your vision of the healing that you see is possible for him. The loving compassion with which you help him become aware of, and analyze, those personal characteristics that are stopping him from reaching his goals can actually release his own unique ability to heal. When your partner can share in your connection with a higher power and your faith in him, he will be empowered to make other behavioral changes that will lead to even more healing in his life.

Past-Life Gifts

You have had many past lifetimes where your survival depended on trusting in a higher power and being sensitive enough to live your life in a way that caused no harm. Many of these incarnations were spent in monasteries or other situations where you were shut away from the hustle and bustle of daily life, and as a result you are very sensitive to noisy environments and feel more comfortable with quiet and serenity.

These lifetimes also offered the opportunity for self-reflection and self-purification. Through these experiences you gained a true understanding of the connection between cause and consequence, and are thereby able to change your persona to be a magnet for attracting different circumstances in your life.

You have had so much time to purify your own weaknesses in behavior and deficiencies in character during these past lives that you are naturally tolerant of the shortcomings of others. Your acceptance and love for people as they are—without judgment—can teach us all the value of oneness and unconditional love.

Confidence in Social Situations

Step into the role of "the gentle healer."
Hold the intention of "How can I help you feel that life is not so threatening?"

⊙

ASPECTS

WHAT IS AN ASPECT?

An aspect is the energetic relationship between two of the planets that is revealed through your individual astrology chart. The planetary urges connect differently within each person, and the nature of these connections—friendly or unfriendly—is shown by the aspects (the degrees of separation) between the planets. For example, if your Moon is square your Sun (an aspect of conflict), your urge for security (represented by the Moon) is in conflict with your urge to lead and creatively express yourself (represented by the Sun).

Imagine that the planets are located in different positions around the outside of a wheel, each one shooting a line of energy straight toward the center. The way the energy connects between the planets in your astrology chart shows the way the "wiring" connects within *you*.

Now imagine that the circle is a clock. A circle has 360 degrees, so if one planet is at the twelve o'clock position and another planet is at the 6 o'clock position, they are 180 degrees apart. In astrology, this is called an opposition between the two forces or urges represented by the planets involved. For example, if your Mars (representing sexuality) is in opposition to your Venus (representing love), you will find yourself involved with partners with whom there is either a strong chemistry (Mars) or a strong love connection (Venus). Inwardly you feel that your romantic partners fall into one of these two categories, but not both.

FREE COMPUTERIZED ASTROLOGY CHART

Go to www.janspiller.com, click the "Free Astrology Charts" icon on the home page, enter your birth information, and your full birth chart will be calculated for you free of charge. Once you have printed out your personal astrology chart—which will include a list of the signs, houses, and aspects for each of your ten planets—you will be able to gain tremendous insight into the inner workings of yourself and others! Using your chart, locate each planet and write down which sign it's in. Then consult the chapters in this part of *Spiritual Astrology* to interpret the significance of each planet in its sign. For example, if you have the planet Mars in the sign of Aries, read the description on page 77.

Knowing the aspects in your chart will provide you with further insight by showing you how two or more urges within yourself relate to each other in a very specific way. For example, if your list of aspects includes "Mars opposed Saturn," you can look up the meaning of "opposition" in this section on the aspects. Then, by reading the information about your Mars (for example, Mars in Aries), and your Saturn (for example, Saturn in Libra), you can understand how this aspect affects you by imagining these two urges in your life opposing each other.

Once you have a copy of your birth chart and list of your aspects, you are ready to go. To better understand the internal urges that create conflict and stress in your life, as well as those urges within you that naturally work harmoniously together and bring easy good fortune, read the description of the planets involved in each of the aspects in your chart in this part of *Spiritual Astrology*.

DIFFICULT ASPECTS

THE SQUARE AND THE OPPOSITION

The major aspects showing the existence of a specific internal conflict are the square and the opposition. The planets involved show the two urges you experience within yourself that are in conflict with each other. This usually results in feelings of tension because you think that either one urge or the other can be satisfied—but not both.

The advantage is that through this energetic conflict, you become consciously aware of these two unique urges. Through this process you gain strength internally and can adopt a more awake approach to life. If your astrology chart shows several difficult aspects, it indicates that this is a learning and growing lifetime for you, filled with excitement and the blossoming of inner awareness. Difficult aspects also provide more stimulus for accomplishing in your life; the drive to work hard to resolve the conflict.

The drawback is that in the two areas of life indicated, you are likely to experience more difficulty in attaining success in the material world. Your own inner conflicts can create external problems in the areas shown by the planets and houses involved. The *resolution* for difficult aspects is to experience each of the planets involved separately and fully, and not try to combine them into one space. With both planets involved, you will need to be willing to allot separate time to each urge for both parts of you to be satisfied.

The Square

Imagine that one planet is at twelve o'clock and another is at three o'clock—ninety degrees apart. This creates the "square aspect," and the urges represented by the planets involved conflict with each other in terms of your internal process.

For example, if Mars is square Venus, you likely feel an internal conflict between love (represented by Venus) and sex (represented by Mars). It may seem as if you can't have both an exciting sexual relationship and a satisfying love relationship with the same person. As another example, if Saturn squares your Moon, you feel an inner conflict between the urge for tangible accomplishment (represented by Saturn) and the desire to fulfill your personal emotional needs (represented by your Moon).

If you have three or more squares in your chart, this is a learning and growing lifetime for you—you're not on vacation! Your challenge is to consciously learn how to integrate these conflicting urges so that you can successfully experience them all in a healthy, balanced way.

It has been said that the unexamined life is not worth living, and this is certainly the case if your chart contains three or more squares. It is only by coming to understand the different needs indicated by these squares on a deep level that you can consciously recombine them and find satisfaction in these areas of your life. A willingness to go through this process of self-examination leads to growth, maturity, wisdom, and the healing of your soul. Externally, this process leads to attaining the prizes the world holds dear as a by-product of your having worked with and mastered the urges involved.

If you have two planets in a square aspect with each other, look up in this part the meaning of each of those planets—in the sign the planet is located in your birth chart—and imagine those two urges conflicting with each other inside yourself. You will gain insight into the way your inner self is wired, empowering you to resolve a lifelong internal conflict.

The Opposition

Imagine that one planet is at twelve o'clock and another is at six o'clock—180 degrees apart. This creates the "opposition aspect," and the urges represented by the planets involved are in direct conflict with each other. For example, if Mercury opposes Moon, what you think logically (represented by Mercury) is in opposition with what you feel and need emotionally (represented by the Moon). Your relationships with others stimulate the energy of the oppositions in your chart.

The opposition always involves a relationship struggle. When you read about the urges within you involved in the opposition in this part, you will gain a clearer understanding of what was involved in any relationship conflicts that are part of your history. Knowledge is power, and when you see that the external struggle is being magnetically propelled by your inner being, you can make conscious choices about handling those parts of you differently. The opposition is like a teeter-totter—first one side is in the air, and then the other rises. If you keep the teeter-totter in motion—not trying to stay stuck on one side or the other—it can be a fun and enlivening ride!

If you have two planets in an opposition aspect with each other, look up the meaning of each of those planets—in the sign the planet is located in your birth chart—and imagine those two urges working together as a source of discord in your relationships. You will gain insight into the way your inner self is wired, empowering you to resolve recurring conflicts with others.

EASY ASPECTS

THE TRINE AND THE SEXTILE

The major aspects revealing the existence of an innate internal cooperation—two parts of yourself that naturally work compatibly together without any thought on your part—are the trine and the sextile. The planets involved show the urges that share this state of harmony and easy expression. These are two parts of yourself that you have already learned to coordinate in a cooperative way through your past-life experiences.

The advantage is that because these two parts of yourself are so compatible, it's easy and natural for you to create success in the external world that satisfies, and fully expresses, both urges.

The drawback is that in these areas of life where things are effortless for you, there can be a tendency to create success out in the world without necessarily developing inner depth along the way. There can also be a feeling of just falling into things without the satisfaction of a sense of self-direction.

The Trine

To find which of your planets are in a TRINE Aspect with one another, go to www .janspiller.com and a full list of your aspects will be calculated for you free of charge.

In the clock illustration, one planet is at twelve o'clock and another is at four o'clock, creating 120 degrees of separation between them. This aspect indicates harmony and good luck. Internally, the urges represented by the planets involved are naturally working together in a harmonious way, and as a result, spontaneous good luck is created in the external world.

You seem to fall into fortunate circumstances in the areas of your life affected by the planets creating the trine. These two urges within you work together and are spontaneously supportive of each other. For example, with the Moon trine Venus, you will seem to effortlessly find relationships where both of your needs for nurturing (represented by the Moon) and for affectionate love (represented by Venus) are satisfied.

If you have two planets in a trine aspect with each other, look up in this part the meaning of each of those planets—in the sign the planet is located in your birth chart—and imagine those two urges working harmoniously with each other inside of yourself. You will gain insight into the way your inner self is wired, empowering you to use and appreciate areas of life in which you are by birthright blessed.

The Sextile

With this aspect, one planet is at twelve o'clock and another is at two o'clock, with sixty degrees of separation between them. The sextile shows an area of innate inner peace that, combined with applied effort, results in good luck and material success in the external world. For example, if your chart shows Mercury sextile Saturn, your thinking (represented by Mercury) perceives the world and the opportunities that present themselves realistically (represented by Saturn). The resulting practical thinking easily creates material success.

To better understand these internal urges that create easy accomplishment in the external world, read the description of the planets involved in this aspect in this part and imagine that the two urges described are working together cooperatively within you. This knowledge can help you maximize your opportunities, since you realize inherent talents at your disposal to call upon.

THE MOST POWERFUL MAJOR ASPECT

THE CONJUNCTION

Imagine that both planets are at twelve o'clock—zero to ten degrees of separation. This creates the "conjunction aspect," and shows the existence of two urges within yourself—shown by the two planets involved—that act together in the same way as conjoined twins. Sometimes the urge represented by one of the planets takes priority while the energy of the second planet backs up the power of its expression—and sometimes the second planet takes center stage.

For example, a person with the conjunction of Mars (representing sexual urges) and Mercury (representing the mind) would likely experience times when he thought about *everything* in terms of sex (when Mars was expressing), and times when tremendous energy propelled his thinking for good or ill (when Mercury is taking center stage).

The advantage is that because these two parts of yourself are in this synergistic relationship, there is an increase of energy that strengthens both urges.

The drawback is that in the two areas of life involved, you lack objectivity. It is very easy to be expressing these parts of yourself unconsciously, and to be unaware of how this affects others. Someone else may perceive you as almost being two different people, as the energy of *both* planets becomes focused on expressing *one* urge, and then the *other urge* comes to the forefront in an equally strong way.

The *key* is to become aware of the different urges involved and begin to consciously fit them together in a way that creates a harmonious whole. The *challenge* is to see each planet as an individual power, so you can consciously blend their energies to produce the most positive outcome. If one of the impersonal planets is involved—Jupiter, Saturn, Uranus, Neptune, or Pluto—the muse of the impersonal planet is destined to transform and bring the personal planet it conjoins to a higher, more evolved level of expression.

If you have two planets in a conjunction aspect with each other, look up in this part the meaning of each of those planets—in the sign the planets are located in your birth chart—and imagine those two urges working together as conjoined twins. You will gain insight into the way your inner self is wired, empowering you to consciously combine different talents in your individuality.

MINOR ASPECTS

Planets in a "minor aspect" to one another have a decided effect, but the process is not as evident as those involved in one of the preceding major aspects. The affects, though they may be profound inwardly, are less outwardly apparent. The minor aspects involve more subtle processes within the self. There are many minor aspects astrologers may incorporate in their readings, but the following two are the most universally used.

QUINCUNX

This aspect creates internal stress because two parts of yourself don't quite mesh. Through the planets indicated, the quincunx shows the areas of your life where additional learning, growing, and self-understanding are required. As you feel the friction of these urges, you are forced to make adjustments and see things differently in your life in order to lessen the internal pressure. The urges involved—shown by the planets—need to be reevaluated consciously, and then given expression at a higher level than that at which the conflict is occurring. For example, if you have the Moon quincunx your Venus (both urges involving your feeling, love nature), the love you are seeking will be satisfied at a more refined level than your programming conditioned you for at birth.

As you gain the awareness needed to uniquely develop these two facets of yourself, it is the inward journey that proves most rewarding. You have the potential to express the urges of these two planets at a higher level that is unique, and perhaps forward-thinking in comparison to the norm.

If you have two planets in a quincunx aspect with each other, look up in this part the meaning of each of those planets—in the sign the planet is located in your birth chart—and imagine those two urges needing to adjust in their spontaneous expression in order to have both needs met and satisfied.

SEMI-SEXTILE

This is a basically positive aspect that indicates two urges—represented by the planets involved—that are not working together as well as they could to build successful results in the material world. When this aspect appears in your chart, your challenge is to gain information about the planets involved and how the urges they represent are expressing in your life. This will allow you to develop a greater awareness of any adjustments you could make that would empower you to consciously use these energies together to create more positive results.

This is an aspect of building. You are seeking to gain new information about how to use these two planetary energies together to create successful material results. To better understand these internal urges that are requiring conscious development, read the description of your planets involved in the semi-sextile in this part.

CONCLUSION

THE ASTROLOGY CHART is an objective picture, a graph of one's personality structure and individuality. It depicts the ego—the personal self—the structure within us that makes us unique (and feeling separate) from everyone else on the planet.

Ultimately, happiness does not come from a sense of feeling separate from one another. Happiness is a by-product of being in touch with the source of happiness within ourselves. This happiness unites us with others. To understand the personality variations between ourselves and others objectively allows us to relate with others with love, rather than feeling that they have to be just like us.

The purpose of part 1 of *Spiritual Astrology* is to define the uniqueness of each of our personalities. It illustrates that there are choices we can make about the quality of our life. Our choices determine the effects that we experience in life. Nothing happens by accident. Because we have the power to attract experiences, we also have the power to change our responses. The key is in accepting personal responsibility, which leads directly to personal empowerment.

A professional astrologer can look at your birth chart and tell you exactly what your mother was like (as you saw her) and the kind of relationship you had with your father. This information is based on the moment of your birth. So did your parents set your destiny?

For example, in my birth chart I have Saturn (the planetary symbol representing my father) in the 10th house, squared by my Neptune opposing Moon in the 1st and 7th houses. This indicates that my father was a harsh authority figure who ruled me with an iron hand (which is true).

On the other hand, my brother's astrology chart has Saturn in a grand trine with Venus and his ascendant. And sure enough, his relationship with our father was harmonious, peaceful, and supportive—quite different from mine. Yet we both had the same father, the same environment, the same circumstances. My brother brought out one facet of him and I brought out another. It had little to do with my father. We just drew from him what we needed to fulfill our own individual personality structures.

Now I can look at my birth chart and say, "Aha! Because of my father I'll have a problem with authority figures my whole life." Or, every time I start feeling shy or repressed because I've attracted someone who is insensitively telling me what to do, I can say, "Wait a minute here! That's *my* Saturn square Neptune opposing Moon. Nobody's doing it *to* me! I'm attracting it! So what can I do to effectively take charge in this situation?" Once I have asked that question, I have given myself the power to deal creatively with the situation in a way that will work for me.

You are in control of the way you use the energies depicted in your birth chart. When you use these energies positively, considering the good of all concerned, life magically shifts to your personal advantage. If you give the responsibility of your happiness to others, you subjugate yourself to the ups and downs of the material world. When you accept sole responsibility for actualizing the energies in your birth chart, you gain the power to navigate your life in a way that is fulfilling and happy.

To use this book to maximize your experience of life, apply the ideas that you resonate with to see if the results shift situations in a positive way. This is a joy in itself! Then your life is lived from the inside out, rather than just being buffeted around by external shifts in your environment.

Instead of playing catch-up, you're playing your *own* game! You still may be relating with the same people, but by becoming more conscious and changing the *way* you are interacting with them (and with yourself) you gain the empowerment of recognizing that through self-direction, you have far more control over producing the results you would like in your world than you had realized. By changing your presentation, you gain more power over your destiny.

FREE ASTROLOGY CHARTS
AND OBTAINING
YOUR BIRTH CERTIFICATE

FOR A FULL copy of your natal birth chart—including the sign and house locations of all your planets and aspects—go to www.janspiller.com and access this free information the following way:

On the home page, click on "Free Astrology Charts" then click on "Free Astrology Birth Chart & Mini-Interpretation." Enter your birth information (date of birth, place of birth, and time of birth if you know it) and your chart will be calculated for you free of charge. In addition to your astrology chart, the printout will include a listing of the position of all your planets and eclipses in their signs and houses, as well as a list of the aspects between your planets. One natal birth chart per day is free, unlimited charts are available to site members.

If you are uncertain about the exact time of your birth, the best sources for obtaining an accurate time are your birth certificate and written family records (baby book and so forth).

There are three copies of your birth certificate on file in the U.S. city in which you were born. Only *one* of these copies has your birth time on it. Therefore, in sending for your birth certificate, *emphasize* that you want the copy that states your *time* of birth.

To obtain a copy of your birth certificate write to:

> County Clerk
> Hall of Records
> County Courthouse
> (city and state in which you were born)

In requesting your birth certificate, include the following:
- your full name (as it was recorded on the birth certificate) and birth date

- your mother's maiden name
- your father's name
- A check or money order for the fee (the service may be slightly more or less depending on the state). You can call the hall of records in your city to find out the current fee for a birth certificate. A money order receives a faster response than a personal check.
- self-addressed, stamped envelope

Note: You can also order online at www.usbirthcertificate.com/.

PRENATAL ECLIPSES: KEY TO LIFE PATH AND DESTINY

Karen McCoy and Jan Spiller

INTRODUCTION TO PART 2

WITHIN THE ECLIPSES of the Sun and the Moon lies one of the keys to the question "Why me?" The new information presented in part 2 concerning the meaning of the solar and lunar eclipses in our lives is the result of many hours of meditation and study. A lecture by astrologer Robert (Buz) Myers in 1982 gave me the initial idea, and for the next four years I researched more than four thousand charts, watching carefully for the effect of the eclipses on personality and behavior. I found that for the vast majority of people, their solar eclipse sign indicated lessons they had come to teach their fellow beings, while their lunar eclipse sign guided them to the lessons they needed to learn in order to continue their own soul growth.

Another aspect of the eclipses that became clear in my research is that the energy pattern of a particular solar eclipse is similar to the energy a birth brings to that child's parents. When a child is born, look closely at the parents' relationship. Notice that the life force represented by the child's Sun sign is the energy that this particular union needs in order to be revitalized.

For example, when a Gemini is born, those parents need to communicate more. This little Gemini child is ruled by the planet of communications. At conception, the parents sent out a signal: We need help learning to communicate more clearly. In a similar manner, at the time of a solar eclipse, the inhabitants of the earth are asking for the help they need for the greatest good of the planet and the continued evolution of our own collective consciousness.

During an eclipse, the sheath of the Earth is broken, and a surge of energy from the collective higher consciousness enters the planet's atmosphere. This energy is sent as a helping hand. The sign in which the eclipse occurs will determine the type of help that is sent, through the souls who enter at that time and the ability the universe has bestowed on them. How aware and evolved these souls are will determine how well they use their gifts.

Remember when looking at these eclipse patterns that a gift received is not necessarily a gift used. Dealing with karma (or soul growth patterns, as I prefer to call them), I find that the more talents or spiritual assets you use to help your fellow beings, the more personal spiritual growth you gain.

The prenatal solar eclipse represents the aspect of the collective higher consciousness that you have to offer your fellow beings. The sign and house of the eclipse will tell you the area of your life and the mode of expression that make these abilities most accessible to you. The prenatal lunar eclipse pattern will show what you need to continue the growth of your soul. The house and sign will show how and where you can best acquire these lessons. These are the points that stimulate growth and build character. The level of awareness the soul has when entering this plane will determine whether it will seek the lessons of its lunar eclipse with compassion and understanding or with resentment.

The body represents the vehicle for the energies of these two eclipses to merge in order to aid in their joint venture of sharing and learning, giving and receiving. And the body also brings with it the genetic memory of all ancestors that have shared and blended together in the past. I believe that everything in this universe can be perceived as having been created in trinities, including body, mind, and soul. The basic principle of this work is to show us how to function as the complete trinity we are. Body represents the physical form and the earth we temporarily make our home; soul, the evolving essence that is constantly striving for perfection; mind, the instrument we use to reach the spark of the collective higher consciousness, to reach out to one another, and to discover our group responsibility. For in each of us, there resides a part of everyone else. There are no throwaways; the puzzle needs all its pieces, so God-speed in letting your spark shine through.

KAREN McCOY

THE FOLLOWING INFORMATION on the influence of the prenatal eclipses in our personal lives is revolutionary. Our purpose in sharing this knowledge is to empower readers with objective information about themselves and those around them that can help clarify their path on Earth. The final authority in determining the validity and usefulness of the material offered is *you*. In the physical realm, facts are objective; in the intangible realms, truth is subjective.

In my experience with astrology over the past three decades, I have noticed that many people are curious and open-minded. Still others, lacking research, tend to discount the validity of astrology, thereby depriving themselves of a unique opportunity for self-understanding and understanding others. Astrology is simply a mathematical tool for viewing the wiring of your unique internal self. As with any tool, there is always the opportunity for misuse. Thus, we have those among us who would use astrology as a means of casting superstition or gaining material power over another. In any field involving healing, there are abusers of the craft. It is up to you to determine whether you are with a professional or an abuser. This is an ancient science, and the astrology chart itself is based on a series of most exacting and precise mathematical formulas. The tool is pure; the practioner makes all the difference.

Astrology is not a matter of belief, it is a system based on objective mathematical calculations. As with any science, you can test its accuracy by running experiments to determine how the theories work when applied to physical reality. There are many nonmaterial realities that have very definite physical effects. Gravity is not visible, yet its existence is self-evident. Whether or not you are a "believer," you are affected by gravity nonetheless. While radio waves are not perceivable by the physical senses—only one hundred years ago, it was fashionable to be a skeptic about the validity of these waves—today no one doubts their existence. In the same way, the final proof of astrology's validity is whether or not it can be of practical use in your own life. The value of the insights gained through astrology can be enormous, empowering us to see ourselves and others without bias. This allows us to change the way we express ourselves—in alignment with our individuality—and thus to alter the effects of what we are manifesting in our lives.

I would like to acknowledge the tremendous contribution to humankind that astrologers, past and present, have made by dedicating their lives to investigating the cause-and-effect relationship between planetary energies and human behavior. Their research has given us all a tool with which we can consciously gain cooperative control over our destinies. The graph of the astrology chart gives us a precise X ray of our unique individual internal wiring that empowers us to use the tools we were born with consciously and at full capacity. Knowing what is true for us objectively takes us out of the realm of confusion and self-suppression. It supports us in self-actualization.

Part 2 is designed to facilitate your understanding of the lessons you have come to learn in order to continue your evolutionary progress. It illuminates the natural gifts you have promised to share with others while you are here. The purpose is to stimulate spiritual awakening. The final authority on the accuracy of the text is the sense of rightness you experience while reading it. Ultimately, truth works, and if experimenting with the suggestions in this book leads to more clarity and ease in your relationships and greater happiness within yourself, then you know you are on the right track.

JAN SPILLER

HOW TO USE PART 2

REINCARNATION

A belief in reincarnation (your soul having previously experienced life in a physical body other than the current one) is not necessary in order to obtain full value from this book. However, an openness to the possibility of permanently transcending old, limiting mental states and conditions is a necessity for receiving the full impact of the change and freedom that is possible.

Terms such as "past incarnations" and "previous lifetimes" are used. Such phrases may be interpreted to mean prior experiences in other bodies or prior realities experienced in the current body (such as experiences in early childhood with parents or siblings, or the unconscious memories of adolescence in dealing with peers, relationships in puberty, and so forth).

A third interpretation is that the experiences of early childhood are merely a re-creation of individual patternings and habitual responses active in past lives, brought into the current incarnation for further growth and resolution.

Any of these viewpoints will work. It depends on your belief system. The main idea is to be willing to take responsibility for mastering the lessons you currently need to work through and resolve to create a happy life for yourself.

ECLIPSES

DETERMINING THE SIGNS OF YOUR ECLIPSES

Check the eclipse tables following this section (see page 423). In the solar eclipse table, locate the eclipse date immediately before your birth date. Note the sign of the eclipse. That is the sign position of your prenatal solar eclipse. For example, if you were born on March 31, 1953, your prenatal solar eclipse would be in the sign of Aquarius, and you would look up the meaning of your eclipse under the section on Aquarius. If born on December 13, 1941, you'd find your prenatal solar eclipse in the sign of Virgo; look up the corresponding meaning under the section on Virgo.

Follow the same procedure for determining the sign in which your pre-natal lunar eclipse is located, using the lunar eclipse tables beginning on page 427. For example, for March 31, 1953, the lunar eclipse is in the sign of Leo; for December 13, 1941, the lunar eclipse is in Pisces.

HOW THE ECLIPSES WORK

When the Moon passes between the Sun and the Earth, a solar eclipse occurs; a lunar eclipse occurs when the Earth passes between the Sun and the Moon. Before your birth (sometime between conception and the first breath of life) there were at least two eclipses—one solar and one lunar. These prenatal eclipses have a profound influence on the unborn child, and the energy pattern dispensed during these eclipses follows you the rest of your life.

At birth, the energy of both the prenatal solar eclipse and the lunar eclipse enter the body. By knowing the sign of the eclipses preceding your birth, you can identify the covenant you made with the universe in exchange for the privilege of having a body and being on the planet.

The sign of your solar eclipse shows a universal destiny: It is the energy of the collective unconscious that needs to be actively expressed on Earth at that time for its own balance. The souls born into each solar eclipse have been infused with that energy and have promised to spread it on Earth to help with the planet's growth and evolution.

Thus, the solar eclipse that preceded your birth reveals the energy the universe has invested in you and that you have promised to share during your travels on Earth. The solar eclipse energy is what you are here to clarify for the collective whole. You must share that energy, as you promised in your cov-enant with the universe. Your only choice lies in whether to share your gift in a positive way or in a negative way. You can go about your life generously sharing this gift with your fellow beings, or you can teach them what not to do by having such negative traits in your behavior and personality that those around you learn what to avoid. If you do choose to teach these lessons in a negative manner, you are creating an imbalance within your own life. It makes learning your life lessons more difficult than is necessary.

You promised to share the energy of the solar eclipse in order to earn the right to come onto this plane and learn the lessons represented by your lunar eclipse. The universe operates in perfect balance—if you give something, you open yourself to receiving something. So when you accepted the gift repre-sented by your solar eclipse and promised to share it with others, you earned the right to learn the lessons you need in order to evolve, as shown by your lunar eclipse. The lunar eclipse is what you need for your own soul growth pattern: what you have come to learn, where you hurt, where you need completion. And as you master these lessons as an individual, the entire planet feels it, learns them, and part of the universal balance is realized.

Evolved souls cooperate with this universal plan, spreading their solar eclipse teachings and mastering their lunar eclipse lessons, thus fulfilling their contracts with the universe. At that point they are freed to enjoy being on the planet without obstructions, open to attract and experience the beauty, fun, and bounty available here.

IMPACT OF THE ECLIPSES

The immense impact of the eclipse on individual destiny seems to be tied in with the workings of the planet Pluto. Although in 2006 Pluto was demoted to the status of "dwarf planet" by the International Astronomical Union, astrologers have never wavered in their observation of the intense impact the planet Pluto has as it travels through the constellations of the zodiac, impacting both individual and global destiny. It's a practical matter, based on mathematical calculations. As Pluto enters different degrees of the zodiac, the corresponding degrees in the birth chart of an individual or a nation explode with predictable timing and effects. Thus, astrologers do not doubt Pluto's effect on humankind.

SOLAR ECLIPSE: YOUR RESPONSIBILITY TO SHARE

The sign of your solar eclipse determines what your responsibility is to the collective whole, the energy you have promised to share with others. It's a gift that the universe gave you so you could teach others, thus raising and balancing the consciousness of humankind. Use it wisely, for by freely sharing your gift, you ease the burden of your own lessons. The section on your solar eclipse will tell you what you have come to share with your fellow beings in this lifetime.

LUNAR ECLIPSE: THE LESSONS YOU NEED TO LEARN

The sign of your lunar eclipse indicates those qualities you need to integrate for personal balance, the lessons you have chosen to learn in this lifetime. You are not judged by how you undertake this journey, for it is you who decided to begin the quest. This is a personal destiny: It is the lesson that your soul wants to integrate into its evolutionary pattern.

UNCONSCIOUS EXPRESSION (SOLAR AND LUNAR)

By unconscious expression, we mean the behaviors displayed when you are bucking the tides of growth and choosing not to integrate your lessons. It is the result of swimming upstream and taking yourself out of the natural flow. This is a picture of what life looks like when you have become willful and are not listening to your inner voice. When you are not paying attention to your life lesson, you set yourself up to learn things the hard way, as depicted by the eclipse energies shown under this category. Many of us begin our process of personal growth at this level, until life becomes too painful and we decide to move on to the conscious level.

CONSCIOUS EXPRESSION (SOLAR AND LUNAR)

By conscious expression we mean the type of experiences and inner reactions that occur when you choose to approach life consciously. At this stage of evolution you have decided to listen to your inner voice and follow the flow of life, embracing your lessons in a gentler way. By learning to read the signs of the times and taking into account the responses of those around you, you become more fluid and allow yourself to cooperate with your own destiny. By being aware and conscious, growth comes more easily.

TRANSPERSONAL EXPRESSION (SOLAR AND LUNAR)

Transpersonal expression refers to the attitudes and experiences that become active when you choose to transcend the ego and function in a way that serves the highest good. Personal growth and maturity lead to a sense of greater ease in life.

Many people begin the process of personal growth on the unconscious level. As you grow, you become less resistant to life, and you naturally learn to operate more from the conscious level. With further experience on the planet, you recognize another option: living your life transpersonally, viewing life in a larger context than that of personal survival.

In this stage you are aware of the support and good intent of the universal forces, including Mother Nature. You become open to receiving the natural bounty of life. You realize that in cooperating for the good of the whole, individual happiness is a natural by-product. Your needs are easily and naturally provided. This is the stage in which you decide to give up the ego functions that separate you from your fellow beings and open yourself as a channel for receiving and sharing light and love. This stage is reached after diligent spiritual growth and self-purification. If it is not attractive now, it may become more alluring after a few more lifetimes.

PHYSICAL INTEGRATION (SOLAR AND LUNAR)

The body helps you fine-tune your lessons and provides you with a way to gauge your behavior. Your physical state can be a personal barometer to soul growth. The body can make your journey easier through the advice it can render. Listen carefully, for it knows you very well.

The section on physical integration provides a physical checkpoint for determining when the psychological energies of the solar or lunar eclipse life lessons are out of balance. It is based on the premise that mental or emotional imbalance, when ignored on the psychological level, can manifest on the physical level in order to gain your attention and muster your resolve to remedy the situation.

In no way are the suggestions made in these sections to be interpreted as a substitute for taking physical precautions and appropriate remedies in handling physical illnesses.

THE DOUBLE SOLAR EFFECT: YOUR TWO GIFTS

This effect occurs when two solar eclipse occur between your birth date and the most recent lunar eclipse. For example, referring to the table on page 428, if you were born on December 12, 1964, your prenatal lunar eclipse would be in Capricorn. This lunar eclipse occurred on June 25, 1964. Note that two solar eclipses occur between this lunar eclipse and your birth date— one on December 4, 1964, in Sagittarius, and one on July 9, 1964, in Cancer. If you were born on this date, you have a double solar eclipse.

This means that you can have a more active path than the rest of us. You have two special gifts, two things you have promised to share. You have accepted the responsibility of sharing two separate sets of lessons. You will draw people to you who need both lessons, and you have promised to handle the responsibility of both. If you could not handle such a task, it would not have been given to you.

THE DOUBLE LUNAR EFFECT: YOUR TWO LESSONS

This effect occurs when two lunar eclipses happen between your birth date and the most recent solar eclipse (refer to the tables on page 423). For example, if you were born on February 18, 1952, your prenatal solar eclipse would be located in Virgo, occurring on September 1, 1951. Note that two lunar eclipses occur between this solar eclipse and your birth date—one in Leo on February 11, 1952, and one in Pisces on September 15, 1951. If you were born on this date, you have a double lunar eclipse.

There is a distinctive psychological effect for those having a double lunar eclipse. You may feel as if you have two strong drawing influences, two roads in life you must travel. Truly, there are two sets of lessons that you have chosen to integrate into your life experience during this incarnation.

Sometimes you feel that you are two distinctively unrelated people, with different directions pulling at you. People close to you may even suggest that you have a split personality, as both parts surface at different times. What actually occurs is that two main issues need to be addressed and both parts of you need fulfillment in this lifetime.

The soul has chosen to walk two paths simultaneously. When you have learned to work on both lessons at once, you can facilitate these lessons traveling a parallel course in your life. A positive use of this energy would be to allow yourself to explore more than one avenue. You could have two careers, two different social environments, or two main areas of interest.

Operating unconsciously, the double lunar eclipse can sometimes give the appearance of having a split personality. This occurs when you have not learned to master and understand the necessity of learning both lessons. Then you flounder back and forth from one to the other instead of taking control and guiding your own life. Having a double lunar eclipse does not mean you have a split personality, however. As long as you are consciously striving to learn your lessons, there will be a bond of unity in your internal diversity. Problems with split personality occur only if you try to avoid responsibility for either of your lessons.

HOUSES: WHAT YOU MUST SHARE

The houses tell you in which area of your life you are learning to share and teach (the house in which your solar eclipse is found) and in which area you are learning to integrate your lessons (the house in which your lunar eclipse is found).

The houses containing your prenatal solar and lunar eclipses cannot be ascertained from the logs in this book. If you do not yet have a copy of your full birth chart containing this information, go to www.janspiller.com, click "Free Astrology Chart" on the home page, and the information will be calculated for you, free of charge. You do need your time of birth to receive an astrology chart showing your correct Ascendant.

SOLAR AND LUNAR ECLIPSES

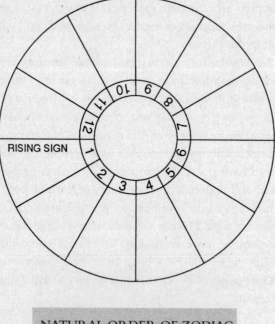

NATURAL ORDER OF ZODIAC

Aries	Libra
Taurus	Scorpio
Gemini	Sagittarius
Cancer	Capricorn
Leo	Aquarius
Virgo	Pisces

Place your rising sign in the slice of the pie labeled 1. Then fill in the other slices, following the natural order of the zodiac in a *counterclockwise* direction, according to where your rising sign begins. Know that the zodiac is a circle that has no beginning or ending, so your rising sign becomes your personal beginning and the other signs follow in their natural chronological order.

If you do not know your rising sign, you can find an approximation of it by using the wheel below.

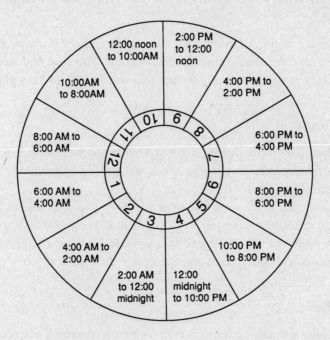

Find on the wheel the time of day you were born. Please subtract one hour from your birth time if you were born during daylight savings time or war time. Write the Sun sign you were born under in the slice of the pie corresponding to that time. Then continue filling in the rest of the zodiac wheel counterclockwise from the place your Sun sign begins. For example, if you were born at 9 A.M. and your Sun is in the sign of Leo, you would write Leo in slice 11. Because Virgo comes after Leo in the zodiac, you would write Virgo in slice 12. Then you would continue around the wheel, following the natural order of the zodiac.

The sign you write in slice 1 will be your approximate rising sign. Your actual rising sign could be the one before or the one after, so when using this approximated method, read all three house placements. After finding your approximated eclipse houses, decide for yourself which ones fit.

♈

ARIES

SOLAR ECLIPSE: WHAT YOUR SOUL CONTRACTED TO TEACH OTHERS

(In order to fully activate your solar eclipse energy in Aries, it may be helpful to read the lunar eclipse in Aries section. You may find information that can help you more fully contribute your solar eclipse in Aries gifts.)

Your Mission

In this incarnation, you are teaching your fellow beings the lessons of assertiveness, independence, courage of convictions, and overcoming the fear of new beginnings.

Through this process you will draw people to you who tend to be clingy and overly dependent. Your job is to assist them in becoming more self-reliant. Simultaneously you are challenged to avoid falling into the trap they set for you so you don't begin to take over the lives of those around you.

Self-Reliance

Teaching self-reliance through example means remaining independent and holding firm to the idea that all positive relationships may be represented by the symbol for infinity—separate yet connected. In a relationship both parties must go out and experience the world, then return and share. Through their experiences, each gains something to share, so each remains of value to the other.

You intuitively understand the value of being independent, self-sufficient, and self-supported. Thus, you tend to draw people to you who are overly dependent on doing things with others.

Through your ability to be independent and assertive, you can teach the value of getting out there and doing what needs to get done, no matter what obstacles are in the way. Or you can teach this lesson through procrastination, always looking for more data, never thinking you have enough information, and remaining too fearful to move on. Either way, the lesson gets taught. And if you teach voluntarily, it can be an accelerating process with your particular pattern, for life can renew itself almost minute by minute.

Courage

To teach your fellow beings to have the courage of their convictions, you use your innate sense of fair play. You will always come to the defense of those who cannot defend themselves, but you will leave them to fight their own battles if you find they are not gaining courage with your support. You intuitively understand it is wrong for you to fight for those who will not stand up for themselves. This would only make your own muscles stronger and not benefit them in a lasting way.

Assisting the weak without allowing them to lean on you can sometimes appear heartless to outsiders. They don't see that you are teaching others true inner courage and strength by letting them stand alone. But you understand that allowing others to become dependent on you is much more cruel in the long run. This is why you fight for your independence as well as for theirs.

Leadership

You are also teaching proper leadership through your example. In positive leadership you must pass the seed to those who are responsible for nurturing it, and then move on. You understand that leaders must never remain behind, or they are not truly leaders, just manipulators.

As a true leader, you begin the process, head it in the proper direction, and set a positive example of courage, assertiveness, and strength of convictions. You go forward with your project without sending another to find the way first. Like Daniel Boone, you are right out there, clearing the path for others to follow. You teach them not to be afraid of something new or of new beginnings, that it is all right to move forward, and that everything must change. Nothing can survive in a static environment.

LUNAR ECLIPSE: WHAT YOUR SOUL IS LEARNING TO EMOTIONALLY EMBRACE

Your Mission

In this incarnation you are learning to be independent and have the courage of your convictions.

Past-Life Influence

You have been overly dependent on the opinions of those around you. Somehow you developed a belief that others were more intelligent and you were less capable. There is also a fear of not being liked, a fear of rejection, and a fear of creating disharmony through conflict.

To compensate for these fears you have let others dominate your life. You are learning that you are entitled to your own thought processes and that there is a definite reason for all of humankind to be thinking uniquely about different areas of life. It is very important that you learn to share your convictions, even if it creates conflicts.

The very process of standing up for your beliefs creates change. With change there is growth. Without growth nothing can exist. Even the universe is constantly expanding and contracting. If you never defend your convictions, how will you ever know to change when you are wrong? How can you help those around you who need to change if you continue backing down whenever you feel someone else is a stronger personality?

Independence

Coming from a history of overdependency on others, you are not accustomed to functioning as a separate being. But if you are to be happy in any relationship, you must first gain your independence, for if you marry before you define yourself, you will surrender before the battle of identity is won. Then you could fall back into past-life patterns of becoming too dependent on those around you and postpone finding your own strength and courage until your mate (or friend, parent, employer, and so forth) decides that she or he is tired of holding you up. If you wait to be shoved out the door, you are making your lesson more difficult than the universe intends it to be.

What you need to learn: to function independently within society and relationships, simultaneously contributing to the whole and benefiting from the whole. If you cannot do this within a relationship, you will find it necessary to separate yourself to learn this lesson before you can live harmoniously with another.

You are learning to find factors of individual identity that allow you to have a sense of self within the context of a relationship. For instance, when you have your own profession, creative project, or a personal area of interest in which you maintain a sense of separate identity, it gives you confidence to be yourself and hold to your own views in the relationship. Do those things that assist you in establishing your own identity, and still be able to have a nurturing relationship.

Assertiveness

Because of a fear of not being right, you allow mates and associates to make all the decisions. You have learned in the past to value the decisions of others over your own. You also tend to attract strong-willed people who are very assertive.

We always draw to us what we need to learn, and if the energy from your mannerisms tells the universe that you are lacking in assertiveness, the universe will send people and situations to you that will force you to incorporate this quality into your being.

It is up to you whether you learn from this or allow yourself to be suppressed by it. In order to survive, you will either learn to assert yourself or "buckle under" to the will of the other person. Either way, the issue of self-assertion will be uppermost in your mind.

You are extremely uncomfortable around raised voices and any form of anger, but you've come to practice asserting yourself when you are right. You are also breaking the habit of backing away from what you want when someone raises his or her voice.

Self-Trust

You are learning that might is not always right and that it is okay to go after what you want. It is not healthy to step aside because someone else wants the same thing you do; you need to learn this assertiveness so you can compete successfully in the world. So strong is your fear of rejection and defeat that when any kind of competition arises, your inclination is to concede. It's important for you to realize that you may have to compete for some of the things you want.

A cause, game, or object cannot say, "I belong to you, come and take me"; you first have to recognize it as a goal and then have the assertiveness to go after it. Part of self-trust involves overcoming the obstacle of being so afraid of losing that you don't get in the running.

The only humiliation in competing comes from not even trying. Once you understand this, you can overcome your fear of competition and learn to enjoy it.

New Beginnings

You are learning not to be afraid to start over. The Aries energy is one of new beginnings. This ability to begin anew must be incorporated into your soul growth pattern. When you need to know all the facts and figures before making any decision, new beginnings can be extremely difficult for you.

In any new beginning there is an element of the unknown. You are learning to trust that you can handle what is ahead. Until you learn to trust the self, life will be a series of forced new beginnings. These forced new beginnings probably seem to occur without rhyme or reason. You may find yourself continually going down dead-end streets, as in going to work for a company that then soon goes into bankruptcy; taking a job that is in the process of being phased out; getting involved in relationships that can't possibly work; forming friendships with people who are about to move.

You only go down dead-end streets, however, when you follow what other people offer rather than getting in touch with the spark within and following those options that make you feel energized inside. When you learn to do what you want—finding those projects and relationships that charge your battery—you will find you are instinctively attracted to those situations that will not let you down.

There will be no relief to the pattern of dead-end streets until you learn that on a subconscious level you already know what you need to do and you have enough faith in yourself to go out in the world without fear of competition and rejection. You must have the courage of your convictions and enough trust in yourself to be able to stand up and try again if something doesn't work out.

Self-trust is the most important lesson for you to learn. Once you develop this attitude, there is very little that you cannot achieve.

Step 1: Unconscious Expression

FALSE INDEPENDENCE

Through your fear of rejection you can manifest a false state of independence, pushing away those people who could be most valuable to you. You may feel that if you push them away first, you won't have to deal with them walking out on you later. Once you learn not to fear your ability to handle whatever life offers, you can allow yourself to be vulnerable enough to receive life's pleasures.

You have come to learn the value of independence in this lifetime. A previous existence of overdependency on others causes you try to connect in unhealthy ways with those around you, not setting your path in motion toward independence. If you indulge this tendency, you will always feel held down by the desires, wants, and needs of others.

If you operate at this unconscious level, you will find very little personal freedom in this lifetime—restrictions and repressions will arise all around you. When this occurs you may externalize intense anger, which can be seen by the trained eye as a volcano on the verge of erupting. In this mode you can develop tremendous amounts of aggression and are capable of a great deal of violence.

SUPPRESSED ANGER

At the same time, you fear anger and external displays of hostility. You may fear standing up for yourself, yet harbor an anger that tends to surface in the wrong places. It often manifests around people who are less powerful than you, as with children, or in restaurants with waiters or waitresses in response to slow service or bad food.

This anger will surface everywhere except where it should: in the relationship in which you have allowed yourself to become dependent. It may be at work or in your marriage—any area of your life where you are letting others do for you what you should be doing for yourself. You suppress this anger, for it is caused by fear of losing that particular situation or person. But the anger comes out in those situations where you feel in control and have no fear of loss. You need to learn to confront and handle anger and resentment at the source.

In so doing, you will harmonize the other areas of your life. One of the better ways to learn to handle anger is by recognizing your great need to master the energy of assertiveness, and realizing that the anger is undirected, unharnessed assertiveness.

Once you embrace self-confidence, you can use your assertive energy to pursue your own direction. Until then you may find yourself allowing others to take what they want while you feel resentful.

PAST-LIFE INFLUENCE

Your mate gave you everything you wanted. In your present existence, you now find that there's only the self to rely on. If you are to have any of your heart's desires, you must be self-sufficient. This means that you must learn to be assertive enough and have enough faith in yourself to compete in life's arena for what brings you happiness.

SELF-NEGATION

You have no faith or trust in yourself. From this lack of self-trust can spring a tendency to lie to yourself and to others. This occurs when you have allowed others to dominate your life and make decisions for you. You then program yourself not to have the confidence, faith, and trust to make your own decisions.

Unconsciously, you have taught yourself that you are not capable of seeing truth. The problem compounds itself when the subconscious does not allow this negative thought to enter, but counteracts it by lying to the self, so that when you twist it around, a false idea becomes your truth. You may twist truths in a self-defeating way, project fears, or act from a base of unwarranted insecurities. You therefore experience mixed signals within because you are not in touch with what is truth and what is not.

One of the pitfalls of the unconscious Aries lunar eclipse can be the way you form relationships. You tend to put others on pedestals, whether it be your boss, your lover, a friend, an employee, or your child. And when that "other" does not function the way you feel he or she should, the pedestal comes tumbling down. Unfortunately, you are usually standing underneath and get hurt. Then, in a burst of anger that can reach extremes of violence, you chastise the person for not living up to your expectations. This pushes people farther away from you, thereby forcing you to take the negative path to your ultimate goal of independence.

TRUTH VERSUS NONTRUTH

Recognize that you need to function independently—not necessarily solo but as a leader. It is not your role to push people out ahead but to lead the way. Your expectations have to be of yourself, not of others. It is imperative that you learn to discern between truth and nontruth.

You achieve this by following your inner voice and learning to trust the self, thereby reprogramming the subconscious to tell the truth always. In the beginning this process can be difficult because your subconscious is programmed to do the opposite. As the subconscious learns that you are ready to accept the truth, it starts projecting with more honesty. But when you first begin to turn things around, there are some gray areas, and you must have the courage to come through these unknown spaces. Once those with this eclipse pattern pass through the gray and into the light, very few ever return to darkness.

Step 2: Conscious Expression

RECOGNIZING YOUR SPECIAL NEED FOR INDEPENDENCE

Operating consciously, you recognize your need to become independent in this lifetime. You realize that it is easier for you to become dependent on others than it is to become self-sufficient. To overcome this you tend to push yourself to be independent and sometimes reject honest assistance. You are learning how to accept help along the way without falling back into past patterns of dependency.

You are usually more comfortable working for yourself than working for another because you are still overcoming a fear of being overly influenced by others. When you learn to trust yourself and to relate with others from a place of strength, you can become very successful in business: Your need to achieve can be a driving force.

You tend to push out into the world and away from the shelter of home and family. You recognize this as a potential weakness for you and deliberately aspire to overcome it. You are likely a very driven, success-oriented, achievement-oriented person. You need to be careful not to push yourself into being an overachiever or workaholic. In your desire to prove your self-worth and become independent, you can suffer from periods of physical burnout. While it is good to push yourself in the direction of achievement, it is not necessary for all the achievement to happen immediately!

You have an ability to recognize truth within yourself and within those around you. Once you have pushed yourself from the nest, you tend to move too quickly and be intolerant of those who learn more slowly. It is important not to lose your sensitivities as you push outward.

As you make your way through life and find your place in the world, you almost always take a stand for the oppressed and truly want to aid all those who are struggling for survival. You work extremely well in areas that call for devotion to principles and in assisting those who need help; you are a friend to those who need to be shown the light or the way to find a new beginning.

STANDING UP FOR YOURSELF

You are learning to stand up for yourself in all life situations. You are breaking a past pattern of being so fearful of rejection and being proven wrong that you were afraid to speak up when your opinion was different from others. Now you are looking to become the best you possibly can be and to feel pride in yourself. You find it necessary to speak up when you are in disagreement with others.

Operating consciously, you recognize the value of developing inner strength. You find it is easier to express your feelings than to live with yourself when you don't. Though it is important that you express yourself, it is also important to learn to think before you talk. To be truly able to speak with the courage of your convictions, you must be firm within your own belief.

Your opposite polarity, Libra, needs to have all the facts before expressing; as a newly emerging Aries, you must learn from your counterpart to look before you leap. If you can retain the qualities of both—the assertiveness of the Aries and the tact of the Libra—you will be well suited on your journey.

As you progress you find yourself exhilarated by the thought of a new beginning, but also fearful of being able to handle it. Yet so strong is the desire to learn to trust the self that you will go through a series of new beginnings until you master the qualities of strength and inner trust. Then the urge to push yourself into new beginnings dissipates, since you are secure, no matter where you are. You know that you can move on at any time if you become uncomfortable.

Step 3: Transpersonal Expression

You have incarnated with the group consciousness of raising the vibration of the planet. You have a sense that many of your fellow beings have lost sight of their origins. You teach renewed faith and trust through your childlike naiveté that all is working according to universal plan.

In this existence you share faith with all your fellow beings, trusting everyone as if all are members of the same family, for you understand that we truly are.

RECOGNIZING OTHERS' WEAKNESSES WITHOUT JUDGING IT

You look upon society as children not yet grown, still learning the rules, regulations, and social amenities of the universe. Yours is a lifetime of teaching—through the way you live—that ours is a family whose members must have as much faith in one another as we have in the God of our consciousness. You teach that unless we support and assist one another, there will always be someone missing at family reunion time.

As a joyful, playful soul, you teach us to love our brothers and sisters, for you have incarnated as the original life source (fresh from the source), still able to see good and innocence in all. You can show us all the spark of light from within.

Physical Integration

You need to listen to your body in the areas of the head, face, and left eye. When you are not consciously learning your lessons or teaching what you promised to teach, there can be a tendency toward weakness in the muscle of the left eye. It may twitch. You may bang your head when you are not paying attention and refusing to listen to your own inner voice. This is all part of your lesson of learning to pay attention and trust your inner self.

If you go for extended periods of time without listening, you can suffer from headaches, from a dull throb to a migraine, depending on how neglectful you have become. When you devalue your own ideals and put too much energy into the ideas of those around you, thereby neglecting the self, you may find yourself urinating frequently or suffering from lower back pains. This is a warning system you have devised to force yourself to pay more attention to your own needs.

☿

TAURUS

SOLAR ECLIPSE: WHAT YOUR SOUL CONTRACTED TO TEACH OTHERS

(In order to fully activate your solar eclipse energy in Taurus, it may be helpful to you to read the lunar eclipse in Taurus section. You may find information that can help you more fully contribute your solar eclipse in Taurus gifts.)

Your Mission

In this incarnation, you are teaching your fellow beings about a proper prosperity consciousness. You have incarnated with a very solid sense of moral, financial, and spiritual values, and tend to draw to you people who need to have their value systems realigned; for example, people having financial difficulties who need to learn to handle their resources properly and to build solid financial foundations.

You understand intuitively that you can climb high only if you have a firm foundation to support you. This is why you can teach those around you how to make sure that every brick has been laid securely and mortared in before they take the next step.

Choosing to Withhold Your Knowledge of Prosperity

You may choose not to share your knowledge and refuse to teach the basic economic structure that you understand so well. Result: You may experience the negative repercussions within your own family. You may be exposed to a wife, husband, son, daughter, father, or mother who has severe financial difficulties. Or, you or someone close to you may have to experience personal bankruptcy.

You are only responsible to teach this lesson through your own example. If you choose to take it a step further, however, and actually assist others with your financial understanding, you are sharing yourself beyond the call of duty, which will lead to your own lessons being eased in other areas.

What is important is for you to keep your sense of value amid the financial havoc that you find all around you. Through this alone you teach people a stronger sense of security and financial patience. Very often you tend to draw to you people who are very impatient with finances; through your example of slowly and securely accomplishing your financial goals, you help to teach them patience. As everything falls apart, those around you recognize that you are still standing on solid ground. Thus, you help others to recognize the value of building on solid ground, and you can assist them in adding security to their lives.

If you choose to teach the lesson of finances in a negative way, you will create havoc in the financial lives of those close to you. If you choose to teach the value of finances on a positive level, you can be of great assistance to your family and associates. You can be extremely intuitive in knowing which investments will reap a profit. Others can benefit greatly if you help them plan for their future in a practical manner that allows room for growth, while retaining a strong foundation.

You do not take risks with anyone's resources. You are not one of the gamblers of the zodiac—you are a builder.

Moral Values

You may choose to teach the lesson of moral values negatively. Result: You will be viewed as a person of low moral character. You may cause disappointment and pain to those around you through lack of a proper value system. But even if you choose this path, you still teach the most negative expression of all by setting yourself up as an example of self-destruction.

If you teach moral values in a positive way, you will set a personal example with an impeccable reputation. In this mode you are extremely monogamous, loyal, family oriented, and concerned with family security and home stability. Due to your strong moral fiber and your stability within your family and community, you are usually found in a position of responsibility and high esteem.

You are also here to teach the importance of having strong spiritual values. You may choose to teach spiritual responsibility in a negative way. Result: You will show yourself as a person having no regard for the collective consciousness or the God-consciousness within yourself. Thus, you will not respect yourself or those around you, and will work only for what you want, not for the good of all concerned.

If you teach this lesson positively, you can show that the thread of universal consciousness and the need to work for the most good for the most people must begin within your own family and extend out to the rest of humanity. You teach that the respect you use in dealing with your fellow beings directly correlates to your own personal sense of self-respect and respect for the universe. You truly can be of spiritual value to those whose lives you touch.

The negative expressions are rare cases in this eclipse pattern, since the majority have been born with an advanced consciousness. You usually choose to teach your lessons by your own good example, by strengthening the values of others, and by being a worthwhile asset to the world.

Recognizing True Value

You can validate the good you see in others, thereby strengthening their positive direction. You naturally recognize the value in everything. Most important, you intuitively understand the worth of the human spirit, the human heart, and the human desire that prods us all to achievement.

Through understanding this value and appreciating your fellow beings, you teach others to treasure themselves. If you do not value yourself, you cannot achieve anything because you think you are not worthy of the achievement.

Quite often in your lifetime you will meet people who are down on their luck and have very little feeling of self-worth. You have the ability to assist them in finding their sense of value from the core of their own being. With sensitivity and patience you can put them in contact with their own inner beauty, the essence of the God-consciousness within. Then, through logic and perseverance, you can aid them in removing the debris that has hidden their true value.

Career Choices

Your innate appreciation for the natural beauty of the Earth allows you to walk on its surface and experience its peaceful nourishment. You are very much in touch with all the senses of the body; through your enjoyment you teach and inspire others to enjoy their senses as well. You would be an excellent artist, for you can physically manifest your appreciation of beauty, art, and nature, thus enabling others to appreciate the beauty you see in all that surrounds us. You are a sculptor, builder, engineer, or architect—if only with sand on the beach. You were born to mold.

Your career choices: You would do well as a loan officer, financial advisor, accountant, bookkeeper, office controller, or a position in the building or financial industries. With your natural ability to understand financial resources, choosing one of these avenues affords you a place to offer your services where you can be of maximum benefit to your fellow beings. Any field that requires building a solid foundation can benefit from your talents.

If you choose not to help others professionally in these areas, you will still be teaching those around you the value of having a strong foundation. You understand in your home life as well as in your business life what it means to say, "The buck stops here."

LUNAR ECLIPSE: WHAT YOUR SOUL IS LEARNING TO EMOTIONALLY EMBRACE

Your Mission

In this incarnation, your lesson is to develop a proper prosperity consciousness.

Past-Life Influence

You are coming from a previous existence that was extremely spiritual but materially poverty-stricken. Some of you took vows of poverty in past incarnations in order to focus your energy fully on your spiritual development. Thus, you came into this incarnation with the false idea that money and spirituality are never to blend.

You studied a great deal on the spiritual level, and exposure to those who misused resources taught you to distrust anyone who had money. Consequently, during this existence you may tend to self-destruct where finances are concerned.

Many of you recognize that your quest is to learn how to handle money, and you have a strong desire and need for it. Yet due to this self-destruct mechanism, when you reach a state of comfort you may do something on a subconscious level to destroy your financial position so you can feel good about yourself spiritually.

You may have misused other people's resources and did not give adequate service for what you charged. In order to overcome a feeling of guilt and a fear of overcharging for your services, you tend to undercharge in this lifetime. You need to understand that in undercharging you are overcompensating and actually stealing from yourself. To bring this into balance, you need to realize that the appropriate fee to charge is the equivalent value of the services rendered.

Combining Spirituality and Money

You are here to learn that money can have spiritual power. When you allow your spirituality to manifest through good works that support your fellow beings, money is a natural by-product of that service. Part of your lesson is to learn that money is not a negative; money is simply another aspect of life that needs to be mastered.

You have mastered how to have nothing and still keep a proper spiritual consciousness. In this lifetime it is your turn to learn how to have. You are discovering that having money isn't what matters; it is what you do with the money and the ways in which you obtain it.

You are learning to recognize that it is all right to have. The universe is concerned only with how you acquire what you have and what you do with it. Your job is to learn to manifest the abundance of the universe and feel free to have and enjoy the comforts of life.

Self-Worth Is Not Measured by Money

You need to learn not to measure your self-worth or the worth of others by their wealth or material possessions. This would be a negative pattern for you, since any judgment you pass on others limits your own sense of freedom and self-worth.

You are learning how to have without judging those around you. You still want to keep your spiritual values, yet you recognize that everyone is walking a different path and that this time your path leads to material prosperity. Now it is time for you to learn to accept money and allow it to validate your efforts and the spiritual energy that you are sharing. You are learning that it is natural for the universe to reward you with money when you give service to others.

Appropriate Sexual Behaviors

In learning to relate morally with others, you may draw to you those who have very poor morals, and you may be used sexually by others. Or, in the reverse, you can regress into past-life patterns and become sexually abusive yourself, having no regard for the other's feelings before entering into a sexual encounter.

Learning to appreciate the wants, needs, and desires of another helps you to eliminate patterns where you think only of self-gratification. Through this process you also become more in touch with your own sexual needs and desires. By learning to interpret correctly the responses of your partner, you can become an extremely sensual person in this existence, mastering the ability to bring pleasure to yourself and your partner. As you learn and grow and accept moral responsibility for your interactions with others, you learn to feel better about yourself and your physical body.

If you choose to learn these lessons negatively, it brings discord into your existence, including the financial aspect of your life, thus creating financial stress. Moral, financial, and spiritual values are all interconnected parts of your life process and your lesson.

On a spiritual level, you are learning to overcome a previous pattern of misusing your spiritual energies. You may have indulged in a direct misuse of power, such as misinforming others about spiritual awareness or psychic insights for the sake of material gain. In this existence you are learning the value of being honest in your spiritual communications to others. You are holding yourself accountable and working off the debt of using others inappropriately, either by taking what did not belong to you or by encouraging others to form a dependency on you for financial rewards.

Spiritual Prosperity Consciousness Brings Balance

In this learning process you are seeking a point of equilibrium from which you do not misuse others and yet do not cheat yourself by giving everything away. You are learning to develop a proper spiritual prosperity consciousness by recognizing the value in everything and everyone, including yourself. You can balance any guilt for prior lifetimes of misusing money and people by consciously using your power in this lifetime to validate your own self-worth and that of others.

You have entered into this existence with an extremely low sense of self-esteem. You are learning to build up your feelings of self-worth and to feel better about yourself. It is very important for you to validate yourself and to accept recognition from others. Your challenge: to give yourself an opportunity to receive the positive reinforcement that benefits you so greatly.

You need to know that you are a valuable asset to humankind; that there is a reason for you to be living other than to eat, sleep, and work; and that your fellow human beings care about you. You can learn to feel better about yourself by helping others and by accepting the verbal and financial gratitude of those you aid. The more self-esteem you feel, the more valuable you become to those around you.

Get in touch with the physical body and the pleasures of physically living in a body on the Earth plane. You will learn to understand about the Earth and the soil. As you learn all about Mother Earth, you discover that just by putting your hands into the ground you feel a sense of belonging. You can smell and appreciate the sweetness of the air you breathe.

Grounding and Appreciation

You are learning: to be aware of the air entering your nostrils and feeding your body; to feel the earth beneath your feet; to appreciate the consistency of the ground you walk on, the soil that brings forth the life that sustains you; to appreciate the fruits of the Earth—even, on a sensual level, the taste of the foods the Earth offers; to look upon the world and appreciate the vastness of its beauty.

You are beginning to hear the sounds and harmony of nature. Through this learning process you will be able to recognize how much the Earth plane offers you in terms of your soul growth. In return, you will pay homage to the Earth by learning to use its resources and enhance its beauty, especially in your own surroundings. By being in touch with nature you find an awareness that is very personally gratifying. Through getting in touch with all your physical senses, you learn what gives you pleasure. This empowers you to teach others the value of taking pleasure from the Earth plane. You are helping those around you to develop a deep, healthy connection with the physicality of the Earth.

Step 1: Unconscious Expression

BLOCKING PROSPERITY

On an unconscious level, you can defeat the purpose of your life lesson by blocking the flow of prosperity. You have come to learn a positive prosperity consciousness, but if you do not allow yourself to develop a secure base for your resources, you will find that you constantly have to reestablish yourself financially.

You are driven to succeed financially, yet you find yourself losing touch with your original plan, failing to build a secure enough foundation, and rushing off to fill your financial desires too quickly. Those with this eclipse are prone to experiences of bankruptcy. You tend not to value the self enough to feel deserving of achievement.

In past lives: You had a spiritual nature. You are aware of wanting to be of great value to your fellow beings in this lifetime, but when unconscious you forget to allow yourself the financial reimbursement due for your services.

FALSE NOTIONS ABOUT MONEY

Those of you who have chosen to learn your financial lessons the hard way may go through life thinking that money is the answer to all your problems. As you feed this negative thought process, you begin to judge those around you by their material possessions. Some of you have an ability to accumulate abundant resources, but due to this judgmental thought process you may find that the money and material possessions you acquire do not bring internal happiness.

If you continue judging yourself and others by these standards, it can put you in a negative frame of mind and expose you to very ruthless people, the kind who use others at their weakest point. If you avoid developing the proper prosperity consciousness, you rob yourself of the pleasures of life, no matter how much wealth you accumulate. It is necessary for you not only to accumulate resources but to develop moral and spiritual values.

While you may be aware that it is necessary for you to accumulate material resources in this lifetime, you still may feel that this somehow makes you unscrupulous. Because of this misconception you may set limitations on yourself, and when you reach a certain point, you unconsciously undermine your success. You may make poor investments or, through poor judgment, walk away from everything you have accumulated. Then you must start all over.

You are capable of starting over, but as time goes on this becomes a tiring process, and with each new beginning you have less motivation and experience less success. This may continue until you finally recognize what a proper prosperity consciousness is all about. Then you can also reevaluate your moral and spiritual values and develop a more sharing attitude toward others. This approach in turn opens you to receiving more material abundance.

CON ARTIST TEMPTATION

On an unconscious level there's a tendency to be a manipulative, scheming con artist when it comes to dealing with other people's resources. This can occur if you neglect your lesson of learning to develop your own resources. You are among the souls who have lost confidence, to the extent that their basic morality has been affected. This particular group can stoop to the most socially unacceptable levels when it comes to financial, moral, or spiritual values.

Some of you can be complete social outcasts. Fearing that you can't do it on your own, you become parasites, feeding off others for your very survival. Manipulative tactics degrade both yourself and others, and undermine the very lessons you came to learn. In these cases, you must undertake a total reevaluation, since you must begin to form proper behavior patterns that allow you to respect yourself again. Once you have reversed the negative process and you begin to value yourself, you can find your way back to social acceptability.

Step 2: Conscious Expression

Operating consciously, you recognize that this is the lifetime to reevaluate and reestablish yourself in the spiritual, financial, and physical realms.

PAST-LIFE INFLUENCE

You are coming from previous existences in which there was an over-abundance of spiritual teachings and a nonattachment to material and physical reality. To balance your growth, in this incarnation you have come to learn how to acquire material things that bring physical comfort and serenity, and to realize that it is not negative to enjoy being in your body. You are learning that it is not wrong to acquire what you want and enjoy having it.

You are developing the understanding that the universe does not care if you go to the river of life with a teaspoon or a bucket. The universe will fill whatever size container you bring, as long as you fulfill your needs while still respecting the self and those around you. There is no negativity in abundance if the resources are honorably gained and honorably used.

MONEY: A WEALTH OF SOLUTIONS ALL AROUND YOU

As you walk through life there may be financial problems, and you will have the opportunity to learn that with each new problem there is a new solution. As you remain open to the guidance that surrounds you, you will gain an understanding of how to build the foundations necessary to achieve financial stability in this lifetime. You can then begin to build this base and acquire great wealth.

Not all of you have a need for great amounts of money, but all have a need to understand the place that money has in the universal scheme. You must come to understand that you govern money—it does not rule you. Those who are conscious accept this reality and free themselves from the misconceptions of the past. Your previous belief system was that having wealth left a person attached to the physical plane and therefore unable to connect with the God presence within. This is a basic misconception you are learning to release through your process of acquiring and enjoying material things without being attached to them.

SEXUAL AND MORAL VALUES

You are also learning about your sexual values and sensuality in relation to your moral values. Past lifetimes of overindulgence on a physical level or a total abstinence of sexual participation have left you with a need to feel, sense, and become comfortable with physical pleasure. By learning to appreciate the senses of the physical body you can bring into balance your tendency to extreme physical behavior. You are learning about the senses themselves and how to be comfortable and appropriate within a physical body.

You have spent many incarnations either abusing yourself physically or totally ignoring your physical body. Now you must find a happy medium. With a need for physical gratification comes a need for moral responsibility. When you consciously recognize that both of these needs must be satisfied, you will work on developing your sensuality while staying aware of the social and moral repercussions of your behavior.

Step 3: Transpersonal Expression

You are here to develop the group consciousness of your fellow beings on the moral and financial levels. You teach us that we all are jointly responsible—morally, financially, and physically—for one another, and you show us how to interact and depend on one another in appropriate ways. You are also teaching us how to appreciate the Earth and its value—not only as the mother that sustains our lives but as a valuable and integral part of the universe.

Through your natural ability to appreciate the value in all things and all persons, you help others to appreciate the value in themselves. You are extremely logical and have an innate sense of appreciation for all that is valuable in both the physical and spiritual realms. You can share these insights in simple ways that enable even children to expand their awareness.

AWARENESS OF THE PHYSICAL WORLD

You are acutely aware of the body, mind, and soul principles as they are activated by walking through a physical existence. You understand your relationship to the Earth plane and gladly accept the stability the Earth offers. When you feel the need to rebalance yourself, you can be found with your hands in the soil, for you have an intuitive awareness that this will put you back in touch with physical reality and with your internal balance.

You understand that until we accept our physical reality we cannot truly set ourselves free from it. The Earth dimension will continue to pull us back until we have learned to appreciate and enjoy it.

You are teaching humankind that until we totally understand and respect the physical body—the plane that gives us life—we cannot free ourselves from coming back to experience another lifetime on the physical plane. You are also teaching the value of the physical plane in relation to the value of the spiritual plane, helping others to understand their interdependency; the value of appreciation and its ability to free us from physical attachment.

Physical Integration

When you resist the lessons you have chosen to learn in this lifetime, you will find that the body communicates to you through the senses. You may find that the ear, neck, and throat areas become extremely sensitive when you are allowing your prosperity consciousness to slip. The skin may produce rashes when you do not allow yourself to experience physical comfort, since the skin is connected to the sense of feeling. The ears may be prone to infections or other irritations when you are not listening to others. The throat may become sore and/or there may be a tendency toward sores in the mouth when you fail to appreciate the sense of taste. The eyes may become swollen and irritated if you resist the foresight you need for success. The nose may become overly sensitive and prone to allergic reactions when you do not remember to value the self.

During your process of growth it would be wise to pay attention to these areas, for through watching the body you can learn things you are not able to perceive intellectually. The senses are most easily sent off balance in this eclipse pattern while you are learning about the senses.

You also need to be mindful of the thyroid—it can become either over- or underactive, depending on how intensely you pursue the lessons of becoming comfortable within your physical body. The ears, neck, and throat areas should be watched most closely when your prosperity consciousness is out of balance, since these are the areas that communicate when your value system needs alignment. By watching these areas for early symptoms you can avoid many obstacles in your life.

$$\text{II}$$

GEMINI

SOLAR ECLIPSE: WHAT YOUR SOUL CONTRACTED TO TEACH OTHERS

(In order to fully activate your solar eclipse energy in Gemini, it may be helpful to read the lunar eclipse in Gemini section. You may find information that can help you more fully contribute your solar eclipse in Gemini gifts.)

Your Mission

In this incarnation, you are teaching your fellow beings the value of communication.

Additionally, you have the ability to understand the importance of the spoken and written word, and one of your responsibilities in this lifetime is to keep information circulating. You have the natural ability to say the right thing at the right time, and you can talk to anyone about anything.

You have a knack for being in the right place at the right time to hear specific information that is needed by someone else. The information that you share with others can change the direction of their lives. Through you they come to understand that they are in total control of their ability to communicate and that they must take responsibility for the frame of mind they allow themselves to have.

As a natural teacher you have the ability to stimulate mental growth processes in others. Through your command of your native language, you awaken in those around you a desire to develop their mental abilities. During this process, those you touch come to understand their fellow beings better and to broaden their consciousness. Thus, you bring the lesson of brotherhood to your social environment and teach us all to deal with one another in a more caring way.

Teaching Freedom of Movement

On some levels you are teaching freedom of movement. You find confinement difficult since you are the storyteller, the jester, the town crier. Part of the uniqueness you offer is levity and a clear direction of consciousness, through teaching others to see the humor within their own being. You have an ability to laugh and to create a change in an atmosphere that could otherwise block communication and understanding between people because of too much severity.

Your eclipse pattern is responsible for humankind's moving about the Earth and interacting with one another in larger numbers than ever before. This broadening of the circle comes from your insatiable need for more information; it keeps you searching far afield and constantly expanding your environment.

You are like the child whose first environment is limited to the home and then broadens to the school and to the neighborhood. Eventually the child grows up and goes away to college, then moves out into the business world, into a relationship, and to another city. Everything is continually expanding so more experience can be assimilated, and you teach the value of this process to others.

This lesson may be taught either positively or negatively; the choice is yours, but the lesson will be taught. You may teach the value of extended horizons, increased communications, alert awareness, and flexible mental abilities by setting an example and taking an expansive approach to how you live your life. Or you may teach these lessons by being an example of what not to do through negative personality traits such as rigidity, improper social behavior, belittling others by making fun of them, and burying yourself in activities without sharing what you are learning.

The Value of Multiple Experiments

You understand intuitively that life is too short for you to become a master in any of the many areas you want to experience. You have chosen in this incarnation not to master any one field, but to experience and taste a bit of everything.

You are teaching those around you the value of having a vast number of experiences, and at the same time, introducing others to these experiences. This allows the people you come into contact with to choose the directions in which they want to broaden their minds. You help people realize that there are more horizons and perspectives than they might originally have been able to see. Actually, you are teaching others to stop, look, listen, and investigate what the options are before setting themselves too firmly in any one place. You are helping people to recognize their choice and to make educated decisions, and not fix themselves in such rigid mind-sets that they can't change course.

You are opening your fellow beings to the perception that they can experience more than one lesson or one set of lessons in a lifetime. You help them to realize that there is no end to the learning experience, just as there is no end to the universe—it is constantly expanding. You help to set us free and teach us that there are more places to go, more knowledge to gain, more information to pass on. It is a never-ending cycle, and you open up our consciousness to the awareness of this concept of infinity.

LUNAR ECLIPSE: WHAT YOUR SOUL IS LEARNING TO EMOTIONALLY EMBRACE

Your Mission

In this incarnation, you are learning how to communicate about the correct use of language and appropriate social behavior.

You are learning not to take things for granted or assume that others perceive things the same way you do. In the process of honoring this lesson, you must depart from your past-life hermit consciousness and embark on a path of

social awareness. In order to integrate your lessons, you must align your consciousness with that of your fellow beings so you can share the knowledge you
have gained in previous existences.

In your journey through life you come to recognize that others seem to
misunderstand your communications. Why? Accustomed to living within your
own mind, you often do not realize that your internal thought processes have
not been expressed verbally. Having thought about something, you sometimes
think you have said it when you haven't. Then you get frustrated because
someone didn't act on it.

Asking for Feedback

To eliminate the frustration of being misunderstood, you need to see if
what you said—or thought you said—was clearly understood. You are learning that communication is more than verbalization; it has to do with the clear,
effective giving and receiving of information.

When people are able to tell you what they have heard, this will ease your
frustration and teach you how to be more articulate. As you learn to communicate more effectively you will be able to reduce the number of times you
solicit feedback.

Fear Makes You Stop Listening

Although you know intuitively that in this lifetime you must learn to relate with society, you still feel fearful. This is because you do not yet trust your
own mental abilities and the soundness of your belief systems. You think that
if you interact too much with others, their views and opinions may rub off on
you. You fear that you can be too easily swayed from your own mental process
and ideas by the communications of others. You are so easily distracted that
as a defense mechanism, you sometimes block out others and don't hear what
they have to say at all.

You also tend to verbalize what you want to have happen instead of what
is actually going on. This is because you want to program only positive information. You must learn that sometimes you need the negative information in
order to put yourself on a positive path!

You are learning to accept the awareness of what is transpiring and the
reason for being in an existence in which you need social interaction. The purpose is to accelerate your own growth process while on the physical plane. And
if you refuse to integrate the so-called negative side of things, then you won't
have the information you need for your own future growth.

Learning When to Say No

As you learn to be sociable, you must understand how people are seeing you so you can adjust your behavior and learn to participate more appropriately in social situations. This isn't something that you were born knowing how to do, but it is particularly important for you to integrate this information into your personality. You often think that being gracious means saying everything nice, while sometimes being gracious means saying "thank you, but no." Or, "No thank you, but may I take a rain check?" Or, simply give the logical, factual reason behind your no, and ask if you could join them at another time.

It is truly more gracious to decline an invitation politely than to accept out of a fear that if you say no, the person will never invite you again. Fear may make you reflect too much sweetness and not enough honesty. It is not your intent to be dishonest; you just don't want to close any doors because you are aware of needing to learn how to interact socially in this lifetime.

As you become more open to learning from others how to socialize with mutually clear communication, you learn that there is a time to say no. This allows you to socialize in a more balanced way and also ensures that you have the time alone that you need. By not overcommitting, your lessons become easier and you avoid social blunders. By learning to say no, you can actually begin to enjoy socializing, for it is no longer a strain: You do it when you want to instead of out of fear.

Needing Time Alone

This is very important for you because when you feel that you have given too much of yourself to others and given away too much of your time—which you value so highly—you may find yourself trapped in a pattern of not showing up, not keeping your appointments, and being unreliable. When you learn to respect your need for time alone and simultaneously integrate the social awareness you are here to learn, you can balance both inner needs.

Another manifestation of this process can be seen in those of you who promise too much of your time, keep all your agreements, and then find yourselves feeling stressed, put upon, and exploited. In this pattern you may even become ill temporarily in order to gain the time alone that you need.

When you have learned to respect your needs, you can integrate your lesson of sociability with your desire to escape from the crowd. By facing both desires openly and communicating your needs to others honestly, you will be able to master the art of communication. This shows that you have learned to communicate with the self—and this is what you have come to learn. It is important to respect your desire to be alone and spend time going within. Through allowing yourself this time, you get in touch with the essence of your own being.

Past-Life Influence

You embodied a very monastic frame of mind. You walked a spiritual path, meditated in the mountains, or integrated a myriad of psychological and philosophical studies. Society has supported your personal spiritual growth in past lifetimes. In return you are bringing the value of all you have learned to your current existence. You have been allowed the gift of spending many lifetimes studying and going within to understand humankind's role on the universal level. For those who study long enough to reach this depth of perception, the gift must come full circle. Now you must find ways to share your knowledge for the good of all.

You have learned the common denominator, the common thread, that runs through all philosophy and all religion. You thereby have the ability to impart an unprejudiced attitude in your interactions with others. Your challenge is to find a way to share this information in the course of your everyday life.

This does not mean that you must stand on a soapbox and preach, but through your mannerisms, your lack of prejudice, and your understanding of theology you can impart this information to those around you. This will only be possible, however, if you have learned your lessons regarding appropriate social interactions. And because of the importance of what you have to share, including your soul awareness and your ability to understand a more universal consciousness, you must take the time to be sure that you are perceived properly and are not misunderstood.

Step 1: Unconscious Expression

FALSE COMMUNICATION

In this incarnation, you could become a pathological liar. You want good so badly in your life and you want so much to please everyone that you can't bring yourself to deal with harsh realities. Everything you say tends to be "flowered" to tell the other person exactly what he or she wants to hear. If you lie, you please the other person, if only for a short while. Even if you don't like the way someone looks, you say: "My, don't you look lovely." Then you feel the gratification of communicating something nice, seeing a smile, and getting pleasure back from the other person. You don't want to hear or communicate any negative thoughts.

You are learning to integrate your communication skills with society in this incarnation. Yet, due to fear of rejection, you sometimes lack the confidence to integrate any negative feedback from the outside. You need to communicate with yourself on a rational level in order to understand that negative response is not a personal rejection.

Accept the spoken word for what it is—information about how the speaker is perceiving something. Then you can see that in every communication there is the potential for growth and learning. Through being objectively receptive to the other person's communication, you can gain the facts you need to continue in your own growth. If you limit your communications only to positive information, there cannot be any growth, only unrelated, Pollyanna-style optimism. This pseudocommunication lacks the depth and honest interchange that leads to mutual growth.

FEELING CHEATED

At times you may feel like the world is cheating you. In defense you tend to take the initiative and do the cheating first. Sometimes you feel that because you work so hard you have the right to take what you want, even if it doesn't belong to you. The basis of this self-defeating pattern goes back to an unconscious belief that you must not rise above your father's station in life.

Thus, you may unconsciously circumvent your success, causing your downfall and putting yourself in situations where you have to do hard physical labor or work very hard to build your reputation. No sooner do you gain a reputation, however, than you do something to destroy it, and then you have to work very hard to get back on top again. Or else you change occupations often, starting new business and always having to build things up from the ground level.

You do this unconsciously because your abilities are so great that if you stayed in one profession you would eventually pass your father's level of success. In your belief system, the "father" is the pinnacle, and your subconscious will not allow you to outshine him. This is due to former existences when you studied theology and gained a tremendous respect for the God-Father. Now there is confusion between that ideal and your earthly father. This misconception on the subconscious level prevents you from seeing yourself on any level as better than your creator.

Through appropriate social interaction and growth in personal awareness, however, you can reestablish your spiritual path and recognize the proper place of love for the Father/father in your life. This frees you to become as successful as you desire in this existence. Then you will no longer feel as though you are being cheated as a result of unrewarded efforts, for you can at last allow yourself to succeed.

HONESTY IS CRUCIAL

It is crucial for you to learn to deal honestly on all levels of awareness and social interaction. If you choose to be dishonest, you separate yourself from the realm of responsible conscious awareness. This means that you would no longer be of any use to the spiritual planes for imparting the information and the consciousness you are to give to others during the later years of this existence.

During the first fifty-six years of life you are allowing the growth process to manifest and build your reputation, sense of social honor, and reliability. If you have established a reputation for being untrustworthy up to this point, you have obligated yourself to learn your lessons with more difficulty than necessary—possibly through social disgrace. If this occurs, it is because you have betrayed your own spirituality.

It is of the utmost importance that you maintain a reputation for honesty and good character. You must accomplish the integration of appropriate social skills by this point, including the development of gentle yet persuasive mannerisms, for it is through these abilities that you can share your spiritual consciousness effectively.

Step 2: Conscious Expression

In this mode, you begin to recognize when you are misunderstood and go about making sure that you are being clear. Education is extremely important to you, for this is the avenue through which you learn to articulate your thoughts and ideas effectively to others. You can also learn the art of communication by developing your writing skills. The physical nature of using pen and paper allows you to bring out your thought processes more clearly. This way of expression is less threatening for you at first than direct communication with others. Writing will help you gain confidence in your communication skills, at which point you will be better able to communicate in the context of social relationships.

MULTITASKING

You might find yourself working in a sales-oriented profession, possibly in customer service or a position in which you afford yourself an opportunity to communicate with people from all walks of life. You may spend a great deal of time reading all forms of printed material and literature, perhaps watching television and simultaneously reading the newspaper.

You are constantly busy and ask many questions. You recognize that your lesson is to learn the art of communication, so you pursue it by going directly to the source: the classroom, television, books, newspapers. You try to expose yourself simultaneously to all the worlds you did not have access to in the past. It is not uncommon for you to watch two, three, even four television programs at the same time, or to read four and five books, since this intensified communication process activates your mind.

Physical movement is also very important to you. It seems that due to confinement in previous existences, movement and the motion of the body accelerates your communicative skills and your whole developmental process in this lifetime.

Step 3: Transpersonal Expression

You are here to teach your fellow beings to communicate with one another, because the consciousness of humankind is in need of realignment. You are working to restore the clarity of communication that existed among all people before the biblical time of Babylon. At that time there was a rift in the consciousness of humankind: The various tribes were split into different tongues (languages) and could no longer communicate with one another. Your consciousness contains the necessary ingredients to reunite all languages, thought processes, and belief systems. In a way, your job is to heal the separation that happened through language in Babylon.

Your communication skills give you the ability to convey to others an understanding of the common thread running through all things in the universe. Operating from a humanitarian base, you can combine the discipline of communication with your sensitivity, manifesting the inspiration that allows others to recognize that they are one, yet separate. This awareness will lead to an interdependency based upon trust and faith in humankind that allows us to see the spiritual consciousness within all.

Physical Integration

If you choose not to learn the lessons of communication, you may experience difficulty with the lungs, the nervous system, and the hands, arms, and shoulders. The body will begin to communicate with you in basically the same way you are supposed to be learning to communicate—by dealing with issues that create or are created by blocks in communication. The nervous system communicates to the different areas of the body. The lungs process oxygen for the entire body, and the hands, arms, and shoulders reach out to communicate to others literally and through body language. Your body communicates with you by drawing your attention to these areas, reminding you that the lesson of communication is being blocked.

THE VALUE OF SELF-QUESTIONING

The way to understand and alleviate these symptomatic physical responses is to reevaluate the way you have been communicating in daily life. When these symptoms occur, ask yourself: Am I communicating everything—or am I holding back? Am I allowing my communications to flow forward, or am I blocking myself due to fear of rejection? Am I dealing with life honestly, or am I manipulating and making excuses so I will not have to deal with the other person's response to an area I feel has not yet been integrated properly in my own consciousness?

You can restore your psychological health and physical balance by recognizing that during this process, you must keep the communication flowing. Remain honest and verbal, remembering to include the other person's insights into your perspective at all times. By learning to see the world through the eyes of others, you become free inside yourself. By integrating the information others give to you on the psychological level, you set your body free, opening the channels of communication to your lungs and nervous system. When all channels of communication are kept open, energy can flow freely through the body, maintaining perfect balance and health within your being.

If in this process you tell yourself that the opinions of others are not useful, then you are unconsciously telling yourself that we are not interconnected but are all separate beings. The body receives the message that it is separate from the mind and the mind is separate from the soul, and so forth. Instead of functioning as a trinity, you begin to function as three separate people, which causes confusion and disorder within the body. Then the body is unable to communicate clearly within itself and send the proper messages to its different parts. Thus, your physical problems manifest mainly in the nervous system, which circulates energy and messages throughout the body.

When you learn to value the opinions of others and integrate what is appropriate, you are teaching your body to function as an integrated unit.

CANCER

SOLAR ECLIPSE: WHAT YOUR SOUL CONTRACTED TO TEACH OTHERS

(In order to fully activate your solar eclipse energy in Cancer, it may be helpful to read the lunar eclipse in Cancer section. You may find information that can help you more fully contribute your solar eclipse in Cancer gifts.)

Your Mission

In this incarnation, you are teaching people to understand, deal with, and express emotions—how to feel.

You are a healer who affects the emotional body of those around you. This helps those you aid to feel more stable and secure in dealing with their feelings. You tend to draw to you those who don't understand their emotional problems because they are too connected to the external world. When confronted with problems on the emotional level, these people don't know how to react. Often you unknowingly heal others by taking on the negativity of their emotional upsets. You have the ability to heal their emotions through absorbing the negativity into yourself, dissipating it, and then releasing the healed energy back into the universe.

As a natural healer you heal the emotions and the soul. You lighten people's hearts; by giving them a shoulder to cry on it relieves their emotional block, allowing the natural balance of their emotional body to emerge.

Your Covenant with the Universe

Your gift is to relieve your fellow beings of their emotional burdens and upsets. To facilitate this process, you have been granted the gift of being able to release this negativity back into the universe. The universe has promised to relieve your emotional burdens in return. You don't need anyone else to process them for you because, as you take on and release the emotional burdens of others, your own emotional burdens are released too.

You tend naturally to attract status quo, business-oriented, reputation-minded, "stiff upper lip" people, since these individuals are unable to throw away anything, even their own negativity, and thus need a receptacle in which to deposit their emotional hurts. Due to their business orientation, they naturally need everything to have a usefulness, and consequently they want even their emotional wounds transformed into something positive. You can facilitate this process.

Your best bet is to recognize and respect the pattern with which those you help are resonating. These are people with an accumulation consciousness, and they have difficulty realizing that the accumulation of emotional debris is a negative process. They must deposit their negative emotions somewhere, so they gravitate to you. It is your job to accept with maternal understanding the negativity of others and then to allow it to be dispersed into the universe.

The Self-Pity Trap

You may fall into the self-pity trap by not appropriately understanding the importance of your role in the universe. You are not supposed to become overly involved in the emotional lessons of those you help, but rather allow yourself to receive their burdens, share your empathy, and get on with your own life.

If you focus on people dumping on you instead of on the gift they are sharing, you can become an actual garbage pail instead of an emotional recycling plant. The universe gave you the job of listening to the emotional ills of others because you have the capacity to release emotional pain—both your own and that of other people. As you serve your universal function you are rewarded by being allowed to experience a great depth of closeness with many people.

The emotional support you provide is extremely important. If others do not find a way to release their emotional debris, they walk through life emotionally constipated and entirely shut off from their feelings. There is no room for their emotions to flow because they have created blockages, so they become cold, calculating, and very unemotional. You relieve these blocks in others, thereby restoring their capacity to feel. You can heal the emotional imbalance in others and simultaneously keep your own emotional flow active by reaching out to share.

Emotional Sensitivity

There is a nurturing energy surrounding you that automatically relaxes other people and makes them feel comfortable. You project the serenity of a calm lake as you become accustomed to your path and willingly take on the role of assisting others in emotional purification. On a spiritual level you are known as Earth mothers and Earth fathers.

You were born with a high degree of emotional sensitivity and need to form behavior patterns that keep your sensitivity in a positive mode. If you are unwilling to share the gift of your sensitivity with others, you may close down and become overly sensitive on a personal level. This can lead to defensive, emotionally exaggerated responses that keep you from the closeness with others that in your birthright.

Learning how to channel your own emotionally sensitivity is very important. When you are helping those who are emotionally out of balance, you can usually process their emotional negativity properly. But you sometimes tend to take others' upsets personally. This happens when you absorb the negativity into your body before the other person asks for emotional assistance.

Jumping in Too Quickly

Sometimes you do not give people a chance to become comfortable and sort out their own emotions before you intervene and try to resolve their upsets for them. They feel this to be an invasion of emotional privacy. You must learn to be more aware of whether those close to you are truly in need of and are seeking your assistance.

When you violate the freedom of others to process their emotions, it leads to situations where you feel defensive and your feelings get hurt. Because you are an emotional healer, you will attract people who are not in touch with their emotions. They need time to process their emotional entanglements. If you try to pull out their negative emotions before they have finished processing and are ready to release the feelings, you pull to yourself more pain than is necessary. You need to allow others the privacy of their emotions before you go in and try to yank them out; you are a receptacle, not an emotional surgeon.

Keeping Perspective

Be wary of allowing your feelings for others to interfere with your own process—your personal integrity, knowing what is right and wrong. When you allow yourself to feed on or overlook wrong action in those you are trying to help because you have no emotional bond with them, you end up retaining their negativity within your own being. On a physical level you may retain water if you restrict your activity and/or opinions due to your dependency on others or their dependency on you. Other people will simply dump their negativity. You must absorb the impact and then respond with your own true feelings about the situation.

It is your responsibility to be yourself, to express your feelings and natural responses regardless of what you anticipate the negative or hurtful reaction of other people will be. You need to absorb their negativity without feeling responsible for the distresses that people go through in their lives. Keeping this perspective allows you to maintain your own ethics, truly helping others to heal their emotions. It also helps you to prevent your own emotional attachments from getting in the way of the healing process. You need to remember that when other people are going through personal suffering, it is simply the universe's way of waking them up and putting them back into alignment with their true purpose.

LUNAR ECLIPSE: WHAT YOUR SOUL IS LEARNING TO EMOTIONALLY EMBRACE

Your Mission

In this incarnation, you are learning to successfully interact with others on an emotional level and to bring stability to your emotional body.

Your temperament contains an accumulated past-life residue of feeling that you have to perform, to be on top and in control of people and situations in order to be accepted by others on an emotional level. In your youth, you may have problems relating to your family because you don't understand your usefulness within the unit. You feel you must earn your way in order to achieve a feeling of belonging with others. In later years this can lead to difficulty in emotional situations if you don't learn to separate your ability to provide from your ability to experience emotional nourishment.

A Foreign Family

You have incarnated into a family you have never been with before, and you therefore feel uncomfortable within your own family unit. You have many lessons to learn about the emotions and the emotional responsibility family members have toward one another. Your discomfort forces you to learn to deal with your emotions. You can either learn to be responsible for your moods and attitudes, choosing not to create friction for those around you because of your extreme emotional sensitivity, or be at odds with everyone in the family and have to learn through constant emotional irritation.

One way to deal with your emotions is to become more aware of the effects your emotional outbursts have on those around you. Understand that everyone deals with emotions differently and has the right to emote in his or her own way. Being overly sensitive, you should refrain from making emotional judgments before digesting everything that has occurred in any given situation. You are learning not to take on feelings that don't belong to you; not to project that others are in a bad mood because of you; and not to feel that you have to defend your own existence because someone in your family is in a bad mood.

If you respond defensively to the moods of others, you annoy the very people with whom you are trying to learn your lessons. As the agitation gets stronger, you feel even less wanted, for you are so sensitive that you feel the annoyance of others and know when they don't want to be around you. But usually you are not in touch with the fact that your own defensive attitude is separating you from your family, not the true essence of who you really are.

Allow other family members emotional freedom and recognize their right to feel differently from you about any given thing. As you become less defensive, others will enjoy being around you, and the learning process can take a positive course that is less painful for everyone involved.

Security Needs

Prior soul memories of tremendous success in business, management, and worldly affairs simultaneously accompanied a neglect of family interaction and warmth. Overemphasis on business and neglect of the family have created an imbalance that necessitates your making emotions a top priority in this life-time. Although you are loved by your family, quite often you don't recognize it because you do not know what emotions feel like. You are here to break the pattern of walking away from emotional situations and hiding in the outside world.

You tend to feel isolated even when with others until you gain a sense of belonging within yourself. One of your first lessons is to learn to be comfortable and centered within your own body so that you can feel emotionally secure when in the company of others. Once you feel that sense of belonging, you will begin to sense your own value in relationships with others. Then you will feel secure enough to confront issues and situations instead of sidestepping everything. When you reach the point of allowing yourself to be cared for, you are well on the road to learning your lessons.

All the fears you have about coming out of your emotional shell are the result of not knowing this inner sense of security. Consequently, when others approach you to share nurturing on an intimate level, you feel uncomfortable unless you know exactly what they expect of you. Before you can allow yourself to feel, you need the security of knowing you can fulfill the other's expectations. At times this can cause you to appear cold and calculating when actually you're softhearted.

Past-Life Influence

On the emotional level, you are a child of the universe. You have natural abilities with business and function very comfortably in that world. Yet back in your home environment, many of you tend to be emotionally immature. The male expects to be mothered by his wife, and the female expects to be coddled by her husband. Through your mate and those in your intimate circle, you seek to replace the emotional nurturing you did not allow yourself to feel as a child. This is why it is important for you to learn to feel secure within your own being; you do not have to go through life seeking approval from those you love. Feeling every adjustment and criticism as a personal rejection can lead to your withdrawing into your inner shell.

You are learning to accept yourself as a being who is going through different phases of life and has ups and downs and makes mistakes just like everyone else. You are realizing that mistakes do not mean you are not worthy of love or are not a useful human being. It just means "whoops, I guess I need to try that again."

Step 1: Unconscious Expression

SELF-PITY

The main way you defeat your own happiness is by wallowing in self-pity. You say to yourself, "Nobody loves me and everybody is criticizing me and everyone wants something from me and nobody appreciates me or accepts me the way I am." Actually, you are unconsciously projecting these fears from inside yourself. These are not facts of objective reality, but your fears can become self-fulfilling prophecies. Your negative outlook may actually draw into your life people who are like that, or you can bring out these qualities in the people close to you.

You may tend to draw takers and users because you are feeling so sorry for yourself that the universe responds to that energy by supporting your expectations. Since your expectations are that you are going to be taken advantage of, life sends you a person or situation to do just that emotionally.

When you get too involved in self-pity, you can go into long periods of brooding that make it difficult to let go of past hurts. This indulgence is your main stumbling block. You have this tendency because self-pity evokes the semblance of self-nurturing feelings. But indulging in this process actually prevents you from future growth, since it is by learning from your unpleasant experiences that you grow beyond the need to repeat them.

DIFFICULTY LETTING GO

A second self-defeating mechanism is your difficulty in letting go of what is familiar. It may be a job, a situation, a person, and so on. Holding on to the old, even if it has become stagnating and emotionally unsatisfying, offers some security. But this can actually prevent the present and future emotional satisfaction that you long for.

By letting go of situations that are no longer conducive to your personal growth and vitality, you become open to receiving the bounty of fulfilling emotional situations into your life.

OVERCOMPENSATING FOR EMOTIONAL INSECURITIES

You inadvertently defeat yourself by overcompensating for your emotional insecurities. You may be unwilling to leave a familiar home environment, even though it is no longer productive for you to be there. In severe cases, some persons with this eclipse pattern suffer from agoraphobia (fear of open spaces). Your insecurity and fear of being rejected by the outside world can leave you with a sense of being unfulfilled. You may also indulge in compensatory activities, such as overeating, substituting food as a source of emotional nurturing and comfort.

Overcompensation can also result in a tendency to retain water for emotional support. There may be a strong desire for dairy products due to their subconscious relationship with mother's milk. These compensating tendencies will continue until you become a truly self-nurturing individual.

Step 2: Conscious Expression

LEARNING TO NURTURE YOURSELF

One of your first steps should be to learn how to nurture yourself. Self-love will build the confidence you need to take the emotional risks necessary for emotional triumphs. One psychological technique that can increase self-love is the practice of creative visualization. Try to remember a time in your childhood when you felt unloved by one or both parents. In your mind, rewrite the script, seeing your parent(s) giving you exactly the kind of nurturing you needed at the time.

Repeat this exercise until you can do it easily and comfortably. Next, practice visualizing yourself as an adult walking up to your child self and hugging that child. These exercises can free you from feeling the need to be accepted by others, which totally frees you to be yourself!

CREATING EMOTIONAL SAFETY

Take responsibility for building emotional safety into your relationships by honestly sharing your emotional responses, fears, and tender feelings. Such verbalizations validate the existence of your feelings, and through this process you gain a sense of inner centeredness and strength. If rejection and disappointment do arise, this empowers you to handle them without the sense of woundedness that would ordinarily drive you back into your shell.

By taking chances in expanding your emotional horizons, you open yourself to the types of relationships that can bring real emotional satisfaction. On a subconscious level, you are teaching yourself to manifest emotional satisfaction through believing that you deserve it and can handle it.

Through difficult emotional experiences you learn to develop a sense of courage that serves to keep you above the dangers of an endless pit of emotional quicksand. A willingness to grow beyond these hurts is a prerequisite for climbing out of the emotional muck that you were born to transcend. It is in fact the difficult emotional experiences that actually earmark the path you must walk and master, one step at a time, in order to obtain the full emotional satisfaction that is your birthright.

Step 3: Transpersonal Expression

Your emotional fiber is actually not personal at all, but your link with the universe. You sense this. As you listen to your emotional body and allow it to be expressed honestly and naturally, without censorship, in whatever environment you find yourself, you restore a healthy emotional balance for those around you. Thus, giving your own feelings a voice, expressing the subtle emotional undercurrents you sense going on around you, you clear the emotional atmosphere for everyone involved.

You do not take the emotions you feel personally by reacting to them or holding on to them. You understand that you are working out the group karma of emotions on the planet and thus process emotional upsets readily and willingly. You realize that you are simultaneously helping to cleanse the emotional body of the planet. You have the capacity to link with the most intimate part of other people—their feelings, hurts, longings, and disappointments—and to establish this link from an objective, humanitarian level. Operating at this level, you can allow the unconditional love and acceptance of the universe to channel through you to heal the emotional wounds of the people who cross your path.

Born under this eclipse pattern, you entered onto the Earth with an etheric coating of emotional hypersensitivity. When this sensitivity is directed inward, from a motive of self-protection, the result is emotional starvation and isolation. When directed outward on the humanitarian level, if your gift of sensitivity is used to be aware of others' emotional essences, your inner serenity becomes your strongest support system. It comes from being motivated to heal the emotions of others. The result is an internal experience of calm self-nurturing, total satisfaction, and fulfillment from within.

Physical Integration

Resistance to learning your lessons can lead to physical symptoms: ulcers and other stomach disturbances such as gastritis, indigestion, heartburn, belching, or water retention. Abscesses, malignant and nonmalignant growths, disturbances in the pancreas, and afflictions of the uterus are other symptoms of imbalance with the Cancerian energies. Occasionally, the breast area may also be affected. Problems with calcium levels can lead to deterioration of the bone marrow, knee problems, or soft teeth.

Of all the eclipse patterns, yours is most positively affected on a physical level by periodic visits to the ocean or other large bodies of water. On a holistic level, the body is physically integrating the pattern of learning to nurture and be nurtured. Every cell in the body is relating to this nurturing process, so the body is constantly absorbing—either someone's negative emotions or food or water. That is why you tend to retain water. Your body will continue to do this until you have integrated your process and no longer have to exaggerate absorption to draw attention to your need to nurture others or to be nurtured. Conversely, you may be a very thin person and have difficulty keeping anything in your system. In this case, the exaggeration is in refusing to accept nurturing.

On a deep psychological level, water retention is actually the cells saying to the inner organs of the body, "We'll love you, we'll coddle you. Feel it, sense it. We'll hold you." As you begin to practice self-nurturing on the psychological level, the need to overnurture on the cellular level will begin to dissipate.

♌

LEO

SOLAR ECLIPSE: WHAT YOUR SOUL CONTRACTED TO TEACH OTHERS

(In order to fully activate your solar eclipse energy in Leo, it may be helpful to read the lunar eclipse in Leo section. You may find information that can help you more fully contribute your solar eclipse in Leo gifts.)

Your Mission

In this incarnation, you have come to teach your fellow beings how to accept love. People drawn to you are extremely aloof and have difficulty accepting too much affection (or what they view as too much affection). They tend to feel that love is limiting, that love would hold them down. They find themselves continually detaching instead of learning that they can accept love and retain freedom simultaneously.

You can help others learn this lesson in different ways. One way is to persevere, not taking no for an answer, and continuing to love and share love when you honestly feel it in your heart, whether those around you are remaining aloof or not.

You can also share love through recognizing the good within others and teaching those around you to feel that they are worthy of accepting love and strong enough not to lose their own identity.

Or you can be very demonstrative, jealous, and possessive where love is concerned, thereby showing those drawn into your life exactly what it is they don't want. Yet this very process encourages the other person to look elsewhere for love that will allow them freedom.

Lightening the Load of Others

Your ability to teach others to lighten up and not take things so seriously can bring happiness into the lives you touch, providing you don't take yourself too seriously. You tend to come into the lives of persons who need cheering up, who feel the everyday duties of life are too mundane for them to handle. Through your ability to find pleasure, you teach others to find it too.

Those of you with this eclipse pattern who choose not to accept your natural ability can teach others the value of happiness through being overly possessive and jealous; this causes people to break from you and find happiness by going their own way.

Loneliness and Self-Pity

When you don't understand what you are teaching, you can find yourself trapped in patterns of loneliness and self-pity. You can create a great deal of unhappiness and loneliness in your own life. Allow your glee and joyfulness to shine through, no matter how much negativity you draw to you. With your ability to spark creativity and love in others, you attract persons who are very down on themselves. Remain centered. Do not allow those around you to knock you off balance and change your way of looking at life. It is your duty to remain buoyant, teaching others to love the self.

If you should find yourself trapped in a pattern of loneliness, you need only to bring romance into your life to feel that spark of love inside. And if those around you refuse to accept your gift, it is important that you share in another area. If you have chosen to stay in a relationship with a person who is unwilling to love the self, you can share your love and creativity in many other areas. You can work with children or go into self-expressive fields such as teaching, creative arts, and acting. There are many areas of life where you can express this wealth of creativity and your ability to stimulate others into rejoicing about the self. You do not have to remain in morose patterns. If you do, it is self-inflicted, and you do not have the right to blame others since you have the strength and ability to climb out.

Fun and Play

The Leo eclipse must let the child shine through. Your example allows others to see that we are all children in life's eyes, and our lessons do not always have to be so serious. As you allow the child energy to manifest, you also allow the creative force from within to flow. You can be extremely creative yourself, and/or you have the ability to spark creativity in those around you, just by validating the child in all. When we are children, our imaginations are not tarnished with the worries and anxieties of everyday life. And when your energy enters into another's life, your playfulness allows him or her to set aside their worries and to play. As you teach this to others, you find those around you becoming more creative when their true inner spark begins to burn.

You are the true teachers of the zodiac. In teaching those around you to lighten up and get in touch with their own creative source, you show them the goodness that lies within and empower them to bring it forth. You have an innate ability to teach people to find their own self-worth and to motivate them to go forward in the world with their own natural abilities proudly shining.

As with the other eclipses, you can teach your lessons from a positive or a negative standpoint. You can share love, sensitivity, and recognition with those around you, teaching them to become proud, creative, loving of self, and thereby able to share love. Or you can go through life invalidating others, taking credit for their creativity, and devaluing those who are close to you. In this way you push others to the point of standing up for themselves and recognizing: "Hey, I'm worth more than this." Either way, the lesson of loving yourself, being proud of yourself, and letting yourself shine is taught.

LUNAR ECLIPSE: WHAT YOUR SOUL IS LEARNING TO EMOTIONALLY EMBRACE

Your Mission

In this incarnation, you have come to learn how to accept love.

Past-Life Influence

You played a very strong role in the humanities and developed a humanitarian type of consciousness. You loved on a more universal level, not taking time to feel individual personal love, personal pride, or self-worth.

In this existence you are learning to accept your own individuality, which includes developing the ego, learning to be proud of the spark of the collective consciousness that you carry within, and allowing your own individual spark to burn brightly to reflect the glory of the whole. You realize that in performing your individual best you are truly honoring the oneness by shining your brightest. When connecting in a group consciousness, we honor one another by doing the best for each other that we possibly can.

Developing the Ego

What motivates us to do this best is to develop the ego. The idea is to develop the ego without selfishness and yet at the same time with self-love. You are finding qualities within that you can feel proud of. You are to value the self and self-expression, but you must begin by learning to love the self.

You are beginning to recognize that the self is worthy of being loved and that it is not a negative thing to accept love and to feel self-pride. Many of you are coming from such a universal consciousness that you think it is negative to care about the self at all or to develop the ego. You may lose sight of the fact that although we are all part of the whole, we are also individuals. You realize that we are all connected and that we must all help one another. Your difficulty lies in recognizing that you have a responsibility to make your individual spark—your individual self—as valuable to your fellow beings as possible. In teaching one another personal pride and self-love, we charge the battery that encourages us all to perform at our highest.

Somehow you developed the spiritual misconception that your role is to be a doormat for society. You feel that if you think too highly of yourself, you will be singling yourself out as being more important than the group. You need to learn in this lifetime that you can only be of use to the group when you feel good about yourself; we all perform best when we feel confident inside.

You are discovering that to truly love all you must first love yourself. You are learning to honor those things in your life that cause your individual spark to grow stronger, shine more brightly, and become as vibrant as it can possibly be. By recognizing your own self-worth, the flow of your creative energy, and your own special essence, you are adding to this plane by allowing the self to shine through.

Those around you can benefit from your ability to inspire others to be more creative and more loving. Once you have found this space for yourself, you can be one of the most inspirational of teachers.

Accepting Love

When you finally recognize that it is all right to love the self, you have reached the point where you can accept love from others. Your lesson is to accept love into the self as well as learn to love the self. You tend to detach from loving situations, fearing that the involvement will be limiting. You need to realize that it is all right for love to remain a constant within your life. It is all right to allow yourself to be loved, and you do not have to be perfect first! You fear that if you are not perfect, you will hold back yourself or the other person, so you may drive yourself to a state of perfection before you allow yourself or another to truly commit.

During this lifetime this thought process needs to be reevaluated and changed. Recognize that we are here to give support to one another by accepting love and support from each other. This support makes our journeys easier, more loving, and more conscious; we are in our most comfortable, productive states when we allow ourselves to feel loved and be supported by those around us. Allow yourself to benefit from this love and support, and not isolate yourself with an unrealistic reality.

There are three basic steps in allowing this love to enter your life. First, recognize that we are all separate entities within a whole. The separate divine spark within each of us needs to have support and love from other members of the whole; we all need love. Second, realize that sharing and being loved are all right. They are not signs of weakness but natural, healthy human traits. This step leads directly to the other major lesson you have come to learn: Procreation, or individual creativity. You are learning that if you are to create anything worthwhile in this life, you must take in the love and support of those around you. Until your being is in total balance and harmony, you cannot connect with your truest creative forces—the forces of procreation. These have the power to create another entity, whether it be another human being, a painting, a book, or a garden. To allow the "child" of your creativity to develop properly, you must reach this level of awareness and accept love.

Within this element of procreation and creativity you are learning to let your own creative spark flow so that you can give back to life the beauty that you see. You can express this spark in art, in writing, in choosing to teach a child how to learn and grow, or perhaps on the stage, sharing love, happiness, laughter, and drama with others.

Because Leo rules the factor of procreation, you are in touch with the creative energies, the Christ-consciousness, the God-consciousness. You are also in touch with the possibility of losing your identity to those you serve, just as actors and actresses often lose the privacy of their own lives by playing roles for the masses.

Recognizing Individuality

In the past you have dispersed your individuality into the whole so that now you have no recognition of individuality. Thus, you need to develop a conscious awareness that there is an individual spark so that this divine particle becomes validated. You may fear coming into the body and developing an ego within the body. The thought is: "Now I'll get caught up in the stream of life and really lose my identity." This fear unconsciously prevents you from coming into your own space. In actuality, once you begin to manifest your individuality, freedom, not entrapment, is the result.

You may fear becoming an individual because more is expected of individuals, and you don't know whether or not you can live up to it. You fear getting caught up in the responsibility of living up to your capabilities. And this is another lesson: not to concern yourself so much with the future outcome of the projection of ego but to live in the integrity of the moment, doing what brings uplifting feelings and happiness to the spark within the individual self. In giving happiness to your own spark—your self—your inner joy and sense of fulfillment will flood out and increase the quality of life for all those around you.

In this lifetime you are allowed to have happiness and love; it's your birthright. It is an individual duty for you to achieve this time. It is the missing factor in your soul growth. You have repaid your debt to society many times over, and what is owed to your soul growth pattern in this existence is individual, separate, personal love and development. You want to become a creative force within the self because in honoring the one, you must procreate. And your job is to create through sharing the joy within yourself.

This correlates directly to the lesson of learning to love the self. The creative energy is so strong within the Leo that if you don't develop your own individuality before your creativeness starts flowing, then others may recognize the spark before you do. This can lead to others ruling your life, which is exactly what you fear.

Step 1: Unconscious Expression

AVOIDING LOVE

Operating unconsciously, you have a great deal of difficulty keeping any consistency in relationships. You are coming from a past-life awareness of relationships holding you down. You fear that becoming involved in the feelings of others means being responsible for their feelings.

What you fail to realize is that learning to interrelate, share feelings, and accept love is an essential part of humanness. You have an awareness of group consciousness and a recognition that the whole must be taken into consideration, not just the individual. That side of you is very well defined. But when it comes to personal self-worth and value, loving the self or allowing others to love you, you tend to run from those experiences.

In order to turn this pattern around, you need to become aware that when you deny yourself the affection and support of another, you are only functioning at half steam, and sooner or later there will be no steam. Science has proven that a being cannot live without love. A simple technique to get in touch with the interchange of personal love is to begin what is known as "hug therapy," allowing yourself to hug and be hugged.

LACK OF SELF-ESTEEM

You may tend to give away your power because of a lack of self-esteem and self-love. You do not recognize the value of your own creativity. You have the ability to create a winning situation for everyone concerned, yet when you give away your power you block your creativity from being used constructively. Sometimes you allow others to take credit for what you have created and often it isn't as constructive and successful as it would have been if you had stayed involved. As you become more in touch with the self and learn to value the self, you can reap the rewards of your own creativity without giving it away. Then you will afford yourself and others the joy of sharing a very special part of yourself.

On the unconscious level, through low self-esteem and being overly serious about the concept of universal consciousness, you can forget that it is all right to enjoy living on this planet. You may have a subconscious fear that if you allow pleasures, it will trap you into a returning cycle. It seems that every part of the process you are going through boils down to allowing love into your life, bringing about a natural healing and balance within the entire personality.

If you continue not allowing yourself to feel love, you will destroy the very essence of your life. And in this destruction there is great sadness. You can find yourself wallowing in periods of depression created by your reticence to accept love. These self-inflicted depressions need to be understood so they can be removed.

It is not necessary, healthy, or even part of your lesson to go without love. The idea is for you to open your eyes to the beauty you have within and understand that because of this beauty you are valuable and worthwhile. Then you can remove the veil of self-inflicted depression and allow your creative juices to flow. As you create, spreading the happiness you feel to others, you are soon able to see what is within you that is worthy of being loved.

The Leo eclipse truly is a humanitarian who has lost sight of individual value, and your challenge is to open your heart to accept individual love. Through an overabundance of service you forgot to take time to regenerate the self.

EXCESSIVE DETACHMENT OR JOY

If you get caught in the negative aspect of learning your lessons, you can be detached, cold, and castrating to those around you. You may also be highstrung, unemotional, defensive, and double-dealing. You may not trust your own creativity but may steal the creative works of others, suffering a lonely, deprived existence.

Until you can climb out of this negative state, you will feel a void around you. When you learn to turn your energies around, you will find an unquenchable desire to assist those who are less fortunate, as if you were paying back the years you deprived yourself of being around anyone. You become a crusader in the humanities and bring forth new and innovative ways to assist, entertain, and give pleasure to all.

Should the pattern of not honoring the love within the self continue, you will find yourself becoming nasty with those around you, rebellious, sarcastic, pushy, and domineering. The reason these patterns begin to surface is that you are not recognizing any self-worth and therefore not recognizing when someone else cares or wants to support you.

You come on very strong and arrogant to get your needs met, but actually, if you opened your heart to those around you, they would be more than willing to assist and even find pleasure in supporting the extremely loving, vibrant, joyful spirit that you are capable of being when you don't block off your own creative energy.

To help reconnect with the flow of your creative energy, stop and ask: "Does this feel right?" Learn to trust your body: If it feels right and is for the highest good of all concerned, do it; if it doesn't feel right, don't do it, no matter what anyone says. Establish this bond of trust with the self; your inner voice has the clarity to raise your self-esteem and self-confidence. Then you begin to follow your inner guidance and satisfy the child's longing within your own heart.

Step 2: Conscious Expression

The idea is to create. You recognize this not based on what others expect, but from that sense of love and joy within. You are here to share love and to share yourself. Indeed, sharing yourself is a form of creation. You understand that the universe created us out of love, and we can't create at our finest until we can function from that base of love. And we cannot accept this universal love going forth to others in an effort to reunite the whole until we can really feel it. In order to feel it we must experience it in conscious awareness.

When you begin your journey into creativity, you find pleasure in sharing your expressions of love, whether in painting, acting, raising children, writing, or just finding creative ways to allow others to feel uplifted and sense the love that is flowing from you. Once you allow yourself to tap that internal source— that spark of the collective consciousness that burns within—there is no end to your ability to create and to manifest exciting experiences in this lifetime.

You develop a way with children that is remarkable to behold. As your enthusiasm for life accelerates, being in your presence can be like riding a roller coaster. Sometimes your expression of creativity exceeds what another would consider human endurance, yet to the driven Leo eclipse, the boredom of noncreativity would be more than you could endure.

You do recognize some obstacles in learning how to accept the responsibility of love into your life. For both the unconscious and the conscious eclipse, you are still learning how to accept love. The conscious eclipse, aware that this is an obstacle to growth, has a driving need to answer the question "why am I doing this?" And you may experience many different relationships, constantly searching for this answer.

TO SEE CLEARLY, GET OUTSIDE THE SELF

You may be involved in self-evaluation techniques, whether it be meditation, yoga, or any other practice that can bring you out of the self. You are more comfortable in detaching. You find that if you can remove yourself from the problem, you can see it more clearly. Once you understand it, you are very capable of healing it.

You are gaining awareness of the self and the issues that block you from loving. In your mind, if you allow anyone to love you, it means that there must be something special about you. And after all, how could any of us be any more special than the next if we are to have the universal consciousness of which you are so proud?

This would seem to invalidate your belief system, but you must realize that through the universal consciousness developed in previous existences, you forgot to recognize that you are also an individual embodiment of the spark of the collective whole, and it is that spark that needs to be seen. Recognition is positive for your growth.

The joy is to allow others to give you love in order to open yourself to the mental and emotional flow of life. Then you are cooperating with the heartfelt factor within you as well as with the tide of external events. By expressing the inner in combination with the events of the outer, a truly vital alchemical combination comes forth that is healing for all concerned.

On the conscious level you are learning to trust that others truly love you and to be open to accepting their love. As you expose the spark within to others, you can discover whether or not those around you truly appreciate you. You may find that there is no need to dominate the situation, so you can allow yourself to trust those around you and interrelate with more harmony.

Through bringing more harmony into your life you allow yourself to develop the true creativity that you have come to express.

Step 3: Transpersonal Expression

You are yearning to honor the divinity of the whole by doing those things that strengthen, honor, and allow for the preferences of the individual spark of divinity within yourself. By respecting the spiritual ember of the collective consciousness that burns in all, you are teaching others the energy of procreation. You have an intuitive understanding and awareness that this divine spark can be found within every living thing.

It is up to us as individuals to respect and pay homage to that spark by fulfilling our personal life experiences to the utmost, by allowing the joy and pleasures of loving and being loved, and by sharing our creative energies with our fellow beings.

You are extremely creative and have an ability to inspire others to bring forth their creative essence. You desire to see all those around you become the best they can be, for if we are all achieving our highest potential, we are simultaneously aiding the whole. You are acutely aware of your place in the collective consciousness and the fact that you have been created in love. The energy of love is what gives life to everything: a child, an idea, or an action. Nothing in the universe can exist without love, since the universal scheme of life is the essence of love. In the transpersonal expression you express this pure essence of love.

Physical Integration

When you choose not to allow yourself to feel love and affection in your life—either by not loving yourself or by not allowing others to love you—the body tends to weaken the heart muscle. The heart muscle seems to correlate directly to your ability to love and be loved. The essence of love is the very essence of survival for you or any other being. It seems to be the most important factor in human existence. Without love, as time passes, you lose the desire to live, thereby creating disorders within the body that directly correlate to the vitality of life.

The spinal column can also become affected. When the vibrancy of love is shut off from the heart center, the heart center isolates itself from the rest of the body. Then it does not allow the spinal column to carry the messages from the brain, thereby cutting off communication and vitality.

By breaking through these obstacles you can regain your vitality and restore health to the entire body. But it takes love to give you the desire to do so. Once you are determined, there is no holding you back from any achievement, including restoring health to the body.

♍

VIRGO

SOLAR ECLIPSE: WHAT YOUR SOUL CONTRACTED TO TEACH OTHERS

(In order to fully activate your solar eclipse energy in Virgo, it may be helpful to read the lunar eclipse in Virgo section. You may find information that can help you more fully contribute your solar eclipse in Virgo gifts.)

Your Mission

You have incarnated this lifetime to teach people how to use their analytical faculties. Thus, you tend to draw gullible people who need to learn how to put things in proper perspective. You attract people who live in illusionary states and need someone to teach them to take more responsibility for their actions. Through your ability to correctly assess most situations and bring reason to the problem-solving process, you can be of great help to those who have lost their direction.

When you accept your gifts, you are a natural-born counselor because you can sense what is needed to help people regain an objective focus. Through bypassing the emotions and gaining direct access to reason, your insights can guide people around emotional responses that might have been blocking them from seeing things more clearly.

You can discern, by noticing people's usage of words and their body language, where they have weaknesses that need to be addressed. You can see where the emotional responses are, and you know how to get around these responses to allow people "in the back door" so they can get to what they really need to deal with. When necessary you can even help them to reprogram their thought processes.

Teaching Integration

You also teach others about assimilation. You show them how to stay more grounded while they integrate new concepts and expand their awareness. By teaching people how to organize their lives, you make sure that everyone is doing his or her part, so that the planet can continue to evolve. You are the one who works hard to get the job done and takes care of all the details. You are a positive example of a hardworking person, showing your best effort by being very precise and analytical.

Just by the way you live your life, you teach those around you how to put things in proper perspective and do the work that needs to be done. You help them to learn not to feel sorry for themselves, not to get lost in a daydream world, and not to be overly sensitive. Your philosophy is: "Hey, we all have to work. Don't feel sorry for yourself. We need to do this, and we can't function unless everyone does his or her part."

The Gift of Alignment

Sometimes you are misunderstood because of your ability to see flaws. If you don't present your insight tactfully, you may not be appreciated by those you help. The idea is to point out flaws so that things can be put back in proper alignment. Since your motivation is the desire that everything and everyone function at the highest level, you will always call attention to something that isn't right. It sometimes seems to others as though you are constantly putting your finger on a sore spot. Those you help may not appreciate you at the time, but later they do appreciate the correction that has been made.

In this process you do not get much validation for your work, and sometimes you wonder if it's all worth it. Yet it is almost a compulsion for you to continue pointing out people's flaws because your contract with the universe is to help put the planet back into alignment. Professionally, as a counselor, you may help to put people's consciousness back into focus. Or as a friend you may try to point out things in a tactful way. You have the ability to see the whole picture, and thus you know how to align the parts properly.

Wherever you are, you find yourself adjusting the individual parts into harmony with the universal whole. You deal most with this aspect of adjustment, since this is the main purpose of your sharing. You go through life creating responses in people that cause them to adjust. There is always a temporary irritation in the adjustment until they feel comfortable in the new groove, and then they appreciate what you have done. You need to know that people do come to appreciate the observations you have shared with them.

Awareness of Timing

If you find that you are being misunderstood and that people are having difficulty getting along with you, it is time to analyze your own behavior. You may have reached a point where you have become so analytical that you have forgotten to be tactful and discerning. A pill is always easier to swallow when there is a little sugar on it. Remembering this will enable you to maximize your ability to be accepted by others, which in turn allows you to be of more assistance.

Timing is of the utmost importance. Remember that there is a proper time and place for criticism—tact alone is not enough. Even if you point out a flaw to someone very sensitively, if you do it at the wrong time and the wrong place, it can still be extremely hurtful. For example, you don't tell someone she has bad breath just before she gives a presentation and there is nothing she can do about it. Don't tell a person about something that can't be corrected at the time if it is going to make him or her self-conscious. You need to afford others their space and respect their ability to be comfortable with themselves so they are able to function at their highest level. By criticizing people at the wrong time, you can knock them off their stride at a time when they most need your support. Wait until their feet are planted firmly on the ground. Your observations will have the most impact when others can translate them into action immediately.

Job Opportunities

On the nonpersonal level, you have the capacity to work in the field of systems analysis. You can work within large corporate structures, on important projects that call for someone who is really attuned to detail. You are also good at putting people and projects together. Because you can understand different processes, you are able to recognize the people and information that belong in those areas. Thus, you would function quite comfortably as a systems analyst or director of human resources.

Work is very important to you, and when your career is on solid ground, other areas of your life automatically become stabilized. You don't need to be a nitpicker at home if your work environment affords you an opportunity to use your discerning eye. This allows your critical ability to be used for its maximum benefit, while keeping it out of the home where it can cause stress. Do not apply your analytical process with those close to you unless you have mastered using a great deal of tact. Being critical toward those in your home can cause detachment within the family.

However, this energy can be used positively in the home in the area of the family's diet—selecting what the family should eat for proper nutrition and maximum health benefits. You also have a talent for keeping the mental stimulation and communication flowing through the family by not allowing blockages to form from emotional responses that have been misunderstood. For this alone, you are a very valuable asset to any family, social, or work environment.

LUNAR ECLIPSE: WHAT YOUR SOUL IS LEARNING TO EMOTIONALLY EMBRACE

Your Mission

In this incarnation, you are learning to not be so gullible and ready to believe what others tell you.

Past-Life Influence

You were overly involved in the spiritual realm, and this time you must adjust and get your feet back on the ground. You need to find out that you can function in the physical world and still retain a spiritual consciousness.

One of your major lessons is to find a balance between the spiritual and the physical worlds. You need to learn that while we are in physical bodies we have physical desires. Your gullibility lies in the fact that you don't take the desires and motives of others into account when you make decisions. You already recognize the God essence in everyone, but you also need to realize that being in the flesh and working on certain lessons adds a different flavor to the spiritual character of every person. This is why you must learn to put things in proper perspective and take the desires and motives of others into account.

Physical Discrimination

You are psychic at birth and have very strong sensitivities. But because of your one-sided approach, many of the signals you receive seem mixed and clouded to you. In understanding and using your psychic awareness, remember that if an insight is useful to you, it is from the universe and you can trust it. If isn't useful, discard it. In this way you can learn and assimilate what works in the physical universe through a process of personal discrimination.

As for your problem with gullibility, it is not necessary to worry about who is telling you the truth and who isn't. You didn't incarnate with the ability to tell who is honest and who is dishonest—you just see everyone's spiritual essence. It is difficult, therefore, for you to sort out fact from fiction when dealing with their physical forms. Again, just concern yourself with whether what you are perceiving, being told, hearing, or reading is useful to you personally. If it is, then you can integrate it into your life and use it. If it isn't, no matter how useful it is to someone else or how truthful the information might be, you must discard it so that something else you need can come in.

Learning Integration

You are teaching yourself to assimilate and integrate information instead of functioning solely from your "inner perception" as you have in previous lifetimes.

By incorporating analytical thinking into your behavior patterns, you can take control over your life, be more decisive, and take charge of the direction in which your life is going. You are combating an inner tendency to be wishy-washy and easily victimized by others through your readiness to trust without first checking out pertinent information. Once you establish an analytical frame of mind, you are no longer plagued by manipulative parasites. You are taking responsibility for your own life instead of waiting around for others to lead you, and you are learning to discern where your associates are headed before agreeing to participate in unrealistic pursuits.

You are learning physical integration on a multitude of levels. When you incorporate your reasoning ability into your behavior patterns, you solidify a sense of adulthood and become an effective focus in the world. It is also important for you to respect your physical body, especially your digestive system, since it correlates most directly to this eclipse pattern. You are learning to take responsibility for the foods you put into your body, just as you need to take responsibility for the thoughts you accept into your consciousness. This cleanliness extends to your physical body and the organization that you bring into your environment. Paying attention to these physical processes gives you confidence in your ability to operate effectively in the world.

Through learning to pay attention to details, you begin putting things in proper perspective—placing them where they belong in your life. The digestive system does the same thing when it sends nutrients to the different areas of the body where they belong. So both internally and externally your job is to ask: What is this? What value is it? Where does it belong? And as you practice keeping your physical environment in order, on a psychological level you are incorporating a sense of order, clarity, and definition that all help you to develop a strong reasoning ability.

Psychic Sensitivity

You were born with psychic abilities and are working to develop reasoning abilities. You have been overly sensitized to the spiritual realms in prior incarnations, which has resulted in a tendency to be spacey and nonobservant in the present. You often overlook details in your environment so you can continue your spiritual quest. But you must retain a sense of discipline, refinement, and responsibility to your fellow beings. You can truly be a spiritual herald for the planet through offering your services once your gifts have been incorporated on the physical level.

You are responsible for helping others to harvest what they have planted on the psychological level. The idea is not to make reality fit into the dream vision but to infuse the dream vision into the present lifetime. To do this you must learn the basics of society's rules and be able to operate effectively within that framework.

Step 1: Unconscious Expression

If you choose to resist the flow of your lessons, you may become trapped in patterns of self-pity, martyrdom, self-indulgence, and other forms of escapism. You can have problems with overindulgence in alcohol, drugs, and/or food. You are drawn to these escape patterns because you feel that the physical world is too harsh. In severe cases you may allow the body to deteriorate and even entertain thoughts of leaving this plane to escape from your lessons. The proper way for you to escape from the unpleasant aspects of physical life is to learn the disciplines that support you in establishing your spiritual visions of happiness on a tangible level in your everyday existence.

SERVICE TO OTHERS

Serving others empowers you to get in touch with the sense of spirituality inside you. With a loving heart, you can help your fellow beings raise their consciousness. Watching others establish positive behavior patterns helps you find proper connection with the physical plane. You are here to serve or suffer—there is no middle path.

When operating unconsciously you may tend to be overly critical, due to a lack of balance in your life. If you don't hone your analytical abilities and develop your sense of tact, you will be constantly disappointed by the behavior of others. Learning not to take the actions of others so personally would greatly enhance your ability to interact with them harmoniously.

Sometimes you are born into a family environment in which there is much harshness and criticism. To survive you may shut down your sensitive nature and function in the critical manner that you were exposed to in your own youth. In these cases you can become very cold and crude in your speech and mannerisms, finding fault with everything and everyone. Your intolerance is so great that you walk through life constantly pointing out the flaws and weaknesses in those around you, without tact or regard for their feelings. Once you recognize this pattern it becomes possible for you to train yourself to be aware of others' feelings. Through this awareness you can learn to get in touch with your own feelings and chip away the crusts with which you have protected your fragile sensitivities.

When you learn to recognize your own sensitivity and that of others, you are able to communicate your discerning observations in ways that strengthen the character and improve the life circumstances of those around you. And this is what you have come to learn and to integrate into your personality.

THE "HOLLOW CYLINDER"

There can sometimes be a "hollow cylinder" aspect to this unconscious eclipse pattern, for there are times when you totally turn off to life experiences. Then you walk through life assimilating nothing and sensing nothing, caught in a void between the spiritual and physical worlds and not functioning in either. At times you may not have any sense of direction or see any reason to be on this planet at all. So strong is this fog that you can't even sense the spiritual realms. You are yearning to feel at home someplace—anyplace—and yet you don't know where "home" is.

The imbalance you find on this planet—and the challenge to readjust your consciousness to the needs of the physical plane so you can be of use here—is sometimes so overwhelming that you totally detach; this is when you seem to be a hollow cylinder. But you are learning to recognize that the Earth plane is home in this incarnation. As you accept being on the Earth and allow yourself to become grounded through effective participation here, you find a true sense of spiritual worth that anchors you in both worlds simultaneously.

Step 2: Conscious Expression

A MISSION TO SERVE HUMANKIND WITH REASON

Operating consciously, you intuitively gravitate to the lessons you came to learn in this lifetime, and you willingly take responsibility for how you interact with others. You find yourself constantly dealing with situations where you have to integrate your analytical abilities within your family, work environment, and social life. You are called upon to use your abilities to discern and discriminate, and you feel a strong sense of urgency to hone these skills so you can be of service.

You intuitively recognize the needs of others and are receptive to filling them. You have a strong sense of loyalty and the desire to be of service, although you often need to be taught how this service can be performed. You are very willing to help others if they will tell you what they need. You are a very growth-oriented being who recognizes the need for putting things in proper perspective, and you have come to learn to do this in your own life as well.

PAST-LIFE INFLUENCE

You have walked a very loving spiritual path in previous existences and are putting that love to work in the here and now. You have a warm space in your heart for your fellow beings; thus, you want to be of service to humankind, and you need to learn how to do this effectively. It is for this purpose that you have come to the physical realm.

In this lifetime you experience a great deal of hard work, and when oper-ating consciously you have very few problems accepting your role as a worker. You recognize that you are integrating the ability to work and function on the physical plane as a productive human being. You feel a sense of being in tune with the universe, and you recognize that everything in the universe has a physical counterpart.

Often you experience some situation in which you require counseling, for there are times when you need assistance in understanding how the mental facul-ties assimilate information. Normally, you seek this counseling yourself, recogniz-ing when you are personally out of alignment, and this is one of your strengths. You are overcoming a need to handle everything by yourself and are voluntarily seeking aid to understand better what it is you are not perceiving accurately.

By allowing someone else to assist in your growth process, you are able to rise above any emotional disturbances or interferences that may block you from functioning at your highest level. Once back on track you rarely need this type of help again. The process that you learn through counseling is how to integrate your reasoning ability into the rest of your being. When you have mastered this you are ready to help others.

FREEDOM THROUGH REASON

From a very early age you have been curious about the workings of the human mind. You are very inquisitive, and sometimes you are told by others that you are troublesome and nosy. But this is a necessary process, and you should not feel guilty, since you need to have as many facts as possible. You re-quire abundant information because you are learning to process things and put them in their proper place. This is an important part of your personal structure, for your greatest freedom lies in mastering your reasoning ability.

You can relinquish the burden of requiring each detail when the assimila-tion process through which you learn to become more aware begins to oper-ate automatically. You can simultaneously assimilate what you need as you pass through an experience, leading to your greatest and most joyful awareness: enjoying the vividness of life through the ability to be totally here now.

As a child born with this eclipse pattern, you need to be allowed to satisfy your curiosity. It is important for others not to impose their own behavior patterns on you (that is, children should be seen and not heard). You need to learn how to integrate socially at a very early age in order to prevent blockages that could cause you difficulty in communicating with others and put you into an unconscious mode. Once in an unconscious mode, it is difficult for you to become conscious again. If this should happen to you, others who make you feel useful and appreciated and who give you responsibility can help you back into the conscious mode. To remain conscious, form habits of defining your goals and purposes and be careful to follow your chosen path.

Step 3: Transpersonal Expression

You are teaching your fellow beings about the digestive process: spiritual, physical, or mental digestion. You are here to teach us to put things in their proper perspective and to put the proper foods into our bodies. You are the consumer advocates of the planet, making sure that our foods are free of pollutants, our water is fit to drink, and our air is clean enough to breathe. You fight against anything that endangers the survival of the physical body, so the spirit will continue to have a vehicle through which to learn its lessons and evolve. You are helping to restore balance and harmony on Earth itself by teaching your fellow beings to take responsibility for what they put on the planet, into the atmosphere, and into their bodies and minds. You are here to teach the planet what to eat and what not to eat on all levels.

You make us aware of those things that will cause problems in the future. If we overeat and put food into our bodies that our bodies cannot use, it will show up later on the hips or someplace else where we don't want it. The Earth, which is part of the universal body, can have the same experience. You are responsible for teaching us what not to put into our bodies and also what not to put on the Earth or into the atmosphere because you intuitively understand what can and cannot be assimilated. What cannot be assimilated is going to lie around and cause us problems in times to come.

Like bees or ants, you work hard physically and keep things together so that as spiritual beings, we have a safe and healthy environment in which to manifest. You bring spiritual energy onto the planet by physically working and doing the labors of love that make the planet a comfortable place for all beings to function. You are charged with the responsibility of manifesting spirituality in a practical, helpful way on Earth. You teach that we can have true spirituality if we are all willing to work together and for one another. We need to acknowledge that we are interdependent—just as the bees and the ants are interdependent—for our survival. When we are on the physical plane, we are our brother's and sister's keeper. You show us that we must learn to accept and incorporate this interdependency and work hand in hand for the greatest success.

Physical Integration

There is a direct correlation between the digestive system and what you need to learn. Thus, the digestive system in the body will communicate—through its own imbalances—when proper psychological integration has not taken place. The entire digestive tract can be affected. The large intestine and even the spleen can develop knots and restrictions when you are not functioning properly on an analytical level. You need to recognize that when you are working to assimilate information on a mental and emotional level, at the same time you are programming your body to integrate nutrients appropriately.

If you teach your body negative patterns for integrating the substances you put into it, the digestive track will rebel. This can show up in problems with elimination. When food is not properly digested, the consequences may be constipation (a result of ignoring problems and not processing them) or diarrhea (the result of overanalyzing a situation).

If you ignore the necessary process of thoughtful assimilation, you risk a severe reaction: intestinal cramps and severe forms of gastritis. A bloated abdomen can indicate the need to reevaluate what is going on in the external world in terms of proper adjustment and assimilation. Inflammatory problems with the appendix can be another way the body communicates an immediate need for you to pay attention to integrating and assimilating what is going on in your life.

If you are too distracted to understand that the body is reflecting what you are experiencing on a psychological level, the lymphatic system may also be affected. This can lower the body's resistance, leaving you open to hidden infections and a breakdown of the immune system. The idea is to recognize that the areas of the body ruled by the eclipse pattern can also be the strongest areas if you choose to pay attention at an early stage to what the body is trying to tell you.

♎

LIBRA

SOLAR ECLIPSE: WHAT YOUR SOUL CONTRACTED TO TEACH OTHERS

(In order to fully activate your solar eclipse energy in Libra, it may be helpful to read the lunar eclipse in Libra section. You may find information that can help you more fully contribute your solar eclipse in Libra gifts.)

Your Mission

In this incarnation, you are here to teach your fellow beings about balance and harmony.

You have an ability to teach the subtleties of developing balance and harmony in people's lives. You have an intuitive sense of what is fair in all areas of life, especially in the area of relationships, and you have come into this existence to teach others how to share. Thus, you will draw to you people who are either selfish, overly independent, or extremely childlike. You can meet with great resistance as you teach these people the give and take of life.

The balance in any one-on-one relationship is a very fine line between giving and receiving, and the majority of those with whom you come in contact are excessively attached to one or the other. Because of your innate need never to settle for less than half or to give more than half, you may find yourself moving from one relationship to the next.

You are conscious of having two separate needs: to share half of yourself in a relationship and to keep half of yourself wholly to yourself. You are not comfortable with the other person giving more than half in a relationship because you fear that you may then be required to give more than half at another time. Essentially, you are teaching others how to keep their own identity in the context of a relationship.

Keeping a Sense of Balance

As you teach this lesson you must keep your sense of fairness in balance, for if you become unbalanced, you can end up teaching the lesson through your own misuse of the sharing energies. Those who are in balance and teaching in a positive mode make excellent lawyers, counselors, and advisers of all kinds, for with your ability to sit on the fence you can truly see both sides and aid both parties in finding an amiable solution.

At times you can appear very stubborn and selfish in relationships because once you have reached that halfway mark in giving or receiving, a herd of elephants could not push you further. In relationships, once you feel that your partner is not coming up with his or her fair share of giving, you begin to lose interest. You will give generously in a primary relationship, but once you feel the other person is asking you to cross the line of fairness, your attentions leave the relationship.

You always have an ongoing relationship, and if your partner does not share fairly with you, you simply begin sharing with someone else. In this situation you teach the value of sharing through removing yourself (physically or emotionally) from the relationship.

Self-Defined Fairness

Through sensitive communication others may be able to coax you into explaining the reasons for any of your decisions in life, even after you have reached the point of anger. When angered, however, you can be almost warlike, as if you were a general plotting a strategy. Before you will walk away from any relationship, you will use whatever means possible to show others just how unfair they have been. This can include treating them as unfairly as they have treated you.

Sharing every part of your life with one other person is your ideal, but when that is not possible, you will not compromise your need for fair play. You are capable of segmenting the different areas of your life. For instance, you are capable of staying within a marriage relationship for financial reasons only, partaking and sharing in the financial end of it so things will remain fair for both parties. Simultaneously, you are capable of taking the loving side of yourself and sharing it outside of that relationship. Monogamy is your ideal, but it is not your motivation. Fair play, sharing, balance, and harmony are your priorities as well as what you are teaching others by the way you live your life.

This also holds true in business relationships. If you have made a commitment to a business deal that is not meeting your financial needs, you will follow through with this commitment but make future investments somewhere else.

You have the ability to teach fairness in any manner in which those who need this lesson can accept it. If people who give too much draw you into their lives, you will take until they realize that "hey, this is not fair." If they are the type of people who take too much, you will also say, "Hey, this is not fair." Whichever role you feel you must play, the lesson is taught.

If you choose to ignore your innate ability to interrelate with others from a standpoint of balance, fair play, and harmony, your behavior patterns can become extremely selfish, insensitive, and self-destructive. You can give off an energy that repels people from becoming involved with you, due to your unwillingness to share any part of yourself. If you choose not to deal with the energy of fairness using personal integrity, you can be very arrogant and self-righteous, thereby teaching the necessity of fairness through your own self-centered behavior.

The Value of Sharing

You teach the value of sharing on a multitude of levels. You teach that when we give up our need for self-containment and come out of ourselves, we double our capacities. In sharing our thought processes with others, we gain additional resources and learn to value their input. In sharing our finances, we double our financial strength. You have an innate understanding of the need to band together and do more sharing, and you have the ability to bring people together who are of value in one another's lives. You help to show those around you the value of teaming up. Being extremely adept at recognizing when a merger is advantageous to both parties in business, friendship, and romance, you make an excellent marriage counselor, business consultant, or matchmaker.

Those who accept the energy of the Libra eclipse have learned to master the fine art of communication. You understand its importance and the value of negotiation, and you teach this through your own communicative skills. Whether in business deals, intimate relationships, or the give-and-take of friendship, you teach others the most valuable part of communication: getting another perspective on their problems. By bringing issues of concern out of the self, people can be detached from their emotional influences; this is very helpful in making intelligent decisions. You also have the ability to teach others the mirroring technique of seeing themselves through another's eyes.

By teaching the interdependency of relationships you show others the value of relating and the value of keeping their own identity. Thus, we learn and grow as individuals and always have something to share with others. If we become overly dependent on a relationship and do not involve ourselves in learning and growing on our own, we have nothing to bring to the relationship and thereby have ended the sharing process. You incarnated with this awareness and are sharing it with others. This is also why, in teaching the lesson of relationships, you find it so necessary to keep your individuality, for you intuitively understand that without that you can teach nothing. Basically, you teach us how to take the other person into account without losing track of ourselves.

LUNAR ECLIPSE: WHAT YOUR SOUL IS LEARNING TO EMOTIONALLY EMBRACE

Your Mission

In this incarnation, you are learning how to be fair in all areas of life, to share your mind, and to recognize the value of bringing your thought processes out of the self to communicate with others. This allows you to see how the opinions and insights of others can help you make intelligent decisions.

Learning Balance between Giving and Taking

In relationships you are learning the proper balance between giving and taking—not to take from another more than you are willing to give or give more than you are willing to take. Through this process comes the realization that taking from another human being when you are not willing to give is a theft of emotion, and this is very unfair to do to another. If you choose to live your life taking the affection of others when you are not willing to return it, you end up filling your life with bodies but no feelings.

On the other hand, if you are constantly giving to people who are not willing to take—people who are fearful of accepting love—it will be easy for you to fall into past patterns of holding on, just to have a body there. You may be fearful that if you give up someone you care about, that place in your life may remain unfilled. But if you continue giving, you can totally drain your vitality and capacity to love. So whether you find selfishness in others and learn about fairness in that way or are selfish yourself until others demand fairness from you, the lesson of fairness in relationships will be learned.

Some of you are learning about balance and harmony in areas of business: how to merge forces in order to work with others. Sometimes you may feel that everything in the business world must be accomplished by yourself and that if you join forces with another, you will lose recognition and become lost in the crowd. Once you have learned to share and work with others you will realize that there is even more success for you in joining forces.

Those of you who come to this lesson from the opposite perspective will tend to give all the credit to your partner in business or your mate at home. You need to learn the value of taking your share of the credit. Whether in a business project or in a relationship, you tend to give all your time and energy and not save any to do what you need to do with your life. If you refuse to learn the lesson of fairness, life may take away whatever is unfair in your life. And life has no regard for whether you are being unfair or another person or situation is being unfair to you. The universe does not care what you have or do not have, only that you learn to share.

Past-Life Influence

You incarnated with great difficulty in learning how to share because you are coming from past lifetimes of being extremely independent. The majority of you want to share, but you are so accustomed to doing things by yourself that it's challenging to learn how to depend on another. It feels awkward for you to slow down enough to allow someone to assist you, but accepting help from another validates that person's reasons for being involved in your life. If you continue to go through life being so self-contained, those around you will feel no need to be with you.

Slow down and allow others to participate in your life, or you will walk through life feeling lonely and keeping yourself from the very thing you promised to learn in this lifetime: relating with others and finding harmony within relationships. Reaching this point of balance within yourself and recognizing value in your partner are prerequisites for you to be able to have a partner in any area of your life.

Your independent attitude comes from a previous existence of just going after what you wanted, walking through other people's territories, with no regard for others. You need to learn the social graces, including tact, sensitivity, and consideration, because yours is a raw, emotional gut instinct. If you ignore your need for relationships, one of two things can happen in your old age: You can be lonely and feel a sense of incompletion, or you can become totally dependent as a last chance to learn the lesson of allowing others to assist you.

Learning to Honor Commitments

In all areas of your life, you are learning to develop a balanced sense of commitment. You can be so insistent on moving forward that you forget about previous commitments, or you can be so tied into commitment that you are unable to function without one. Here again, balance and fairness are the operative words. Commitment, whether it be by spoken word or legal contract, can be a sore spot until the concept of responsibility is accepted and demanded. You need to keep the commitments you have made and to demand that others keep their commitments to you. By being aware of the need for all involved to keep their promises, you are freed to interrelate in a positive way.

Step 1: Unconscious Expression

Operating unconsciously can bring you many relationship problems. You tend to go from relationship to relationship, never understanding why they don't work out. You can be extremely unfair to others without even recognizing it. You can be so self-centered that you take from life and relationships whatever you want, with no regard or consideration for the other people involved. This can affect your business affairs if you become unconscious of how you are interacting with people on a financial level. This tendency can cause many financial and relationship problems, causing you to go from job to job, wondering: Why is everyone being unfair to me? Why is everyone picking on me? Why is no one thinking of my interests? Why is everyone being so demanding of me and holding me down?

IMBALANCED RELATIONSHIPS

If your are operating unconsciously, you need to stand still for five minutes and take a look around. Look behind you and see the expressions on the faces of people whom you have just raced past without even saying, "Excuse me" or "How are you?" or "How was your day?" Incorporate some basic considerations into your makeup. One of those considerations is slowing down long enough to allow other people to catch up to you.

On the other side of the scale, you can set yourself up as the martyr in relationships, not recognizing that you are always giving without asking for anything in return. You do not recognize that it is a form of selfishness not to give others an opportunity to aid you or feel they are an intricate part of your life. This is just as negative as going through life taking everything you want without regard for others. You tend to take over in relationships, providing everything you think your partner needs without even asking, "Is this what you want?" You feel you are doing a fabulous job aiding the relationship, bettering your partner, and doing nothing for yourself, when in reality you are taking over without regard for the other. The only difference is that you're leading from behind, with a big push from the back.

In both cases, you are learning to take other people into account in forming relationships. Stop, look, and listen as you become involved in any relationship. In this way you can take others into consideration without either ruling their lives or taking off in your own direction.

One useful technique: Sitting down with a pencil and paper and figuring out what you are willing to give to a relationship and what you expect from one—before you become involved. Through this process you can learn what interrelating is all about. Taking time to think about it and saying, "These are my personality traits; this is why I expect; this is what I will not accept," empowers you to relate with more clarity and to be truly yourself.

Step 2: Conscious Expression

AIMING FOR SUCCESSFUL RELATIONSHIPS

Operating consciously, you are aware that you have difficulties relating. You are trying to overcome these problems by asking questions and getting feedback on what others think of you. In this lifetime you have reached the realization of what you want and where you are going. You are coming from previous existences of being in constant motion, and in this life you must learn to appreciate relationships. Life is a journey, and in order to enjoy it you need to take others along with you. Otherwise you find yourself on a lonely path that has no end.

Consciously you realize that you want a mate, another person to make this journey with you. But you also realize that you have never learned how to relate. As you begin to learn how to open yourself to another, there may be periods of opening, shutting down, going inside to evaluate what has been learned, and then coming out again. These periods of inward shutdowns are very necessary, for you are just beginning to learn how to interact. Do not become discouraged by this process, since it is very easy for you to pull back into your strong sense of self-containment and self-sufficiency.

The key is to really stay attuned to your desire to share. Always seek honesty in your communications; you can tend to rationalize what is going on around you so you remain in a past pattern of not taking others into account. You are learning to meet in the middle and to be willing to adjust yourself to the needs of those around you. Even the most conscious of you find it a challenge to adjust to another. Yet if you remain true to your inner desire to share, this process does eventually take place.

While learning how to relate you come to understand that communication is the key. You ask questions, get feedback, and find out who you are through others' eyes. You come into this existence finding it difficult to see yourself until another reflects your image. Through this need for reflection you are prodded on your path of learning to relate and communicate.

SUCCESSFUL BUSINESS RELATIONSHIPS

You are also learning to share and relate with your coworkers and business partners, to give yourself an avenue of added success by incorporating the lessons of others into the lessons that you are learning. This way, you double your resources. As this process becomes a more integral part of your business, social, and romantic life, you become adept at relating to others and an avid spokesperson for teaching those around you the value of being conscious of their fellow beings.

Step 3: Transpersonal Expression

You are aware of the needs and the delicate balances of those around you. You no longer relate only on a personal level but seek to find those modes of mutual expression that create a higher balance and harmony in each of your relationships.

On the level of group consciousness, you are teaching those of the physical realm to connect and communicate with all realms. You intuitively understand the need to watch, respect, and nurture nature itself and our interdependency with the Earth.

You are also aware of the interdependency we have with one another and the necessity of communicating clearly to aid one another's process on this plane. You understand our spiritual connection with the universe and the need to remain true to our spiritual self, staying clear on our journey into consciousness.

You are here to teach those of the physical realm to understand the interrelationship of the physical and spiritual realms, as well as the role the Earth plays in the universal plan. When you assist those on this plane to gain a higher understanding of the value that all things have to one another, you are truly a valued spiritual worker.

Physical Integration

When you learn to pay attention to the subtleties of the body, you begin to understand the essence of sharing and communication. The body is an intricate communication system, and through listening to it you can learn when something is out of balance.

When there is an imbalance in the external world, the physical world will reflect this imbalance. The body will draw attention to the kidneys and adrenal glands, and also the ovaries for women and the prostate for men. Just as we live our everyday lives integrating our external relationships, deciding which are positive and which are not, our kidneys and adrenal glands do a similar job with our internal relationships. The kidneys filter the impurities of deception, whether self-deception or the deception of others.

You can learn a very valuable lesson by listening to the body because it doesn't lie. By lying to yourself you do as much damage as if you are being unfair with another person, and your body will teach you this lesson. If you refuse to learn your lessons in the external world, your internal universe will impose them on you.

With the eclipse pattern of Libra, it is wise to remember that the essence of this pattern is honesty. When your energies are out of balance with the self and those around you, and when you are not looking with clearness of vision and being true to yourself and those around you, you disturb the delicate balance of your body. This can cause your physical equilibrium to become unbalanced; you can be subject to swaying from side to side, an inability to walk securely, and various other balance problems. This is because the balance the equilibrium represents within the internal physical world is an exact reflection of how you are dealing with your external worlds.

♏

SCORPIO

SOLAR ECLIPSE: WHAT YOUR SOUL CONTRACTED TO TEACH OTHERS

(In order to fully activate your solar eclipse energy in Scorpio, it may be helpful to read the lunar eclipse in Scorpio section. You may find information that can help you more fully contribute your solar eclipse in Scorpio gifts.)

Your Mission

In this incarnation, you have come to teach your fellow beings about the proper use of power, the right use of will, and how not to misuse energy. Scorpio holds a tremendous amount of energy, which can be used for positive or negative ends. You teach those who hold this energy how to use it properly. It is all about healthy boundaries for yourself and others.

When this energy is used properly—whether it is used for mental, physical, spiritual, or financial healing—its potential is extreme. If used in a negative way, it can be devastating. It is your job to use it in a positive way and teach others to do the same. If used for personal gain without regard for others, the involution can be just as extreme. We also have a responsibility to create our own destiny and manifest our desires on the physical plane, but we must do this without interfering with the destinies of others. You teach those around you to take total charge of themselves; to be accountable for their actions; to understand that whatever is given out comes back to the self.

The concept that every energy expelled from the physical being, the spiritual being, or the emotional being comes full circle to the source is very important. The Scorpio eclipse rules this energy of "what goes around comes around." You teach that we are all held accountable for our actions, our desires, and even our creations, for we are responsible for whatever we manifest.

You have the unnerving ability to see into the essence of a person and recognize what needs repair, and thus you are able to teach moral, financial, and spiritual responsibility. You draw people to you who need to know if there are any cracks in their foundations, for in bringing the Scorpio energy into their lives, they become aware of any personal weaknesses.

The Responsibilities of a Surgeon

Remember that you are responsible for shedding light in areas where you expose ills. You do not have the right to inflict pain without cause. You are the eclipse pattern of the surgeon, and it would be just as great a karmic debt for a surgeon to open a living body and walk away as it is for you to expose a wound without shedding insight and using your energy for transformation and regeneration.

If you are functioning from negativity, you are capable of using the resources of others with little regard for how it may weaken them. On the negative plane you can be highly manipulative, forfeiting your free will to a cycle out of which it seems to be almost impossible to climb. If you yield to the temptation of altering your own behavior in order to elicit a certain response from others, you can find yourself trapped in a vicious cycle: When you use your ability to understand the psychological mechanisms of another for the purpose of manipulation, the result is mutual entrapment. You may continue this pattern until you recognize what it really does: The energy of manipulation actually limits your own life experience.

Remain true to your own desires, whether or not those around you have the same ones. Others need the freedom to have separate goals, and you must avoid the temptation to sway them from their path. Your power comes from keeping the purest of personal integrity. Keeping your personal integrity intact allows you to come from a positive place in sharing your knowledge of the workings of the universe, the depth of your spiritual awareness, your understanding of the cycles of life and death, and the motivation for the behavior patterns of those around you. In this way you can add insight and clarity to the lives you touch without giving in to the temptation of using your power to bend the will of others.

When you are in a state of high integrity, you have the ability to help those around you locate what needs healing in themselves, which enables them to become clearer about their own motives. Then they are able to take responsibility for their actions and rise to a new level of personal power.

Helping Others Find Their Moral Direction

You tend to draw people to you who have an improper prosperity consciousness; you teach them to rise above the financial muck that they have imposed upon themselves. You can recognize when they have taken a wrong turn in terms of their values. You see when they need help to realign their own pathways with moral principles that will serve them.

You are willing to lead people out of places that others would fear to enter, for you can see future consequences from present actions. You can see where others are on the wrong track, and you have the integrity and courage to show them how they can realign themselves with their own best interests. You are teaching that it is more important to help others remove blocks to personal empowerment than it is to be tactful or to ignore the obstructions.

Because of your ability to help people who are out of alignment, you tend to attract all sorts of "lost sheep." If you are coming from negativity, you can incur a great deal of negative karma from misusing people in their moments of weakness. You are teaching the correct use of power and must take care not to misuse it yourself, since you will be held accountable at a later date.

Your Gift of Healing

You heal people's value systems—moral, financial, and spiritual. During this process you empower others to tap their own creative resources and thus become successful. Many of you work within financial, counseling, and rehabilitative institutions of all kinds, whether physical, spiritual, or financial. These could include mortgage companies, metaphysical counseling, the medical profession, collection agencies, the Internal Revenue Service, or other investigative agencies.

People are drawn to you whose values are contrary to those of society. This is because they need contact with healing energy to come back into alignment with themselves and their own constructive use of power. These people sense that their energy is harmful to society, yet their spiritual essence does not want to harm society, so they are looking for help. The universe wants to heal all its children, and therefore it empowers you with the energy to confront people with weakened values and to help them see how their actions affect other people.

You are teaching people that until their values are in alignment with correct universal principles, all of their actions will be self-defeating, fruitless, or disappointing in some way. You can show them where their internal base for relating with others is out of alignment with what would help them establish their own personal power.

The Proper Use of Sexual Energy

This is another lesson you are teaching, since you have a natural understanding of why people join on a physical level. You know unconsciously that when we are not embodied, we are androgynous—not male or female but a completion of both energies. Upon incarnating, one of those energies lies dormant within us unless we become aware enough to claim it and stop projecting it onto the opposite sex. But until this transformation takes place, there is the need for the joining of bodies to attain a sense of spiritual completion.

Sexual energy is so powerful because it creates a vehicle for another soul to enter this plane. You understand that when two bodies are joining, so are their souls. This is why the male energy blending with the female energy allows both a sense of completion.

Sexual union incurs a great deal of responsibility because there is also a blending of the actual juices of life. The fluids of the male enter the female, and on a much more subtle level, the fluids of the female enter the male. Through this blending, there is a completion of body, mind, and soul—an interweaving of energies on all three levels. If the couple is compatible, there is truly a feeling of satisfaction for both. If there is no compatibility, a disharmony is created within both. You are aware of the magnitude of sexual interchange on the spiritual as well as the physical level. You have the capacity to share this knowledge with others and intuitively understand that the act of sex is a form of spiritual completion.

LUNAR ECLIPSE: WHAT YOUR SOUL IS LEARNING TO EMOTIONALLY EMBRACE

Your Mission

In this incarnation, you are learning lessons relating to your value system: not being swayed in your values; how to share your values; overcoming negative manipulative traits; and taking responsibility for your sexual behavior.

You need to learn appropriate spiritual values and gain the understanding that as part of an intricate whole, these values affect all those around you. As the energies you emit come back to you, you are learning that what goes around comes around. Learning to plant positive seeds is important, since negative seeds grow like weeds and need no nurturing.

Realigning your principles is sometimes difficult, for you are coming from previous existences of being concerned with setting proper foundations for the self and the family. In this incarnation, however, you need to learn that society is interdependent and you are responsible for more than just yourself. We must all aid one another; the strong must help the weak, and the weak must learn how to be strong.

Discovering Boundaries for Yourself and Others

You also need to discover what the boundaries are for yourself and for others. You have a strong desire to push others to their limit because you want to know the boundaries: How far can I push you? At what point will you give in? Will you stand up to me? If they give in, you have no use for them and will move on to someone or something new. You do this because, without a sense of your own boundaries, you are afraid of misusing your power unless someone else sets limits for you. Your energy is like raw power—a rushing flood of water. Until you find something or someone to contain it, it just creates havoc in its path. When you do find containment, you become totally content. Once you know your limits you can direct your power from within them. Only then do you feel safe enough to claim your power fully.

Children born with this eclipse pattern need special guidance in discovering their boundaries. Whatever limits are set must always be enforced. As children mature and boundaries are expanded, they must be told that the boundaries are being expanded and why. With this assistance they are able to learn their proper place in their family, play, school environments, and society.

Once the boundaries are set, however, these children will still try to test the strength of the walls. They will continually have to be told: "You can only go this far. I say it and I mean it, and you cannot cross that line." If they are allowed to cross that line even once, there's no turning back. If these children see weakness, they will push twice as hard the next time, even if you stand up to them. They will not stop pushing those close to them until you tell them, "That's enough!"

Even when you become an adult, your parents, lovers, and bosses must never back down from your power. If they can stand their ground and teach you the value of your place within their reality, you will trust them. Then they will find you are an invaluable ally, for you will do anything for those you trust; your loyalty is immeasurable, and you would trust them with your life. If they are careless enough to make a fool of you in any situation, they will find out that you only remained within the boundaries they set because you respected them.

Respecting Others

One of your lessons is learning to respect others. You are looking for something within the human race that is deserving of respect. Yours is the energy of destruction, and you incarnated thinking that everything here is bad and needs to be rebuilt. Now you want to know who and what is of value here. The purpose of these thoughts is to purge and restructure yourself, keeping what is good and destroying what is not. You are looking for something or someone worthy of your respect. When you find it, you honor it, but when you find that you can't respect something, you try to destroy it.

You need to define those qualities in others that are valuable to you and begin building them in yourself. You do this by testing others to discover the limits of their integrity, strength, values, and moral fiber. You are seeking to find if there is something really good and worthwhile in those around you and if they have the integrity to live their principles as well as teach them. You are looking to find what values give other people the strength and self-confidence to work for the good of the planet so you can emulate them and find peace.

Past-Life Influence

In this lifetime you are becoming aware that in other incarnations you have allowed your values to slip. You have a misuse of power from past lives on your conscience. You feel that either you, or those you have been exposed to, deal in negative manipulative energy, and you want to transform the essence of your soul totally. You are desperately looking for something of value—something good—because this is the energy of transformation and regeneration. You want to get rid of what isn't good within you so you can rebuild yourself and be of value to others and to society.

If you don't meet with any limitations and don't find anyone with a strong enough value system to guide you in your youth, your life can become very difficult. You may even become imprisoned or institutionalized in places that will take responsibility for providing a structure for you and for giving you a substantial set of values. But with luck you will find something good in people and society that is worthy of your allegiance and support.

Once your energy is aligned with something you believe in, something you have tested and know to be worthwhile and beyond reproach in its integrity, you pledge yourself to it with your whole heart. That principle, person, or cause then becomes your value: It can contain your energy and make use of your tremendous strength, and you can find peace within it.

Mastering Power

When Scorpio energy is silent and reserved, it is because you are angry inside. You realize the extent of your power and know that if you let loose, society will lock you up. When you are resentful, it is because your energy has no outlet you can believe in. Your energy desperately needs a focus and a cause that you can pledge your power to, and in the process of building this cause, your energy finds its own radiant expression. This is why the Scorpio energy is often the power behind the throne; your power is strong enough to lift anyone to success if you believe in him strongly enough. You have no need to be in the limelight yourself, but you have a tremendous need to find someone or something to believe in.

You have come to learn that there is good in the world. You are aware of the bad, and you have an intuitive ability to see anything that needs to be repaired or destroyed. You need to learn that there are things around you that have strong, solid bases you can believe in. You feel such a need to share your tremendous energy because the Scorpio energy is one of joint values. You want to find someone to believe in so you can share your values and build a strong power base.

Being in the limelight is not important to you, but you do want to operate from a strong base of power; you therefore tend to go through life gathering people around you whom you trust. If you give people your trust, there is something very special inside of them, because you don't trust easily. You may trust certain people with one area of your life and not trust them with another. If that is your relationship with them, you will always have one eye on them. You won't be the power behind the throne for these people, but if you see value in them, you will let them be part of your army. Every member of your support group is someone who is indebted to you. You have an exaggerated fear of failing in money matters, reputation, career—so you always have "markers" in your pocket as backup (people who owe you favors).

You need to develop more trust in the universe so you are not constantly running scared. Then you can relax and allow the universe to help you build what you feel is truly good and worthwhile, so you can find peace and enjoyment in life. You are learning that you cannot depend on other people to set your boundaries and contain your energy. You need to get in touch with what is good for you and begin to act within your own boundaries and be responsible for your own energy.

Human frailty frustrates you. You are driven to self-perfection, and you think that weaknesses in the physical body limit your power. You seek a sense of mastery over yourself and your environment, and you strive to master the physical body and learn its limits. You also push others to their limits, but never beyond where you yourself have gone.

Learning to feel your body and listen to it is important so you won't push yourself to the point of breaking down physically. You may tend to push your body past its limits to exhaustion, and then you have to rebuild your strength from scratch. You feel that you have to know how far your body will take you in a pinch. In your search for limits, therefore, the first place you tend to look is your physical body.

Late Financial Bloomer

You are often a late bloomer financially. This is because you spend so much time doing favors for others and securing your power base that you don't spend time building your own success through your own merit. You expend time and energy on people you hope will support you because you are so fearful of having the rug pulled out from under you. But in actuality, you are giving away your power, a little bit here and a little bit there.

As you learn to trust yourself you will know that you are strong enough to get back up again if you fall. You are beginning to realize that you don't need the support of all those around you because you are a mountain of power within yourself. When you connect with the power within you and learn to go with your natural inborn flow, you will find that the universe does support you and there is good in the world—and in you. That is what you are here to learn: discovery and belief in your own goodness.

You are also learning to stop projecting your goodness outward by looking for someone else to believe in. As you learn to support and trust yourself by being true to your own sense of goodness, you can begin to construct your own boundaries and contain your own energy. This gives you the freedom to be more trusting of those around you, since it eliminates the need to give away your power. This will also lead to the realization that it is all right for you to be successful and to be in the limelight. Then you can be the power behind your own throne and rise to success. From this position you can support those around you—but from a purer motive, since you no longer feel that you need them to ensure your own strength. Now when you support others it will be from a place of true caring, and you will no longer be involved in a process that gives your power away.

The caliber of the people around you will also change. As long as you thought you needed others to support you, you unknowingly held yourself down by having opportunists around you, feeding off your energy. This is why so often you have been disappointed in human nature. When you feel you are buying favors from others rather than simply giving freely, without strings attached, you deprive those around you of giving of their own volition and love when you need their help. By not giving freely, you have robbed yourself of the opportunity to experience the law of cause and effect in a positive way.

Whatever you give to another has to come back to you—if not through the person you gave it to, then through someone else when you need it. As you learn to unblock the flow within yourself by giving freely, you will see the goodness in others as you experience them giving freely back to you. This feels very different from begrudging indebtedness and obligation! You need to learn that if you look for the worst in people, you will agitate them until you bring out the quality you fear (at least in your own mind). But if you expect the best, you are powerful enough to evoke that quality in others.

By learning to give freely and without ulterior motives, you are letting go of the energy of manipulation. You can spend so much time manipulating the lives of those around you that you become caught in this mode of expression, thereby stunting your own growth. As you release this negative energy, you realize that just because people travel their own separate paths doesn't mean they can't care about and support one another. You start to understand that if others truly care about you, they will be there when you need them, and if they're not, then maybe they don't care as much as they say or as you think they do. This helps you to sort out the people who really care about you from those who don't, and also broadens your awareness of the many different ways people show they care.

When you reach this awareness, you will operate from a sense of your full power, and there will be no holding you back. You also are learning about the proper use of power in this incarnation: that it is negative to use your power over those who are weaker, and positive to share your power to assist others in coming into their own strength. In empowering others, you gain a sense of your own strength in a way that breeds self-esteem.

Step 1: Unconscious Expression

Operating unconsciously, you may have a negative behavior pattern of building your success on the misfortune of others. If you are not aware of the lessons you have come to learn, you may find yourself surrounded with very negative people or being a very negative person. You may be someone who uses others in their weakest moments, such as a loan shark (legal or not), pimp, drug dealer, con artist, or ambulance chaser. Another manifestation of this eclipse could be various forms of psychic manipulation, such as voodoo, the casting of spells or hexes, and so forth.

We must all learn our life's lessons, but how we choose to learn them is up to us. Coming from negativity, using others would be an unconscious method for learning your lessons. Through this pattern you would learn the lesson of cause and effect. You can find yourself being forced into rehabilitation or suffering tremendous losses through your own schemes.

Many of you are coming directly from a previous incarnation in which your value system had a cracked foundation. Your moral, financial, and spiritual values have been shattered through abuse of your ethics, and you are here to strengthen them in this lifetime. If you don't go about this in a positive way, however, you may find yourself becoming something that you despise.

If you choose to operate in a negative fashion, your body may deteriorate as you set out to prove that there is no one you can depend on, not even yourself. You try to prove to yourself that there is nothing good on this plane and that everything must be destroyed.

RESILIENCY

When you finally reach bottom, you have an amazing ability (more so than any other eclipse pattern) to pull yourself out of the muck. Unfortunately, you may need to create a crisis in your life in order to do it, unless you seek some sort of counseling or run into someone you respect enough to allow him or her to show you the light. Once you accept that there is good in the world—or once you have fallen as far as you can physically, emotionally, or financially—then you begin to make upward progress. The idea is for you to do this before you ruin your life.

One way to facilitate your growth is to begin to value yourself: Once you feel you are worth saving, you are more than capable of pulling yourself up. You know your faults all too well. You need to understand what is right about yourself and to get in touch with the goodness inside you. You are gentle, you have an understanding of the workings of the universe, you are sensitive (even if you try to hide it), you care about others (even if you pretend not to), and you have a basic goodness of intent. If someone can tell you one positive thing every time you do something negative, it gives you the recognition of your good intent without validating your antisocial behavior. Once you can see this spark of good, you will have enough faith in yourself to climb out of the worst situations. You are capable of overcoming circumstances that would bury the average person.

When operating unconsciously, you have difficulty handling other people's jealousy. This is because you are also working on issues of jealousy and know only too well that feeling of hatred for someone who is more successful than you. You are trying hard to overcome this and be sensitive to it because you don't like that part of yourself, but you tend to judge yourself too harshly.

Often when you get angry it is because someone got hurt and you want to protect or be loyal to that person. Negative reactions may come from not knowing socially acceptable responses to these situations. You care so much about your fellow beings that when you see a misuse of power, you feel compelled to assault it physically or to confront it and remove it. You want to destroy anything that is not positive.

It is important for you to recognize the good within yourself because this eclipse rules the energy of destruction, and until you see the spark of good within you, you will continue on a self-destructive path. You don't see your own value until someone else reflects it. You are here to learn your value as a human being, to society, and to others.

Step 2: Conscious Expression

You know instinctively that you are here to learn how to use the energy of transformation and regeneration in a positive mode. The energy of transformation is also the energy of destruction, and you intuitively understand that something must die for something else to be reborn. You recognize from a prior lifetime, where you were dealing with your internal values, that an integral part of your soul growth pattern was left out—the ability to incorporate your values with those of others. In this life you have come to learn how to recognize what is valuable to all, not just what is valuable to the self. You tend to deal with this lesson by removing from your consciousness what is no longer useful and replacing it with something more positive.

WHAT YOU GIVE RETURNS TO YOU

The Scorpio energy is a very powerful one. It is the energy of surging water, which knows no limits until it is contained. Thus, you can come on too strong within society and must learn how to control your energy. Until society or someone you respect tells you that you have reached the set limits, you will not stop pushing. Others must deal openly and honestly with you and not be afraid to stand up to you, because you can learn your boundaries only through other people setting limits and holding their ground. It does you no good when people let you run over them, since this teaches you nothing.

Operating consciously, you know that you must treat others the way you want to be treated. You recognize that just because other people do not always stand up to you—or are not always able to contain your energy—does not mean that you must destroy them. If you do try to destroy them, at another time, someone else more powerful will try to destroy you. You understand that everything in the universe works as a cycle, and everything you give returns to you. This also holds true for positive actions, thought, and emotions—whatever leaves the body on a mental, physical, or spiritual level comes back. Through this recognition you are learning the proper use of power.

PARTNERSHIP

You are learning the lessons of joint manifestation. By intertwining your energies with another, you are learning how to trust and be trusted. You are learning how to overcome past patterns of possessiveness that lead to jealousy. This is very important, because if you do not learn to let go, it can pull you into a pattern of jealousy that prevents growth and holds you down.

If instead you learn to develop trust, including self-trust, it allows you to overcome these negative possessive traits. This will give you the strength of personal integrity to deal very successfully with people on a joint level, for you know that truly trusting another means trusting the self.

If you do not trust others, unconsciously you are telling yourself that they have the power to affect your life, and you give them power over you. Then you recognize that you can relate with those around you without letting their actions affect you to the point where you become incapable of handling any situation. Through this process you learn to trust your own integrity and internal strength enough to know that you can rise above any depth, to any height you choose. You are the energy of the scorpion transforming itself to the eagle and then to the phoenix.

Step 3: Transpersonal Expression

You have the capacity to teach people to recognize and honor the good that lies in their own individuality. You teach that by honoring the good in oneself, each of us honors the whole. You help others to remove whatever is invalidating the self, so that their spiritual essence can shine through; by validating what is right in themselves, they validate the whole. You teach that we are all part of a collective whole and have a spark of the collective consciousness within us. In keeping our own sparks kindled, we add power to the whole.

You are using your power to transform the consciousness of humankind by removing old subconscious patterns that hold down the evolution of the individual soul as well as the evolution of planetary consciousness. Your ability to see through to the core of any situation can expose the diseases that prohibit a healthy body, mind, or spirit, and the result is purifying and healing. On the highest levels you are the psychic healers and spiritual regenerators, reconnecting the minds of your fellow beings to a magnetic relationship with the whole.

Physical Integration

You need to remain aware of your spiritual responsibility to the universal plan. If you put this responsibility aside, your reproductive organs may tend to deteriorate, since these correlate with the universal energy of creation and expansion. Incorporating this principle into your everyday life—if not on a spiritual level, at least in your interactions with others—is your key to good health. Thus, it is important that you learn to let go of your creations, whether trusting those around you with what you value or sharing your spiritual concepts. If you choose to ignore the responsibility of sharing these vital parts of yourself, your body will communicate to you by drawing attention to its reproductive areas.

If you are not dealing with the energy of transformation and regeneration—the energy of purging the old to make way for the energy of birth and rebirth—you may have problems with your rectum, colon, small intestine, or bowel. If on a spiritual level you are allowing yourself to create blockages, the body will reflect what you are doing. In order to let go of the obstruction and not experience physical problems from holding back what needs to be released, you must learn that you cannot control everything around you.

$\nearrow$

SAGITTARIUS

SOLAR ECLIPSE: WHAT YOUR SOUL CONTRACTED TO TEACH OTHERS

(In order to fully activate your solar eclipse energy in Sagittarius, it may be helpful to read the lunar eclipse in Sagittarius section. You may find information that can help you more fully contribute your solar eclipse in Sagittarius gifts.)

Your Mission

In this incarnation, you have accepted the responsibility for teaching your fellow beings how to understand the common thread that runs through all the philosophies and various belief systems of humankind.

You are spreading the awareness that we are all one, we are all heading in the same direction, and at the same time we have all come to learn something on our own unique paths. You are teaching that a spark of the collective consciousness burns strongly within all of us. We need to learn to respect one another, without prejudices, and to recognize that no matter which path a person has chosen, we are all traveling to the same destination. All the ways up the mountain lead to the same summit.

The lives you touch in this lifetime are automatically stimulated to a higher consciousness. You have incarnated without any prejudices, and you need to be careful not to develop prejudices. The idea is to recognize that you already have the proper philosophy. In this lifetime, because of your philosophical nature and your personal belief system, you will tend to attract very glib people. You will draw those who are socially oriented and overly status conscious. It is natural for you to try to change them because the various eclipse patterns always attract people who need to learn the lesson they are teaching.

Holding to Truth

It is important that you do not compromise your belief system, for yours is the philosophy that actually reflects the higher consciousness. It is your privilege to raise those around you to your level of spiritual awareness and not allow yourself to be influenced by others.

During your spiritual travels it is important for you to stay aware and not become stuck in thinking that one way is the only way. You truly understand that all souls are driven by the desire for perfection of self—to be one with the source—reunited with the God of their consciousness. It is important for those of you who have chosen to be spiritual teachers in this lifetime to remain clear and unprejudiced. Thus, you may help your fellow beings to clarify their awareness and guide them on their journeys with the freedom to travel the path they have chosen. You have the strength and the understanding to assist people on their chosen paths without the ego involvement that might tempt you to bring them to your path.

It is not uncommon for you to experience the restrictions of religious indoctrination in your youth. The rigidity of this approach provides the stimulus for you to break free later and begin your search for the common thread that underlies all belief systems and religions. In your resistance to the idea that one way is the only way, you serve humanity by heralding the spirit of tolerance for—and understanding of—religious philosophies.

Motion is essential. You can be interested in taking care of the physical body but usually only because you understand the need to keep it moving. You recognize that all things on Earth must continually be in motion, for through your spiritual development you have learned that nothing is static within the universe. To be of the utmost usefulness to the soul and to the spark of God within it, the physical body must be fluid and move with the least restriction possible. In movement there is freedom, and through freedom comes the awareness to conceptualize many different ideas. Through allowing others in your environment true freedom of expression you receive the reward of bringing out the highest and the best in those around you.

Career Options

Professionally, you make excellent philosophers, counselors, professors, spiritual teachers, and gurus. You are not at all desirous of people following you, however, even though you exude the type of energy that draws people to you. Your purpose is not to be a spiritual leader but to embody spiritual awareness and to give people back their spiritual freedom.

You do wish not to personify their consciousness and replace what or who they followed before. You want to set people free to find their own paths, believing that instead of having any individual gurus on this plane, humankind needs to find a greater sense of awareness from within.

You are therefore comfortable in any profession that affords you the opportunity to help people develop a greater sense of reality and actualize their beliefs. You can help others deal with being different and support their needs to expand in unfamiliar areas. Because you do not feel guilty about being different, you give others permission to truly be themselves.

Awareness of Truth

You are a seer of reality. Through your innate ability to see the underlying truth in everything around you, you can teach others to remove the veils of illusion that obstruct clear thinking. Using logical deduction you are able to see a more exact reality, and you teach these techniques to others. This enables them to perceive truthful and precise information, and thus to make intelligent decisions. You have the ability to see the answer and to distill information, and you can help those around you to reach their goals by tuning in to the wider perspective that you can show them.

You have tremendous decision-making abilities since you can see the resolution at a great distance. The adept person can learn a great deal about fundamental logic, and you get great pleasure in sharing this ability with all who are willing to learn from you. You tend, however, to expound your beliefs and must be mindful that sometimes you express your ideas too strongly. This can frighten the more timid souls away from the very freedom and awareness you are trying so hard to offer them. You have a great love for your fellow beings and a strong sense of responsibility for helping them to develop their conscious awareness.

You often need to break the everyday structure of your environment since you fear being trapped in it. Because of this ability to exist within yet separate from the normal concepts of society, you remain a curiosity to those around you. This stimulates others to ask the questions that they need to have answered. You are truly happy in this role because you do not seek students, they seek you. This way, no dependency is formed, for students are often not aware that they have met a teacher until the teacher has moved on.

Should you choose to walk through this life asleep and unwilling to assist others in achieving more advanced states of awareness, you will be known for your shallowness of perception. In this way you still teach the same lesson, only you do it by being a negative example of how those around you do not want to live their lives.

LUNAR ECLIPSE: WHAT YOUR SOUL IS LEARNING TO EMOTIONALLY EMBRACE

Your Mission

You have come into this life to break all prejudices and to learn to understand the common thread that runs through all forms of philosophy, religion, and spirituality. You have an unquenchable thirst for knowledge, higher insights, and information regarding conscious awareness.

Past-Life Influences

You need to unlearn the prejudices that you absorbed in previous lifetimes. In the past your perceptions were limited and narrow-minded; your ideas were based only on information from your own immediate environment. Due to this limited framework you became judgmental about how others should live and how things should be done.

In this life, you are exposed to many things outside your own belief systems. Once this happens it greatly accelerates your process and an inquisitive side comes to the fore. It is as if you begin a crash course to expand your horizons and your consciousness. The way you go about this process can be different at different times of your life, yet the thrust is the same: to acquire the knowledge and information that can set you free from limiting past belief systems that kept you from connecting with a universal sense of wholeness.

Some of you acquire the information you need by traveling to foreign countries and exposing yourself to different cultures, philosophies, and theologies. As you explore these different cultures you investigate their belief systems, seeking the history of the various religions to find the common thread behind the different rules and regulations of their doctrines.

For example, you may ask: "Why did Catholicism say not to eat meat on Fridays?" When you think about it from a practical point of view, you realize that when the rule was made, people were not aware that the human body needs a rest and that it takes a long time to digest a piece of meat. In this way you can break down the practices behind organized religion and understand that they were formulated to teach humankind how to be sociable, how to be civilized, and how to take care of the physical body so that the soul within could thrive.

A Draw to Foreign Countries

You want to experience foreign countries firsthand. You are drawn to better understand the individual cultures, background, and motivations of the people. This helps you to put your philosophy, ideas, and attitudes in alignment. For you, book knowledge is not enough. You want to see how people are living, if the culture works, and whether you respect the moral fiber of the people.

You want to be aware of how the philosophy is integrated into the culture: "Does what I have read and studied really fit with the people that have this philosophy and practice this religion? What type of personal consciousness does this belief system manifest?" You are accustomed to functioning within different social groups and understanding social behavior patterns on a surface level. Now you are taking your understanding to a deeper level and gaining an awareness of the larger pattern. You are attracted to foreign countries so you can find the common thread that runs through each of the different societies and cultures. This gives you a sense of belonging to an abstract consciousness that is inclusive of all social cultures.

The more cultures you are exposed to the better, because you are distilling all the different belief systems and integrating what works for you. You are actually looking for your own direction and your own philosophy because you have lost your way. You became so accustomed to living on a superficial social level that you lost your drive to find your own path. And the only way you seem to be able to find your path in this lifetime is to distill what you need from many different philosophies.

When you have a compilation of the things that you like, you experiment with what works for you spiritually, philosophically, and practically—what perceptions make you feel happy and confident. When you experience other religions and philosophies—without being judgmental, it is hoped—you learn that some things work and some things don't on an individual, personal level. You are developing your own religion, your own inner connection with truth.

Learning to overcome a tendency to prejudices, narrow-mindedness, and superficiality is very important to you in this lifetime. You want to know the whys behind the different philosophies and religions in order to gain a greater understanding. In a previous existence you had exposure to only tidbits of everything but no depth of information, so in this incarnation you have an unquenchable thirst for more information on a philosophical level. You are seeking the common denominator of truth beneath the social interactions and the pieces of information that you already have.

You came to the planet with your mind-set in a precise social structure, believing that things should be a certain way. You look at your own family environment and say: "Okay, this philosophy seems to work for my family. But I notice that my friends' families have different philosophies that seem to work for them. How can that be? How come they're not doing things the same way I am?" This exposure in your youth to different people with different belief systems really started you thinking.

Seeking the Common Denominator

You need the common thread so you can find peace. You feel a strong sense of separation from the from the universe while in the body. You want to be back on a spiritual plane but are not totally sure how to get there. You are looking for answers, wanting to identify with something larger than the inconsistency of social interactions. You are looking for truth, and you feel the only way to find truth is to investigate everything personally. This is not investigation for its own sake but to gain the information you feel you need in order to make educated decisions.

As a spiritual teacher you have an innate understanding that you are here to awaken the consciousness of your fellow beings, yet you don't automatically understand what you are supposed to awaken or exactly how you are to do it. Your quest for knowledge will eventually guide you to an understanding of how best to teach your lesson. You need to be very careful, however, not to become so strongly attached to any one path that you lead those around you down only that path. You have a great deal of persuasiveness because you mastered the lesson of salesmanship in previous existences and now you are concentrating on mastering the abilities of the mind.

You can best aid your fellow beings by helping them to find their own paths. You need to recognize that each individual has his or her own route: No two can travel exactly the same path because each passageway supports only an individual consciousness. To become whole, each of us must come from our own direction and find our way back to the initial existence. Part of the developmental process that you have come to learn and to share with those around you is that there are a multitude of paths and directions but only one center. Thus, it is most important for you to avoid using your powers of persuasion to try to get people to share your trail. You need to be aware and responsible regarding what you say to others because you could be pulling them from their chosen paths onto yours. In this way you can be detrimental rather than helpful to those around you.

As you learn to listen more carefully to the needs of others, their motives, and where they are coming from, you begin to understand why each person needs to travel his or her pathway in an individual way. By allowing those around you the freedom to choose their own paths, you relieve yourself of the karmic burden of being the self-appointed pied piper of the planet. In this way you allow yourself to have exactly what you came to obtain: personal freedom. You are learning how to be free without carrying the burden of decision for your fellow beings.

Your job in this lifetime is not to steer others down any particular trail but to share your philosophy of freedom and expansion. In this way you help to set others free to find their own chosen passageway. You accumulate information, throw it into one large pot, and when it is all melted down you find a lump of gold. You are learning to distill information into truth. Through your investigations into different religions and philosophies, you have learned to accept what truly serves humankind and to discard what is too limiting. You are learning to break through man-made religious and philosophical structures to a more universal consciousness. In this way you find your own individual path.

Although you hope to find those of like consciousness along your way, you tend to be a lonely soul, for your journey into consciousness seems to be traveled by few. As you learn to set aside your prejudices and open yourself to new experiences, you are allowed to see the light of others around you. Then your feelings of loneliness are alleviated.

Step 1: Unconscious Expression

YOUR LESSON

You have come to learn how to break down your prejudices and expand your narrow-mindedness. If you choose to learn these lessons the hard way, you can go through life being exposed to a great many narrow-minded people. You seem to run headlong into difficulties with others over their belief systems, often arguing with those who are just as limited in their views as you are. This helps you to recognize the narrow scope of your own beliefs.

If you resist your lesson, you may have to deal with the consequences of your prejudices against people from foreign countries or other religions. You tend to think that anyone who speaks with a dialect that sounds different from yours is below you on an intellectual level. For example, you may think that slow speech patterns indicate a lack of mental alertness. Another example of this type of prejudice would be a reticence to hire someone who speaks with a foreign accent, fearing that the person would not do the job properly or could not communicate clearly with others. This attitude may lead to your missing out on the best person for the job. If the pattern is deeply ingrained from previous incarnations, you may be of a minority group yourself in this lifetime and have the experience of being on the receiving end of prejudice.

You need to accept that you have incarnated to change belief systems that leave no room for expansion of diversity. Your job is to stop being judgmental and self-righteous, and recognize that your way is not the only way. Just because you have chosen a particular route does not mean you cannot benefit from illumination or added insight from others who are on a different path. You are learning to accept the awareness that every human being is one of God's beings, and we all have the spark of the collective consciousness within us. We are all evolving and have the right to grow on our own set path: Not all the flowers of the earth can flourish in the same pot.

ISOLATION

Your social snobbery is similar to those who belong to an elite group or an established country club that does not allow members who do not meet certain social criteria. With this type of consciousness you cannot respect the essence of your fellow beings or appreciate their contributions, which can be new, different, and exciting. For you, everything must remain the same and be within the social graces.

It is important for you to outgrow this tendency so you will no longer be limited to a pathway of narrow-mindedness and isolation. Once you begin to integrate a more expanded awareness, it becomes important for you to share your new insights with others on a human level and not to speak in an overly clinical way. You need to avoid technical terminology, which puts everything on such a lofty level that those around you cannot benefit from your new-found knowledge.

Another potential self-defeating mechanism is your tendency to stop listening to others. You can become so attached to your chosen trail that you end up with a form of tunnel vision—seeing only what you want to see and going straight ahead. You forget that you learn through interacting with other people and being exposed to their cultural beliefs.

You can get so wrapped up in expanding your consciousness that you forget to enjoy and benefit from the essential human element. Also, information that originally increased your awareness can become a limitation if you do not remain receptive to new levels of awareness. It is through interacting with others that you gain what you need to continue in your own personal growth.

Because of habitual past-life limitations to your immediate social environment, you can experience some fear when expanding your horizons beyond what is familiar. Going to parties with different types of people and eating new types of foods can cause you anxiety. You limit yourself if you fail to appreciate other dimensions of life and what those outside of your familiar circle have to offer. In journeying past your immediate environment, you gain some of your most pleasant and expansive experiences and insights.

Step 2: Conscious Expression

You go looking for intellectual fulfillment, and you are constantly learning and progressing on your path. You can be found in various institutions of learning, studying philosophy, theology, and the customs and cultures of different lands. You are learning to be more open and aware, and you find that interactions with others and exposure to their philosophies expands your mental capabilities.

You have a natural curiosity about spiritual matters, but you are most interested in understanding what motivates humankind to feel such a link to the spiritual realms while in the flesh. You need to align the principles of the body, mind, and soul in this lifetime. Thus, you actively point yourself in the direction of this alignment and do what is necessary in order to attain it. You enjoy physical activities and understand the body and its functions. You know that the body must be physically agile so that the mind can perform at its highest level.

You acknowledge your respect for the God-consciousness and realize that you are part of the collective whole. You are aware that there are lessons the soul wants to incorporate in this existence, and thus you allow yourself to be prodded to learn more about these three aspects of yourself and to organize them into an integrated whole. Yours is a quest for understanding body, mind, and soul—what their connections are and how they interact.

FREEDOM AND LIBERATION

Operating at a conscious level, you incorporate the philosophy that individuals travel the only road they are capable of conceptualizing at any given time. You realize that if you cannot see it or dream it, you cannot aspire to it. To satisfy your need to achieve higher levels of enlightenment you experience as much as you possibly can in your lifetime. In this way you broaden your ability to conceptualize, thereby increasing your options.

You are highly motivated to attain the degree of consciousness that will free you from having to return to this plane. Thus, you spend a great deal of time and energy investigating all the options that lead to total freedom and liberation. The desire to be one with the whole and not to be a separate entity is intense, matching the intensity of the sorrow stemming from your feelings of separation.

You are seeking the path that will led you to the truth within yourself and thus to the feeling of connectedness with the whole. You want to understand the pathways of all those around you so you can ascertain whether you have chosen the right route.

Step 3: Transpersonal Expression

You have actively aligned yourself with discovering the truth in this incarnation. You operate from the position of understanding that all trails are the right ones, and you make yourself available to others who need help in gaining this same core awareness. You realize that our state of consciousness is limited only by our concepts, so you work to expand other people's concepts. This increases the win potential for everyone, and you recognize that unless we all win, no one wins.

You also encourage others through your own natural state of joy, which adds a lightness and sense of adventure to the road you travel. By doing what you can to lift the mood of those around you, you share the joy and light-heartedness you have found through your own connection with truth. It is not your philosophy that uplifts others as much as your freedom from rigid belief systems and prejudices.

You intuitively understand that your role is to practice tolerance. You recognize that you are working off karma by breaking old, prejudicial patterns and establishing a more progressive mental attitude while on the physical plane. You constantly keep things in motion by helping to release humanity from its past so we can move into the future. You support the trend to bring more freedom and personal accountability into religion and philosophy. In fact, freedom with personal responsibility is the key phrase of the transpersonal eclipse pattern in Sagittarius.

Physical Integration

Your body communicates to you through irritations in the areas of the hips, thighs, and liver. If you choose not to release your prejudices, the liver, which filters impurities from the blood, will cease to function in a way that is supportive to the entire being. This is a reflection of the way that prejudice is not supportive to your psychological or philosophical well-being.

Problems with mobility and the hip joints can result if you allow yourself to slip into past patterns of being unaware, supporting the status quo, and remaining stagnant on a social level. To alert your consciousness to the fact that there has been immobility in your mental and spiritual processes, you may find problems with movement in the hip and thigh areas. These can cause restrictions and irritations varying from a slight degree of discomfort to an extreme amount of deterioration. The tendency toward mental stagnation can be remedied by expanding your consciousness and releasing prejudices and rigid beliefs.

Prejudice manifests as a rash. On another level you can be prone to skin eruptions on different parts of the body. Acne, boils, and other impurities may surface if you are reluctant to get old concepts out of your system. The body is given to us by our parents, but the cell memory within the body has a certain level of awareness on its own. If you seem to have prejudices other than those imparted from your early family environment, this may be why. The body will have skin eruptions because it recognizes that these patterns are detrimental to the overall health of the being, and it works to reject them from the body. Consequently, on the physical level you may develop skin eruptions of all kinds as the body eliminates what it does not want to carry. This is necessary if you have taken an overabundance of prejudices on a cellular level through your family heredity.

♑

CAPRICORN

SOLAR ECLIPSE: WHAT YOUR SOUL CONTRACTED TO TEACH OTHERS

(In order to fully activate your solar eclipse energy in Capricorn, it may be helpful to read the lunar eclipse in Capricorn section. You may find information that can help you more fully contribute your solar eclipse in Capricorn gifts.)

Your Mission

You have come into this incarnation to teach your fellow beings the value of having a good reputation. You have an intuitive sense that if you don't present yourself properly in public, your behavior can come back to haunt you at the most inopportune times.

Operating negatively, you teach this lesson through suffering the consequences instead of reaping the rewards. Others can learn the value of a good reputation by seeing yours demeaned as a consequence of your own improper public behavior.

Operating positively, you teach by presenting yourself with dignity and reserve while you are in the company of others, even within your own family unit. Every action is well thought out. You are so self-disciplined that you can bring a good friend to the airport and refrain from kissing him or her goodbye just so it cannot possibly be misconstrued. Heaven forbid that anyone should say to the wrong person, "I saw John and Mary Lou kissing at the airport." You make sure that others have no opportunity to weaken your standing in any way. You are always aware of your reputation, and that is why you are so reserved in public. Yet you are very demonstrative behind closed doors; you really let the tiger out of the cage when the bedroom door is closed and the shades are pulled.

The Protocol of Achievement

You are teaching the true definition and necessity of protocol through your intuitive understanding that when climbing the ladder of success, certain acknowledgments need to be made along the way. Recognizing that anyone above you on the ladder has a fear of looking down, you understand that this fear comes from not wanting to be on a lower rung.

Whether striving for spiritual, material, or emotional success, everyone is comfortable in his or her chosen upward path. When someone else is encountered moving upward, it can either remind the person of where he or she was or cause the fear of not being recognized for accomplishments. Those who are not secure in their current status can be very dangerous adversaries because those who have fears are capable of pulling others down with them, just as a man who is drowning sometimes drowns the person who has come to save him.

In recognizing this need to respect another's achievements, you secure the ground for those with whom you work. This allows others to be more comfortable and gives them a clear vision to their own path, with no unnecessary obstacles in their way. Through this intuitive awareness of recognizing that all must be respected and acknowledged, your path to the top can be an easier, if sometimes slower, journey. But the route you have chosen to the top is clear to you because you understand the necessity of protocol, and teach the lesson of respecting those who have gone before and their accomplishments.

A Role Model

You also understand and teach that if you want to succeed in this lifetime, you must always conduct yourself as if someone were watching. Whatever examples you are setting, you find yourself living a very visible lifetime—or at least your behavior would indicate that this is so.

You appreciate that it is in your best interests to act as if everything you do will be uncovered. Those around you learn that if they choose to go to the top, they must always conduct themselves as if every aspect of their lives were broadcast on television. Because you are teaching the value of maintaining a good reputation, your energy automatically draws attention to you so that others can learn. It's up to you to choose whether you depict yourself positively or negatively, but either way people learn about the importance of reputation through watching you.

Others can learn from you how to climb the ladder of success in all areas of life. You recognize that no forward motion can be taken until current ground is secured, whether it be in affairs of the heart or in business. You teach others that before the next step is taken in a business venture or in a relationship they must always be secure where they are. This is similar to the actions of a mountain goat who sometimes goes sideways or takes a few steps backward, but gets to the top without falling because it does not step on insecure ground.

You are here to lead an exemplary lifetime and model in your own behavior the principles for which you stand. Through your ability to commit to an ideal and uphold it by virtue of the way you live your life, you teach others that it is possible to stand for a principle that is larger than their personal lives while still going about their day-to-day activities. You teach them the value of commitment since you have the capacity to materialize your goals through the power of your pledge and the ability to keep your goal solidly in mind. This level of awareness allows you to use everything that comes across your path to assist you in reaching your goal. In this way you teach those around you the value of adversity.

People drawn to you tend to be overly emotional and sensitive, and they need to learn to function in the material world. Through your natural ability to teach responsibility and protocol you show them how to succeed in areas where previously they floundered. You aid others in not taking the external world so personally that they allow its harshness to cause them emotional upsets.

You teach those around you to be responsible for their actions because you know that whatever you do in life will be judged by others. You understand that society tends to be judgmental, and you are teaching others to get along with society, to interrelate, and to be successful. Through you they learn that by living within the limits society sets, they will be judged by those around them. It is very important to you to teach others to be useful and act in a manner that serves society, since by doing this you feel you are living a responsible life.

Seeing the Usefulness

For you, usefulness is of the utmost importance. Everything in your life must be useful, and you do not believe in waste, especially the waste of character. If people are not using their potential, not putting their best foot forward, or are losing their good reputation, it is a waste. You do not want to squander your time around people of poor character, for you recognize that society judges you not only by who you are but by those with whom you associate. You teach people the value of being responsible for the way they achieve their goals through a correct relationship with the society in which they live.

LUNAR ECLIPSE: WHAT YOUR SOUL IS LEARNING TO EMOTIONALLY EMBRACE

Your Mission

You have incarnated to learn the value of having a good reputation in this lifetime. Your lessons are how to fit in with society; how to be responsible for your actions; and how to be useful and keep your integrity in the external world.

Past-Life Influence

In past lives, you were very comfortable and secure within the home environment. Thus, in this existence, you need to overcome a dependency on

home and mother, and go out into the world to become a valuable member
of society.

If you choose to learn these lessons in a negative way, it will be through
society's restricting you, perhaps even through periods of incarceration. There
may be times when you are constantly demeaned by those around you or
when your reputation is ruined, or when others find you of no value whatso-
ever and have no qualms about letting you know. Through these experiences
you learn that it is very important to give and not just take. If you go through
life taking and not giving, you encourage resentments and restrictions. These
restrictions are really self-imposed when you choose to give nothing back to
the society that can give you an avenue, a direction, and a place to claim a
name for yourself.

If you learn your lessons positively, in the beginning it may be through
trial and error in how you relate to other people. By persevering on the positive path of establishing a proper reputation, giving, sharing, and making a useful contribution to your environment, you will earn a valued place in society.
You learn not to take your reputation personally but to allow its rise and fall
to teach you where you are off the track in your behavior. When others begin
to lose respect for you, it is your signal to step back, pay attention, and note the
areas in your life where you need to make some adjustments.

You are learning how to climb the ladder of success. Though you are eager
to meet this challenge, you need to learn patience and responsibility in order
to make progress. There is a tendency for those of you who are rushing your
success to forget to acknowledge those who have gone before you; through
this acknowledgment you can gain assistance and support. If you try to climb
the success ladder without recognizing these people, you will learn that they
are stronger than you are and can make your journey very difficult. As you
learn the proper use of recognition, respect, and protocol, you learn to take
your time on a more deliberate upward path.

You are also learning how to control your environment positively, for by
taking responsibility for your actions you have power over the outcome of
your own reality. Control is an important issue for you since in past incarnations you allowed your environment to run you. In this lifetime you must
learn how to discipline yourself without trying to manage those around you.
If you try to control others, life becomes a very heavy experience. You get
dragged down and become bitter and resentful of all your burdens, recognizing
that those around you have become dependent on you but not recognizing
that you have imposed this dependency. If you use your energy to take charge
of your life, you will have the strength and perseverance to climb to the top in
any field of endeavor.

A Visible Lifetime

When you realize that this is a very visible lifetime, you learn how truly important it is to always put your best foot forward. You discover that because you have chosen to learn about the value of reputation and success in this existence, society holds you responsible for all your actions, personal and business. Society doesn't care whether its view of your personal life affects your ability to become successful in business or if your business reputation interferes with your personal life. Experience quickly teaches you always to protect your good name.

Because yours is such a visible life, people may tend to be judgmental, and you are unconsciously asking to be judged. You feel that the only way to know how you are doing is to be judged by the members of your own community, and measure your success by how much people respect you. It is important for you to recognize that not everyone is searching for the community approval that you feel is so necessary and for you to learn to live and let live.

Part of your need to become successful in this lifetime will be clear to you only after you recognize that it is not success alone you are striving for; it is recognition, respect, and a need to be useful. When you incorporate this awareness, you become a very important person who is held in high esteem in your community. You are learning to develop character along the way to achieving your goals.

Step 1: Unconscious Expression

Your lesson is to learn the value of a good reputation. You can suffer a great deal if you invalidate yourself to society by not being concerned with your reputation. It is important for you to recognize that this is a very visible lifetime for you and that you are going to be held accountable for your actions. Thus, you have set yourself up to be judged; this is the only way you can find the meaning of your reputation within society. You must be willing to grow personally from these social judgments rather than to keep striving forward blindly.

When you choose to remain unconscious and not become useful within society, you can become a drain on the social order. You may decide not to take care of yourself financially and be on public assistance—not for legitimate reasons but by refusing to take responsibility for yourself. You can be the person culture belittles for not pulling your fair share or the person society incarcerates for stealing, embezzlement, violence, or another socially unacceptable behavior.

ATTACHMENT TO THE HOME

Some of you may hide within the home, refusing to go out into the world and make a way for yourself. In these and other ways you may never learn to be independent and may be a burden to those within your family unit. Whether you choose to function in the home or out in the world, you must learn to become useful. If you are not taught to be helpful within your home environment as a child, it makes it more difficult for you to learn to be useful within the community.

You may have difficulty dealing with anyone in a position of authority because you are learning the purpose and need for self-authority in this lifetime. Coming from a previous existence where others were always your authority, you are accustomed to giving your power too easily to others. In this lifetime there is a natural rebellion against those in power until your sense of personal power has been incorporated into your soul growth pattern. It is very important for you to become respected and useful within the community so you can incorporate the resulting sense of authority into your own being.

By operating unconsciously in the business world you may tend to manipulate as many business affairs as you possibly can. This is most likely to occur if you begin making your own way before you are confident of your ability to become a respected asset in the community.

You can manipulate situations so you are the only one with access to key bits of information that would complete the puzzle for others. If you indulge in the need to control your environment, you may hold back at least one piece of this vital information, thinking this makes you indispensable. If you can learn to rise above this tendency and have enough faith in yourself to share completely, you will gain the respect and dignity you so strongly desire.

THE DOWNSIDE OF WINNING

Under stress you can have such an exaggerated need for success that you feel you must win at all costs. In this mode you sometimes engage in extremely unscrupulous behavior. Just as you can achieve the height of success, when functioning negatively you can become the very lowest kind of person. In this negative consciousness you are capable of creating financial or emotional scams that can devastate the lives of other people. Playing a simple game of cards with you when you are in this pattern can be like being involved in a game of treachery, for this energy can drive you to cheat in even the friendliest of games. Sooner or later you must accept responsibility for your actions. When you become conscious, you willingly pay back your debt to society and are capable of being of great aid to humankind.

Even when not taken to this extreme, your need dominate is so great that even when not operating in a proper consciousness you often try to control the lives of others. You have an inward fear that if anyone around you was allowed to stand on his or her own two feet for any length of time, that person would surpass you. You gain your greatest prestige by overcoming this need to control the direction of other people's lives.

One way to work toward this goal is by volunteering your time to such service organizations as the Small Business Administration, your local chamber of commerce, or any type of association that assists others in business growth potentials; this puts your positive energy and experience back into the community.

Step 2: Conscious Expression

Knowing that you must incorporate the lessons of accountability into your personality, you begin by accepting responsibility for your actions and relationships on a social level. Those that are conscious from childhood first become responsible at an early age within the family unit. These are the children who have paper routes and lemonade stands or who are very aware of the home and are willing to help whenever needed. Children with this pattern can be aided by giving them additional responsibilities within the home, along with appropriate respect and recognition. This is a wonderful way to help them begin on the positive path.

You are industrious by nature and recognize the value of having a good reputation. Business success is extremely important to you, and you understand that to succeed in the outside world you must always be cognizant of your behavior in public. But even the most responsible may have to learn this lesson the hard way. You also learn that in order to achieve, each foot must be secure on its path before the other one leaves the ground. In this way you discover how to build your own security, and this includes the area of personal relationships.

PAST-LIFE INFLUENCE

There was an overemphasis on emotions; this has left you with a fear of passion. Although the most conscious of you can appear rigid and uncaring to the untrained eye, you actually have a wealth of feeling and sensitivity.

As you begin your upward journey to success, one of the most valuable lessons for you to take on your path is an understanding of the roles of respect and acknowledgment because you can have a fear of authority. It is important for you to respect persons of lesser, equal, and greater authority and not become an elitist, which is a very lonely pattern. If you remain conscious of the personal dignity of those around you while you are on your way to the top, when you get there you will have the esteem of the community behind you and the goodwill of all who look up to your accomplishments.

In affairs of the heart you are learning to find a balance between your natural reserve, the respect that you need, and the feelings and sensitivity that you are trying to incorporate. You are learning that your love life does not have to be set aside in order to achieve success, and you may find yourself attracting very dignified, respectable, sensitive, nurturing, supportive mates.

You feel at your strongest with someone by your side, and you recognize that your home base must be secure in order for you to achieve your greatest success in the outside world.

SHARING RESPECT

Once you have reached success, you tend to want to play the father role in the community or within your business. Thus, you give others a chance to gain personal success by supplying jobs or scholarships, or just by sharing your personal resources in the community.

By honestly giving respect and admiration where it is due, you find that you can gain a great deal of insight and information from those to whom you pay homage. In recognizing and acknowledging the success of others, you tap into a more universal support system where you can access what you need for your personal growth. Thus, the lessons that teach you to become a more responsible, useful, respected member of the community will become assimilated in a much gentler way.

You are learning to view social judgments not as set and rigid conclusions but as indicators of how useful your current behavior actually is to others. To this end you are learning to accept criticism or disapproval as a temporary gauge of your effectiveness and to be open to modifying your behavior accordingly.

Step 3: Transpersonal Expression

Operating at the highest level, your destiny is to be a pioneer on new spiritual paths. You are a natural-born guide and teacher, and can bring the heights of spirituality into the practical form necessary to show others the value of spirituality in their lives and to teach them how to walk the path on a useful daily level.

You understand the need for the group consciousness of this planet to teach its inhabitants to accept responsibility for one another. You teach others to become individually responsible for their consciousness and growth, to understand the necessity of learning their lessons and doing whatever is needed to achieve a sense of oneness with the whole. Through your expanded awareness of universal concepts you can help those on this plane accept that we all are responsible for one another—that if just one is left out, we are still not whole.

Through your consciousness of perseverance and determination you teach that we must be responsible for our thoughts, actions, and deeds so we will not think of ourselves as being more important than the next person. Then we can all stand shoulder to shoulder with arms and hearts extended, completing the circle of love within the universal consciousness.

Physical Integration

You stand for stability and responsibility, just like the bone structure in the physical body. Without the stability of the bones, the body could not move or be responsible for itself; it would be nothing but a limp pile. You intuitively understand the need for taking responsibility when you are in alignment with yourself. But stay aware of your physical structure, for if you are not accepting or teaching responsibility in a proper way, you are not teaching the body to be responsible for itself. If the structure malfunctions, it can weaken the knees, or you may become susceptible to problems with the bones, teeth, or anything that has to do with calcium in the body. You can also be prone to bruises, rashes, skin cancer, dry skin, eczema, spleen disorders, and rheumatism.

Such symptoms are the body's way of drawing attention to the need to reevaluate how you have claimed and maintained a sense of authority in your life. Has it been a rigid, closed, and fearful authority, or a sense of authority based on flexibility and openness to the input of others? When you are not functioning on a positive level, you may become resentful. The energy of resentment can dissipate calcium and cause difficulty with arthritis, bone marrow disorders, and general disfigurement of the bones, including the teeth and jaw line. When functioning positively you can experience a great deal of physical strength and stamina, and remain in extremely good physical condition until very late in life.

If resentments in the body begin to build up, there is an automatic warning mechanism so that you have time to reverse the process before it does any permanent damage. This warning system is in the stomach. When you are having problems with your stomach, you need to reevaluate your life, make some decisions for change, and correct patterns. If you do this, there should be no further negative manifestations in the body.

AQUARIUS

SOLAR ECLIPSE: WHAT YOUR SOUL CONTRACTED TO TEACH OTHERS

(In order to fully activate your solar eclipse energy in Aquarius, it may be helpful to read the lunar eclipse in Aquarius section. You may find information that can help you more fully contribute your solar eclipse in Aquarius gifts.)

Your Mission

You have incarnated to teach the lesson of detachment. You intuitively understand that your greatest awareness comes through motion and movement, and interaction with many people from all walks of life, with your "rolling stone," cavalier attitude. You teach those around you to break their inflexible patterns and appreciate the beauties of life.

This lesson can be taught through different modes of personal behavior. You may stifle those close to you to the point that you become unbearable. This teaches them the lesson of detaching from those influences that bring them pain or retard their growth. You may also teach others to be objective by constantly detaching and moving forward yourself. Thus, your personal example helps people gain awareness of the ebb and flow of the universe, through either your own freedom or your lack of it.

Seeking New Knowledge

The lesson to be learned is that of moving forward and not becoming fixated in unproductive experiences, even though letting go can be painful. To those who are unaware of your process you may appear to be very ungrounded as you move from one experience to the next.

Actually, your process has the potential to revitalize every life you touch. You share what you have learned from your last experience in the present one, and you accumulate new information in the present to bring into the next situation.

Sometimes being with a person who has an Aquarian solar eclipse can feel like an explosion or a shattering of old perceptions of reality that have stopped the other person from experiencing the fullness of life. At other times you may teach this lesson through explosive behavior patterns that leave those around you feeling devastated until the smoke clears and they realize they have been set free.

You tend to draw very possessive, jealous people who need to learn detachment from their overinflated egos. Your nature can help them to incorporate a more universal approach to sharing love in relationships. Through loyalty to a universal sense of brother/sisterhood that precludes any unhealthy attachment to individual form, you understand how to love freely and fully without possessiveness. You have an open channel to universal awareness and are able to see the highest good for the most people. You are able to introduce new ideas and concepts, thereby helping to usher in the Aquarian age.

Teaching Detachment

By teaching detachment you help people to understand that we may not hold on to anything on the physical plane. Whatever we have accumulated must be passed on; all we can actually take with us is experience, and all we really have is time. You intuitively understand that we must make the best use of our time by not holding on to the past and choosing the most positive experiences in the present.

Aquarius is the sign that represents the inventor, and you are innovative in your thinking, recognizing that we do not need to be held down by old thought patterns. Through your need for new experiences you teach others to break old, limited ways of thinking and open the doors to tomorrow. Narrow-minded people, unwilling to believe that there can be a better way to do anything, are attracted to you. When you come into their lives, you help them open themselves to new ideas. You are so persistent and persevering in your enthusiastic approach to newness that you wear down those around you until they accept the prospect of change, or leave.

You also have a very strong sense of fair play, which is why you get so upset at the unfairness you see in the world. You have the ability to teach your fellow beings to be fair with one another by showing fairness in your dealings and by trusting those around you to be fair with you.

However, you are not shy about speaking up when you feel that the other person has not been fair with you. People always start with a clean slate as far as you are concerned, and it is up to them what they want to write on it. But once they have been unfair to you, you hold them accountable. Through their behavior they have established their character in your eyes.

In your mind, all of us begin as equals, with no one having more rights than another. As we live our lives, it is our behavior that allows us to keep— or causes us to lose—our rights. What you are teaching your fellow beings through this philosophy is that we can only hold ourselves accountable for our life situations. If we build a good character by being honest, trustworthy, and honorable, we will create a good situation for ourselves in this lifetime. If we want to change our life situation, our character is something that we are capable of refining through changing our behavior.

LUNAR ECLIPSE: WHAT YOUR SOUL IS LEARNING TO EMOTIONALLY EMBRACE

Your Mission

Your lesson in this lifetime is detachment. Your challenge is to release your tendencies toward possessiveness and jealousy.

The pace at which you learn your lessons is quite accelerated. It essential that you allow things and people to flow through your life, because you need to experience a great deal in this one incarnation. Nothing is allowed to crystallize in this life experience.

Also, it is not permissible for you to consider only yourself when making decisions. The good of the whole is to be your main consideration, and the universe will take care of your personal needs when you are fulfilling this role. If you can learn this detachment during this lifetime, it is not necessary for you to return to the Earth plane.

Past-Life Influences

Part of your lesson is learning to detach from old, set patterns of thinking. You are coming from a past consciousness of royal heritage—not necessarily of being a king or queen, but set family patterns of "you must do this because it is what your ancestors have always done."

You are learning to detach from belief systems that have held you down in the past, whether they were imposed by religion, family, or society. You realize that you do not need to conform to the beliefs of others. As long as you keep the good of the whole in mind and do not hurt others, you have the right to explore and enjoy your natural desire to experiment with life.

A Humanitarian Destiny

While learning your lessons you also have to satisfy a strong sense of curiosity. You have a need to understand the why behind everything. You feel that if you understand the reason for things, you can improve them, and you have an innate desire to improve the quality of life for all.

You are the true humanitarian of the world. In learning to become a humanitarian, you become adept at adjusting your consciousness to that of the masses. You are learning to detach from the ego enough to be able to think of what is for the good of all and at the same time retain a strong enough sense of ego to prod yourself to achieve what you have set out to accomplish.

You are here to achieve the transition from thinking of yourself and your family alone to thinking of humanity. You are learning to take responsibility for directing your fellow beings into more positive areas of exploration on a planetary level as well as considering the expansion of your own family unit. This is an important lesson that must be learned with great respect and love for humankind.

You are also learning to develop a more universal consciousness regarding love. You must break past patterns of how you believed love should be. Previously, you were very jealous and possessive where love was concerned. You felt that things had to remain the way they always had been, which left no room for growth. Now you are learning that you do not need to hold on so tightly in affairs of the heart.

To become a true futuristic thinker and be able to help expand the consciousness of others, you must always give freedom to those around you. If you want the freedom to expand and explore the world around you, you have to be open to others doing the same. By trying to hold on too tightly to anyone you care for, you will meet with such resistance that it can lead to a separation.

Love without Attachment

Giving love without attachment to whether or not it makes the other person love you more is a difficult lesson. You are seeking to separate yourself from an unconscious, self-defeating need for approval. Yours is the lesson of doing what is best for the most concerned and not for the individual gratification of personal love.

You are in the process of accepting your humanitarian role on the planet, and as you practice giving love freely because you feel love for the other person, you learn to act without self-interest. You need to learn to share love for the sheer joy of the experience and not with the expectation of attachment or adoration.

In previous lifetimes you were adored and put on a pedestal, and you have become attached to that kind of attention. Without this adoration you tend to confuse attachment with loyalty. You sometimes take the wrong path because you feel the need of loyalty from others so strongly and think that if you are not loyal to their path, they won't be loyal to you. Because of this misconception you tend to take old paths that you have already finished. It will help you to remember that above all, everyone needs to follow his or her own path— "to thine own self be true." Self-loyalty is a very important lesson for you in this lifetime. You can keep yourself stuck in a rut for a long time because of this fixation on being loyal. You demand loyalty from others and from yourself, but you forget to be loyal to yourself!

For an example of attachment to special attention and adoration, imagine a young dancing girl who relished the special attention her exuberant youth brought her. Later, when it was time for her to shift into the role of teacher to the young dancers who came after her (and to let go of the spotlight), she had to make a choice. She could either be a useful, vital part of the company or a bitter, detached, isolated being. You are in the position of choosing what your response will be to the role of supporting others, rather than being the spotlighted player on the stage.

When handling this on a positive level, you gain an understanding of the timing and cycles of life. There is a time for the spotlight, a time for stepping back, a time for teaching, a time for sharing, a time for loving—a time for every need. The idea is to be able to let go of attachment and proceed to the next level.

Receiving Love

In this lifetime the need to love for the sake of love is very strong. You must learn to detach from the habit of dictating the behavior of those who fall in love with you. In previous lifetimes you were loved either because of your position in society or for what you could give in return. This time, in learning to be loved just for your own self, you are learning to let go of your attachment to certain behavior patterns that came with these previous expressions of love. This also frees you to love without pressure and to open yourself to being loved for yourself and not for a role you play. A king is loved because of his position and prestige; a leader because of his or her role of strength. In this lifetime you can finally experience the joy of being loved just for yourself.

Part of your lesson is to let go of needing those who are close to you to behave in a certain way. In learning to love without attachment to the behavior patterns of those you love, you are beginning to understand what it means to live and let live. In doing this you are fulfilling your own destiny and becoming a very loving, beautiful free spirit.

Your process is truly embodied in the caterpillar becoming the butterfly. You are learning that love is like a butterfly: If you hold on to it too tightly, you kill it. On the other hand, if you allow those you love the freedom you demand for yourself, you find that both energies are satisfied. This is the way to attract a lifelong, loyal mate—both of you able to expand, explore, and grow separately while sharing love together.

Step 1: Unconscious Expression

If you choose to resist the flow of these lessons, you may find yourself experiencing a series of losses—things and people being unexpectedly removed from your life—until you learn to detach and let go. In tenaciously holding on to familiar experiences and people, you block new and vitalizing situations from coming into your life because there is no room for them.

You are seeing that the next lesson is not always so terrible and that when you start something new, you don't always have to know how to do it perfectly from the very beginning. You are learning how to ease into things and not base your judgment on your first impression. Aquarius is a fixed sign, giving you a tendency to attachment and difficulty in letting go. It is all right to allow yourself to get used to new things, people, ideas, and places. But you must learn to detach from one experience and move on to the next.

PAST-LIFE INFLUENCES

Your creative tendencies were so extreme that you had to put all your attention into that one area of your life. You focused your energy on one narrow path and learned how to block out everything else. You bring with you into this lifetime that tendency to focus on only one area at a time, along with your intense creativity. Due to your fear of letting go, you may not recognize that this creativity is a talent the soul has developed—you can't lose it, and you can bring it to any area or project that you choose.

The trick is to use your talents not just for your own personal gratification but for humanity. Once you make the betterment of humankind your life's goal, you will be able to flow easily with what is for the greater good. In this process you will discover that your own life begins to flow with more clarity of vision and a stronger sense of stability; you will no longer feel that things are being wrenched from you.

EGO PRIDE—A BOTTOMLESS PIT

There's a tendency to find yourself stuck in old patterns of ego gratification. You can become obsessed with the idea that others should pay homage to you. This attitude causes you to become stubborn, ego centered, and very unpleasant to be around. In this negative state you are fighting the very lesson you came to learn, which is giving up personal desires for the good of all concerned. You must learn to be less selfish and to detach from a need for glory before you can find happiness in this lifetime. Once you learn to consider others you find a renewed sense of happiness. Instead of feeling like an outsider begging to be noticed, you find the confidence and sense of belonging that comes from acting for the good of the whole.

If you choose not to learn the lesson of releasing old mind-sets and making way for new, innovative thinking, you may find yourself caught in a pattern of constantly conforming your behavior and thinking to those around you. Unconsciously, you can be enslaved by performing the role that is expected of you and not understand why you are constantly nervous and irritable. This is because inside you feel as if everything in your life is just a waste of time.

Basically, Aquarius is a very time-oriented sign. You have a strong sense of needing to accomplish certain things in certain periods of time. When you can let go of situations in which you have learned your lessons and allow yourself to move on to the next, you will begin to waste less and less time. The wasted time is the time spent in holding on, not the lesson itself. Time is wasted by not moving forward, and ultimately it is this recognition that frees you to operate on a conscious level and helps you to gain mastery over your life.

You have come to use your creativity and inventiveness in areas that better the quality of life for all. You cannot even begin to do this, however, until you learn to think with more open-mindedness. The first step is to overcome your habit of not wanting to listen to anyone else's ideas and dreams. Then, give up the stubborn attachment to old, worn-out thought processes.

LISTENING AND LETTING GO

When you refuse to listen to the ideas of others, it's because you feel that if someone has a concept different from yours, she is attacking the very basis of your thinking process. You are learning that when minds come together there is more strength, more reasoning ability, and more intellect. You need to recognize that two minds are better than one because each can show the other the weaknesses and strengths that each possesses. This gives you double the brain power. Once you are willing to open up and listen you can process what you have heard and begin to use information from others.

With each old thought that you let go, with each new concept that you accept, you learn how to integrate new awareness, concepts, and insights from outside the self. As you learn to make room for these new concepts, you realize that you never let go of anything that truly belonged to you. Every thought belongs to the universe. You never have to lose a thought to gain a new one—you just make room for more. At this point you become free to tap into the universal consciousness that can teach and guide you from a higher level, and your future growth becomes easier and easier.

Operating unconsciously, you can be very judgmental and untrusting, fearing that everyone is out to take advantage of you. You may be class oriented and feel that others will never be any better or worse than the family they were born into. This class consciousness stems from your sense of royalty, which comes from a past lifetime when you were royalty or a person of high prestige in your community. These feelings are left over from a time when in fact it was not possible for people to rise above the social station dictated by their birth. This is possible in our society—the time of monarchy and keeping the people down is over. Now you need to release this consciousness; in doing so you help release this negative energy from the planet.

Upholding the old consciousness can result in holding down your own growth. Your lesson is to break a pattern of thinking that is oriented to the status quo and to develop a freer way of viewing life that allows change and growth for everyone. You will realize eventually that we are all created equal.

Step 2: Conscious Expression

You understand the process of letting go and allowing people and things to flow through your life. This enables you to incorporate a great number of experiences in this lifetime. You understand that this process must take place if you are to get past the point of allowing physical and emotional desires to stop your personal growth. Once you have committed yourself to your growth process, the universe finds you to be a receptacle open to receiving your true heart's desire.

You are constantly striving to improve your ability to relate to life on a more universal level. You intuitively sense that humankind has spent too much time in selfish pursuits, and you feel that you must find a way to correct the world. You find yourself involved in humanitarian causes such as the Peace Corps, studying diseases that plague humanity, working to save the seals, or being the case worker for an underprivileged family. You have a strong desire to find out what you can do to help, and act on this desire.

THE EXCHANGE OF LOVE

You want so much to help others that quite often you forget to spend time building a personal life. You love your fellow beings and are motivated to get your ego under control so you can be of service to humankind as a whole.

You may feel that it is selfish to allow yourself time for love, and you tend to become detached and aloof where affairs of the heart are concerned. You may fear that if you do allow yourself to attach and feel personal love, you will not be able to accomplish all that you want to do. What you really need is to acquire a balance between the two because everyone needs love. You have such a strong need to be loved that you spend all your time doing things for your fellow beings so they will love you. But you forget to spend time on personal love and may not allow anyone to get close enough to give it.

From a conscious position you understand that humankind is just as delicate as love. You have a strong altruistic connection to humanity and understand that we should all do whatever is necessary to facilitate each other's process. You have a group-consciousness orientation. It is important to you that all your fellow beings become more aware of their responsibility to the planet as a whole. You can be a very active environmentalist, working to change the way we treat the Earth, or you may put your energies into your local school system.

The aware Aquarian eclipse has an ability to recognize where change is needed, the courage to bring this awareness into the open, and the energy to make it happen. You will not settle for stagnation or unfairness.

THE POWER OF OBJECTIVITY

Many of you find it easier to relate to humankind by finding some abstract study or tool to use in fulfilling your urge to be of assistance. While you desire to help, you still need to remain detached enough not to fall into past patterns of allowing your will to take over, thereby not really being of any help to those you work with.

Thus, especially while you are in the early stages of your own growth process, it is recommended that you find an objective tool through which you can see yourself as well as assist others (that is, astrology, psychology, tarot, a research foundation, and so forth). You need an external structure that allows you to see yourself objectively while you are developing your universal consciousness. You find great joy and satisfaction in helping others along the path, and when you can be learning and assisting others at the same time, you feel you are truly on the path yourself.

You have come into this lifetime feeling as if there is something inside that you must set straight. You recognize that on some level you still see humanity as segregated into different classes and that this is why you feel such a separateness from your fellow beings. Once you recognize that all of us are created equal and have the spark of the collective consciousness within, you can function more comfortably as an interdependent, beneficial part of the society within which you have chosen to incarnate.

PAST-LIFE INFLUENCE

You had an overdeveloped ego that caused you to feel you were better than those around you. But in this existence you must learn to incorporate your own worth with the worth of all and detach from the need to feel that your accomplishments and needs are more important than those of others. It's as if you are stepping down from the past lifetimes of royalty to understand the lesson of being one of the many.

Part of this lesson is to recognize that all of us were born naked and dependent on others to sustain our lives. Some begin in affluence and end in poverty; some begin in poverty and end in affluence; still others maintain the status quo. Through this realization you can gain the awareness that we can make of our lives whatever we choose. You begin to notice that a person's class does not necessarily determine his or her happiness, and that the only consistent factor in those who remain happy is that they have built a strong character.

Thus, through observation you learn that the development of individual character is much more important that social status. A strong character frees a person to achieve his or her heart's desire, and that is your most important lesson.

Step 3: Transpersonal Expression

You intuitively understand that the universe has a great deal for you to learn, so you willingly accept the experiences and the lessons. You realize that if you are to evolve past the physical plane and the need to live on Earth and go through its experiences, you must detach from every phase of the physical body. Those who allow this detaching process to manifest may work as channels, bringing in outside news for the Aquarian age.

At the most evolved level you serve as receptacles of information, which you pass on as though you were a receiving station from the universe and a transmitting station to the planet. When you have freed yourself enough to allow this process to materialize within the body, the information from the universe flows through you so you can pass it on directly to your fellow beings. In this way you help to bring the energies of the Aquarian age into the world.

Physical Integration

Resistance to your lessons can lead to health warnings designed to alert you to the necessity of learning to let go and let God. Such health warnings may include nervous tension, hypoglycemia, diabetes, swelling of the ankles, problems with circulation, and a craving for sugar. It is important to take walks in order to keep your circulation flowing and balanced. This also assists in aligning yourself with your own spiritual lesson of learning that everything in the universe must circulate and that you can't keep anything confined in one location. The universe cannot exist in a static environment, and neither can the individual with an Aquarian eclipse. A person with this eclipse can be subject to misdiagnosis as being mentally unbalanced, due to the possible fluctuating sugar level in the body.

$$\mathcal{H}$$

PISCES

SOLAR ECLIPSE: WHAT YOUR SOUL CONTRACTED TO TEACH OTHERS

(In order to fully activate your solar eclipse energy in Pisces, it may be helpful to read the lunar eclipse in Pisces section. You may find information that can help you more fully contribute your solar eclipse in Pisces gifts.)

Your Mission

You have incarnated to help your fellow beings develop their sensitivities. You tend to draw to you very critical, overly analytical people, and you can teach these individuals to develop deeper levels of empathy. This also allows them to develop new ways of expressing their analytical abilities that will be more acceptable to others so they won't set themselves up for rejection as often. You are very sensitive to the energies around you and pick up vibes because you are so psychically developed. Thus, you need to be careful not to absorb the negativity of others.

With this natural gift of inborn intuition you can teach others the value of following their hunches and the usefulness of this awareness. Your hunches are accurate although often you are not even aware of why you are saying things and where the information is coming from. But you are enough in tune with your energies to know you should follow your hunches.

For example, if an upcoming investment was mentioned and you said, "Don't purchase this one, purchase that one instead," it would be a good bet to follow this advice. This is true when you are following your hunches, not your mind. When such advice comes from a hunch, you have no idea why you said it. It's an intuitive instinct, and following it is extremely beneficial to the life processes of those you touch.

You are adept in sensing when someone is in a state of distress. You would be an excellent counselor or advisor because of your deep level of sensitivity. What you give your fellow beings is the freedom to be in distress without being judged. As you walk through life you draw to you people who are very self-judgmental and in need of seeing the larger whole. Through your natural compassion you can help others to regain their sense of self-worth.

Occasionally, even those born with this eclipse pattern lose their way and seem to be caught in a pattern of self-delusion. When this occurs you may tend to indulge in self-pity and destructive patterns of escapism. Unfortunately, you still draw critical people to you, so you will not be as lucky as those who find their way to you for help. If you lose your way, you need to seek professional assistance to get back to reality and to form more positive behavior patterns.

A Victim by Default

Because your innate nature is so sensitive, assistance not given in a loving, supportive manner can drive you deeper inside yourself. This can lead to a self-imposed state of martyrdom. You may feel it is only right that someone take the burden, and you set yourself up to be the victim. Ironically, even when negatively expressed in victimhood, you model the principles of sensitivity and concern for your fellow beings and often evoke qualities of concern and compassion in others. It is your choice whether to teach this lesson through your negative behavior or your positive behavior.

You are teaching these lessons on many levels: we are all God's children and to dishonor one is to dishonor the source; all human beings are part of the collective whole and contain within themselves the spark of the divine consciousness; we must have regard for all who are lost, even ourselves; we must have respect, love, and compassion for one another.

Even if you feel lost, you are teaching that we are all lost along our earthly path. Since we have traveled away from the less confining spiritual realms into the denser physical worlds, we are constantly struggling to regain the feeling of connectedness with one another.

Like a magnet you absorb the negativity of those around you, then send back love, support, understanding, and whatever words of insight you think will ease the other person's pain. Your gift is that of healing through compassion, and people feel better simply by being in your presence. You allow people the freedom to be themselves because you recognize that everyone is in the state of being they need to be in to work on their lessons in this lifetime.

Creating Oneness

In relationships, you teach people not to analyze everything to death, remembering that too much separateness leads to unnecessary strains in relationships. You teach that unconnected categories can be self-isolating structures, and you help people to let go of feeling that they have to define themselves in order to relate.

You also help others to accept the subtleties of life. Through your own psychic receptivity, intuitive insights, and sensitive connectedness to others and to the whole, you validate that there are realms of perception beyond the norm of day-to-day living. You teach others to sense and to feel and to get in touch with the spirit inside themselves and become one with the universe. You can do this through many different modes of expression: as a spiritual teacher and leader; as a living example of compassion and sensitivity; as a person who is supportive and validating to the processes of those around you. Regardless of the mode, you teach others to relate with one another from an awareness of their inner divinity.

Basically, yours is the gift of modeling the principle of surrender in its highest, most loving form. Others are inspired by you to allow the principle of let go and let God to operate in their lives. You teach others to accept divine inspiration, either through a negative or a positive response flow.

On the negative level: You may play the devil's advocate by totally ignoring divine inspiration, not accepting any universal help, and ignoring the spiritual gifts with which you incarnated. You may push away the compassion that others offer and remain a separate, detached entity. On the positive level: You allow spiritual assistance and human compassion to aid you and truly surrender to a higher power.

The Pull to Addiction

You teach your fellow beings how to remain in spiritual consciousness while incarnated. When you get into escapism patterns (drugs, alcohol, and so forth), you are actually seeking to regain an altered state of consciousness that you know you are capable of reaching. At some time during your life you have felt that gift of being connected with a kind of bliss consciousness, and when it gets lost, you can fall into patterns of escapism because you are seeking so desperately to regain it. It is not the drugs or the alcohol that you want to experience, but you want to reconnect with the spiritual state that the drugs and alcohol artificially simulate.

This won't give you the sense of spiritual fulfillment you are seeking, however. It only takes the edge off the reality of the physical realm that is so difficult for you to deal with when you feel disconnected from your spiritual center. What you are really seeking is the altered state of consciousness that is the deep inner serenity and security of feeling the spiritual realm while in the flesh.

You help people learn to go with the flow. Your philosophy is that everything in the universe is working out exactly as it should and that if we will only let go, the current will take each of us to our proper destination. You teach that by trusting the universal guidance and letting go of attachment to the ego, we can go with the flow of life and thereby receive the positive rewards we truly deserve.

LUNAR ECLIPSE: WHAT YOUR SOUL IS LEARNING TO EMOTIONALLY EMBRACE

Your Mission

In this incarnation you have come to learn to deal with sensitivities.

Past-Life Influence

You have been overly critical and have spent too much time putting everything in its proper perspective. Now it is time to recognize that everything blends together and is in reality an interacting part of everything else. When you realize this, you will be able to activate the "let go and let God" principle in your life.

In the lessons of this eclipse pattern you must learn to allow sensitivity to flow within your being—to listen to the inner voice and discern truth from fiction. During these lessons it is important to retain your analytical abilities in order to ascertain whether each piece of information is useful; if it is not useful, it is from the imagination.

This guiding principle frees you to let these thoughts or spiritual inspirations flow into your mind and to decide if you will act on them. Through this process you can release the fear of becoming too sensitive and losing your grip on reality. You are allowed to develop these sensitivities and keep your feet on the ground at the same time.

Learning to Let Go and Let God

You are learning not to be afraid to look at what the universe is trying to show you. Look and listen when you have premonitions, intuitions, and so forth. Once you learn to let go and let God and trust the intuitive information that comes through, you will recognize that the purpose is not to make you suffer because of what you see (if it's something painful), but to allow you to correct your direction or the direction of others before unnecessarily painful repercussions take place.

The idea is that life, or the God-consciousness, would prefer each of us to learn our lessons as gently as possible. You are learning to be a type of seer, either later on in this existence or in the next, who can warn us or allow us to see that we are headed down the wrong path. When you allow yourself to let go and be guided, others who don't have this gift of psychic foresight can be aided through your guidance.

As you become more open to what is around you, you may in some ways become overly sensitive. Some of your feelings may not belong within your environment, so it is important to exercise your ability to discern and discriminate, which you spent so much time developing in the past. This discerning attitude must be brought along on your journey into sensitivity, for without it you can get lost in the muddle and confusion.

By becoming more aware of your sensitivities you will tend to attract the emotional debris of those with whom you will come into contact. Your living environment may be too close to another's home or apartment that has conflict. If you forget to be discerning, you can absorb the negativity of those around you and claim it as your own. You need to stop and think, not just feel the energy pattern. When you become distracted and disoriented and sense anger within, ask yourself: "Where is this anger coming from? Is it mine? Do I own it? Is it something that I need to handle? Or am I picking up something from someone around me?"

Remember that as you develop psychically and become a very sensitized being, you will need to take your strongest ally with you on this journey. This ally is your analytical ability, which will assist you in understanding what is going on around you. The universe would never have allowed you to enter onto the path of developing such acute sensitivity if you had not already developed your analytical abilities. The sensitivity that you are learning to develop is best supported by remembering to keep your feet on the ground.

Past-Life Influence

You overcategorized others, which has led to a tendency to need those around you to have set behavior patterns that allow you to keep things in order. Learning to trust your fellow beings is a challenge.

In developing new patterns of trust you will come to grips with the fact that the universe unfolds differently for each person. Realizing this empowers you to increase your faith in the universal plan, which in turn allows you greater access to universal awareness. You can use this guidance for yourself and for those around you.

Provided that you overcome your tendency to be too critical and set aside your judgments of human behavior patterns, you can be among the fine psychics and mystics on the planet. You can also become an excellent diagnostician by using the best of your abilities to categorize, analyze, synthesize, and feel the energies of others.

If you wish to get on the path to learning these lessons, you may begin by trusting your own intuition and practicing in the context of your daily activities. For example, if you are accustomed to traveling a certain road from one location to the next and have an intuition to take a different route on a certain day for no apparent logical reason, the experiment would be to trust your instincts and follow that different route. Perhaps the universe has a reason for you not to travel your usual route.

In following this inner guidance you validate your feelings and assure your higher self that you want this guidance and are able to accept it. This is important because it strengthens the connection. It is on these mundane levels that you train yourself to trust.

Another effective way to begin this training is to physically manifest your intuitions. For example, if your inner voice says that someone needs to hear from you, pick up the phone and call that person. The idea is to physically act on what your inner voice is telling you to do, as long as it is not harmful to anyone. In this way you let your higher consciousness know directly that you are willing for it to take a more active part in your life.

DREAM POWER

You have the gift of becoming more aware of what you are learning, sensing, and perceiving from the dream state. Keeping a journal of your dreams will help you to combine your intuitive facilities with the practicalities of your daily life in a powerful way. And this is an easy place to begin this lesson!

When you learn to get in touch with these energies and to make sense of the continuity of the dream state, you may begin a meditation program that will help you become aware of these energies while awake. Then, during the normal course of the day, you can take control of the energy and receive guidance and inspiration whenever you feel the need.

This will help you in overcoming a tendency to be overly self-critical, which can result in too much time being spent in finding flaws with the self. You need to understand that you are also a physical being working on this planet to evolve. The idea is to let go of the need for perfection so you can accept the spiritual guidance you came to learn. This will make your whole existence much easier and more gentle. Once you accept your imperfect state without guilt, you are ready to accept spiritual guidance, which can facilitate your growth process into a higher level of perfection.

Step 1: Unconscious Expression

You can resist the flow of your lesson by remaining overly critical and overly analytical, and refraining from any form of participation in the spiritual realms. There is a temptation to negate everything that comes through from spiritual consciousness by analyzing it to the point where it is impossible to perceive the true message. This keeps you from having the vision you need to realign your behavior in a way that would empower you to join with others as part of the whole.

Not recognizing the aid and the assistance you are given from the spiritual realms delays you from allowing a sensitive nature to develop within your own being. This can lead to your being harsh and insensitive, and you may reject all assistance from those around you, including those who are trying to receive aid from the spiritual realms. When this happens there is a repetition of old errors because you have disallowed the new insight that would break the self-defeating patterns.

OPENING UP TOO SOON

On the other hand, you may have come into this lifetime so aware of the need to become sensitive that you open yourself too quickly from the very beginning. Opening and expanding too widely without prior physical, emotional, or spiritual training can "blow your circuits" and frighten you off your path. You may feel that you have been knocked off the path through too intense an encounter with the spiritual realms because of your lack of education and inability to understand what is happening. In this case a reevaluation is necessary and a step-by-step, grounded process of psychic opening needs to take place. If handled in a way that honors both the spiritual and the physical realms, this process can be rewarding and illuminating, and add a great deal of satisfaction to your life.

It is equally as important not to develop too rapidly as it is not to stay in old mind-sets of rigid separation. The idea is to gently become aware of wholeness. To leave behind your discerning abilities could lead to forms of escapism and overindulgence, whether it be food, alcohol, drugs, television, or prolonged sleeping patterns that are inappropriate to your lifestyle. If you resist the lesson of learning to add sensitivity to your interactions with others, you may tend to alienate others through your harsh manner and rough behavior.

One of the lessons you are learning is that through sensitivity you will be able to communicate with your fellow beings and to achieve what you have always wanted: to aid others in reaching their own individual states of perfection or at least to help others in regaining their direction so that they may become more secure beings.

FEELING OVERWHELMED

When you first open to your sensitivity and compassion, unless you do it very consciously you can at times feel overwhelmed with the need to take on the burdens of others. Not understanding where this feeling is coming from, you may accept too much emotional debris from those around you, thereby making your burden heavier than it needs to be. You can recognize when this is happening because you will resent those coming to you for assistance. When you feel this sense of resentment, it's important to get in touch: "Am I accepting more than I really want to? Have I made myself a self-appointed martyr? Am I shifting resentment and anger to those who are coming to me for help?"

If the answer is yes, then it is an important lesson, because you begin to deal with the problems of friends, family, and coworkers only when you truly wish to help and to give only the assistance that you truly wish to give. When you give more than you have, you deplete your own energy and resent those who are "taking" from you, failing to realize that no one is taking, you are giving, and at all times we must be responsible for what we give. You are learning to be sensitive to the self as well as to others by learning when to say no.

You have an innate ability to recognize when something needs strengthening or readjusting. From previous lifetimes spent being harsh and overly critical, however, you can develop a pattern of finding flaws in everything and everyone. When you overdo this type of analysis, you repulse those around you because insensitive criticism is one of the most difficult things to accept.

You are learning in this lifetime to present your awarenesses in a different manner so that those you are trying to aid will not reject your advice solely because of the way it has been presented. If you confront someone with a weakness in a harsh or cold manner, it forces that person to put up a protective shell. You need to take care not to present your insights in a manner that is either humiliating or emotionally damaging. Otherwise, you will have placed such a barrier between yourself and the other person that no matter how beneficial your insights are, you will never be able to penetrate the wall the other person has erected for emotional self-protection. An essential part of your lesson is to develop tact and sensitivity in your mannerisms.

Step 2: Conscious Expression

You recognize that you need to incorporate sensitivity into your mannerisms. You are aware of the inspirational and intuitive side of your nature, and if you allow yourself an intelligent avenue to explore this intuition and sensitivity, these traits can be properly incorporated into your being. Only then can these gifts be used to aid and assist your fellow beings.

By recognizing where corrections need to be made, you can couple your previous exposure to the analytical mind and your awareness to detail with your ability to distill facts into a useful perspective. Once the intuitive faculty has been added, you are able to be of great service to others. As your life progresses, sensitivity, spirituality, and psychic awareness become more and more a part of your being, and you become of even greater assistance to those around you. Some of your abilities are similar to those who have premonitions, since you can perceive what will be happening in the future and can then share your insights with those affected. Then they have the opportunity to make a more educated decision about the direction they would like their lives to take.

A NATURAL GUIDE

Once your sensitivity and tact are developed you would make a good counselor, since you are able to discern information, analyze it intelligently, and guide others into a proper perspective. When operating at a conscious level, you are developing the ability to take the element of human frailty into account as you critique those around you. When you do this, the information is accepted and used by others, and you are deeply appreciated by those who need direction.

When expressing this eclipse pattern consciously, you are aware of subtleties that are transpiring within your being. You notice that you are becoming more intuitive as the days pass, having learned to listen to your intuitive guidance through trial and error. With awareness of this guidance, as you watch and critique what is transpiring, you can learn to feel and sense the difference between imagination and intuition.

SPIRITUAL VALUES

Those of you who are more evolved appreciate the spiritual values and are curious to develop them. Many take courses in spiritual awareness, psychic abilities, dream analysis, reading spiritual books, and meditation. All of these are excellent for opening up your consciousness, broadening your perspective and awareness, and empowering you to receive more information through your psychic faculties. As your psychic abilities grow, there are deeper insights into how you can most benefit your fellow beings and yourself with these aware-nesses. You perceive that you are developing these gifts so you can help oth-ers, and as you continue your work you may find many of your dreams to be precognitive in nature.

You are a sensitive, responsible being, and when operating at a conscious level, you may be drawn to occupations or situations where you can use this special sensitivity. You are aspiring to truly emanate love and compassion from your being.

Step 3: Transpersonal Expression

You are bringing great amounts of spiritual awareness to this planet through your ability to share love, peace, and harmony with those you come in contact with and through the very way you think and live your life. You are born open and psychically aware of universal concepts that the average person is not even capable of imagining. You perceive the wholeness in everything and everyone. You truly understand and are able to conceptualize this aware-ness of this wholeness: that everything is whole within itself yet an integral part of another whole that encompasses yet another.

This awareness endows you with the ability to appreciate today, for to-morrow will always be part of a cycle yet to happen, and today is all we need to concern ourselves with when we have established enough faith in the uni-versal plan and in our own integrity as a whole being.

You have a natural ability to walk through this lifetime without losing the sense of belonging to a greater whole; you remain assured that you are a loved and honored part of this universal oneness. Thus, you are able to impart to oth-ers a sense of belonging to something greater than the self. This allows them to feel more confidence and freedom in exploring their chosen lessons, knowing they are always really home.

Physical Integration

When you are resisting the developmental process you chose to acquire in this lifetime, your body will communicate to you that you are on the wrong track by drawing attention to the feet and the lymphatic system. Before these areas of the body becoming activated and oversensitized, you will have warn-ing signals or symptoms in the digestive system. This is to let you know that you are overanalyzing and not allowing your psychic sensibilities to enter the picture.

Through becoming more aware of your overdigestive process beginning on the psychological and then the physical level, you can form more sensitive habit patterns and thereby free the digestive process to assimilate properly. You can do this by allowing spiritual energy to flow through you.

If you resist or ignore this awareness, the result may be problems with the feet (including the arches and the instep) in the form of corns, calluses, swelling, sweatiness, and general irritations. Next, the lymphatic system of the body would become symptomatic. Pisces, being the last sign of the zodiac, is equivalent on the physical level to the last line of resistance within the body itself—the lymphatic system, which controls the immune system. If you choose to ignore your decision to develop spiritually in this lifetime, you may break down your lymphatic system. If you allow yourself to lose touch with your inner guidance, you could bring on these problems.

HOUSES CONTAINING
YOUR ECLIPSES

1ST HOUSE

For additional insight into the 1st house eclipse, read the eclipse in Aries section (page 216).

SOLAR ECLIPSE

You share what you have come to teach through direct one-to-one interactions, and you act out these life lessons through your physical mannerisms. When asked a direct question, you respond with full honesty—regardless of the repercussions—and you carry a childlike enthusiasm for accomplishing the tasks you have accepted.

In this lifetime you are drawn to teach others how to expand their self-identity. Your natural understanding of how important it is for people to follow their sense of independence and set their own goals gives you the ability to enhance that awareness in others. In this way you encourage those who are in need of expanding to reach a new point of self-realization and self-direction.

You can teach those around you how to be successfully assertive and express themselves in a way that helps them attain their goals. You also motivate others to develop a stronger and more effective self-identity, which frees them to take assertive action in their lives.

LUNAR ECLIPSE

You are learning your lessons by noticing how people respond to your personality. Those you come in contact with will force you to take responsibility for your actions and will hold you accountable for your behavior and interactions with others. You are learning to integrate into your personality the qualities described by the sign of your lunar eclipse. Once this is accomplished your presentation will become well rounded, and you will feel much more comfortable with other people.

You may find yourself going through life searching for who you really are, but by studying the sign of your lunar eclipse, your search for identity and self-sufficiency can be shortened.

2ND HOUSE

For additional insight into the 2nd house eclipse, read the eclipse in Taurus section (page 225).

SOLAR ECLIPSE

You are here to help those around you get in touch with their own deepest values. Through either a positive or a negative experience with you, others can learn the importance of building a strong foundation in whatever area is weak in their personality structure. You teach them how to build a strong foundation by laying the blocks one at a time.

You can be especially helpful to others in the areas of the emotions and in building feelings of self-worth. They can learn from you how to determine what needs to be incorporated into their personalities to strengthen and broaden their emotional makeup. Through you, people can get in touch with what their emotional needs actually are, for you intuitively understand that in order to manifest anything you must know what you want.

You have a natural understanding of moral, financial, and spiritual values, and a knack for helping people recognize ways to strengthen their values and feel better about themselves. Being able to look at life with clear logic and an understanding of what is and what is not reality, you can quickly calculate the assets and liabilities of those with whom you come in contact. And you can teach others how to use their assets and eliminate their weaknesses.

LUNAR ECLIPSE

There is some basic flaw in your internal value system that you have come to restructure. Your challenge is to strengthen your foundation in whatever area is weak.

It's like a missing brick that needs to be filled in so that at some stressful time in your life your internal structure doesn't topple over. What you are looking for is that missing brick in the basic foundation of your life—your values. Studying the sign of your lunar eclipse will help you, and when you have found and fixed this missing link, you will also be restored to balance and harmony within your being.

3RD HOUSE

For additional insight into the 3rd house eclipse, read the eclipse in Gemini (page 235).

SOLAR ECLIPSE

You have the ability to teach people the necessity of sharing the experiences, ideas, and feelings in their everyday lives.

In your environment you are usually the one counted on to keep the conversation flowing, and you teach those around you the importance of keeping information and knowledge circulating. You keep everyone informed about what is going on, and the type of information you focus on is determined by the sign of your solar eclipse.

You teach that there are no limits. We can have as much as we want in any area of life—money, love, knowledge, and so forth—as long as we don't plug up our own flow by holding on to what we believe in or have now. You show us that as long as we keep it circulating, something new and better will always take its place.

LUNAR ECLIPSE

You are here to learn to allow things to flow through you in this lifetime. You have come to remove blockages, to communicate, to socialize and interact with your environment, especially in areas ruled by the sign of your lunar eclipse. Yours is the lesson of letting go and trusting the universe to provide what you need and replenish what you release.

This is a lifetime for breaking stagnated energy patterns such as not sharing your resources, feeling you were the only one privy to certain information, being unable to communicate your feelings, or fearing that the energy flowing from you would not be reciprocated. In this existence you came to find the bounty available from the energy of circulation.

4TH HOUSE

For additional insight into the 4th house eclipse, read the eclipse in Cancer (page 245).

SOLAR ECLIPSE

You are teaching people how to become comfortable within their home base. You show them how to recognize their security needs and take responsibility for fulfilling these needs for their inner security. Through you, others can get in touch with their inner nature and lay strong foundations to grow from so they will not be easily swept off balance by their external surroundings. You teach people to develop a deeper understanding of themselves, which gives them security in relating to the world. You have the ability to teach those around you to feel comfortable with themselves, whether they need to learn lessons of detachment, attainment, or sharing. You help them to see that their souls are at exactly the right point in their evolution, regardless of their circumstances.

Your innate ability to be comfortable in the areas related to the sign of your solar eclipse allows you to teach people to be comfortable with that energy within themselves. You are a nurturer and can teach others to nurture their own self-esteem. You make people feel at ease and good about themselves, and secure about the foundations from which they are emerging. You bring out their capacity to feel and validate their sensitivities.

LUNAR ECLIPSE

You came into this incarnation with low self-esteem, and you are learning self-worth and self-identity in this lifetime. Learning to be comfortable within your family will help you to be comfortable within the essence of your soul. If you are an overachiever, it may be because you feel there is so much to improve. You may spend too much time judging yourself when what you really need to learn is how to build your self-esteem. The idea is to spend as much time building self-esteem as you spend building in the external world. Remember to do those things that make you feel good about yourself and to validate your successes internally along the way. Learning to enjoy the process as much as reaching the goal is important for you.

As you begin to recognize your own self-worth you become less defensive, especially within the family unit. Allowing others to nurture you helps you to feel better about yourself. You are extremely good at seeing flaws within the self, and you need to learn to nurture your own identity and accept your soul's reason for being part of the universe. There is goodness in your essence, and you have much to share as you learn to express yourself from your own center.

5TH HOUSE

For additional insight into the 5th house eclipse, read the eclipse in Leo (page 253).

SOLAR ECLIPSE

You have the responsibility of teaching others how to play in life. By following your heart you teach those around you how to approach life in a more carefree way. You are an extremely creative being, and you help other people to bring forth their own creativity. You have good organizational abilities, work well with children, and are comfortable with affairs of the heart. Generally an easygoing person, you possess depth and intensity, and are success oriented. Perhaps the most important lesson you teach others is to accept the pleasures that life offers and to stay out of self-denial.

You can dramatize your own life in a way that inspires others to take chances and risks in their own lives. You demonstrate the lesson of risk taking and have the ability to break people out of old, stagnant patterns. Yours is the energy of the child who knows better than to neglect the pleasure and enjoyment of life. By enjoying your life you help others to remove the crust from around their hearts and accept love into their lives.

LUNAR ECLIPSE

You are learning how to take life less seriously and to play. You are also learning to accept good fortune and love. You tend to want to know the motive behind everything that comes to you and to doubt whether you are really worthy of receiving it. By learning to release old emotional insecurities, you are more willing to take chances, stepping out into life for the sheer enjoyment of pursuing a new pathway.

The lesson of accepting is a difficult one for you, yet it is essential that it be learned. If you are going to love the universe, you must first learn to love yourself. To begin to love yourself means first getting over your hesitancy about accepting love, gifts, and praise from others. When you live in a state of acceptance, you are truly able to give love not only on an individual level but on a universal level. At that time you will come into your own true power and have the ability to teach universal concepts.

This lifetime you are learning how to deal with affairs of the heart, children, and your own creativity. Through procreation you learn how to incorporate the joy of your creativity into this existence. As you begin to allow yourself to be proud and accept love from what you create in this existence, you also allow yourself to develop an ego and self-identity through what you create. This helps you get more in touch with your creator and other universal energies. Learning to recognize that you have the ability to create puts you in touch with your power to manifest your own positive destiny. Through consciously creating what makes your life happy, vital, and alive, you learn to accept responsibility for creating your own reality.

6TH HOUSE

For additional insight into the 6th house eclipse, read the eclipse in Virgo (page 263).

SOLAR ECLIPSE

You are teaching others how to organize their lives by having clearly defined goals, putting things in proper perspective, and disciplining their visions to a practical application. You have the capacity to observe details and to see the larger picture involved. You're teaching those around you how to learn from their own lives, find their own flaws, and find their own remedies. This gives them the power to put things back in order for themselves.

Your concern with finding a healthy balance between the needs of mind and body teaches others to do the same. You also teach the value of self-improvement since you are willing to learn and grow from your various life experiences. Especially in the areas of work, service, and health, you share with others the gifts shown by the sign of your solar eclipse.

LUNAR ECLIPSE

You need to learn to make lifestyle adjustments that will let you have a healthy body, sensible work habits, and a positive attitude toward this service-oriented lifetime. In the process you will open to learning the lessons you seek through the signs of your lunar eclipse. In previous lifetimes you have neglected certain things concerning health, work, and service, and you need to reevaluate your ideals and intentions in these areas. You may need to learn about the body (what you can and cannot put into it) or break laziness patterns from previous incarnations.

Instead of wishing your life away you are learning to physically manifest what you want in this lifetime. You are putting your mind back into productive focus toward a direction or goal, and in the process you will learn the lessons dictated by the sign of your lunar eclipse.

7TH HOUSE

For additional insight into the 7th house eclipse, read the eclipse in Libra (page 273).

SOLAR ECLIPSE

You are here to teach others how to relate. Yours is the gift of interaction and teaching others how to have successful partnerships and relationships. You are teaching the benefits of promises and contracts, and how necessary it is to honor commitments.

Through your innate ability to relate with others in the spirit of harmony, goodwill, and consideration of the other person, you can share your solar eclipse gift. You teach people that to see the self, or at least how the self is viewed by others, they must learn how to relate. Thus, you are teaching humankind how to use the mirror of "the other" to help reevaluate the self.

LUNAR ECLIPSE

You are learning how to master the lesson of your eclipse through your close relationships with others.

You can experience the energy of relating by being aware of the effect you have on the lives and attitudes of those around you, and by learning to understand the roles that others play in your life. The meaning of commitment and the value of follow-through are becoming clearer to you as you learn to take the needs of others into consideration.

8TH HOUSE

For additional insight into the 8th house eclipse, read the eclipse in Scorpio (page 282).

SOLAR ECLIPSE

In this lifetime you are teaching the energies of transformation. When you enter into powerful psychological interactions with others (whether business or sexual), you give them access to your gifts.

The financial, moral, and spiritual responsibility we have for one another is the lesson you teach. You make others aware of how their values affect those with whom they come in contact, and you help them to understand the importance of finding common values on all three levels. You can also use your powerful energy as a healer or metaphysician.

By your example you can teach those around you the value of investing time, money, and awareness in humankind as a whole. You have a natural intuitive awareness of the values and needs of those around you and understand their importance on a moral, financial, and spiritual level.

LUNAR ECLIPSE

You are learning to take responsibility for how your values affect the other people in your life.

You need to learn why it is important for the strong to be responsible for the weak. As you enter into areas of joint responsibility and mutual empowerment, you gain access to what you need in order to learn the lessons determined by the sign of your lunar eclipse. You are also learning to take responsibility for how you express yourself sexually in this lifetime.

9TH HOUSE

For additional insight into the 9th house eclipse, read the eclipse in Sagittarius (page 294).

SOLAR ECLIPSE

You are teaching others to have adventures in life, to take chances, and to be free. By encouraging others to pursue their sense of individual adventure and not to become fixed on one ideal or one location, you teach them how much can be learned by allowing their consciousness to expand and their body to travel while they are on the planet.

You encourage others to incorporate as many different lessons and experiences as possible into one existence by circulating in different cultures and environments. They follow your example of sharing what you have learned from other environments, showing that each type of culture has its own positive awareness and value. In the process of living an adventurous lifestyle, you open yourself to share the gifts shown by the sign of your solar eclipse.

LUNAR ECLIPSE

You have incarnated with the responsibility to expand your awareness of both conditioned ideals and other cultures and social environments.

You are here to realize that there is more to life than what you already know. Thus, you will feel a desire for freedom and movement and a curiosity for new experiences in this lifetime. You are reaching for idealistic goals, and in the process of pursuing your sense of adventure, you will encounter lessons you need to learn as indicated by the sign of your lunar eclipse.

10TH HOUSE

For additional insight into the 10th house eclipse, read the eclipse in Capricorn (page 304).

SOLAR ECLIPSE

You teach others about professional ethics and community responsibility. You are a leader in the community, teaching your peers to be aware of the interdependency that members of the community have with one another.

You have the ability to be a politician, religious leader, or the parent who runs the PTA. You are capable of achieving goals easily in this lifetime, and through the process of your achievement you teach the qualities of your solar eclipse sign to others.

LUNAR ECLIPSE

You need to learn about community responsibility. You are learning to communicate your thoughts and feelings with a high level of integrity within your chosen fields of endeavor. The sign of your lunar eclipse shows the areas where you need the most work. You are learning to set and achieve career goals and to pursue these goals with a single-mindedness that empowers you to develop character and learn your lessons along the way.

It is important not to allow your insecurities to get in the way. Sometimes you may find yourself feeling sidetracked or having to take a few steps backward. Understand that this is natural in the process of learning how to use everything in your path to attain your goal.

11TH HOUSE

For additional insight into the 11th house eclipse, read the eclipse in Aquarius (page 314).

SOLAR ECLIPSE

You are teaching your fellow beings to develop a group consciousness and to be more aware of the needs of others. You teach many of your lessons in group situations, helping others to develop group-oriented awareness. Much of your work is in humanitarian endeavors that are for the highest good of the most people. You can help bring about the realization that when the masses are taken care of, individual lives will also be fulfilled. One example of this is the family unit. If decisions are made that make the family happy, the individuals within the family are happy too.

In pursuing your own high ideals and aspirations, you help others to become goal oriented. You make them aware that nothing can be achieved in this life unless you strive for it. Through your own zest for life and accomplishment you teach other people to reach for the stars, and you show them that nothing is beyond their reach if they really focus their energy on it.

You encourage others to pursue their dreams, aspirations, and ideals, and are extremely supportive of your friends and acquaintances. You often put a great deal of time and energy into the efforts of those you feel have worthy goals or those with whom you feel a kinship. You encourage others to fulfill their dreams in ways explained in the sign of your solar eclipse.

LUNAR ECLIPSE

Besides learning to dream, you are also are learning that it is all right to improve the life you were born to and acquire more than you have. Dreaming is a very healthy pastime for you because it helps to build your soul growth pattern. Regardless of the sign of your eclipse, when it is in the 11th house you must learn how to dream in order to aspire to new heights in this lifetime.

You are also learning about group consciousness and how to incorporate the good of all into your aspirations. You are recognizing that in fulfilling the group need, your own individual needs are automatically satisfied. As you begin to take into consideration the desires, goals, and aspirations of those around you (the group, not just individuals), you will discover your need to find your relatedness to the whole—either by giving to or receiving from them. You are learning to be aware of the group as a mutually supportive emotional system in terms of your dreams and aspirations.

You are beginning to allow your life to merge with the flow of the universe. If you follow your own inner guidance and intuition, you will be directed to the precise path you are to follow to reach your own personal goals.

12TH HOUSE

For additional insight into the 12th house eclipse, read the eclipse in Pisces (page 324).

SOLAR ECLIPSE

Through the principle of "let go and let God" you are teaching others to have trust and confidence in the universal unfolding of events. You help other people learn how to cope with unexpected changes and the ups and downs of life. You show them how to deal with limitations, how to listen to the inner world within, and how to appreciate the inspiration that can be received only when we are willing to listen to the inner voice. You teach others to accept and even to appreciate the confines of their own mind.

People can learn from you how to contact peace and inner serenity through meditation and how to gain the awareness that the universe can unfold to those who are willing to slow down and listen by going within. You also have the ability to deal with institutions of all kinds. You are excellent at counseling others because you are aware of their self-defeating patterns and can offer emotional encouragement according to the nature of the sign in which your solar eclipse is found.

LUNAR ECLIPSE

You are learning how to get in touch with the self by quieting the psyche long enough to go within and listen for inspiration and guidance. It is important for you to experience the serenity of meditation, to make time to be alone and go within. This process will empower you to discover your own self-defeating mechanisms so you can learn the lessons in the sign of your lunar eclipse.

Rooting out anything from a previous incarnation that is still buried within your psyche will help you to get rid of self-limiting habit patterns. You are learning to free yourself from internal mechanisms that lead to unconscious withdrawal from situations rather than active participation. By going inward you are able to remove these blockages so you can participate in life with a free flow of energy.

If you don't learn to contact your inner self on your own, you may find it necessary to have the imposed structure of an institution. It's important for you to find healthy modes of going within instead of developing escapism patterns such as drugs, alcohol, television, sleeping too much, or self-pity.

Through learning to make the corrections within yourself, you find that your external circumstances cease to pose any kind of a block to your own expression. As an added benefit you will develop at a rapid pace spiritually and psychically, and find yourself aiding others in areas that were once weaknesses for you.

ASPECT PATTERNS

T HE ASPECTS INDICATE the nature of the psychological relationship between your solar and lunar eclipses. There are four major aspects
possible between the lunar eclipse and the solar eclipse in your individual
chart: conjunction, semi-sextile, quincunx (or inconjunct), and opposition.

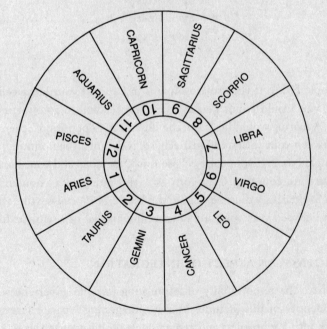

For the purpose of understanding the relationship between your solar and lunar eclipses, these aspects are to be calculated by sign only, not the degrees. They are calculated by the distance between the signs. To determine the aspect between your prenatal solar and lunar eclipses, use the diagram wheel on the previous page.

Counting your prenatal solar eclipse as "1," count each sign until you reach your prenatal lunar eclipse (it will be counted also), going in a counter-clockwise direction. Then refer to the list below to find the aspect between your prenatal solar and lunar eclipses.

The definitions of meanings of the aspects are in the text that follows the list.

LIST OF ASPECTS AS THEY RELATE TO THE ECLIPSES

> 1 = conjunction
> 2 = semi-sextile
> 6 = inconjunct
> 7 = opposition
> 8 = inconjunct
> 12 = semi-sextile

Example No. 1: If your solar eclipse is in Leo and your lunar eclipse is in Aquarius, you would count Leo as 1, and, proceeding in a counterclockwise direction, Aquarius would be 7. On the list 7 is an "opposition"; therefore, the aspect between your solar and lunar eclipses is that of an opposition.

Example No. 2: If your solar eclipse is in Capricorn and your lunar eclipse is in Sagittarius, counting Capricorn as 1 and going in a counterclockwise direction, Sagittarius would be 12. On the list, 12 is a "semi-sextile"; therefore, the aspect between your solar and lunar eclipses is that of a semi-sextile.

CONJUNCTION: AN ASPECT OF INTEGRATION

You have the responsibility of assimilating past-life experiences into the personal identity of this lifetime. You are integrating separate facets of your personality into a wholeness and centeredness within yourself. It is as though the self was so involved with other projects and identities in prior incarnations that it lost its focus. Thus, in the present incarnation the urge is toward unity, self-sufficiency, and a sense of completion within the self.

After having been dispersed, the identity is now ready to integrate itself at a higher level than was available in past lifetimes. Your greatest growth comes not through objective awareness but through subjective experiences of your life situations.

Your job is to allow the circumstances of your life to aid you in building a separate identity that will give you a true sense of individuality. When you reunite with that spark of identity within yourself, you find an inner strength emerging. This self-reliance will heal the nagging sense of incompletion you feel when you allow yourself to become dependent on others for your personal growth.

It is important for you to practice being real with the self because this is a lifetime for you to become fully conscious of reaping what you sow. You will get out of life only what you are willing to put into it, in the sense of expressing what is really going on inside you. The degree of realness that you are willing to share with others reflects the realness that the universe will be willing to unfold to you.

If you can become capable of total honesty, your ability to perceive and share advanced spiritual concepts will be unlimited, since the universe will unfold itself to you without reserve. If you choose to separate yourself from your own truth and reality, you can find yourself living a life of confusion and delusion, and possibly needing counseling to remove the veils you have placed over your own identity.

SEMI-SEXTILE: AN ASPECT OF BUILDING

The healing of your own identity is your primary concern during this lifetime, since you need to gain a sense of wholeness within yourself.

To this end you are continually putting your energies into building the things that are important to you, either financially, morally, or spiritually. When what you are striving for is out of alignment with your own true needs and values, you fall into self-defeating patterns that result in the dissolution of everything you have worked so hard to build. You are learning to build carefully and in more conscious alignment with your own personal identity.

Your work needs to be focused primarily on yourself. It is fine for you to work with others in partnership as long as you don't come to rely on them. You are learning that your destiny is an outgrowth of the strength of your inner character.

Your job is to clear out self-defeating patterns from past lifetimes. You encounter these patterns when building those things that you want for a sense of stability in the material world. If a project begins to fail, it is your job to identify the specific self-defeating pattern that has caused this turn of fortune, correct it, and eliminate it from your unconscious behavior.

On one level you are making new beginnings during this lifetime, and on another you are experiencing how to make effective completions. When the direction of your life is in alignment with your purpose, you go through a succession of tedious new beginnings that, when the proper energy is applied, culminate in successful endings. You have many similarities with the entrepreneur who is continually starting a new business and selling or dissolving the old in order to enter into the next new venture.

You need to build without attachment to the physical plane—including whatever you are building—and you find that you have the internal motivation and energy needed to propel you to new projects. When you attain completion of a project, you immediately start looking at ways to dissolve it, for you do not want to become attached to anything in this lifetime. You feel that attachment will hold you down since you realize that the process of dissolving things is at least half of what you came here to learn.

It is important that you do not judge yourself by what you have attained in the physical world. Instead, you should integrate the personal growth that has emerged from the combination of what you have acquired and what you have released in terms of material attachment.

It is also important for you to understand that it is all right for you to have material possessions. Your purpose in this life is not to renounce the material plane but to understand and develop a proper value system by constantly letting go of what is not congruent with the deeper values you have incorporated into this lifetime. When this process is complete, you can acquire great wealth and also be very spiritually aware, taking responsibility for assisting those who are less fortunate.

You can be truly charitable with both heart and pocketbook. Learn to rely on yourself to move into new stages of personal growth. You cannot rely on others to prod you along; you must motivate yourself both mentally and physically. This is truly an aspect of learning self-reliance.

QUINCUNX (INCONJUNCT): AN ASPECT OF ADJUSTMENT

You have accepted the responsibility of teaching your fellow beings to become more aware. This is a karmic aspect. You are among those bringing in the New Age—the agitators and activists, the healers, the new thinkers.

It is a lifetime of "pearl and oyster": Through constant adjustments to the irritations of life you are able to create much beauty and awareness for yourself and other people. Because you are so sensitive to irritations you learn to adjust so that you can heal them quickly; this creates a great deal of growth in one lifetime, which is what you wanted. Your realization that through aiding others your own growth pattern is speeded up is the reason you can be one of the light workers and help to lay the foundation for a positive future for all.

This is a "serve or suffer" lifetime. The most growth and awareness come to you when you are providing a service and helping others to grow and understand. When you are not, you can be deteriorating in one of three areas: your physical health, your mental and emotional health, or your financial situation. More than any other aspect pattern you are subject to these types of instabilities if you neglect taking responsibilities for your own growth.

Your insights do not necessarily come directly through the people who you are aiding and teaching in this lifetime. Your duty is to assist where you can, and the universe will reward you with another source to provide the knowledge you need, either directly through your own spirit or through some other person. As you help others to gain the awareness they need to grow and adjust to their personal life circumstances, you open yourself to receiving the awareness you need. You recognize that your rewards do not come from those you assist.

You are happiest when you are involved in some sort of service, and you are best suited for a profession that involves healing on some level. This could encompass many areas: working in a health-food store or being a dietitian, farmer, or doctor; assisting with psychological healing as a psychiatrist, psychologist, or astrologer; working with spiritual or emotional healing as a minister; or healing other people's financial, moral, or spiritual values.

You are one of the worker bees on the planet. You are preparing the way for the New Age in the same way a farmer clears the ground and makes it ready for the new seeds. You are learning a sense of humility in your role on Earth. You are also learning to appreciate the honor of being able to play a part in the evolution of humankind and the access this gives you to higher sources of information.

In this lifetime you are gaining a larger perspective of the interrelatedness of all things. You are incorporating the feelings of equality and appreciation that come from realizing that everything on the Earth is part of the same life force. Just as the plants are food for us now, we will someday become food for them. Understanding this kind of relatedness keeps you humble, free, and happy in your life role.

OPPOSITION: AN ASPECT OF LEARNING OBJECTIVITY THROUGH RELATIONSHIPS

You are learning from the people you teach. Your major avenue for personal growth evolves from the intensity of your relationship with those around you. As you work with others on a one-to-one basis, the people you support also provide the support you are seeking in your own life. Mutual growth occurs through this process of reciprocity.

The abstract goals of humankind are not your concern. Your challenge is in finding out how to relate to those around you in a way that produces harmony and justice for both parties. Extending your identity to include others gives you a greater sense of self-completion. The self, as developed in prior incarnations, is now ready for another major growth step, and input from the energy of other people is necessary. You are learning to accept the support and assistance of others in gaining awareness of what you need to complete your own development. This requires humility and grace because you must change personal patterns that separate you from those around you and allow, even invite, them to facilitate your growth process. As you become more open to this assistance, you find that the other person also gains self-awareness.

You are seeking to balance a feeling of self-importance in this lifetime by recognizing that all things are of equal importance. You learn this by accepting responsibility for making yourself as complete as you possibly can while remembering that others are doing the same thing and are just as important as you are.

As you work on ego development and relate with others, you find that those around you remind you of your lesson by saying, "Hey, I'm important too." This brings you back to Earth and helps you become more aware of your flaws, for without this awareness you cannot grow. By relating with others you can become the best you can possibly be. At the same time you gain awareness of the needs of others, which facilitates the social balance you are seeking.

You are also learning the value of diplomacy when expressing yourself to others, which leads to more mutually pleasant experiences. This is an equal-time issue; you are learning to share. In the process you gain a sense of ease about life and an ability to enjoy others while pursuing your own goals.

THE TRANSITING ECLIPSES

WHY THE ECLIPSES WORK

Through the years since we have written *Spiritual Astrology,* many of our clients have asked us to help them understand what the difference is between prenatal eclipse and the eclipses that happen every year. The difference can actually be explained very simply: One is a lifelong mission, and the other is a temporary assignment.

The eclipses depict an intimate relationship *between* the Sun, the Moon, and the Earth. The Sun, Moon, and Earth are the trio that represents our ego (Sun), emotions (Moon), and our physical form (Earth) in our birth charts. The transiting eclipses represent our collective egos, our collective emotions, and our collective karma. Karma on an individual level is how we work things out in our physical lives and bodies, and on a collective level how we serve the planet and work things out.

TIPS ON USING THE TRANSITING SOLAR ECLIPSES

On a day-to-day basis, the house the solar eclipse falls in shows the arena in your life that will be the most highly active during the six-month period when the transiting solar eclipse resides in that house. For example, in the chart on page 357, when the transiting eclipse is at fifteen degrees of Cancer, the 2nd house will become activated. Issues of money will come to the forefront of your life. You will be faced with the necessity of dealing with your finances directly. In addition to involvement with money issues, you will also be concerned with other 2nd house matters: You will automatically become aware of your values and whether or not some of your priorities need to change to more properly suit who you are at this point in your life.

Issues involving significant relationships will arise to be dealt with during the time the transiting solar eclipse occupies the 7th house in your birth chart.

In whichever house the transiting solar eclipse falls, that arena of your life will be activated and the issues of that house will come to the forefront of your attention. For a list of the areas of your life ruled by the different houses, see page 356.

Foreknowledge of where the current eclipse will affect you gives you an edge on using time to your advantage. For example, when an eclipse falls in your 2nd house, you will be drawn to deal with money issues. Without anticipating where timing is unfolding to your advantage, it may be two to three months before you get proactively involved in these matters; you miss the full benefit of the cycle. By knowing in advance what will be the next area paramount in your life, you can consciously cooperate with the energy and use it at the beginning of each cycle, before outer circumstances force you to deal with it.

HELPFUL INFORMATION

> Transiting lunar eclipse = emotional integration
> Transiting solar eclipse = ego (personality/consciousness)
>   integration; self-expression
> Time frame transiting eclipses are in effect = approximately
>   six months.
> They will last from one solar eclipse to the next, or from
>   one lunar eclipse to the next.

You can locate the current transiting eclipse by consulting the eclipse tables on page 423. For a free copy of your natal birth chart, go to www .janspiller.com. Natal charts containing your prenatal eclipses are part of the free chart services on this site. With your natal chart in hand, you can locate the house in which the current transiting eclipse is affecting your life personally by using the technique shown at the end of this section on page 357. Other astrology Web sites also offer natal charts.

SOLAR ECLIPSE

The house a solar eclipse falls in describes the area of your life where you will be asked to address and set an example for the collective. When there is a transiting solar eclipse we as a collective are asked to integrate the same consciousness adjustment.

An example: The solar eclipse falls in your 4th house of home, family, your mother, and emotions. If you are a good example in that area of life, it will be a time when you will shine so you can be a good role model to others. If you handle that area of your life poorly, you will be exposed and held accountable to show others that such behavior will not be tolerated, thereby assisting those that are moving in a negative direction to make an adjustment. Either way the result is always a lesson learned the easy way or the hard way. The choice is always ours.

LUNAR ECLIPSE

When there is a transiting lunar eclipse we as a collective are allowed to feel the same emotion. Although we are feeling a collective emotion, it will affect each of us differently, for it will fall in a different house—a different area—of our lives. There are twelve different houses in our astrological charts and each house represents a different area of life. The twelve different signs show the qualities of character we are being asked to embrace.

THE SIGNS

There are twelve signs in the zodiac and these eclipses will always be in one of these twelve signs. The sign will talk about what is being affected—what part of your personality and character are being activated and prompted to express and grow. Again, the sign of the transiting lunar eclipse shows the qualities we are learning to emotionally embrace, and the sign of the transiting solar eclipse reveals what we are learning to express at a more refined and effective level.

Aries = Will be your independence, sense of self

Taurus = Will be your senses, money, possessions

Gemini = Will be your thought process, communication skills

Cancer = Will be your feeling center, how you emote

Leo = Will be your sense of pride, your ego, and creativity

Virgo = Will be your attention to detail, corrections, and work ethic

Libra = Will be your sense of fairness, relationship skills, and the balance in your life

Scorpio = Will be your use of power, transformation, and regeneration

Sagittarius = Will be your sense of freedom, judgment, and
   exploration
Capricorn = Will be your sense of priority, responsibility,
   and status
Aquarius = Will be your sense of the greater good, your genius, and letting go
Pisces = Will be your intuition, compassion, and sensitivity

THE HOUSES

The house the transiting solar eclipse falls in reveals the area in which
issues will arise for you to respond to from a higher level of your own self-
expression. This arena will come to your attention during the six months
when the solar eclipse resides in the house, requiring you to reevaluate the
matters of the house involved and deal with them, head-on, in a new and more
effective way.

The house in your birth chart the lunar eclipse falls in will talk about the
arena of your life that is being activated so you can embrace a higher emotional level of the sign the lunar eclipse falls in.

1st house: your physical body, appearance, and personality
2nd house: your values: moral, financial, and spiritual
3rd house: your siblings, neighbors, education, and communication skills
4th house: your home life, family, mother, and emotions
5th house: your children, creativity, and personal love
6th house: your health and work ethic
7th house: your significant others: best friends, spouse, partners; lawyers
8th house: your bonded relationships: financial, physical, and spiritual; transformation, inheritances
9th house: your higher education, travel, philosophical belief system, and
judges
10th house: your father, authority figures, careers, and standing in the community
11th house: your hopes, wishes, aspirations, friends, groups, and humanitarian
love
12th house: your secrets, self-sabotaging behaviors, sanctuary, place of private
regeneration, inner world (both spiritual and hiding place), surrender to a
higher power

HOW TO FIND THE HOUSE LOCATION OF
THE CURRENT ECLIPSE

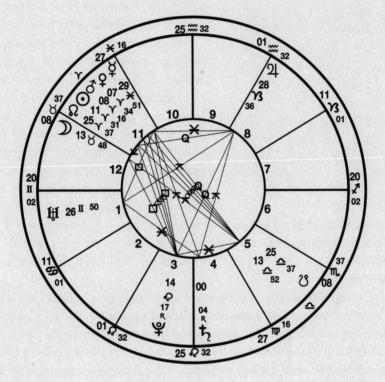

EXAMPLE BIRTH CHART

First, consult the tables on page 423 to determine the sign and degree of the current eclipses. Keep in mind that you will want to make a note of the solar and lunar eclipses that *precede* the current day. Then you are ready to continue with discovering the house in your chart being affected and stimulated by the most recent eclipses.

As you can see, the above wheel has been divided into twelve sections. In astrology, those sections are called houses. You will also see that each house is numbered one through twelve. That is your way of knowing which house a planet is within.

Next you will see that on the farthest edge of the perimeter, we have numbers and squiggle lines. The squiggly lines are called glyphs. They are the symbols for the signs. On the next page, you will find a legend for these glyphs.

SIGN		
Aries	=	♈
Taurus	=	♉
Gemini	=	♊
Cancer	=	♋
Leo	=	♌
Virgo	=	♍
Libra	=	♎
Scorpio	=	♏
Sagittarius	=	♐
Capricorn	=	♑
Aquarius	=	♒
Pisces	=	♓

The numbers next to these glyphs are referred to as degrees. Each sign in the zodiac has thirty degrees. There are twelve signs, which added together make a full circle. **Example**: 30 x 12 = 360, the equivalent of a whole circle.

If you look at the bolder of the numbers next to the glyphs for the signs, you will see the degree that house begins with.

Example No. 1: The 1st house begins with 20 degrees of Gemini, so if you are looking up an eclipse in the back of the book, whether it is transiting or prenatal, and that eclipse is 18 degrees of Gemini, you can see that it is in the 12th house, for the first house begins at 20 degrees. With 18 being before 20 it is easy to figure out this fact. Now if the eclipse is 29 degrees of Gemini, you can be assured that the eclipse is in the 1st house, for 29 is greater than 20. You can do this with every eclipse and every house the same way.

Example No. 2: The eclipse you want to look up is 2 degrees of Cancer. It is plain to see the 2nd house has the sign of Cancer on it, so all we need to figure out is if 2 degrees falls before or after the beginning of the 2nd house. In our example chart the house starts at 11 degrees. The 11th degree is greater than the 2nd, so again it is easy for us to see that the eclipse falls before the 2nd house begins, making it a 1st-house eclipse.

Remember how smart you are and have fun with this. This is a wonderful brain exerciser and a consciousness expander. The universal consciousness is numbers. Let the wonders of numbers open your eyes. Or order a chart and have someone do it for you. Either way enjoy the results.

WORKSHEET

Example of how to use the formula: Transiting Libra lunar eclipse in your 3rd house. *Solar or lunar?* This example is *lunar,* so we will write *emotional integration* on our list. Then we look at the sign. We see it is Libra, so we look at our key words for the sign of Libra: *fairness, relationship skills, balance.* Finally we look at which house this is transpiring in (though as you can see, even if you do not know which house this is happening in, there is already useful information just on the type of eclipse and the sign, and both are easily found in this book). As stated above, it is taking place in the 3rd house. Key words for the 3rd house are: *siblings and communication skills.*

During this cycle it is time for you to learn to *emotionally integrate* better *communication skills* dealing with your *relationships.*

Remember that we always have choices about whether we put our energy into learning our lessons the easy way or the hard way. As in the above example, we could choose the hard way, not paying attention to how our *emotional communications* affect our *relationships* and suffer deep difficulty in our *relationships,* possibly even breakups during this particular eclipse cycle. On the other hand, if we put our energy into learning the easy way, we start paying attention to how our *emotional communications* are affecting our *relationships,* make some adjustments, and improve the quality of our relationships. The choice is always ours—we were born with free will. Either way, the universe is not connected to our choices, only to the lessons we set for ourselves before we were born.

Please use the charts below to assist you in figuring out your transiting eclipses as explained above.

Example		Key Words
Solar or Lunar	Solar	Personality-ego
Sign		Relationship-Balance
Libra		
House		Communication
Third		

Solar or Lunar	Lunar	Emotional Integration
Sign		Relationship-Balance
Libra		
House		Communication
Third		

Solar or Lunar		
Sign		
House		

CONCLUSION:
EAVESDROPPING ON THE SIGNS

UPON ENTERING THE Earth plane, these are the remarks heard from the various eclipse and Sun signs:

Aries: "Everybody out of my way!"
Taurus: "What's mine?"
Gemini: "Listen to me."
Cancer: "Does anybody really care?"
Leo: "Who wants to play?"
Virgo: "We're not doing it right!"
Libra: "Is this the right direction?"
Scorpio: "Let's get to the bottom of it."
Sagittarius: "I know where you're coming from."
Capricorn: "I deserve better."
Aquarius: "I'm just curious."
Pisces: "What am I doing here?"

MATHEMATICAL TABLES: FINDING THE SIGNS IN WHICH YOUR PLANETS AND ECLIPSES ARE LOCATED

INTRODUCTION TO PART 3

THE PURPOSE OF part 3 is to supply mathematical tables that will enable you to find the signs in which your planets and eclipses are located. In providing these tables it is our intention to allow you to gain maximum self-sufficiency and freedom in being able to read birth charts. This in no way invalidates the furthering of your education through a reading with a qualified professional astrologer or through additional classes and studies. The purpose is to offer a beginning place for self-actualization and an astrological key that will assist you on your path of soul awareness.

If you would like your entire natal astrology chart calculated and printed for you, go to www.janspiller.com. On the home page, click on "Free Astrology Charts" and you will be connected with a page that will calculate your entire birth chart for you free of charge. For further information on the signs and symbols of astrology, go to "Astrology 101" on www.janspiller.com.

HOW TO USE PART 3

THE MATHEMATICAL TABLES for looking up the sign positions of all your planets and prenatal solar and lunar eclipses are accurate within twenty-four hours of the cutoff dates indicated, depending on your exact time and place of birth. If you have a planet located on a cutoff date—either the first date of a new period or the last date of the old—read both sign descriptions. For total accuracy in determining your sign positions as well as finding the houses in which your planets and eclipses are located, see how to obtain a free copy of your natal birth chart on page 363.

It is easy to use part 3. Using your birth date, simply find the sign location for each of your planets and eclipses. Then look up the corresponding *meaning* of each of your planets in part 1, and of each of your eclipses in part 2.

THE PLANETS

THE SUN

Where was the Sun when you were born?

DATE	SUN SIGN
1/01 to 1/19	Capricorn
1/20 to 2/18	Aquarius
2/19 to 3/20	Pisces
3/21 to 4/19	Aries
4/20 to 5/20	Taurus
5/21 to 6/20	Gemini
6/21 to 7/21	Cancer
7/22 to 8/22	Leo
8/23 to 9/22	Virgo
9/23 to 10/22	Libra
10/23 to 11/21	Scorpio
11/22 to 12/20	Sagittarius
12/21 to 12/31	Capricorn

If you were born on a "cusp"—the last day of one sign and the first day of another—you can accurately determine your Sun sign by going to www .janspiller.com. Click on "Free Astrology Charts" on the home page. Enter your contact information and birth information, and a full chart will be printed for you including your aspects, free of charge.

THE MOON

The Moon moves rapidly through the constellations of the zodiac, spending only two and a half days in each sign. Due to the Moon's rapid motion, tables are not printed in this book. You can find the sign and house position your Moon is in by going to www.janspiller.com. Click on "Free Astrology Charts" on the home page. A free birth chart, including your aspects, will be calculated for you.

MERCURY

Relative to the Earth, Mercury always travels in a constellation very near the one occupied by the Sun. Consequently, on the date of your birth, Mercury could only be in one of three signs: the sign your Sun is in, or one sign away, ahead or behind. The following table will tell you which sign Mercury was in when you were born.

For the positions of Mercury prior to 1936, go to "Free Astrology Charts" on www .janspiller.com.

DATE	ZODIAC SIGN	DATE	ZODIAC SIGN
1936		6/13 to 6/30	Gemini
1/1 to 1/5	Capricorn	6/30 to 7/14	Cancer
1/5 to 3/12	Aquarius	7/14 to 7/31	Leo
3/12 to 3/30	Pisces	7/31 to 10/7	Virgo
3/30 to 4/14	Aries	10/7 to 10/25	Libra
4/14 to 4/30	Taurus	10/25 to 11/13	Scorpio
4/30 to 7/8	Gemini	11/13 to 12/3	Sagittarius
7/8 to 7/23	Cancer	12/3 to 12/31	Capricorn
7/23 to 8/7	Leo		
8/7 to 8/27	Virgo	*1938*	
8/27 to 11/1	Libra	1/1 to 1/6	Capricorn
11/1 to 11/20	Scorpio	1/6 to 1/12	Sagittarius
11/20 to 12/9	Sagittarius	1/12 to 2/8	Capricorn
12/9 to 12/31	Capricorn	2/8 to 2/26	Aquarius
		2/26 to 3/14	Pisces
1937		3/14 to 4/1	Aries
1/1	Capricorn	4/1 to 4/23	Taurus
1/1 to 1/9	Aquarius	4/23 to 5/16	Aries
1/9 to 2/13	Capricorn	5/16 to 6/7	Taurus
2/13 to 3/6	Aquarius	6/7 to 6/22	Gemini
3/6 to 3/22	Pisces	6/22 to 7/6	Cancer
3/22 to 4/6	Aries	7/6 to 7/26	Leo
4/6 to 6/13	Taurus	7/26 to 9/2	Virgo

DATE	ZODIAC SIGN	DATE	ZODIAC SIGN
9/2 to 9/10	Leo	9/13 to 10/3	Libra
9/10 to 9/30	Virgo	10/3 to 12/9	Scorpio
9/30 to 10/18	Libra	12/9 to 12/28	Sagittarius
10/18 to 11/6	Scorpio	12/28 to 12/31	Capricorn
11/6 to 12/31	Sagittarius		

1939

		1941	
		1/1 to 1/16	Capricorn
1/1 to 1/11	Sagittarius	1/16 to 2/3	Aquarius
1/11 to 2/1	Capricorn	2/3 to 3/6	Pisces
2/1 to 2/18	Aquarius	3/6 to 3/16	Aquarius
2/18 to 3/6	Pisces	3/16 to 4/11	Pisces
3/6 to 5/14	Aries	4/11 to 4/28	Aries
5/14 to 5/30	Taurus	4/28 to 5/12	Taurus
5/30 to 6/13	Gemini	5/12 to 5/29	Gemini
6/13 to 6/29	Cancer	5/29 to 8/5	Cancer
6/29 to 9/6	Leo	8/5 to 8/20	Leo
9/6 to 9/22	Virgo	8/20 to 9/6	Virgo
9/22 to 10/10	Libra	9/6 to 9/27	Libra
10/10 to 10/31	Scorpio	9/27 to 10/29	Scorpio
10/31 to 12/2	Sagittarius	10/29 to 11/11	Libra
12/2 to 12/13	Scorpio	11/11 to 12/2	Scorpio
12/13 to 12/31	Sagittarius	12/2 to 12/21	Sagittarius
		12/21 to 12/31	Capricorn

1940

1/1 to 1/5	Sagittarius	**1942**	
1/5 to 1/24	Capricorn	1/1 to 1/9	Capricorn
1/24 to 2/11	Aquarius	1/9 to 3/16	Aquarius
2/11 to 3/3	Pisces	3/16 to 4/4	Pisces
3/3 to 3/7	Aries	4/4 to 4/20	Aries
3/7 to 4/16	Pisces	4/20 to 5/4	Taurus
4/16 to 5/6	Aries	5/4 to 7/12	Gemini
5/6 to 5/21	Taurus	7/12 to 7/28	Cancer
5/21 to 6/4	Gemini	7/28 to 8/12	Leo
6/4 to 6/26	Cancer	8/12 to 8/30	Virgo
6/26 to 7/20	Leo	8/30 to 11/6	Libra
7/20 to 8/11	Cancer	11/6 to 11/25	Scorpio
8/11 to 8/28	Leo	11/25 to 12/14	Sagittarius
8/28 to 9/13	Virgo	12/14 to 12/31	Capricorn

DATE	ZODIAC SIGN	DATE	ZODIAC SIGN
1943		2/4 to 2/22	Aquarius
1/1 to 1/2	Capricorn	2/22 to 3/10	Pisces
1/2 to 1/27	Aquarius	3/10 to 5/16	Aries
1/27 to 2/15	Capricorn	5/16 to 6/3	Taurus
2/15 to 3/10	Aquarius	6/3 to 6/18	Gemini
3/10 to 3/27	Pisces	6/18 to 7/3	Cancer
3/27 to 4/11	Aries	7/3 to 7/26	Leo
4/11 to 4/30	Taurus	7/26 to 8/16	Virgo
4/30 to 5/25	Gemini	8/16 to 9/9	Leo
5/25 to 6/13	Taurus	9/9 to 9/27	Virgo
6/13 to 7/5	Gemini	9/27 to 10/14	Libra
7/5 to 7/20	Cancer	10/14 to 11/3	Scorpio
7/20 to 8/4	Leo	11/3 to 12/31	Sagittarius
8/4 to 8/26	Virgo		
8/26 to 9/24	Libra	*1946*	
9/24 to 10/11	Virgo	1/1 to 1/9	Sagittarius
10/11 to 10/30	Libra	1/9 to 1/28	Capricorn
10/30 to 11/18	Scorpio	1/28 to 2/15	Aquarius
11/18 to 12/7	Sagittarius	2/15 to 3/3	Pisces
12/7 to 12/31	Capricorn	3/3 to 4/1	Aries
		4/1 to 4/16	Pisces
1944		4/16 to 5/11	Aries
1/1 to 2/12	Capricorn	5/11 to 5/26	Taurus
2/12 to 3/2	Aquarius	5/26 to 6/9	Gemini
3/2 to 3/18	Pisces	6/9 to 6/27	Cancer
3/18 to 4/3	Aries	6/27 to 9/3	Leo
4/3 to 6/10	Taurus	9/3 to 9/19	Virgo
6/10 to 6/26	Gemini	9/19 to 10/7	Libra
6/26 to 7/10	Cancer	10/7 to 10/29	Scorpio
7/10 to 7/28	Leo	10/29 to 11/20	Sagittarius
7/28 to 10/4	Virgo	11/20 to 12/12	Scorpio
10/4 to 10/21	Libra	12/12 to 12/31	Sagittarius
10/21 to 11/9	Scorpio		
11/9 to 12/1	Sagittarius	*1947*	
12/1 to 12/23	Capricorn	1/1 to 1/2	Sagittarius
12/23 to 12/31	Sagittarius	1/2 to 1/21	Capricorn
		1/21 to 2/7	Aquarius
1945		2/7 to 4/15	Pisces
1/1 to 1/13	Sagittarius	4/15 to 5/3	Aries
1/13 to 2/4	Capricorn		

DATE	ZODIAC SIGN	DATE	ZODIAC SIGN
5/3 to 5/18	Taurus	7/24 to 8/8	Leo
5/18 to 6/2	Gemini	8/8 to 8/28	Virgo
6/2 to 8/10	Cancer	8/28 to 11/3	Libra
8/10 to 8/26	Leo	11/3 to 11/21	Scorpio
8/26 to 9/11	Virgo	11/21 to 12/11	Sagittarius
9/11 to 10/1	Libra	12/11 to 12/31	Capricorn
10/1 to 12/7	Scorpio		
12/7 to 12/26	Sagittarius		
12/26 to 12/31	Capricorn	**1950**	
		1/1 to 1/1	Capricorn
		1/1 to 1/14	Aquarius
1948		1/14 to 2/14	Capricorn
1/1 to 1/13	Capricorn	2/14 to 3/7	Aquarius
1/13 to 2/1	Aquarius	3/7 to 3/24	Pisces
2/1 to 2/19	Pisces	3/24 to 4/7	Aries
2/19 to 3/17	Aquarius	4/7 to 6/14	Taurus
3/17 to 4/8	Pisces	6/14 to 7/2	Gemini
4/8 to 4/24	Aries	7/2 to 7/16	Cancer
4/24 to 5/8	Taurus	7/16 to 8/1	Leo
5/8 to 5/27	Gemini	8/1 to 8/27	Virgo
5/27 to 6/28	Cancer	8/27 to 9/10	Libra
6/28 to 7/11	Gemini	9/10 to 10/9	Virgo
7/11 to 8/2	Cancer	10/9 to 10/26	Libra
8/2 to 8/16	Leo	10/26 to 11/14	Scorpio
8/16 to 9/3	Virgo	11/14 to 12/4	Sagittarius
9/3 to 9/26	Libra	12/4 to 12/31	Capricorn
9/26 to 10/16	Scorpio		
10/16 to 11/9	Libra	**1951**	
11/9 to 11/29	Scorpio	1/1 to 2/9	Capricorn
11/29 to 12/18	Sagittarius	2/9 to 2/28	Aquarius
12/18 to 12/31	Capricorn	2/28 to 3/15	Pisces
		3/15 to 4/1	Aries
1949		4/1 to 5/1	Taurus
1/1 to 1/5	Capricorn	5/1 to 5/14	Aries
1/5 to 3/13	Aquarius	5/14 to 6/8	Taurus
3/13 to 4/1	Pisces	6/8 to 6/23	Gemini
4/1 to 4/16	Aries	6/23 to 7/8	Cancer
4/16 to 5/1	Taurus	7/8 to 7/27	Leo
5/1 to 7/9	Gemini	7/27 to 10/2	Virgo
7/9 to 7/24	Cancer	10/2 to 10/19	Libra

DATE	ZODIAC SIGN	DATE	ZODIAC SIGN
10/19 to 11/7	Scorpio	12/10 to 12/30	Sagittarius
11/7 to 12/1	Sagittarius	12/30 to 12/31	Capricorn
12/1 to 12/12	Capricorn		
12/12 to 12/31	Sagittarius		
		1954	
		1/1 to 1/17	Capricorn
1952		1/17 to 2/4	Aquarius
1/1 to 1/12	Sagittarius	2/4 to 4/12	Pisces
1/12 to 2/2	Capricorn	4/12 to 4/29	Aries
2/2 to 2/20	Aquarius	4/29 to 5/14	Taurus
2/20 to 3/7	Pisces	5/14 to 5/30	Gemini
3/7 to 5/14	Aries	5/30 to 8/7	Cancer
5/14 to 5/31	Taurus	8/7 to 8/22	Leo
5/31 to 6/14	Gemini	8/22 to 9/7	Virgo
6/14 to 6/29	Cancer	9/7 to 9/28	Libra
6/29 to 9/7	Leo	9/28 to 11/4	Scorpio
9/7 to 9/23	Virgo	11/4 to 11/10	Libra
9/23 to 10/11	Libra	11/10 to 12/3	Scorpio
10/11 to 10/31	Scorpio	12/3 to 12/23	Sagittarius
10/31 to 12/31	Sagittarius	12/23 to 12/31	Capricorn
1953		**1955**	
1/1 to 1/6	Sagittarius	1/1 to 1/10	Capricorn
1/6 to 1/25	Capricorn	1/10 to 3/17	Aquarius
1/25 to 2/11	Aquarius	3/17 to 4/6	Pisces
2/11 to 3/2	Pisces	4/6 to 4/21	Aries
3/2 to 3/15	Aries	4/21 to 5/6	Taurus
3/15 to 4/17	Pisces	5/6 to 7/13	Gemini
4/17 to 5/7	Aries	7/13 to 7/30	Cancer
5/7 to 5/22	Taurus	7/30 to 8/14	Leo
5/22 to 6/5	Gemini	8/14 to 9/1	Virgo
6/5 to 6/25	Cancer	9/1 to 11/7	Libra
6/25 to 7/28	Leo	11/7 to 11/26	Scorpio
7/28 to 8/11	Cancer	11/26 to 12/15	Sagittarius
8/11 to 8/30	Leo	12/15 to 12/31	Capricorn
8/30 to 9/15	Virgo		
9/15 to 10/4	Libra	**1956**	
10/4 to 10/31	Scorpio	1/1 to 1/3	Capricorn
10/31 to 11/6	Sagittarius	1/3 to 2/2	Aquarius
11/6 to 12/10	Scorpio	2/2 to 2/14	Capricorn

DATE	ZODIAC SIGN	DATE	ZODIAC SIGN
2/14 to 3/10	Aquarius	5/16 to 6/5	Taurus
3/10 to 3/28	Pisces	6/5 to 6/19	Gemini
3/28 to 4/12	Aries	6/19 to 7/4	Cancer
4/12 to 4/29	Taurus	7/4 to 7/25	Leo
4/29 to 7/6	Gemini	7/25 to 8/23	Virgo
7/6 to 7/20	Cancer	8/23 to 9/10	Leo
7/20 to 8/5	Leo	9/10 to 9/28	Virgo
8/5 to 8/26	Virgo	9/28 to 10/15	Libra
8/26 to 9/29	Libra	10/15 to 11/4	Scorpio
9/29 to 10/10	Virgo	11/4 to 12/31	Sagittarius
10/10 to 10/30	Libra		
10/30 to 11/18	Scorpio	*1959*	
11/18 to 12/7	Sagittarius	1/1 to 1/10	Sagittarius
12/7 to 12/31	Capricorn	1/10 to 1/30	Capricorn
		1/30 to 2/16	Aquarius
1957		2/16 to 3/4	Pisces
1/1 to 2/12	Capricorn	3/4 to 5/12	Aries
2/12 to 3/3	Aquarius	5/12 to 5/28	Taurus
3/3 to 3/20	Pisces	5/28 to 6/11	Gemini
3/20 to 4/4	Aries	6/11 to 6/28	Cancer
4/4 to 6/12	Taurus	6/28 to 9/4	Leo
6/12 to 6/28	Gemini	9/4 to 9/20	Virgo
6/28 to 7/12	Cancer	9/20 to 10/8	Libra
7/12 to 7/29	Leo	10/8 to 10/30	Scorpio
7/29 to 10/5	Virgo	10/30 to 11/24	Sagittarius
10/5 to 10/23	Libra	11/24 to 12/13	Scorpio
10/23 to 11/11	Scorpio	12/13 to 12/31	Sagittarius
11/11 to 12/1	Sagittarius		
12/1 to 12/28	Capricorn	*1960*	
12/28 to 12/31	Sagittarius	1/1 to 1/3	Sagittarius
		1/3 to 1/22	Capricorn
1958		1/22 to 2/8	Aquarius
1/1 to 1/13	Sagittarius	2/8 to 4/15	Pisces
1/13 to 2/6	Capricorn	4/15 to 5/4	Aries
2/6 to 2/24	Aquarius	5/4 to 5/18	Taurus
2/24 to 3/12	Pisces	5/18 to 6/2	Gemini
3/12 to 4/2	Aries	6/2 to 6/30	Cancer
4/2 to 4/10	Taurus	6/30 to 7/5	Leo
4/10 to 5/16	Aries	7/5 to 8/10	Cancer

DATE	ZODIAC SIGN	DATE	ZODIAC SIGN
8/10 to 8/26	Leo	*1963*	
8/26 to 9/11	Virgo	1/1	Capricorn
9/11 to 10/1	Libra	1/1 to 1/19	Aquarius
10/1 to 12/7	Scorpio	1/19 to 2/14	Capricorn
12/7 to 12/26	Sagittarius	2/14 to 3/8	Aquarius
12/26 to 12/31	Capricorn	3/8 to 3/25	Pisces
		3/25 to 4/9	Aries
1961		4/9 to 5/2	Taurus
1/1 to 1/14	Capricorn	5/2 to 5/10	Gemini
1/14 to 2/1	Aquarius	5/10 to 6/14	Taurus
2/1 to 2/24	Pisces	6/14 to 7/3	Gemini
2/24 to 3/17	Aquarius	7/3 to 7/17	Cancer
3/17 to 4/9	Pisces	7/17 to 8/2	Leo
4/9 to 4/26	Aries	8/2 to 8/26	Virgo
4/26 to 5/10	Taurus	8/26 to 9/16	Libra
5/10 to 5/28	Gemini	9/16 to 10/10	Virgo
5/28 to 8/3	Cancer	10/10 to 10/28	Libra
8/3 to 8/18	Leo	10/28 to 11/15	Scorpio
8/18 to 9/4	Virgo	11/15 to 12/5	Sagittarius
9/4 to 9/27	Libra	12/5 to 12/31	Capricorn
9/27 to 10/21	Scorpio		
10/21 to 11/10	Libra	*1964*	
11/10 to 11/30	Scorpio	1/1 to 2/10	Capricorn
11/30 to 12/19	Sagittarius	2/10 to 2/29	Aquarius
12/19 to 12/31	Capricorn	2/29 to 3/16	Pisces
		3/16 to 4/1	Aries
1962		4/1 to 6/9	Taurus
1/1 to 1/7	Capricorn	6/9 to 6/24	Gemini
1/7 to 3/14	Aquarius	6/24 to 7/8	Cancer
3/14 to 4/2	Pisces	7/8 to 7/26	Leo
4/2 to 4/17	Aries	7/26 to 10/2	Virgo
4/17 to 5/2	Taurus	10/2 to 10/19	Libra
5/2 to 7/10	Gemini	10/19 to 11/7	Scorpio
7/10 to 7/26	Cancer	11/7 to 11/30	Sagittarius
7/26 to 8/10	Leo	11/30 to 12/16	Capricorn
8/10 to 8/29	Virgo	12/16 to 12/31	Sagittarius
8/29 to 11/4	Libra		
11/4 to 11/23	Scorpio	*1965*	
11/23 to 12/12	Sagittarius	1/1 to 1/12	Sagittarius
12/12 to 12/31	Capricorn	1/12 to 2/2	Capricorn

DATE	ZODIAC SIGN	DATE	ZODIAC SIGN
2/2 to 2/20	Aquarius	5/1 to 5/15	Taurus
2/20 to 3/8	Pisces	5/15 to 5/31	Gemini
3/8 to 5/15	Aries	5/31 to 8/8	Cancer
5/15 to 6/1	Taurus	8/8 to 8/23	Leo
6/1 to 6/15	Gemini	8/23 to 9/9	Virgo
6/15 to 7/1	Cancer	9/9 to 9/29	Libra
7/1 to 7/30	Leo	9/29 to 12/5	Scorpio
7/30 to 8/2	Virgo	12/5 to 12/24	Sagittarius
8/2 to 9/8	Leo	12/24 to 12/31	Capricorn
9/8 to 9/24	Virgo		
9/24 to 10/12	Libra	*1968*	
10/12 to 11/1	Scorpio	1/1 to 1/11	Capricorn
11/1 to 12/31	Sagittarius	1/11 to 2/1	Aquarius
		2/1 to 2/11	Pisces
1966		2/11 to 3/17	Aquarius
1/1 to 1/7	Sagittarius	3/17 to 4/6	Pisces
1/7 to 1/26	Capricorn	4/6 to 4/22	Aries
1/26 to 2/12	Aquarius	4/22 to 5/6	Taurus
2/12 to 3/2	Pisces	5/6 to 5/29	Gemini
3/2 to 3/21	Aries	5/29 to 6/13	Cancer
3/21 to 4/17	Pisces	6/13 to 7/12	Gemini
4/17 to 5/9	Aries	7/12 to 7/30	Cancer
5/9 to 5/24	Taurus	7/30 to 8/14	Leo
5/24 to 6/7	Gemini	8/14 to 9/1	Virgo
6/7 to 6/26	Cancer	9/1 to 9/28	Libra
6/26 to 8/31	Leo	9/28 to 10/7	Scorpio
8/31 to 9/16	Virgo	10/7 to 11/7	Libra
9/16 to 10/5	Libra	11/7 to 11/27	Scorpio
10/5 to 10/29	Scorpio	11/27 to 12/16	Sagittarius
10/29 to 11/12	Sagittarius	12/16 to 12/31	Capricorn
11/12 to 12/11	Scorpio		
12/11 to 12/31	Sagittarius	*1969*	
		1/1 to 1/4	Capricorn
1967		1/4 to 3/12	Aquarius
1/1	Sagittarius	3/12 to 3/29	Pisces
1/1 to 1/19	Capricorn	3/29 to 4/13	Aries
1/19 to 2/5	Aquarius	4/13 to 4/30	Taurus
2/5 to 4/14	Pisces	4/30 to 7/7	Gemini
4/14 to 5/1	Aries	7/7 to 7/22	Cancer

DATE	ZODIAC SIGN	DATE	ZODIAC SIGN
7/22 to 8/6	Leo	7/26 to 8/29	Virgo
8/6 to 8/26	Virgo	8/29 to 9/10	Leo
8/26 to 10/6	Libra	9/10 to 9/29	Virgo
10/6 to 10/9	Virgo	9/29 to 10/17	Libra
10/9 to 11/1	Libra	10/17 to 11/5	Scorpio
11/1 to 11/19	Scorpio	11/5 to 12/31	Sagittarius
11/19 to 12/9	Sagittarius		
12/9 to 12/31	Capricorn		

1972

		1/1 to 1/11	Sagittarius
1970		1/11 to 1/31	Capricorn
1/1 to 1/3	Capricorn	1/31 to 2/18	Aquarius
1/3 to 1/4	Aquarius	2/18 to 3/5	Pisces
1/4 to 2/13	Capricorn	3/5 to 5/12	Aries
2/13 to 3/5	Aquarius	5/12 to 5/28	Taurus
3/5 to 3/21	Pisces	5/28 to 6/11	Gemini
3/21 to 4/5	Aries	6/11 to 6/28	Cancer
4/5 to 6/13	Taurus	6/28 to 9/4	Leo
6/13 to 6/29	Gemini	9/4 to 9/21	Virgo
6/29 to 7/13	Cancer	9/21 to 10/8	Libra
7/13 to 7/30	Leo	10/8 to 10/30	Scorpio
7/30 to 10/7	Virgo	10/30 to 11/28	Sagittarius
10/7 to 10/24	Libra	11/28 to 12/12	Scorpio
10/24 to 11/12	Scorpio	12/12 to 12/31	Sagittarius
11/12 to 12/2	Sagittarius		
12/2 to 12/31	Capricorn		

1973

		1/1 to 1/4	Sagittarius
1971		1/4 to 1/23	Capricorn
1/1 to 1/2	Capricorn	1/23 to 2/9	Aquarius
1/2 to 1/13	Sagittarius	2/9 to 4/16	Pisces
1/13 to 2/7	Capricorn	4/16 to 5/5	Aries
2/7 to 2/25	Aquarius	5/5 to 5/20	Taurus
2/25 to 3/13	Pisces	5/20 to 6/3	Gemini
3/13 to 4/1	Aries	6/3 to 6/26	Cancer
4/1 to 4/18	Taurus	6/26 to 7/15	Leo
4/18 to 5/16	Aries	7/15 to 8/11	Cancer
5/16 to 6/6	Taurus	8/11 to 8/28	Leo
6/6 to 6/21	Gemini	8/28 to 9/13	Virgo
6/21 to 7/5	Cancer	9/13 to 10/2	Libra
7/5 to 7/26	Leo	10/2 to 12/8	Scorpio

DATE	ZODIAC SIGN
12/8 to 12/28	Sagittarius
12/28 to 12/31	Capricorn

1974

DATE	ZODIAC SIGN
1/1 to 1/15	Capricorn
1/15 to 2/2	Aquarius
2/2 to 3/2	Pisces
3/2 to 3/17	Aquarius
3/17 to 4/11	Pisces
4/11 to 4/27	Aries
4/27 to 5/11	Taurus
5/11 to 5/28	Gemini
5/28 to 8/4	Cancer
8/4 to 8/19	Leo
8/19 to 9/5	Virgo
9/5 to 9/27	Libra
9/27 to 10/26	Scorpio
10/26 to 11/11	Libra
11/11 to 12/1	Scorpio
12/1 to 12/20	Sagittarius
12/20 to 12/31	Capricorn

1975

DATE	ZODIAC SIGN
1/1 to 1/8	Capricorn
1/8 to 3/15	Aquarius
3/15 to 4/4	Pisces
4/4 to 4/19	Aries
4/19 to 5/3	Taurus
5/3 to 7/11	Gemini
7/11 to 7/27	Cancer
7/27 to 8/11	Leo
8/11 to 8/30	Virgo
8/30 to 11/5	Libra
11/5 to 11/24	Scorpio
11/24 to 12/13	Sagittarius
12/13 to 12/31	Capricorn

1976

DATE	ZODIAC SIGN
1/1 to 1/2	Capricorn
1/2 to 1/24	Aquarius

DATE	ZODIAC SIGN
1/24 to 2/15	Capricorn
2/15 to 3/9	Aquarius
3/9 to 3/26	Pisces
3/26 to 4/9	Aries
4/9 to 4/29	Taurus
4/29 to 5/19	Gemini
5/19 to 6/13	Taurus
6/13 to 7/4	Gemini
7/4 to 7/18	Cancer
7/18 to 8/3	Leo
8/3 to 8/25	Virgo
8/25 to 9/20	Libra
9/20 to 10/10	Virgo
10/10 to 10/28	Libra
10/28 to 11/16	Scorpio
11/16 to 12/5	Sagittarius
12/5 to 12/31	Capricorn

1977

DATE	ZODIAC SIGN
1/1 to 2/10	Capricorn
2/10 to 3/1	Aquarius
3/1 to 3/17	Pisces
3/17 to 4/2	Aries
4/2 to 6/10	Taurus
6/10 to 6/25	Gemini
6/25 to 7/9	Cancer
7/9 to 7/27	Leo
7/27 to 10/3	Virgo
10/3 to 10/21	Libra
10/21 to 11/9	Scorpio
11/9 to 11/30	Sagittarius
11/30 to 12/20	Capricorn
12/20 to 12/31	Sagittarius

1978

DATE	ZODIAC SIGN
1/1 to 1/13	Sagittarius
1/13 to 2/4	Capricorn
2/4 to 2/22	Aquarius
2/22 to 3/10	Pisces

DATE	ZODIAC SIGN	DATE	ZODIAC SIGN
3/10 to 5/15	Aries	5/31 to 8/8	Cancer
5/15 to 6/3	Taurus	8/8 to 8/24	Leo
6/3 to 6/17	Gemini	8/24 to 9/9	Virgo
6/17 to 7/2	Cancer	9/9 to 9/29	Libra
7/2 to 7/26	Leo	9/29 to 12/5	Scorpio
7/26 to 8/12	Virgo	12/5 to 12/24	Sagittarius
8/12 to 9/9	Leo	12/24 to 12/31	Capricorn
9/9 to 9/26	Virgo		
9/26 to 10/13	Libra	**1981**	
10/13 to 11/2	Scorpio	1/1 to 1/12	Capricorn
11/2 to 12/31	Sagittarius	1/12 to 1/31	Aquarius
		1/31 to 2/15	Pisces
1979		2/15 to 3/17	Aquarius
1/1 to 1/8	Sagittarius	3/17 to 4/7	Pisces
1/8 to 1/28	Capricorn	4/7 to 4/23	Aries
1/28 to 2/14	Aquarius	4/23 to 5/7	Taurus
2/14 to 3/3	Pisces	5/7 to 5/28	Gemini
3/3 to 3/27	Aries	5/28 to 6/22	Cancer
3/27 to 4/17	Pisces	6/22 to 7/12	Gemini
4/17 to 5/10	Aries	7/12 to 8/1	Cancer
5/10 to 5/25	Taurus	8/1 to 8/16	Leo
5/25 to 6/8	Gemini	8/16 to 9/2	Virgo
6/8 to 6/26	Cancer	9/2 to 9/26	Libra
6/26 to 9/2	Leo	9/26 to 10/13	Scorpio
9/2 to 9/18	Virgo	10/13 to 11/9	Libra
9/18 to 10/6	Libra	11/9 to 11/28	Scorpio
10/6 to 10/29	Scorpio	11/28 to 12/17	Sagittarius
10/29 to 11/17	Sagittarius	12/17 to 12/31	Capricorn
11/17 to 12/12	Scorpio		
12/12 to 12/31	Sagittarius	**1982**	
		1/1 to 1/5	Capricorn
1980		1/5 to 3/13	Aquarius
1/1	Sagittarius	3/13 to 3/31	Pisces
1/1 to 1/20	Capricorn	3/31 to 4/15	Aries
1/20 to 2/6	Aquarius	4/15 to 5/1	Taurus
2/6 to 4/14	Pisces	5/1 to 7/8	Gemini
4/14 to 5/1	Aries	7/8 to 7/23	Cancer
5/1 to 5/16	Taurus	7/23 to 8/8	Leo
5/16 to 5/31	Gemini	8/8 to 8/27	Virgo

DATE	ZODIAC SIGN	DATE	ZODIAC SIGN
8/27 to 11/2	Libra	12/1 to 12/7	Capricorn
11/2 to 11/21	Scorpio	12/7 to 12/31	Sagittarius
11/21 to 12/10	Sagittarius		
12/10 to 12/31	Capricorn		
		1985	
		1/1 to 1/11	Sagittarius
1983		1/11 to 1/31	Capricorn
1/1	Capricorn	1/31 to 2/18	Aquarius
1/1 to 1/11	Aquarius	2/18 to 3/6	Pisces
1/11 to 2/13	Capricorn	3/6 to 5/13	Aries
2/13 to 3/6	Aquarius	5/13 to 5/30	Taurus
3/6 to 3/23	Pisces	5/30 to 6/13	Gemini
3/23 to 4/7	Aries	6/13 to 6/29	Cancer
4/7 to 6/13	Taurus	6/29 to 9/6	Leo
6/13 to 7/1	Gemini	9/6 to 9/22	Virgo
7/1 to 7/15	Cancer	9/22 to 10/10	Libra
7/15 to 7/31	Leo	10/10 to 10/31	Scorpio
7/31 to 8/28	Virgo	10/31 to 12/4	Sagittarius
8/28 to 9/5	Libra	12/4 to 12/11	Scorpio
9/5 to 10/8	Virgo	12/11 to 12/31	Sagittarius
10/8 to 10/26	Libra		
10/26 to 11/13	Scorpio	**1986**	
11/13 to 12/3	Sagittarius	1/1 to 1/5	Sagittarius
12/3 to 12/31	Capricorn	1/5 to 1/24	Capricorn
		1/24 to 2/10	Aquarius
1984		2/10 to 3/2	Pisces
1/1 to 2/8	Capricorn	3/2 to 3/11	Aries
2/8 to 2/27	Aquarius	3/11 to 4/17	Pisces
2/27 to 3/14	Pisces	4/17 to 5/7	Aries
3/14 to 3/31	Aries	5/7 to 5/21	Taurus
3/31 to 4/24	Taurus	5/21 to 6/5	Gemini
4/24 to 5/15	Aries	6/5 to 6/26	Cancer
5/15 to 6/7	Taurus	6/26 to 7/23	Leo
6/7 to 6/21	Gemini	7/23 to 8/11	Cancer
6/21 to 7/6	Cancer	8/11 to 8/29	Leo
7/6 to 7/25	Leo	8/29 to 9/14	Virgo
7/25 to 9/30	Virgo	9/14 to 10/3	Libra
9/30 to 10/17	Libra	10/3 to 12/9	Scorpio
10/17 to 11/6	Scorpio	12/9 to 12/29	Sagittarius
11/6 to 12/1	Sagittarius	12/29 to 12/31	Capricorn

DATE	ZODIAC SIGN
1987	
1/1 to 1/17	Capricorn
1/17 to 2/3	Aquarius
2/3 to 3/11	Pisces
3/11 to 3/13	Aquarius
3/13 to 4/12	Pisces
4/12 to 4/29	Aries
4/29 to 5/13	Taurus
5/13 to 5/29	Gemini
5/29 to 8/6	Cancer
8/6 to 8/21	Leo
8/21 to 9/7	Virgo
9/7 to 9/28	Libra
9/28 to 10/31	Scorpio
10/31 to 11/11	Libra
11/11 to 12/3	Scorpio
12/3 to 12/22	Sagittarius
12/22 to 12/31	Capricorn
1988	
1/1 to 1/9	Capricorn
1/9 to 3/15	Aquarius
3/15 to 4/4	Pisces
4/4 to 4/19	Aries
4/19 to 5/4	Taurus
5/4 to 7/11	Gemini
7/11 to 7/28	Cancer
7/28 to 8/12	Leo
8/12 to 8/30	Virgo
8/30 to 11/6	Libra
11/6 to 11/24	Scorpio
11/24 to 12/13	Sagittarius
12/13 to 12/31	Capricorn
1989	
1/1 to 1/2	Capricorn
1/2 to 1/28	Aquarius
1/28 to 2/14	Capricorn
2/14 to 3/10	Aquarius

DATE	ZODIAC SIGN
3/10 to 3/27	Pisces
3/27 to 4/11	Aries
4/11 to 4/29	Taurus
4/29 to 5/28	Gemini
5/28 to 6/11	Taurus
6/11 to 7/5	Gemini
7/5 to 7/19	Cancer
7/19 to 8/4	Leo
8/4 to 8/25	Virgo
8/25 to 9/26	Libra
9/26 to 10/10	Virgo
10/10 to 10/30	Libra
10/30 to 11/17	Scorpio
11/17 to 12/7	Sagittarius
12/7 to 12/31	Capricorn
1990	
1/1 to 2/11	Capricorn
2/11 to 3/3	Aquarius
3/3 to 3/19	Pisces
3/19 to 4/3	Aries
4/3 to 6/11	Taurus
6/11 to 6/27	Gemini
6/27 to 7/11	Cancer
7/11 to 7/28	Leo
7/28 to 10/5	Virgo
10/5 to 10/22	Libra
10/22 to 11/10	Scorpio
11/10 to 12/1	Sagittarius
12/1 to 12/25	Capricorn
12/25 to 12/31	Sagittarius
1991	
1/1 to 1/13	Sagittarius
1/13 to 2/5	Capricorn
2/5 to 2/23	Aquarius
2/23 to 3/11	Pisces
3/11 to 5/16	Aries
5/16 to 6/4	Taurus

DATE	ZODIAC SIGN	DATE	ZODIAC SIGN
6/4 to 6/18	Gemini	8/25 to 9/10	Virgo
6/18 to 7/3	Cancer	9/10 to 9/30	Libra
7/3 to 7/26	Leo	9/30 to 12/6	Scorpio
7/26 to 8/19	Virgo	12/6 to 12/26	Sagittarius
8/19 to 9/10	Leo	12/26 to 12/31	Capricorn
9/10 to 9/27	Virgo		
9/27 to 10/15	Libra		
10/15 to 11/3	Scorpio	***1994***	
11/3 to 12/31	Sagittarius	1/1 to 1/13	Capricorn
		1/13 to 1/31	Aquarius
		1/31 to 2/21	Pisces
1992		2/21 to 3/18	Aquarius
1/1 to 1/9	Sagittarius	3/18 to 4/9	Pisces
1/9 to 1/29	Capricorn	4/9 to 4/25	Aries
1/29 to 2/15	Aquarius	4/25 to 5/9	Taurus
2/15 to 3/3	Pisces	5/9 to 5/28	Gemini
3/3 to 4/3	Aries	5/28 to 7/2	Cancer
4/3 to 4/14	Pisces	7/2 to 7/10	Gemini
4/14 to 5/10	Aries	7/10 to 8/2	Cancer
5/10 to 5/26	Taurus	8/2 to 8/17	Leo
5/26 to 6/9	Gemini	8/17 to 9/3	Virgo
6/9 to 6/26	Cancer	9/3 to 9/26	Libra
6/26 to 9/2	Leo	9/26 to 10/18	Scorpio
9/2 to 9/18	Virgo	10/18 to 11/10	Libra
9/18 to 10/6	Libra	11/10 to 11/29	Scorpio
10/6 to 10/29	Scorpio	11/29 to 12/18	Sagittarius
10/29 to 11/21	Sagittarius	12/18 to 12/31	Capricorn
11/21 to 12/11	Scorpio		
12/11 to 12/31	Sagittarius	***1995***	
		1/1 to 1/6	Capricorn
1993		1/6 to 3/14	Aquarius
1/1 to 1/2	Sagittarius	3/14 to 4/1	Pisces
1/2 to 1/20	Capricorn	4/1 to 4/16	Aries
1/20 to 2/7	Aquarius	4/16 to 5/2	Taurus
2/7 to 4/15	Pisces	5/2 to 7/10	Gemini
4/15 to 5/3	Aries	7/10 to 7/25	Cancer
5/3 to 5/17	Taurus	7/25 to 8/9	Leo
5/17 to 6/1	Gemini	8/9 to 8/28	Virgo
6/1 to 8/9	Cancer	8/28 to 11/3	Libra
8/9 to 8/25	Leo	11/3 to 11/22	Scorpio

DATE	ZODIAC SIGN	DATE	ZODIAC SIGN
11/22 to 12/11	Sagittarius	*1998*	
12/11 to 12/31	Capricorn	1/1 to 1/12	Sagittarius
		1/12 to 2/2	Capricorn
1996		2/2 to 2/19	Aquarius
1/1	Capricorn	2/19 to 3/7	Pisces
1/1 to 1/16	Aquarius	3/7 to 5/14	Aries
1/16 to 2/14	Capricorn	5/14 to 5/31	Taurus
2/14 to 3/6	Aquarius	5/31 to 6/14	Gemini
3/6 to 3/23	Pisces	6/14 to 6/30	Cancer
3/23 to 4/7	Aries	6/30 to 9/7	Leo
4/7 to 6/13	Taurus	9/7 to 9/23	Virgo
6/13 to 7/1	Gemini	9/23 to 10/11	Libra
7/1 to 7/15	Cancer	10/11 to 11/1	Scorpio
7/15 to 8/1	Leo	11/1 to 12/31	Sagittarius
8/1 to 8/25	Virgo		
8/25 to 9/11	Libra	*1999*	
9/11 to 10/8	Virgo	1/1 to 1/6	Sagittarius
10/8 to 10/26	Libra	1/6 to 1/25	Capricorn
10/26 to 11/14	Scorpio	1/25 to 2/12	Aquarius
11/14 to 12/4	Sagittarius	2/12 to 3/2	Pisces
12/4 to 12/31	Capricorn	3/2 to 3/17	Aries
		3/17 to 4/17	Pisces
1997		4/17 to 5/8	Aries
1/1 to 2/8	Capricorn	5/8 to 5/23	Taurus
2/8 to 2/27	Aquarius	5/23 to 6/6	Gemini
2/27 to 3/15	Pisces	6/6 to 6/26	Cancer
3/15 to 4/1	Aries	6/26 to 7/31	Leo
4/1 to 5/4	Taurus	7/31 to 8/10	Cancer
5/4 to 5/11	Aries	8/10 to 8/31	Leo
5/11 to 6/8	Taurus	8/31 to 9/16	Virgo
6/8 to 6/23	Gemini	9/16 to 10/4	Libra
6/23 to 7/7	Cancer	10/4 to 10/30	Scorpio
7/7 to 7/26	Leo	10/30 to 11/9	Sagittarius
7/26 to 10/1	Virgo	11/9 to 12/10	Scorpio
10/1 to 10/19	Libra	12/10 to 12/30	Sagittarius
10/19 to 11/7	Scorpio	12/30 to 12/31	Capricorn
11/7 to 11/30	Sagittarius		
11/30 to 12/13	Capricorn	*2000*	
12/13 to 12/31	Sagittarius	1/1 to 1/18	Capricorn
		1/18 to 2/4	Aquarius

DATE	ZODIAC SIGN	DATE	ZODIAC SIGN
2/4 to 4/12	Pisces	4/29 to 7/6	Gemini
4/12 to 4/29	Aries	7/6 to 7/21	Cancer
4/29 to 5/13	Taurus	7/21 to 8/5	Leo
5/13 to 5/29	Gemini	8/5 to 8/26	Virgo
5/29 to 8/6	Cancer	8/26 to 10/1	Libra
8/6 to 8/21	Leo	10/1 to 10/10	Virgo
8/21 to 9/7	Virgo	10/10 to 10/31	Libra
9/7 to 9/28	Libra	10/31 to 11/18	Scorpio
9/28 to 11/6	Scorpio	11/18 to 12/8	Sagittarius
11/6 to 11/8	Libra	12/8 to 12/31	Capricorn
11/8 to 12/3	Scorpio		
12/3 to 12/22	Sagittarius		
12/22 to 12/31	Capricorn	**2003**	
		1/1 to 2/12	Capricorn
		2/12 to 3/4	Aquarius
2001		3/4 to 3/21	Pisces
1/1 to 1/10	Capricorn	3/21 to 4/5	Aries
1/10 to 1/31	Aquarius	4/5 to 6/12	Taurus
1/31 to 2/6	Pisces	6/12 to 6/28	Gemini
2/6 to 3/16	Aquarius	6/28 to 7/13	Cancer
3/16 to 4/5	Pisces	7/13 to 7/30	Leo
4/5 to 4/21	Aries	7/30 to 10/6	Virgo
4/21 to 5/5	Taurus	10/6 to 10/23	Libra
5/5 to 7/12	Gemini	10/23 to 11/11	Scorpio
7/12 to 7/29	Cancer	11/11 to 12/2	Sagittarius
7/29 to 8/13	Leo	12/2 to 12/30	Capricorn
8/13 to 8/31	Virgo	12/30 to 12/31	Sagittarius
8/31 to 11/7	Libra		
11/7 to 11/26	Scorpio	**2004**	
11/26 to 12/15	Sagittarius	1/1 to 1/13	Sagittarius
12/15 to 12/31	Capricorn	1/13 to 2/6	Capricorn
		2/6 to 2/25	Aquarius
2002		2/25 to 3/11	Pisces
1/1 to 1/3	Capricorn	3/11 to 3/31	Aries
1/3 to 2/3	Aquarius	3/31 to 4/12	Taurus
2/3 to 2/13	Capricorn	4/12 to 5/15	Aries
2/13 to 3/11	Aquarius	5/15 to 6/5	Taurus
3/11 to 3/29	Pisces	6/5 to 6/19	Gemini
3/29 to 4/12	Aries	6/19 to 7/4	Cancer
4/12 to 4/29	Taurus	7/4 to 7/25	Leo

DATE	ZODIAC SIGN	DATE	ZODIAC SIGN
7/25 to 8/24	Virgo	12/7 to 12/27	Sagittarius
8/24 to 9/9	Leo	12/27 to 12/31	Capricorn
9/9 to 9/28	Virgo		
9/28 to 10/15	Libra	**2007**	
10/15 to 11/4	Scorpio	1/1 to 1/14	Capricorn
11/4 to 12/31	Sagittarius	1/14 to 2/1	Aquarius
		2/1 to 2/26	Pisces
2005		2/26 to 3/17	Aquarius
1/1 to 1/9	Sagittarius	3/17 to 4/10	Pisces
1/9 to 1/29	Capricorn	4/10 to 4/26	Aries
1/29 to 2/16	Aquarius	4/26 to 5/10	Taurus
2/16 to 3/4	Pisces	5/10 to 5/28	Gemini
3/4 to 5/11	Aries	5/28 to 8/4	Cancer
5/11 to 5/27	Taurus	8/4 to 8/19	Leo
5/27 to 6/10	Gemini	8/19 to 9/5	Virgo
6/10 to 6/27	Cancer	9/5 to 9/27	Libra
6/27 to 9/4	Leo	9/27 to 10/23	Scorpio
9/4 to 9/20	Virgo	10/23 to 11/10	Libra
9/20 to 10/8	Libra	11/10 to 12/1	Scorpio
10/8 to 10/29	Scorpio	12/1 to 12/20	Sagittarius
10/29 to 11/25	Sagittarius	12/20 to 12/31	Capricorn
11/25 to 12/12	Scorpio		
12/12 to 12/31	Sagittarius	**2008**	
		1/1 to 1/7	Capricorn
2006		1/7 to 3/14	Aquarius
1/1 to 1/3	Sagittarius	3/14 to 4/2	Pisces
1/3 to 1/22	Capricorn	4/2 to 4/17	Aries
1/22 to 2/8	Aquarius	4/17 to 5/2	Taurus
2/8 to 4/16	Pisces	5/2 to 7/10	Gemini
4/16 to 5/4	Aries	7/10 to 7/25	Cancer
5/4 to 5/19	Taurus	7/25 to 8/9	Leo
5/19 to 6/2	Gemini	8/9 to 8/28	Virgo
6/2 to 6/28	Cancer	8/28 to 11/4	Libra
6/28 to 7/10	Leo	11/4 to 11/22	Scorpio
7/10 to 8/10	Cancer	11/22 to 12/11	Sagittarius
8/10 to 8/27	Leo	12/11 to 12/31	Capricorn
8/27 to 9/12	Virgo		
9/12 to 10/1	Libra	**2009**	
10/1 to 12/7	Scorpio	1/1	Capricorn
		1/1 to 1/20	Aquarius

DATE	ZODIAC SIGN	DATE	ZODIAC SIGN
1/20 to 2/14	Capricorn	3/9 to 5/15	Aries
2/14 to 3/8	Aquarius	5/15 to 6/2	Taurus
3/8 to 3/25	Pisces	6/2 to 6/16	Gemini
3/25 to 4/9	Aries	6/16 to 7/1	Cancer
4/9 to 4/30	Taurus	7/1 to 7/28	Leo
4/30 to 5/13	Gemini	7/28 to 8/7	Virgo
5/13 to 6/13	Taurus	8/7 to 9/8	Leo
6/13 to 7/3	Gemini	9/8 to 9/25	Virgo
7/3 to 7/17	Cancer	9/25 to 10/12	Libra
7/17 to 8/2	Leo	10/12 to 11/2	Scorpio
8/2 to 8/25	Virgo	11/2 to 12/31	Sagittarius
8/25 to 9/17	Libra		
9/17 to 10/9	Virgo	*2012*	
10/9 to 10/27	Libra	1/1 to 1/7	Sagittarius
10/27 to 11/15	Scorpio	1/7 to 1/27	Capricorn
11/15 to 12/5	Sagittarius	1/27 to 2/13	Aquarius
12/5 to 12/31	Capricorn	2/13 to 3/1	Pisces
		3/1 to 3/23	Aries
2010		3/23 to 4/16	Pisces
1/1 to 2/9	Capricorn	4/16 to 5/8	Aries
2/9 to 3/1	Aquarius	5/8 to 5/23	Taurus
3/1 to 3/17	Pisces	5/23 to 6/6	Gemini
3/17 to 4/2	Aries	6/6 to 6/25	Cancer
4/2 to 6/9	Taurus	6/25 to 8/31	Leo
6/9 to 6/24	Gemini	8/31 to 9/16	Virgo
6/24 to 7/9	Cancer	9/16 to 10/4	Libra
7/9 to 7/27	Leo	10/4 to 10/28	Scorpio
7/27 to 10/3	Virgo	10/28 to 11/13	Sagittarius
10/3 to 10/20	Libra	11/13 to 12/10	Scorpio
10/20 to 11/8	Scorpio	12/10 to 12/31	Sagittarius
11/8 to 11/30	Sagittarius		
11/30 to 12/18	Capricorn	*2013*	
12/18 to 12/31	Sagittarius	1/1	Sagittarius
		1/1 to 1/18	Capricorn
2011		1/18 to 2/5	Aquarius
1/1 to 1/12	Sagittarius	2/5 to 4/13	Pisces
1/12 to 2/3	Capricorn	4/13 to 5/1	Aries
2/3 to 2/21	Aquarius	5/1 to 5/15	Taurus
2/21 to 3/9	Pisces	5/15 to 5/30	Gemini

DATE	ZODIAC SIGN	DATE	ZODIAC SIGN
5/30 to 8/8	Cancer	8/27 to 11/1	Libra
8/8 to 8/23	Leo	11/1 to 11/20	Scorpio
8/23 to 9/8	Virgo	11/20 to 12/9	Sagittarius
9/8 to 9/28	Libra	12/9 to 12/31	Capricorn
9/28 to 12/4	Scorpio		
12/4 to 12/23	Sagittarius		
12/23 to 12/31	Capricorn	**2016**	
		1/1	Capricorn
		1/1 to 1/8	Aquarius
2014		1/8 to 2/13	Capricorn
1/1 to 1/11	Capricorn	2/13 to 3/4	Aquarius
1/11 to 1/31	Aquarius	3/4 to 3/21	Pisces
1/31 to 2/12	Pisces	3/21 to 4/5	Aries
2/12 to 3/17	Aquarius	4/5 to 6/12	Taurus
3/17 to 4/7	Pisces	6/12 to 6/29	Gemini
4/7 to 4/22	Aries	6/29 to 7/13	Cancer
4/22 to 5/7	Taurus	7/13 to 7/30	Leo
5/7 to 5/28	Gemini	7/30 to 10/6	Virgo
5/28 to 6/16	Cancer	10/6 to 10/24	Libra
6/16 to 7/12	Gemini	10/24 to 11/12	Scorpio
7/12 to 7/31	Cancer	11/12 to 12/2	Sagittarius
7/31 to 8/15	Leo	12/2 to 12/31	Capricorn
8/15 to 9/1	Virgo		
9/1 to 9/27	Libra	**2017**	
9/27 to 10/10	Scorpio	1/1 to 1/4	Capricorn
10/10 to 11/8	Libra	1/4 to 1/12	Sagittarius
11/8 to 11/27	Scorpio	1/12 to 2/6	Capricorn
11/27 to 12/16	Sagittarius	2/6 to 2/25	Aquarius
12/16 to 12/31	Capricorn	2/25 to 3/13	Pisces
		3/13 to 3/31	Aries
		3/31 to 4/20	Taurus
2015		4/20 to 5/15	Aries
1/1 to 1/4	Capricorn	5/15 to 6/6	Taurus
1/4 to 3/12	Aquarius	6/6 to 6/20	Gemini
3/12 to 3/30	Pisces	6/20 to 7/5	Cancer
3/30 to 4/14	Aries	7/5 to 7/25	Leo
4/14 to 4/30	Taurus	7/25 to 8/31	Virgo
4/30 to 7/8	Gemini	8/31 to 9/9	Leo
7/8 to 7/23	Cancer	9/9 to 9/29	Virgo
7/23 to 8/7	Leo	9/29 to 10/16	Libra
8/7 to 8/27	Virgo		

DATE	ZODIAC SIGN	DATE	ZODIAC SIGN
10/16 to 11/5	Scorpio	**2020**	
11/5 to 12/31	Sagittarius	1/1 to 1/16	Capricorn
		1/16 to 2/2	Aquarius
2018		2/2 to 3/3	Pisces
1/1 to 1/10	Sagittarius	3/3 to 3/15	Aquarius
1/10 to 1/31	Capricorn	3/15 to 4/10	Pisces
1/31 to 2/17	Aquarius	4/10 to 4/27	Aries
2/17 to 3/5	Pisces	4/27 to 5/11	Taurus
3/5 to 5/13	Aries	5/11 to 5/28	Gemini
5/13 to 5/29	Taurus	5/28 to 8/4	Cancer
5/29 to 6/12	Gemini	8/4 to 8/19	Leo
6/12 to 6/28	Cancer	8/19 to 9/5	Virgo
6/28 to 9/5	Leo	9/5 to 9/26	Libra
9/5 to 9/21	Virgo	9/26 to 10/27	Scorpio
9/21 to 10/9	Libra	10/27 to 11/10	Libra
10/9 to 10/30	Scorpio	11/10 to 12/1	Scorpio
10/30 to 11/30	Sagittarius	12/1 to 12/20	Sagittarius
11/30 to 12/12	Scorpio	12/20 to 12/31	Capricorn
12/12 to 12/31	Sagittarius		
		2021	
2019		1/1 to 1/7	Capricorn
1/1 to 1/4	Sagittarius	1/7 to 3/15	Aquarius
1/4 to 1/23	Capricorn	3/15 to 4/3	Pisces
1/23 to 2/9	Aquarius	4/3 to 4/18	Aries
2/9 to 4/16	Pisces	4/18 to 5/3	Taurus
4/16 to 5/6	Aries	5/3 to 7/11	Gemini
5/6 to 5/20	Taurus	7/11 to 7/27	Cancer
5/20 to 6/4	Gemini	7/27 to 8/11	Leo
6/4 to 6/26	Cancer	8/11 to 8/29	Virgo
6/26 to 7/18	Leo	8/29 to 11/5	Libra
7/18 to 8/11	Cancer	11/5 to 11/24	Scorpio
8/11 to 8/28	Leo	11/24 to 12/13	Sagittarius
8/28 to 9/13	Virgo	12/13 to 12/31	Capricorn
9/13 to 10/2	Libra		
10/2 to 12/8	Scorpio	**2022**	
12/8 to 12/28	Sagittarius	1/1	Capricorn
12/28 to 12/31	Capricorn	1/1 to 1/25	Aquarius
		1/25 to 2/14	Capricorn
		2/14 to 3/9	Aquarius

DATE	ZODIAC SIGN	DATE	ZODIAC SIGN
3/9 to 3/26	Pisces	*2024*	
3/26 to 4/10	Aries	1/1 to 1/13	Sagittarius
4/10 to 4/29	Taurus	1/13 to 2/4	Capricorn
4/29 to 5/22	Gemini	2/4 to 2/22	Aquarius
5/22 to 6/13	Taurus	2/22 to 3/9	Pisces
6/13 to 7/4	Gemini	3/9 to 5/15	Aries
7/4 to 7/19	Cancer	5/15 to 6/2	Taurus
7/19 to 8/3	Leo	6/2 to 6/16	Gemini
8/3 to 8/25	Virgo	6/16 to 7/2	Cancer
8/25 to 9/23	Libra	7/2 to 7/25	Leo
9/23 to 10/10	Virgo	7/25 to 8/14	Virgo
10/10 to 10/29	Libra	8/14 to 9/8	Leo
10/29 to 11/16	Scorpio	9/8 to 9/25	Virgo
11/16 to 12/6	Sagittarius	9/25 to 10/13	Libra
12/6 to 12/31	Capricorn	10/13 to 11/2	Scorpio
		11/2 to 12/31	Sagittarius
2023			
1/1 to 2/10	Capricorn	*2025*	
2/10 to 3/2	Aquarius	1/1 to 1/7	Sagittarius
3/2 to 3/18	Pisces	1/7 to 1/27	Capricorn
3/18 to 4/3	Aries	1/27 to 2/14	Aquarius
4/3 to 6/10	Taurus	2/14 to 3/2	Pisces
6/10 to 6/26	Gemini	3/2 to 3/29	Aries
6/26 to 7/10	Cancer	3/29 to 4/15	Pisces
7/10 to 7/28	Leo	4/15 to 5/10	Aries
7/28 to 10/4	Virgo	5/10 to 5/25	Taurus
10/4 to 10/21	Libra	5/25 to 6/8	Gemini
10/21 to 11/9	Scorpio	6/8 to 6/26	Cancer
11/9 to 12/1	Sagittarius	6/26 to 9/2	Leo
12/1 to 12/22	Capricorn	9/2 to 9/17	Virgo
12/22 to 12/31	Sagittarius	9/17 to 10/6	Libra
		10/6 to 10/28	Scorpio
		10/28 to 11/18	Sagittarius
		11/18 to 12/11	Scorpio
		12/11 to 12/31	Sagittarius

VENUS

Like Mercury, Venus stands between the Earth and the Sun. Consequently, Venus is located either in the same sign as your Sun or as much as two signs ahead of or behind your Sun. Venus takes 225 days to pass once around the zodiac, spending approximately 19 days in each sign.

For the positions of Venus prior to 1936, go to "Free Astrology Charts" on www.janspiller .com.

DATE	ZODIAC SIGN	DATE	ZODIAC SIGN
1936			
1/1 to 1/3	Scorpio	9/24 to 10/19	Virgo
1/3 to 1/28	Sagittarius	10/19 to 11/12	Libra
1/28 to 2/21	Capricorn	11/12 to 12/6	Scorpio
2/21 to 3/17	Aquarius	12/6 to 12/30	Sagittarius
3/17 to 4/10	Pisces	12/30 to 12/31	Capricorn
4/10 to 5/4	Aries		
5/4 to 5/29	Taurus	*1938*	
5/29 to 6/22	Gemini	1/1 to 1/22	Capricorn
6/22 to 7/17	Cancer	1/22 to 2/15	Aquarius
7/17 to 8/10	Leo	2/15 to 3/11	Pisces
8/10 to 9/3	Virgo	3/11 to 4/5	Aries
9/3 to 9/28	Libra	4/5 to 4/29	Taurus
9/28 to 10/22	Scorpio	4/29 to 5/24	Gemini
10/22 to 11/16	Sagittarius	5/24 to 6/18	Cancer
11/16 to 12/11	Capricorn	6/18 to 7/13	Leo
12/11 to 12/31	Aquarius	7/13 to 8/9	Virgo
		8/9 to 9/6	Libra
1937		9/6 to 10/13	Scorpio
1/1 to 1/5	Aquarius	10/13 to 11/15	Sagittarius
1/5 to 2/1	Pisces	11/15 to 12/31	Scorpio
2/1 to 3/9	Aries		
3/9 to 4/13	Taurus	*1939*	
4/13 to 6/3	Aries	1/1 to 1/4	Scorpio
6/3 to 7/7	Taurus	1/4 to 2/5	Sagittarius
7/7 to 8/4	Gemini	2/5 to 3/5	Capricorn
8/4 to 8/30	Cancer	3/5 to 3/30	Aquarius
8/30 to 9/24	Leo	3/30 to 4/25	Pisces

DATE	ZODIAC SIGN
4/25 to 5/20	Aries
5/20 to 6/13	Taurus
6/13 to 7/8	Gemini
7/8 to 8/2	Cancer
8/2 to 8/26	Leo
8/26 to 9/19	Virgo
9/19 to 10/13	Libra
10/13 to 11/6	Scorpio
11/6 to 11/30	Sagittarius
11/30 to 12/24	Capricorn
12/24 to 12/31	Aquarius

1940

DATE	ZODIAC SIGN
1/1 to 1/18	Aquarius
1/18 to 2/11	Pisces
2/11 to 3/8	Aries
3/8 to 4/4	Taurus
4/4 to 5/6	Gemini
5/6 to 7/5	Cancer
7/5 to 7/31	Gemini
7/31 to 9/8	Cancer
9/8 to 10/6	Leo
10/6 to 11/1	Virgo
11/1 to 11/26	Libra
11/26 to 12/20	Scorpio
12/20 to 12/31	Sagittarius

1941

DATE	ZODIAC SIGN
1/1 to 1/13	Sagittarius
1/13 to 2/6	Capricorn
2/6 to 3/2	Aquarius
3/2 to 3/26	Pisces
3/26 to 4/19	Aries
4/19 to 5/14	Taurus
5/14 to 6/7	Gemini
6/7 to 7/2	Cancer
7/2 to 7/26	Leo
7/26 to 8/20	Virgo
8/20 to 9/14	Libra

DATE	ZODIAC SIGN
9/14 to 10/10	Scorpio
10/10 to 11/5	Sagittarius
11/5 to 12/5	Capricorn
12/5 to 12/31	Aquarius

1942

DATE	ZODIAC SIGN
1/1 to 4/6	Aquarius
4/6 to 5/5	Pisces
5/5 to 6/1	Aries
6/1 to 6/27	Taurus
6/27 to 7/22	Gemini
7/22 to 8/16	Cancer
8/16 to 9/10	Leo
9/10 to 10/4	Virgo
10/4 to 10/28	Libra
10/28 to 11/21	Scorpio
11/21 to 12/15	Sagittarius
12/15 to 12/31	Capricorn

1943

DATE	ZODIAC SIGN
1/1 to 1/7	Capricorn
1/7 to 1/31	Aquarius
1/31 to 2/25	Pisces
2/25 to 3/21	Aries
3/21 to 4/15	Taurus
4/15 to 5/10	Gemini
5/10 to 6/7	Cancer
6/7 to 7/7	Leo
7/7 to 11/9	Virgo
11/9 to 12/7	Libra
12/7 to 12/31	Scorpio

1944

DATE	ZODIAC SIGN
1/1 to 1/2	Scorpio
1/2 to 1/27	Sagittarius
1/27 to 2/21	Capricorn
2/21 to 3/16	Aquarius
3/16 to 4/10	Pisces
4/10 to 5/4	Aries

DATE	ZODIAC SIGN
5/4 to 5/28	Taurus
5/28 to 6/22	Gemini
6/22 to 7/16	Cancer
7/16 to 8/10	Leo
8/10 to 9/3	Virgo
9/3 to 9/27	Libra
9/27 to 10/22	Scorpio
10/22 to 11/15	Sagittarius
11/15 to 12/10	Capricorn
12/10 to 12/31	Aquarius

1945

DATE	ZODIAC SIGN
1/1 to 1/5	Aquarius
1/5 to 2/1	Pisces
2/1 to 3/10	Aries
3/10 to 4/7	Taurus
4/7 to 6/4	Aries
6/4 to 7/7	Taurus
7/7 to 8/3	Gemini
8/3 to 8/30	Cancer
8/30 to 9/24	Leo
9/24 to 10/18	Virgo
10/18 to 11/11	Libra
11/11 to 12/5	Scorpio
12/5 to 12/29	Sagittarius
12/29 to 12/31	Capricorn

1946

DATE	ZODIAC SIGN
1/1 to 1/22	Capricorn
1/22 to 2/15	Aquarius
2/15 to 3/11	Pisces
3/11 to 4/4	Aries
4/4 to 4/28	Taurus
4/28 to 5/23	Gemini
5/23 to 6/17	Cancer
6/17 to 7/13	Leo
7/13 to 8/8	Virgo
8/8 to 9/6	Libra
9/6 to 10/15	Scorpio

DATE	ZODIAC SIGN
10/15 to 11/7	Sagittarius
11/7 to 12/31	Scorpio

1947

DATE	ZODIAC SIGN
1/1 to 1/5	Scorpio
1/5 to 2/5	Sagittarius
2/5 to 3/4	Capricorn
3/4 to 3/30	Aquarius
3/30 to 4/24	Pisces
4/24 to 5/19	Aries
5/19 to 6/13	Taurus
6/13 to 7/8	Gemini
7/8 to 8/1	Cancer
8/1 to 8/25	Leo
8/25 to 9/19	Virgo
9/19 to 10/13	Libra
10/13 to 11/6	Scorpio
11/6 to 11/30	Sagittarius
11/30 to 12/24	Capricorn
12/24 to 12/31	Aquarius

1948

DATE	ZODIAC SIGN
1/1 to 1/17	Aquarius
1/17 to 2/11	Pisces
2/11 to 3/7	Aries
3/7 to 4/4	Taurus
4/4 to 5/6	Gemini
5/6 to 6/28	Cancer
6/28 to 8/2	Gemini
8/2 to 9/8	Cancer
9/8 to 10/6	Leo
10/6 to 10/31	Virgo
10/31 to 11/25	Libra
11/25 to 12/19	Scorpio
12/19 to 12/31	Sagittarius

1949

DATE	ZODIAC SIGN
1/1 to 1/12	Sagittarius
1/12 to 2/5	Capricorn
2/5 to 3/1	Aquarius

DATE	ZODIAC SIGN	DATE	ZODIAC SIGN
3/1 to 3/25	Pisces	*1952*	
3/25 to 4/19	Aries	1/1 to 1/2	Scorpio
4/19 to 5/13	Taurus	1/2 to 1/27	Sagittarius
5/13 to 6/6	Gemini	1/27 to 2/20	Capricorn
6/6 to 7/1	Cancer	2/20 to 3/16	Aquarius
7/1 to 7/26	Leo	3/16 to 4/9	Pisces
7/26 to 8/20	Virgo	4/9 to 5/3	Aries
8/20 to 9/14	Libra	5/3 to 5/28	Taurus
9/14 to 10/9	Scorpio	5/28 to 6/21	Gemini
10/9 to 11/5	Sagittarius	6/21 to 7/16	Cancer
11/5 to 12/5	Capricorn	7/16 to 8/9	Leo
12/5 to 12/31	Aquarius	8/9 to 9/2	Virgo
		9/2 to 9/27	Libra
1950		9/27 to 10/21	Scorpio
1/1 to 4/6	Aquarius	10/21 to 11/15	Sagittarius
4/6 to 5/5	Pisces	11/15 to 12/10	Capricorn
5/5 to 6/1	Aries	12/10 to 12/31	Aquarius
6/1 to 6/26	Taurus		
6/26 to 7/22	Gemini	*1953*	
7/22 to 8/16	Cancer	1/1 to 1/4	Aquarius
8/16 to 9/9	Leo	1/4 to 2/1	Pisces
9/9 to 10/3	Virgo	2/1 to 3/14	Aries
10/3 to 10/27	Libra	3/14 to 3/30	Taurus
10/27 to 11/20	Scorpio	3/30 to 6/4	Aries
11/20 to 12/14	Sagittarius	6/4 to 7/6	Taurus
12/14 to 12/31	Capricorn	7/6 to 8/3	Gemini
		8/3 to 8/29	Cancer
1951		8/29 to 9/23	Leo
1/1 to 1/7	Capricorn	9/23 to 10/18	Virgo
1/7 to 1/31	Aquarius	10/18 to 11/11	Libra
1/31 to 2/24	Pisces	11/11 to 12/5	Scorpio
2/24 to 3/20	Aries	12/5 to 12/29	Sagittarius
3/20 to 4/14	Taurus	12/29 to 12/31	Capricorn
4/14 to 5/10	Gemini		
5/10 to 6/6	Cancer	*1954*	
6/6 to 7/7	Leo	1/1 to 1/21	Capricorn
7/7 to 11/9	Virgo	1/21 to 2/14	Aquarius
11/9 to 12/7	Libra	2/14 to 3/10	Pisces
12/7 to 12/31	Scorpio	3/10 to 4/3	Aries

DATE	ZODIAC SIGN	DATE	ZODIAC SIGN
4/3 to 4/28	Taurus	10/31 to 11/25	Libra
4/28 to 5/23	Gemini	11/25 to 12/19	Scorpio
5/23 to 6/17	Cancer	12/19 to 12/31	Sagittarius
6/17 to 7/12	Leo		
7/12 to 8/8	Virgo	**1957**	
8/8 to 9/6	Libra	1/1 to 1/12	Sagittarius
9/6 to 10/23	Scorpio	1/12 to 2/5	Capricorn
10/23 to 10/26	Sagittarius	2/5 to 3/1	Aquarius
10/26 to 12/31	Scorpio	3/1 to 3/25	Pisces
		3/25 to 4/18	Aries
1955		4/18 to 5/12	Taurus
1/1 to 1/5	Scorpio	5/12 to 6/6	Gemini
1/5 to 2/5	Sagittarius	6/6 to 6/30	Cancer
2/5 to 3/4	Capricorn	6/30 to 7/25	Leo
3/4 to 3/29	Aquarius	7/25 to 8/19	Virgo
3/29 to 4/24	Pisces	8/19 to 9/13	Libra
4/24 to 5/19	Aries	9/13 to 10/9	Scorpio
5/19 to 6/12	Taurus	10/9 to 11/5	Sagittarius
6/12 to 7/7	Gemini	11/5 to 12/6	Capricorn
7/7 to 7/31	Cancer	12/6 to 12/31	Aquarius
7/31 to 8/25	Leo		
8/25 to 9/18	Virgo	**1958**	
9/18 to 10/12	Libra	1/1 to 4/6	Aquarius
10/12 to 11/5	Scorpio	4/6 to 5/4	Pisces
11/5 to 11/29	Sagittarius	5/4 to 5/31	Aries
11/29 to 12/23	Capricorn	5/31 to 6/26	Taurus
12/23 to 12/31	Aquarius	6/26 to 7/21	Gemini
		7/21 to 8/15	Cancer
1956		8/15 to 9/9	Leo
1/1 to 1/17	Aquarius	9/9 to 10/3	Virgo
1/17 to 2/10	Pisces	10/3 to 10/27	Libra
2/10 to 3/7	Aries	10/27 to 11/20	Scorpio
3/7 to 4/3	Taurus	11/20 to 12/13	Sagittarius
4/3 to 5/7	Gemini	12/13 to 12/31	Capricorn
5/7 to 6/23	Cancer		
6/23 to 8/3	Gemini	**1959**	
8/3 to 9/7	Cancer	1/1 to 1/6	Capricorn
9/7 to 10/5	Leo	1/6 to 1/30	Aquarius
10/5 to 10/31	Virgo	1/30 to 2/23	Pisces
		2/23 to 3/20	Aries

DATE	ZODIAC SIGN	DATE	ZODIAC SIGN
3/20 to 4/14	Taurus	12/4 to 12/28	Sagittarius
4/14 to 5/10	Gemini	12/28 to 12/31	Capricorn
5/10 to 6/6	Cancer		
6/6 to 7/8	Leo	*1962*	
7/8 to 9/19	Virgo	1/1 to 1/21	Capricorn
9/19 to 9/24	Leo	1/21 to 2/14	Aquarius
9/24 to 11/9	Virgo	2/14 to 3/10	Pisces
11/9 to 12/7	Libra	3/10 to 4/3	Aries
12/7 to 12/31	Scorpio	4/3 to 4/27	Taurus
		4/27 to 5/22	Gemini
1960		5/22 to 6/16	Cancer
1/1	Scorpio	6/16 to 7/12	Leo
1/1 to 1/26	Sagittarius	7/12 to 8/8	Virgo
1/26 to 2/20	Capricorn	8/8 to 9/6	Libra
2/20 to 3/15	Aquarius	9/6 to 12/31	Scorpio
3/15 to 4/8	Pisces		
4/8 to 5/3	Aries	*1963*	
5/3 to 5/27	Taurus	1/1 to 1/6	Scorpio
5/27 to 6/21	Gemini	1/6 to 2/5	Sagittarius
6/21 to 7/15	Cancer	2/5 to 3/3	Capricorn
7/15 to 8/8	Leo	3/3 to 3/29	Aquarius
8/8 to 9/2	Virgo	3/29 to 4/23	Pisces
9/2 to 9/26	Libra	4/23 to 5/18	Aries
9/26 to 10/21	Scorpio	5/18 to 6/12	Taurus
10/21 to 11/14	Sagittarius	6/12 to 7/6	Gemini
11/14 to 12/9	Capricorn	7/6 to 7/31	Cancer
12/9 to 12/31	Aquarius	7/31 to 8/24	Leo
		8/24 to 9/17	Virgo
1961		9/17 to 10/11	Libra
1/1 to 1/4	Aquarius	10/11 to 11/5	Scorpio
1/4 to 2/1	Pisces	11/5 to 11/29	Sagittarius
2/1 to 6/5	Aries	11/29 to 12/23	Capricorn
6/5 to 7/6	Taurus	12/23 to 12/31	Aquarius
7/6 to 8/3	Gemini		
8/3 to 8/29	Cancer	*1964*	
8/29 to 9/23	Leo	1/1 to 1/16	Aquarius
9/23 to 10/17	Virgo	1/16 to 2/10	Pisces
10/17 to 11/10	Libra	2/10 to 3/7	Aries
11/10 to 12/4	Scorpio	3/7 to 4/3	Taurus

DATE	ZODIAC SIGN	DATE	ZODIAC SIGN
4/3 to 5/8	Gemini	10/26 to 11/19	Scorpio
5/8 to 6/17	Cancer	11/19 to 12/13	Sagittarius
6/17 to 8/4	Gemini	12/13 to 12/31	Capricorn
8/4 to 9/7	Cancer		
9/7 to 10/5	Leo	**1967**	
10/5 to 10/30	Virgo	1/1 to 1/6	Capricorn
10/30 to 11/24	Libra	1/6 to 1/30	Aquarius
11/24 to 12/18	Scorpio	1/30 to 2/23	Pisces
12/18 to 12/31	Sagittarius	2/23 to 3/19	Aries
		3/19 to 4/13	Taurus
1965		4/13 to 5/9	Gemini
1/1 to 1/11	Sagittarius	5/9 to 6/6	Cancer
1/11 to 2/4	Capricorn	6/6 to 7/8	Leo
2/4 to 2/28	Aquarius	7/8 to 9/9	Virgo
2/28 to 3/24	Pisces	9/9 to 10/1	Leo
3/24 to 4/18	Aries	10/1 to 11/9	Virgo
4/18 to 5/12	Taurus	11/9 to 12/6	Libra
5/12 to 6/5	Gemini	12/6 to 12/31	Scorpio
6/5 to 6/30	Cancer		
6/30 to 7/25	Leo	**1968**	
7/25 to 8/19	Virgo	1/1	Scorpio
8/19 to 9/13	Libra	1/1 to 1/26	Sagittarius
9/13 to 10/9	Scorpio	1/26 to 2/19	Capricorn
10/9 to 11/5	Sagittarius	2/19 to 3/15	Aquarius
11/5 to 12/6	Capricorn	3/15 to 4/8	Pisces
12/6 to 12/31	Aquarius	4/8 to 5/2	Aries
		5/2 to 5/27	Taurus
1966		5/27 to 6/20	Gemini
1/1 to 2/6	Aquarius	6/20 to 7/15	Cancer
2/6 to 2/24	Capricorn	7/15 to 8/8	Leo
2/24 to 4/6	Aquarius	8/8 to 9/1	Virgo
4/6 to 5/4	Pisces	9/1 to 9/26	Libra
5/4 to 5/31	Aries	9/26 to 10/20	Scorpio
5/31 to 6/25	Taurus	10/20 to 11/14	Sagittarius
6/25 to 7/21	Gemini	11/14 to 12/9	Capricorn
7/21 to 8/15	Cancer	12/9 to 12/31	Aquarius
8/15 to 9/8	Leo		
9/8 to 10/2	Virgo	**1969**	
10/2 to 10/26	Libra	1/1 to 1/4	Aquarius
		1/4 to 2/1	Pisces

DATE	ZODIAC SIGN	DATE	ZODIAC SIGN
2/1 to 6/5	Aries	11/28 to 12/22	Capricorn
6/5 to 7/6	Taurus	12/22 to 12/31	Aquarius
7/6 to 8/2	Gemini		
8/2 to 8/28	Cancer	*1972*	
8/28 to 9/22	Leo	1/1 to 1/16	Aquarius
9/22 to 10/17	Virgo	1/16 to 2/9	Pisces
10/17 to 11/10	Libra	2/9 to 3/6	Aries
11/10 to 12/4	Scorpio	3/6 to 4/3	Taurus
12/4 to 12/27	Sagittarius	4/3 to 5/10	Gemini
12/27 to 12/31	Capricorn	5/10 to 6/11	Cancer
		6/11 to 8/5	Gemini
1970		8/5 to 9/7	Cancer
1/1 to 1/20	Capricorn	9/7 to 10/4	Leo
1/20 to 2/13	Aquarius	10/4 to 10/30	Virgo
2/13 to 3/9	Pisces	10/30 to 11/24	Libra
3/9 to 4/2	Aries	11/24 to 12/18	Scorpio
4/2 to 4/27	Taurus	12/18 to 12/31	Sagittarius
4/27 to 5/22	Gemini		
5/22 to 6/16	Cancer	*1973*	
6/16 to 7/12	Leo	1/1 to 1/11	Sagittarius
7/12 to 8/7	Virgo	1/11 to 2/4	Capricorn
8/7 to 9/6	Libra	2/4 to 2/28	Aquarius
9/6 to 12/31	Scorpio	2/28 to 3/24	Pisces
		3/24 to 4/17	Aries
1971		4/17 to 5/11	Taurus
1/1 to 1/6	Scorpio	5/11 to 6/5	Gemini
1/6 to 2/5	Sagittarius	6/5 to 6/29	Cancer
2/5 to 3/3	Capricorn	6/29 to 7/24	Leo
3/3 to 3/29	Aquarius	7/24 to 8/18	Virgo
3/29 to 4/23	Pisces	8/18 to 9/12	Libra
4/23 to 5/18	Aries	9/12 to 10/8	Scorpio
5/18 to 6/11	Taurus	10/8 to 11/5	Sagittarius
6/11 to 7/6	Gemini	11/5 to 12/7	Capricorn
7/6 to 7/30	Cancer	12/7 to 12/31	Aquarius
7/30 to 8/24	Leo		
8/24 to 9/17	Virgo	*1974*	
9/17 to 10/11	Libra	1/1 to 1/29	Aquarius
10/11 to 11/4	Scorpio	1/29 to 2/28	Capricorn
11/4 to 11/28	Sagittarius	2/28 to 4/6	Aquarius

DATE	ZODIAC SIGN	DATE	ZODIAC SIGN
4/6 to 5/4	Pisces	9/1 to 9/25	Libra
5/4 to 5/30	Aries	9/25 to 10/20	Scorpio
5/30 to 6/25	Taurus	10/20 to 11/13	Sagittarius
6/25 to 7/20	Gemini	11/13 to 12/9	Capricorn
7/20 to 8/14	Cancer	12/9 to 12/31	Aquarius
8/14 to 9/7	Leo		
9/7 to 10/2	Virgo	**1977**	
10/2 to 10/26	Libra	1/1 to 1/4	Aquarius
10/26 to 11/18	Scorpio	1/4 to 2/1	Pisces
11/18 to 12/12	Sagittarius	2/1 to 6/5	Aries
12/12 to 12/31	Capricorn	6/5 to 7/6	Taurus
		7/6 to 8/2	Gemini
1975		8/2 to 8/28	Cancer
1/1 to 1/5	Capricorn	8/28 to 9/22	Leo
1/5 to 1/29	Aquarius	9/22 to 10/16	Virgo
1/29 to 2/22	Pisces	10/16 to 11/9	Libra
2/22 to 3/19	Aries	11/9 to 12/3	Scorpio
3/19 to 4/13	Taurus	12/3 to 12/27	Sagittarius
4/13 to 5/9	Gemini	12/27 to 12/31	Capricorn
5/9 to 6/5	Cancer		
6/5 to 7/8	Leo	**1978**	
7/8 to 9/2	Virgo	1/1 to 1/20	Capricorn
9/2 to 10/3	Leo	1/20 to 2/13	Aquarius
10/3 to 11/9	Virgo	2/13 to 3/9	Pisces
11/9 to 12/6	Libra	3/9 to 4/2	Aries
12/6 to 12/31	Scorpio	4/2 to 4/26	Taurus
		4/26 to 5/21	Gemini
		5/21 to 6/15	Cancer
1976		6/15 to 7/11	Leo
1/1	Scorpio	7/11 to 8/7	Virgo
1/1 to 1/25	Sagittarius	8/7 to 9/6	Libra
1/25 to 2/19	Capricorn	9/6 to 12/31	Scorpio
2/19 to 3/14	Aquarius		
3/14 to 4/7	Pisces	**1979**	
4/7 to 5/2	Aries	1/1 to 1/6	Scorpio
5/2 to 5/26	Taurus	1/6 to 2/4	Sagittarius
5/26 to 6/20	Gemini	2/4 to 3/3	Capricorn
6/20 to 7/14	Cancer	3/3 to 3/28	Aquarius
7/14 to 8/7	Leo	3/28 to 4/22	Pisces
8/7 to 9/1	Virgo	4/22 to 5/17	Aries

DATE	ZODIAC SIGN	DATE	ZODIAC SIGN
5/17 to 6/11	Taurus	10/8 to 11/5	Sagittarius
6/11 to 7/5	Gemini	11/5 to 12/8	Capricorn
7/5 to 7/30	Cancer	12/8 to 12/31	Aquarius
7/30 to 8/23	Leo		
8/23 to 9/16	Virgo		
9/16 to 10/10	Libra	*1982*	
10/10 to 11/3	Scorpio	1/1 to 1/22	Aquarius
11/3 to 11/28	Sagittarius	1/22 to 3/1	Capricorn
11/28 to 12/22	Capricorn	3/1 to 4/6	Aquarius
12/22 to 12/31	Aquarius	4/6 to 5/4	Pisces
		5/4 to 5/30	Aries
		5/30 to 6/25	Taurus
1980		6/25 to 7/20	Gemini
1/1 to 1/15	Aquarius	7/20 to 8/13	Cancer
1/15 to 2/9	Pisces	8/13 to 9/7	Leo
2/9 to 3/6	Aries	9/7 to 10/1	Virgo
3/6 to 4/3	Taurus	10/1 to 10/25	Libra
4/3 to 5/12	Gemini	10/25 to 11/18	Scorpio
5/12 to 6/4	Cancer	11/18 to 12/12	Sagittarius
6/4 to 8/6	Gemini	12/12 to 12/31	Capricorn
8/6 to 9/7	Cancer		
9/7 to 10/4	Leo		
10/4 to 10/29	Virgo	*1983*	
10/29 to 11/23	Libra	1/1 to 1/5	Capricorn
11/23 to 12/17	Scorpio	1/5 to 1/29	Aquarius
12/17 to 12/31	Sagittarius	1/29 to 2/22	Pisces
		2/22 to 3/18	Aries
		3/18 to 4/12	Taurus
1981		4/12 to 5/8	Gemini
1/1 to 1/10	Sagittarius	5/8 to 6/5	Cancer
1/10 to 2/3	Capricorn	6/5 to 7/9	Leo
2/3 to 2/27	Aquarius	7/9 to 8/26	Virgo
2/27 to 3/23	Pisces	8/26 to 10/5	Leo
3/23 to 4/17	Aries	10/5 to 11/8	Virgo
4/17 to 5/11	Taurus	11/8 to 12/6	Libra
5/11 to 6/4	Gemini	12/6 to 12/31	Scorpio
6/4 to 6/29	Cancer		
6/29 to 7/24	Leo		
7/24 to 8/18	Virgo	*1984*	
8/18 to 9/12	Libra	1/1	Scorpio
9/12 to 10/8	Scorpio	1/1 to 1/25	Sagittarius

DATE	ZODIAC SIGN	DATE	ZODIAC SIGN
1/25 to 2/18	Capricorn	8/7 to 9/6	Libra
2/18 to 3/14	Aquarius	9/6 to 12/31	Scorpio
3/14 to 4/7	Pisces		
4/7 to 5/1	Aries	**1987**	
5/1 to 5/26	Taurus	1/1 to 1/6	Scorpio
5/26 to 6/19	Gemini	1/6 to 2/4	Sagittarius
6/19 to 7/13	Cancer	2/4 to 3/2	Capricorn
7/13 to 8/7	Leo	3/2 to 3/28	Aquarius
8/7 to 8/31	Virgo	3/28 to 4/22	Pisces
8/31 to 9/25	Libra	4/22 to 5/16	Aries
9/25 to 10/19	Scorpio	5/16 to 6/10	Taurus
10/19 to 11/13	Sagittarius	6/10 to 7/5	Gemini
11/13 to 12/8	Capricorn	7/5 to 7/29	Cancer
12/8 to 12/31	Aquarius	7/29 to 8/23	Leo
		8/23 to 9/16	Virgo
		9/16 to 10/10	Libra
1985		10/10 to 11/3	Scorpio
1/1 to 1/3	Aquarius	11/3 to 11/27	Sagittarius
1/3 to 2/1	Pisces	11/27 to 12/21	Capricorn
2/1 to 6/5	Aries	12/21 to 12/31	Aquarius
6/5 to 7/5	Taurus		
7/5 to 8/1	Gemini	**1988**	
8/1 to 8/27	Cancer	1/1 to 1/15	Aquarius
8/27 to 9/21	Leo	1/15 to 2/9	Pisces
9/21 to 10/16	Virgo	2/9 to 3/5	Aries
10/16 to 11/9	Libra	3/5 to 4/3	Taurus
11/9 to 12/3	Scorpio	4/3 to 5/17	Gemini
12/3 to 12/26	Sagittarius	5/17 to 5/26	Cancer
12/26 to 12/31	Capricorn	5/26 to 8/6	Gemini
		8/6 to 9/6	Cancer
		9/6 to 10/4	Leo
1986		10/4 to 10/29	Virgo
1/1 to 1/19	Capricorn	10/29 to 11/23	Libra
1/19 to 2/12	Aquarius	11/23 to 12/17	Scorpio
2/12 to 3/8	Pisces	12/17 to 12/31	Sagittarius
3/8 to 4/1	Aries		
4/1 to 4/26	Taurus	**1989**	
4/26 to 5/21	Gemini	1/1 to 1/10	Sagittarius
5/21 to 6/15	Cancer	1/10 to 2/3	Capricorn
6/15 to 7/11	Leo	2/3 to 2/27	Aquarius
7/11 to 8/7	Virgo		

DATE	ZODIAC SIGN	DATE	ZODIAC SIGN
2/27 to 3/23	Pisces	8/21 to 10/6	Leo
3/23 to 4/16	Aries	10/6 to 11/8	Virgo
4/16 to 5/10	Taurus	11/8 to 12/5	Libra
5/10 to 6/4	Gemini	12/5 to 12/31	Scorpio
6/4 to 6/28	Cancer		
6/28 to 7/23	Leo	*1992*	
7/23 to 8/17	Virgo	1/1	Scorpio
8/17 to 9/12	Libra	1/1 to 1/24	Sagittarius
9/12 to 10/8	Scorpio	1/24 to 2/18	Capricorn
10/8 to 11/4	Sagittarius	2/18 to 3/13	Aquarius
11/4 to 12/9	Capricorn	3/13 to 4/6	Pisces
12/9 to 12/31	Aquarius	4/6 to 5/1	Aries
		5/1 to 5/25	Taurus
1990		5/25 to 6/18	Gemini
1/1 to 1/16	Aquarius	6/18 to 7/13	Cancer
1/16 to 3/3	Capricorn	7/13 to 8/6	Leo
3/3 to 4/5	Aquarius	8/6 to 8/31	Virgo
4/5 to 5/3	Pisces	8/31 to 9/24	Libra
5/3 to 5/29	Aries	9/24 to 10/19	Scorpio
5/29 to 6/24	Taurus	10/19 to 11/13	Sagittarius
6/24 to 7/19	Gemini	11/13 to 12/8	Capricorn
7/19 to 8/13	Cancer	12/8 to 12/31	Aquarius
8/13 to 9/6	Leo		
9/6 to 10/1	Virgo	*1993*	
10/1 to 10/25	Libra	1/1 to 1/3	Aquarius
10/25 to 11/17	Scorpio	1/3 to 2/2	Pisces
11/17 to 12/11	Sagittarius	2/2 to 6/5	Aries
12/11 to 12/31	Capricorn	6/5 to 7/5	Taurus
		7/5 to 8/1	Gemini
1991		8/1 to 8/27	Cancer
1/1 to 1/4	Capricorn	8/27 to 9/21	Leo
1/4 to 1/28	Aquarius	9/21 to 10/15	Virgo
1/28 to 2/21	Pisces	10/15 to 11/8	Libra
2/21 to 3/18	Aries	11/8 to 12/2	Scorpio
3/18 to 4/12	Taurus	12/2 to 12/26	Sagittarius
4/12 to 5/8	Gemini	12/26 to 12/31	Capricorn
5/8 to 6/5	Cancer		
6/5 to 7/10	Leo	*1994*	
7/10 to 8/21	Virgo	1/1 to 1/19	Capricorn
		1/19 to 2/12	Aquarius

DATE	ZODIAC SIGN	DATE	ZODIAC SIGN
2/12 to 3/8	Pisces	*1997*	
3/8 to 4/1	Aries	1/1 to 1/9	Sagittarius
4/1 to 4/25	Taurus	1/9 to 2/2	Capricorn
4/25 to 5/20	Gemini	2/2 to 2/26	Aquarius
5/20 to 6/14	Cancer	2/26 to 3/22	Pisces
6/14 to 7/10	Leo	3/22 to 4/15	Aries
7/10 to 8/7	Virgo	4/15 to 5/10	Taurus
8/7 to 9/7	Libra	5/10 to 6/3	Gemini
9/7 to 12/31	Scorpio	6/3 to 6/28	Cancer
		6/28 to 7/23	Leo
1995		7/23 to 8/17	Virgo
1/1 to 1/7	Scorpio	8/17 to 9/11	Libra
1/7 to 2/4	Sagittarius	9/11 to 10/7	Scorpio
2/4 to 3/2	Capricorn	10/7 to 11/4	Sagittarius
3/2 to 3/27	Aquarius	11/4 to 12/11	Capricorn
3/27 to 4/21	Pisces	12/11 to 12/31	Aquarius
4/21 to 5/16	Aries		
5/16 to 6/10	Taurus	*1998*	
6/10 to 7/4	Gemini	1/1 to 1/9	Aquarius
7/4 to 7/29	Cancer	1/9 to 3/4	Capricorn
7/29 to 8/22	Leo	3/4 to 4/5	Aquarius
8/22 to 9/15	Virgo	4/5 to 5/3	Pisces
9/15 to 10/9	Libra	5/3 to 5/29	Aries
10/9 to 11/2	Scorpio	5/29 to 6/24	Taurus
11/2 to 11/27	Sagittarius	6/24 to 7/19	Gemini
11/27 to 12/21	Capricorn	7/19 to 8/12	Cancer
12/21 to 12/31	Aquarius	8/12 to 9/6	Leo
		9/6 to 9/30	Virgo
1996		9/30 to 10/24	Libra
1/1 to 1/14	Aquarius	10/24 to 11/17	Scorpio
1/14 to 2/8	Pisces	11/17 to 12/11	Sagittarius
2/8 to 3/5	Aries	12/11 to 12/31	Capricorn
3/5 to 4/3	Taurus		
4/3 to 8/6	Gemini	*1999*	
8/6 to 9/6	Cancer	1/1 to 1/4	Capricorn
9/6 to 10/3	Leo	1/4 to 1/28	Aquarius
10/3 to 10/29	Virgo	1/28 to 2/21	Pisces
10/29 to 11/22	Libra	2/21 to 3/17	Aries
11/22 to 12/16	Scorpio	3/17 to 4/12	Taurus
12/16 to 12/31	Sagittarius		

DATE	ZODIAC SIGN	DATE	ZODIAC SIGN
4/12 to 5/8	Gemini	*2002*	
5/8 to 6/5	Cancer	1/1 to 1/18	Capricorn
6/5 to 7/12	Leo	1/18 to 2/11	Aquarius
7/12 to 8/15	Virgo	2/11 to 3/7	Pisces
8/15 to 10/7	Leo	3/7 to 3/31	Aries
10/7 to 11/8	Virgo	3/31 to 4/25	Taurus
11/8 to 12/5	Libra	4/25 to 5/20	Gemini
12/5 to 12/30	Scorpio	5/20 to 6/14	Cancer
12/30 to 12/31	Sagittarius	6/14 to 7/10	Leo
		7/10 to 8/6	Virgo
2000		8/6 to 9/7	Libra
1/1 to 1/24	Sagittarius	9/7 to 12/31	Scorpio
1/24 to 2/17	Capricorn		
2/17 to 3/12	Aquarius	*2003*	
3/12 to 4/6	Pisces	1/1 to 1/7	Scorpio
4/6 to 4/30	Aries	1/7 to 2/4	Sagittarius
4/30 to 5/25	Taurus	2/4 to 3/2	Capricorn
5/25 to 6/18	Gemini	3/2 to 3/27	Aquarius
6/18 to 7/12	Cancer	3/27 to 4/21	Pisces
7/12 to 8/6	Leo	4/21 to 5/15	Aries
8/6 to 8/30	Virgo	5/15 to 6/9	Taurus
8/30 to 9/24	Libra	6/9 to 7/4	Gemini
9/24 to 10/18	Scorpio	7/4 to 7/28	Cancer
10/18 to 11/12	Sagittarius	7/28 to 8/21	Leo
11/12 to 12/7	Capricorn	8/21 to 9/15	Virgo
12/7 to 12/31	Aquarius	9/15 to 10/9	Libra
		10/9 to 11/2	Scorpio
2001		11/2 to 11/26	Sagittarius
1/1 to 1/3	Aquarius	11/26 to 12/20	Capricorn
1/3 to 2/2	Pisces	12/20 to 12/31	Aquarius
2/2 to 6/5	Aries		
6/5 to 7/5	Taurus	*2004*	
7/5 to 8/1	Gemini	1/1 to 1/14	Aquarius
8/1 to 8/26	Cancer	1/14 to 2/8	Pisces
8/26 to 9/20	Leo	2/8 to 3/5	Aries
9/20 to 10/14	Virgo	3/5 to 4/3	Taurus
10/14 to 11/8	Libra	4/3 to 8/6	Gemini
11/8 to 12/1	Scorpio	8/6 to 9/6	Cancer
12/1 to 12/25	Sagittarius	9/6 to 10/3	Leo
12/25 to 12/31	Capricorn	10/3 to 10/28	Virgo

DATE	ZODIAC SIGN	DATE	ZODIAC SIGN
10/28 to 11/22	Libra	1/27 to 2/20	Pisces
11/22 to 12/16	Scorpio	2/20 to 3/17	Aries
12/16 to 12/31	Sagittarius	3/17 to 4/11	Taurus
		4/11 to 5/7	Gemini
2005		5/7 to 6/5	Cancer
1/1 to 1/9	Sagittarius	6/5 to 7/14	Leo
1/9 to 2/2	Capricorn	7/14 to 8/8	Virgo
2/2 to 2/26	Aquarius	8/8 to 10/7	Leo
2/26 to 3/22	Pisces	10/7 to 11/8	Virgo
3/22 to 4/15	Aries	11/8 to 12/5	Libra
4/15 to 5/9	Taurus	12/5 to 12/30	Scorpio
5/9 to 6/3	Gemini	12/30 to 12/31	Sagittarius
6/3 to 6/27	Cancer		
6/27 to 7/22	Leo	**2008**	
7/22 to 8/16	Virgo	1/1 to 1/23	Sagittarius
8/16 to 9/11	Libra	1/23 to 2/17	Capricorn
9/11 to 10/7	Scorpio	2/17 to 3/12	Aquarius
10/7 to 11/4	Sagittarius	3/12 to 4/5	Pisces
11/4 to 12/15	Capricorn	4/5 to 4/30	Aries
12/15 to 12/31	Aquarius	4/30 to 5/24	Taurus
		5/24 to 6/17	Gemini
2006		6/17 to 7/12	Cancer
1/1	Aquarius	7/12 to 8/5	Leo
1/1 to 3/4	Capricorn	8/5 to 8/30	Virgo
3/4 to 4/5	Aquarius	8/30 to 9/23	Libra
4/5 to 5/2	Pisces	9/23 to 10/18	Scorpio
5/2 to 5/29	Aries	10/18 to 11/12	Sagittarius
5/29 to 6/23	Taurus	11/12 to 12/7	Capricorn
6/23 to 7/18	Gemini	12/7 to 12/31	Aquarius
7/18 to 8/12	Cancer		
8/12 to 9/5	Leo	**2009**	
9/5 to 9/29	Virgo	1/1 to 1/3	Aquarius
9/29 to 10/23	Libra	1/3 to 2/2	Pisces
10/23 to 11/16	Scorpio	2/2 to 4/11	Aries
11/16 to 12/10	Sagittarius	4/11 to 4/23	Pisces
12/10 to 12/31	Capricorn	4/23 to 6/5	Aries
		6/5 to 7/4	Taurus
2007		7/4 to 7/31	Gemini
1/1 to 1/3	Capricorn	7/31 to 8/26	Cancer
1/3 to 1/27	Aquarius		

DATE	ZODIAC SIGN	DATE	ZODIAC SIGN
8/26 to 9/20	Leo	*2012*	
9/20 to 10/14	Virgo	1/1 to 1/13	Aquarius
10/14 to 11/7	Libra	1/13 to 2/7	Pisces
11/7 to 12/1	Scorpio	2/7 to 3/4	Aries
12/1 to 12/25	Sagittarius	3/4 to 4/3	Taurus
12/25 to 12/31	Capricorn	4/3 to 8/7	Gemini
		8/7 to 9/6	Cancer
2010		9/6 to 10/2	Leo
1/1 to 1/18	Capricorn	10/2 to 10/28	Virgo
1/18 to 2/11	Aquarius	10/28 to 11/21	Libra
2/11 to 3/7	Pisces	11/21 to 12/15	Scorpio
3/7 to 3/31	Aries	12/15 to 12/31	Sagittarius
3/31 to 4/24	Taurus		
4/24 to 5/19	Gemini	*2013*	
5/19 to 6/13	Cancer	1/1 to 1/8	Sagittarius
6/13 to 7/9	Leo	1/8 to 2/1	Capricorn
7/9 to 8/6	Virgo	2/1 to 2/25	Aquarius
8/6 to 9/8	Libra	2/25 to 3/21	Pisces
9/8 to 11/7	Scorpio	3/21 to 4/14	Aries
11/7 to 11/29	Libra	4/14 to 5/9	Taurus
11/29 to 12/31	Scorpio	5/9 to 6/2	Gemini
		6/2 to 6/27	Cancer
2011		6/27 to 7/22	Leo
1/1 to 1/7	Scorpio	7/22 to 8/16	Virgo
1/7 to 2/3	Sagittarius	8/16 to 9/10	Libra
2/3 to 3/1	Capricorn	9/10 to 10/7	Scorpio
3/1 to 3/26	Aquarius	10/7 to 11/4	Sagittarius
3/26 to 4/20	Pisces	11/4 to 12/31	Capricorn
4/20 to 5/15	Aries		
5/15 to 6/9	Taurus	*2014*	
6/9 to 7/3	Gemini	1/1 to 3/5	Capricorn
7/3 to 7/28	Cancer	3/5 to 4/5	Aquarius
7/28 to 8/21	Leo	4/5 to 5/2	Pisces
8/21 to 9/14	Virgo	5/2 to 5/28	Aries
9/14 to 10/8	Libra	5/28 to 6/23	Taurus
10/8 to 11/1	Scorpio	6/23 to 7/18	Gemini
11/1 to 11/26	Sagittarius	7/18 to 8/11	Cancer
11/26 to 12/20	Capricorn	8/11 to 9/5	Leo
12/20 to 12/31	Aquarius	9/5 to 9/29	Virgo
		9/29 to 10/23	Libra

DATE	ZODIAC SIGN	DATE	ZODIAC SIGN
10/23 to 11/16	Scorpio	2/3 to 4/2	Aries
11/16 to 12/10	Sagittarius	4/2 to 4/28	Pisces
12/10 to 12/31	Capricorn	4/28 to 6/5	Aries
		6/5 to 7/4	Taurus
2015		7/4 to 7/31	Gemini
1/1 to 1/3	Capricorn	7/31 to 8/25	Cancer
1/3 to 1/27	Aquarius	8/25 to 9/19	Leo
1/27 to 2/20	Pisces	9/19 to 10/13	Virgo
2/20 to 3/16	Aries	10/13 to 11/6	Libra
3/16 to 4/11	Taurus	11/6 to 11/30	Scorpio
4/11 to 5/7	Gemini	11/30 to 12/24	Sagittarius
5/7 to 6/5	Cancer	12/24 to 12/31	Capricorn
6/5 to 7/18	Leo		
7/18 to 7/31	Virgo	**2018**	
7/31 to 10/8	Leo	1/1 to 1/17	Capricorn
10/8 to 11/8	Virgo	1/17 to 2/10	Aquarius
11/8 to 12/4	Libra	2/10 to 3/6	Pisces
12/4 to 12/29	Scorpio	3/6 to 3/30	Aries
12/29 to 12/31	Sagittarius	3/30 to 4/24	Taurus
		4/24 to 5/19	Gemini
2016		5/19 to 6/13	Cancer
1/1 to 1/23	Sagittarius	6/13 to 7/9	Leo
1/23 to 2/16	Capricorn	7/9 to 8/6	Virgo
2/16 to 3/11	Aquarius	8/6 to 9/8	Libra
3/11 to 4/5	Pisces	9/8 to 10/31	Scorpio
4/5 to 4/29	Aries	10/31 to 12/2	Libra
4/29 to 5/23	Taurus	12/2 to 12/31	Scorpio
5/23 to 6/17	Gemini		
6/17 to 7/11	Cancer	**2019**	
7/11 to 8/5	Leo	1/1 to 1/6	Scorpio
8/5 to 8/29	Virgo	1/6 to 2/3	Sagittarius
8/29 to 9/23	Libra	2/3 to 3/1	Capricorn
9/23 to 10/17	Scorpio	3/1 to 3/26	Aquarius
10/17 to 11/11	Sagittarius	3/26 to 4/20	Pisces
11/11 to 12/7	Capricorn	4/20 to 5/14	Aries
12/7 to 12/31	Aquarius	5/14 to 6/8	Taurus
		6/8 to 7/3	Gemini
2017		7/3 to 7/27	Cancer
1/1 to 1/2	Aquarius	7/27 to 8/20	Leo
1/2 to 2/3	Pisces		

DATE	ZODIAC SIGN	DATE	ZODIAC SIGN
8/20 to 9/14	Virgo	4/5 to 5/2	Pisces
9/14 to 10/8	Libra	5/2 to 5/28	Aries
10/8 to 11/1	Scorpio	5/28 to 6/22	Taurus
11/1 to 11/25	Sagittarius	6/22 to 7/17	Gemini
11/25 to 12/19	Capricorn	7/17 to 8/11	Cancer
12/19 to 12/31	Aquarius	8/11 to 9/4	Leo
		9/4 to 9/28	Virgo
2020		9/28 to 10/22	Libra
1/1 to 1/13	Aquarius	10/22 to 11/15	Scorpio
1/13 to 2/7	Pisces	11/15 to 12/9	Sagittarius
2/7 to 3/4	Aries	12/9 to 12/31	Capricorn
3/4 to 4/3	Taurus		
4/3 to 8/7	Gemini	*2023*	
8/7 to 9/5	Cancer	1/1 to 1/2	Capricorn
9/5 to 10/2	Leo	1/2 to 1/26	Aquarius
10/2 to 10/27	Virgo	1/26 to 2/19	Pisces
10/27 to 11/21	Libra	2/19 to 3/16	Aries
11/21 to 12/15	Scorpio	3/16 to 4/10	Taurus
12/15 to 12/31	Sagittarius	4/10 to 5/7	Gemini
		5/7 to 6/5	Cancer
2021		6/5 to 10/8	Leo
1/1 to 1/8	Sagittarius	10/8 to 11/7	Virgo
1/8 to 2/1	Capricorn	11/7 to 12/4	Libra
2/1 to 2/25	Aquarius	12/4 to 12/29	Scorpio
2/25 to 3/21	Pisces	12/29 to 12/31	Sagittarius
3/21 to 4/14	Aries		
4/14 to 5/8	Taurus	*2024*	
5/8 to 6/2	Gemini	1/1 to 1/22	Sagittarius
6/2 to 6/26	Cancer	1/22 to 2/16	Capricorn
6/26 to 7/21	Leo	2/16 to 3/11	Aquarius
7/21 to 8/15	Virgo	3/11 to 4/4	Pisces
8/15 to 9/10	Libra	4/4 to 4/28	Aries
9/10 to 10/6	Scorpio	4/28 to 5/23	Taurus
10/6 to 11/4	Sagittarius	5/23 to 6/16	Gemini
11/4 to 12/31	Capricorn	6/16 to 7/11	Cancer
		7/11 to 8/4	Leo
2022		8/4 to 8/29	Virgo
1/1 to 3/5	Capricorn	8/29 to 9/22	Libra
3/5 to 4/5	Aquarius	9/22 to 10/17	Scorpio

DATE	ZODIAC SIGN	DATE	ZODIAC SIGN
10/17 to 11/11	Sagittarius	6/5 to 7/4	Taurus
11/11 to 12/6	Capricorn	7/4 to 7/30	Gemini
12/6 to 12/31	Aquarius	7/30 to 8/25	Cancer
		8/25 to 9/19	Leo
2025		9/19 to 10/13	Virgo
1/1 to 1/2	Aquarius	10/13 to 11/6	Libra
1/2 to 2/3	Pisces	11/6 to 11/30	Scorpio
2/3 to 3/26	Aries	11/30 to 12/24	Sagittarius
3/26 to 4/30	Pisces	12/24 to 12/31	Capricorn
4/30 to 6/5	Aries		

MARS

The planet Mars spends close to two years traveling one time through the zodiac, spending nearly two months in each sign. The following table will tell you in which sign Mars was located on the specific day and year when you were born.

For the positions of Mars prior to 1936, go to "Free Astrology Charts" on www.janspiller.com.

DATE	ZODIAC SIGN	DATE	ZODIAC SIGN
1936		*1937*	
1/1 to 1/14	Aquarius	1/1 to 1/5	Libra
1/14 to 2/21	Pisces	1/5 to 3/12	Scorpio
2/21 to 4/1	Aries	3/12 to 5/14	Sagittarius
4/1 to 5/12	Taurus	5/14 to 8/8	Scorpio
5/12 to 6/25	Gemini	8/8 to 9/29	Sagittarius
6/25 to 8/9	Cancer	9/29 to 11/11	Capricorn
8/9 to 9/26	Leo	11/11 to 12/21	Aquarius
9/26 to 11/14	Virgo	12/21 to 12/31	Pisces
11/14 to 12/31	Libra		

DATE	ZODIAC SIGN	DATE	ZODIAC SIGN
1938		*1942*	
1/1 to 1/30	Pisces	1/1 to 1/11	Aries
1/30 to 3/11	Aries	1/11 to 3/6	Taurus
3/11 to 4/23	Taurus	3/6 to 4/25	Gemini
4/23 to 6/6	Gemini	4/25 to 6/13	Cancer
6/6 to 7/22	Cancer	6/13 to 7/31	Leo
7/22 to 9/7	Leo	7/31 to 9/16	Virgo
9/7 to 10/24	Virgo	9/16 to 11/1	Libra
10/24 to 12/11	Libra	11/1 to 12/15	Scorpio
12/11 to 12/31	Scorpio	12/15 to 12/31	Sagittarius
1939		*1943*	
1/1 to 1/28	Scorpio	1/1 to 1/26	Sagittarius
1/28 to 3/20	Sagittarius	1/26 to 3/8	Capricorn
3/20 to 5/24	Capricorn	3/8 to 4/16	Aquarius
5/24 to 7/21	Aquarius	4/16 to 5/26	Pisces
7/21 to 9/23	Capricorn	5/26 to 7/7	Aries
9/23 to 11/19	Aquarius	7/7 to 8/23	Taurus
11/19 to 12/31	Pisces	8/23 to 12/31	Gemini
1940		*1944*	
1/1 to 1/3	Pisces	1/1 to 3/27	Gemini
1/3 to 2/16	Aries	3/27 to 5/22	Cancer
2/16 to 4/1	Taurus	5/22 to 7/11	Leo
4/1 to 5/17	Gemini	7/11 to 8/28	Virgo
5/17 to 7/2	Cancer	8/28 to 10/13	Libra
7/2 to 8/19	Leo	10/13 to 11/25	Scorpio
8/19 to 10/5	Virgo	11/25 to 12/31	Sagittarius
10/5 to 11/20	Libra		
11/20 to 12/31	Scorpio	*1945*	
		1/1 to 1/5	Sagittarius
1941		1/5 to 2/13	Capricorn
1/1 to 1/4	Scorpio	2/13 to 3/24	Aquarius
1/4 to 2/17	Sagittarius	3/24 to 5/2	Pisces
2/17 to 4/1	Capricorn	5/2 to 6/10	Aries
4/1 to 5/15	Aquarius	6/10 to 7/22	Taurus
5/15 to 7/1	Pisces	7/22 to 9/7	Gemini
7/1 to 12/31	Aries	9/7 to 11/11	Cancer
		11/11 to 12/26	Leo
		12/26 to 12/31	Cancer

DATE	ZODIAC SIGN	DATE	ZODIAC SIGN
1946		*1950*	
1/1 to 4/22	Cancer	1/1 to 3/27	Libra
4/22 to 6/19	Leo	3/27 to 6/11	Virgo
6/19 to 8/9	Virgo	6/11 to 8/10	Libra
8/9 to 9/24	Libra	8/10 to 9/25	Scorpio
9/24 to 11/6	Scorpio	9/25 to 11/5	Sagittarius
11/6 to 12/16	Sagittarius	11/5 to 12/14	Capricorn
12/16 to 12/31	Capricorn	12/14 to 12/31	Aquarius
1947			
1/1 to 1/24	Capricorn	*1951*	
1/24 to 3/4	Aquarius	1/1 to 1/22	Aquarius
3/4 to 4/11	Pisces	1/22 to 3/1	Pisces
4/11 to 5/20	Aries	3/1 to 4/9	Aries
5/20 to 6/30	Taurus	4/9 to 5/21	Taurus
6/30 to 8/13	Gemini	5/21 to 7/3	Gemini
8/13 to 9/30	Cancer	7/3 to 8/17	Cancer
9/30 to 11/30	Leo	8/17 to 10/4	Leo
11/30 to 12/31	Virgo	10/4 to 11/23	Virgo
		11/23 to 12/31	Libra
1948			
1/1 to 2/11	Virgo	*1952*	
2/11 to 5/18	Leo	1/1 to 1/19	Libra
5/18 to 7/16	Virgo	1/19 to 8/27	Scorpio
7/16 to 9/3	Libra	8/27 to 10/11	Sagittarius
9/3 to 10/16	Scorpio	10/11 to 11/21	Capricorn
10/16 to 11/26	Sagittarius	11/21 to 12/30	Aquarius
11/26 to 12/31	Capricorn	12/30 to 12/31	Pisces
1949			
1/1 to 1/4	Capricorn	*1953*	
1/4 to 2/11	Aquarius	1/1 to 2/7	Pisces
2/11 to 3/21	Pisces	2/7 to 3/19	Aries
3/21 to 4/29	Aries	3/19 to 4/30	Taurus
4/29 to 6/9	Taurus	4/30 to 6/13	Gemini
6/9 to 7/22	Gemini	6/13 to 7/29	Cancer
7/22 to 9/6	Cancer	7/29 to 9/14	Leo
9/6 to 10/26	Leo	9/14 to 11/1	Virgo
10/26 to 12/25	Virgo	11/1 to 12/19	Libra
12/25 to 12/31	Libra	12/19 to 12/31	Scorpio

DATE	ZODIAC SIGN	DATE	ZODIAC SIGN
1954		**1958**	
1/1 to 2/9	Scorpio	1/1 to 2/3	Sagittarius
2/9 to 4/12	Sagittarius	2/3 to 3/16	Capricorn
4/12 to 7/2	Capricorn	3/16 to 4/26	Aquarius
7/2 to 8/24	Sagittarius	4/26 to 6/6	Pisces
8/24 to 10/21	Capricorn	6/6 to 7/20	Aries
10/21 to 12/3	Aquarius	7/20 to 9/20	Taurus
12/3 to 12/31	Pisces	9/20 to 10/28	Gemini
		10/28 to 12/31	Taurus
1955		**1959**	
1/1 to 1/14	Pisces	1/1 to 2/10	Taurus
1/14 to 2/25	Aries	2/10 to 4/9	Gemini
2/25 to 4/10	Taurus	4/9 to 5/31	Cancer
4/10 to 5/25	Gemini	5/31 to 7/19	Leo
5/25 to 7/10	Cancer	7/19 to 9/5	Virgo
7/10 to 8/26	Leo	9/5 to 10/20	Libra
8/26 to 10/12	Virgo	10/20 to 12/3	Scorpio
10/12 to 11/28	Libra	12/3 to 12/31	Sagittarius
11/28 to 12/31	Scorpio		
		1960	
1956		1/1 to 1/13	Sagittarius
1/1 to 1/13	Scorpio	1/13 to 2/22	Capricorn
1/13 to 2/28	Sagittarius	2/22 to 4/1	Aquarius
2/28 to 4/14	Capricorn	4/1 to 5/10	Pisces
4/14 to 6/2	Aquarius	5/10 to 6/19	Aries
6/2 to 12/5	Pisces	6/19 to 8/1	Taurus
12/5 to 12/31	Aries	8/1 to 9/20	Gemini
		9/20 to 12/31	Cancer
1957		**1961**	
1/1 to 1/28	Aries	1/1 to 2/4	Cancer
1/28 to 3/17	Taurus	2/4 to 2/6	Gemini
3/17 to 5/4	Gemini	2/6 to 5/5	Cancer
5/4 to 6/21	Cancer	5/5 to 6/28	Leo
6/21 to 8/7	Leo	6/28 to 8/16	Virgo
8/7 to 9/23	Virgo	8/16 to 10/1	Libra
9/23 to 11/8	Libra	10/1 to 11/13	Scorpio
11/8 to 12/22	Scorpio	11/13 to 12/24	Sagittarius
12/22 to 12/31	Sagittarius	12/24 to 12/31	Capricorn

DATE	ZODIAC SIGN	DATE	ZODIAC SIGN
1962		3/9 to 4/17	Aries
1/1 to 2/1	Capricorn	4/17 to 5/28	Taurus
2/1 to 3/11	Aquarius	5/28 to 7/10	Gemini
3/11 to 4/19	Pisces	7/10 to 8/25	Cancer
4/19 to 5/28	Aries	8/25 to 10/12	Leo
5/28 to 7/8	Taurus	10/12 to 12/3	Virgo
7/8 to 8/21	Gemini	12/3 to 12/31	Libra
8/21 to 10/11	Cancer		
10/11 to 12/31	Leo		
		1967	
		1/1 to 2/12	Libra
1963		2/12 to 3/30	Scorpio
1/1 to 6/2	Leo	3/30 to 7/19	Libra
6/2 to 7/26	Virgo	7/19 to 9/9	Scorpio
7/26 to 9/11	Libra	9/9 to 10/22	Sagittarius
9/11 to 10/25	Scorpio	10/22 to 12/1	Capricorn
10/25 to 12/4	Sagittarius	12/1 to 12/31	Aquarius
12/4 to 12/31	Capricorn		
		1968	
1964		1/1 to 1/8	Aquarius
1/1 to 1/12	Capricorn	1/8 to 2/16	Pisces
1/12 to 2/19	Aquarius	2/16 to 3/27	Aries
2/19 to 3/28	Pisces	3/27 to 5/8	Taurus
3/28 to 5/7	Aries	5/8 to 6/20	Gemini
5/7 to 6/16	Taurus	6/20 to 8/5	Cancer
6/16 to 7/30	Gemini	8/5 to 9/21	Leo
7/30 to 9/14	Cancer	9/21 to 11/8	Virgo
9/14 to 11/5	Leo	11/8 to 12/29	Libra
11/5 to 12/31	Virgo	12/29 to 12/31	Scorpio
1965			
1/1 to 6/28	Virgo	*1969*	
6/28 to 8/20	Libra	1/1 to 2/24	Scorpio
8/20 to 10/3	Scorpio	2/24 to 9/20	Sagittarius
10/3 to 11/13	Sagittarius	9/20 to 11/4	Capricorn
11/13 to 12/22	Capricorn	11/4 to 12/15	Aquarius
12/22 to 12/31	Aquarius	12/15 to 12/31	Pisces
1966		*1970*	
1/1 to 1/29	Aquarius	1/1 to 1/24	Pisces
1/29 to 3/9	Pisces	1/24 to 3/6	Aries

DATE	ZODIAC SIGN	DATE	ZODIAC SIGN
3/6 to 4/18	Taurus	4/19 to 6/8	Cancer
4/18 to 6/1	Gemini	6/8 to 7/27	Leo
6/1 to 7/17	Cancer	7/27 to 9/12	Virgo
7/17 to 9/2	Leo	9/12 to 10/27	Libra
9/2 to 10/19	Virgo	10/27 to 12/10	Scorpio
10/19 to 12/6	Libra	12/10 to 12/31	Sagittarius
12/6 to 12/31	Scorpio		

1971

1/1 to 1/22	Scorpio		
1/22 to 3/11	Sagittarius		

1975

1/1 to 1/21	Sagittarius
3/11 to 5/3	Capricorn
1/21 to 3/2	Capricorn
5/3 to 11/6	Aquarius
3/2 to 4/11	Aquarius
11/6 to 12/26	Pisces
4/11 to 5/20	Pisces
12/26 to 12/31	Aries
5/20 to 6/30	Aries

1972

6/30 to 8/14	Taurus
8/14 to 10/16	Gemini
1/1 to 2/10	Aries
10/16 to 11/25	Cancer
2/10 to 3/26	Taurus
11/25 to 12/31	Gemini
3/26 to 5/12	Gemini
5/12 to 6/28	Cancer
6/28 to 8/14	Leo

1976

8/14 to 9/30	Virgo
1/1 to 3/18	Gemini
9/30 to 11/15	Libra
3/18 to 5/15	Cancer
11/15 to 12/30	Scorpio
5/15 to 7/6	Leo
12/30 to 12/31	Sagittarius
7/6 to 8/23	Virgo
8/23 to 10/8	Libra

1973

10/8 to 11/20	Scorpio
11/20 to 12/31	Sagittarius
1/1 to 2/11	Sagittarius
2/11 to 3/26	Capricorn

1977

3/26 to 5/7	Aquarius
1/1	Sagittarius
5/7 to 6/20	Pisces
1/1 to 2/8	Capricorn
6/20 to 8/12	Aries
2/8 to 3/19	Aquarius
8/12 to 10/29	Taurus
3/19 to 4/27	Pisces
10/29 to 12/23	Aries
4/27 to 6/5	Aries
12/23 to 12/31	Taurus
6/5 to 7/17	Taurus
7/17 to 8/31	Gemini

1974

8/31 to 10/26	Cancer
1/1 to 2/26	Taurus
10/26 to 12/31	Leo
2/26 to 4/19	Gemini

DATE	ZODIAC SIGN	DATE	ZODIAC SIGN
1978		10/20 to 12/15	Virgo
1/1 to 1/25	Leo	12/15 to 12/31	Libra
1/25 to 4/10	Cancer		
4/10 to 6/13	Leo	*1982*	
6/13 to 8/3	Virgo	1/1 to 8/2	Libra
8/3 to 9/19	Libra	8/2 to 9/19	Scorpio
9/19 to 11/1	Scorpio	9/19 to 10/31	Sagittarius
11/1 to 12/12	Sagittarius	10/31 to 12/9	Capricorn
12/12 to 12/31	Capricorn	12/9 to 12/31	Aquarius
1979		*1983*	
1/1 to 1/20	Capricorn	1/1 to 1/17	Aquarius
1/20 to 2/27	Aquarius	1/17 to 2/24	Pisces
2/27 to 4/6	Pisces	2/24 to 4/5	Aries
4/6 to 5/15	Aries	4/5 to 5/16	Taurus
5/15 to 6/25	Taurus	5/16 to 6/28	Gemini
6/25 to 8/8	Gemini	6/28 to 8/13	Cancer
8/8 to 9/24	Cancer	8/13 to 9/29	Leo
9/24 to 11/19	Leo	9/29 to 11/17	Virgo
11/19 to 12/31	Virgo	11/17 to 12/31	Libra
1980		*1984*	
1/1 to 3/11	Virgo	1/1 to 1/10	Libra
3/11 to 5/3	Leo	1/10 to 8/17	Scorpio
5/3 to 7/10	Virgo	8/17 to 10/4	Sagittarius
7/10 to 8/28	Libra	10/4 to 11/15	Capricorn
8/28 to 10/11	Scorpio	11/15 to 12/24	Aquarius
10/11 to 11/21	Sagittarius	12/24 to 12/31	Pisces
11/21 to 12/30	Capricorn		
12/30 to 12/31	Aquarius	*1985*	
		1/1 to 2/2	Pisces
1981		2/2 to 3/14	Aries
1/1 to 2/6	Aquarius	3/14 to 4/25	Taurus
2/6 to 3/16	Pisces	4/25 to 6/8	Gemini
3/16 to 4/24	Aries	6/8 to 7/24	Cancer
4/24 to 6/4	Taurus	7/24 to 9/9	Leo
6/4 to 7/17	Gemini	9/9 to 10/27	Virgo
7/17 to 9/1	Cancer	10/27 to 12/14	Libra
9/1 to 10/20	Leo	12/14 to 12/31	Scorpio

DATE	ZODIAC SIGN	DATE	ZODIAC SIGN
1986		*1990*	
1/1 to 2/1	Scorpio	1/1 to 1/29	Sagittarius
2/1 to 3/27	Sagittarius	1/29 to 3/11	Capricorn
3/27 to 10/8	Capricorn	3/11 to 4/20	Aquarius
10/8 to 11/25	Aquarius	4/20 to 5/30	Pisces
11/25 to 12/31	Pisces	5/30 to 7/12	Aries
		7/12 to 8/30	Taurus
		8/30 to 12/13	Gemini
1987		12/13 to 12/31	Taurus
1/1 to 1/8	Pisces		
1/8 to 2/20	Aries		
2/20 to 4/5	Taurus	*1991*	
4/5 to 5/20	Gemini	1/1 to 1/20	Taurus
5/20 to 7/6	Cancer	1/20 to 4/2	Gemini
7/6 to 8/22	Leo	4/2 to 5/26	Cancer
8/22 to 10/8	Virgo	5/26 to 7/15	Leo
10/8 to 11/23	Libra	7/15 to 8/31	Virgo
11/23 to 12/31	Scorpio	8/31 to 10/16	Libra
		10/16 to 11/28	Scorpio
		11/28 to 12/31	Sagittarius
1988			
1/1 to 1/8	Scorpio		
1/8 to 2/21	Sagittarius	*1992*	
2/21 to 4/6	Capricorn	1/1 to 1/8	Sagittarius
4/6 to 5/21	Aquarius	1/8 to 2/17	Capricorn
5/21 to 7/13	Pisces	2/17 to 3/27	Aquarius
7/13 to 10/23	Aries	3/27 to 5/5	Pisces
10/23 to 11/1	Pisces	5/5 to 6/14	Aries
11/1 to 12/31	Aries	6/14 to 7/26	Taurus
		7/26 to 9/11	Gemini
		9/11 to 12/31	Cancer
1989			
1/1 to 1/18	Aries		
1/18 to 3/10	Taurus	*1993*	
3/10 to 4/28	Gemini	1/1 to 4/27	Cancer
4/28 to 6/16	Cancer	4/27 to 6/22	Leo
6/16 to 8/3	Leo	6/22 to 8/11	Virgo
8/3 to 9/19	Virgo	8/11 to 9/26	Libra
9/19 to 11/3	Libra	9/26 to 11/8	Scorpio
11/3 to 12/17	Scorpio	11/8 to 12/19	Sagittarius
12/17 to 12/31	Sagittarius	12/19 to 12/31	Capricorn

DATE	ZODIAC SIGN	DATE	ZODIAC SIGN
1994		**1998**	
1/1 to 1/27	Capricorn	1/1 to 1/24	Aquarius
1/27 to 3/6	Aquarius	1/24 to 3/4	Pisces
3/6 to 4/14	Pisces	3/4 to 4/12	Aries
4/14 to 5/23	Aries	4/12 to 5/23	Taurus
5/23 to 7/3	Taurus	5/23 to 7/5	Gemini
7/3 to 8/16	Gemini	7/5 to 8/20	Cancer
8/16 to 10/4	Cancer	8/20 to 10/7	Leo
10/4 to 12/11	Leo	10/7 to 11/26	Virgo
12/11 to 12/31	Virgo	11/26 to 12/31	Libra
1995		**1999**	
1/1 to 1/22	Virgo	1/1 to 1/26	Libra
1/22 to 5/25	Leo	1/26 to 5/5	Scorpio
5/25 to 7/20	Virgo	5/5 to 7/4	Libra
7/20 to 9/6	Libra	7/4 to 9/2	Scorpio
9/6 to 10/20	Scorpio	9/2 to 10/16	Sagittarius
10/20 to 11/30	Sagittarius	10/16 to 11/25	Capricorn
11/30 to 12/31	Capricorn	11/25 to 12/31	Aquarius
1996		**2000**	
1/1 to 1/7	Capricorn	1/1 to 1/3	Aquarius
1/7 to 2/14	Aquarius	1/3 to 2/11	Pisces
2/14 to 3/24	Pisces	2/11 to 3/22	Aries
3/24 to 5/2	Aries	3/22 to 5/3	Taurus
5/2 to 6/12	Taurus	5/3 to 6/16	Gemini
6/12 to 7/25	Gemini	6/16 to 7/31	Cancer
7/25 to 9/9	Cancer	7/31 to 9/16	Leo
9/9 to 10/29	Leo	9/16 to 11/3	Virgo
10/29 to 12/31	Virgo	11/3 to 12/23	Libra
		12/23 to 12/31	Scorpio
1997			
1/1 to 1/2	Virgo	**2001**	
1/2 to 3/8	Libra	1/1 to 2/14	Scorpio
3/8 to 6/18	Virgo	2/14 to 9/8	Sagittarius
6/18 to 8/13	Libra	9/8 to 10/27	Capricorn
8/13 to 9/28	Scorpio	10/27 to 12/8	Aquarius
9/28 to 11/8	Sagittarius	12/8 to 12/31	Pisces
11/8 to 12/17	Capricorn		
12/17 to 12/31	Aquarius		

DATE	ZODIAC SIGN	DATE	ZODIAC SIGN
2002		*2006*	
1/1 to 1/18	Pisces	1/1 to 2/17	Taurus
1/18 to 3/1	Aries	2/17 to 4/13	Gemini
3/1 to 4/13	Taurus	4/13 to 6/3	Cancer
4/13 to 5/27	Gemini	6/3 to 7/22	Leo
5/27 to 7/13	Cancer	7/22 to 9/7	Virgo
7/13 to 8/29	Leo	9/7 to 10/23	Libra
8/29 to 10/15	Virgo	10/23 to 12/5	Scorpio
10/15 to 12/1	Libra	12/5 to 12/31	Sagittarius
12/1 to 12/31	Scorpio		
		2007	
2003		1/1 to 1/16	Sagittarius
1/1 to 1/16	Scorpio	1/16 to 2/25	Capricorn
1/16 to 3/4	Sagittarius	2/25 to 4/5	Aquarius
3/4 to 4/21	Capricorn	4/5 to 5/15	Pisces
4/21 to 6/16	Aquarius	5/15 to 6/24	Aries
6/16 to 12/16	Pisces	6/24 to 8/6	Taurus
12/16 to 12/31	Aries	8/6 to 9/28	Gemini
		9/28 to 12/31	Cancer
2004			
1/1 to 2/2	Aries	*2008*	
2/2 to 3/20	Taurus	1/1	Cancer
3/20 to 5/6	Gemini	1/1 to 3/3	Gemini
5/6 to 6/23	Cancer	3/3 to 5/9	Cancer
6/23 to 8/9	Leo	5/9 to 7/1	Leo
8/9 to 9/25	Virgo	7/1 to 8/18	Virgo
9/25 to 11/10	Libra	8/18 to 10/3	Libra
11/10 to 12/25	Scorpio	10/3 to 11/15	Scorpio
12/25 to 12/31	Sagittarius	11/15 to 12/26	Sagittarius
		12/26 to 12/31	Capricorn
2005			
1/1 to 2/6	Sagittarius	*2009*	
2/6 to 3/20	Capricorn	1/1 to 2/4	Capricorn
3/20 to 4/30	Aquarius	2/4 to 3/14	Aquarius
4/30 to 6/11	Pisces	3/14 to 4/22	Pisces
6/11 to 7/27	Aries	4/22 to 5/31	Aries
7/27 to 12/31	Taurus	5/31 to 7/11	Taurus
		7/11 to 8/25	Gemini
		8/25 to 10/16	Cancer
		10/16 to 12/31	Leo

DATE	ZODIAC SIGN	DATE	ZODIAC SIGN
2010		**2014**	
1/1 to 6/6	Leo	1/1 to 7/25	Libra
6/6 to 7/29	Virgo	7/25 to 9/13	Scorpio
7/29 to 9/14	Libra	9/13 to 10/25	Sagittarius
9/14 to 10/27	Scorpio	10/25 to 12/4	Capricorn
10/27 to 12/7	Sagittarius	12/4 to 12/31	Aquarius
12/7 to 12/31	Capricorn		
		2015	
		1/1 to 1/11	Aquarius
2011		1/11 to 2/19	Pisces
1/1 to 1/15	Capricorn	2/19 to 3/31	Aries
1/15 to 2/22	Aquarius	3/31 to 5/11	Taurus
2/22 to 4/1	Pisces	5/11 to 6/24	Gemini
4/1 to 5/10	Aries	6/24 to 8/8	Cancer
5/10 to 6/20	Taurus	8/8 to 9/24	Leo
6/20 to 8/2	Gemini	9/24 to 11/12	Virgo
8/2 to 9/18	Cancer	11/12 to 12/31	Libra
9/18 to 11/10	Leo		
11/10 to 12/31	Virgo	**2016**	
		1/1 to 1/3	Libra
		1/3 to 3/5	Scorpio
2012		3/5 to 5/27	Sagittarius
1/1 to 7/3	Virgo	5/27 to 8/2	Scorpio
7/3 to 8/23	Libra	8/2 to 9/26	Sagittarius
8/23 to 10/6	Scorpio	9/26 to 11/8	Capricorn
10/6 to 11/16	Sagittarius	11/8 to 12/18	Aquarius
11/16 to 12/25	Capricorn	12/18 to 12/31	Pisces
12/25 to 12/31	Aquarius		
		2017	
2013		1/1 to 1/27	Pisces
1/1 to 2/1	Aquarius	1/27 to 3/9	Aries
2/1 to 3/11	Pisces	3/9 to 4/20	Taurus
3/11 to 4/19	Aries	4/20 to 6/4	Gemini
4/19 to 5/30	Taurus	6/4 to 7/20	Cancer
5/30 to 7/13	Gemini	7/20 to 9/4	Leo
7/13 to 8/27	Cancer	9/4 to 10/22	Virgo
8/27 to 10/14	Leo	10/22 to 12/8	Libra
10/14 to 12/7	Virgo	12/8 to 12/31	Scorpio
12/7 to 12/31	Libra		

DATE	ZODIAC SIGN	DATE	ZODIAC SIGN
2018		*2022*	
1/1 to 1/26	Scorpio	1/1 to 1/24	Sagittarius
1/26 to 3/17	Sagittarius	1/24 to 3/5	Capricorn
3/17 to 5/15	Capricorn	3/5 to 4/14	Aquarius
5/15 to 8/12	Aquarius	4/14 to 5/24	Pisces
8/12 to 9/10	Capricorn	5/24 to 7/4	Aries
9/10 to 11/15	Aquarius	7/4 to 8/19	Taurus
11/15 to 12/31	Pisces	8/19 to 12/31	Gemini
2019		*2023*	
1/1	Pisces	1/1 to 3/24	Gemini
1/1 to 2/13	Aries	3/24 to 5/20	Cancer
2/13 to 3/30	Taurus	5/20 to 7/9	Leo
3/30 to 5/15	Gemini	7/9 to 8/27	Virgo
5/15 to 7/1	Cancer	8/27 to 10/11	Libra
7/1 to 8/17	Leo	10/11 to 11/23	Scorpio
8/17 to 10/3	Virgo	11/23 to 12/31	Sagittarius
10/3 to 11/18	Libra		
11/18 to 12/31	Scorpio	*2024*	
		1/1 to 1/4	Sagittarius
		1/4 to 2/12	Capricorn
2020		2/12 to 3/22	Aquarius
1/1 to 1/2	Scorpio	3/22 to 4/30	Pisces
1/2 to 2/15	Sagittarius	4/30 to 6/8	Aries
2/15 to 3/30	Capricorn	6/8 to 7/20	Taurus
3/30 to 5/12	Aquarius	7/20 to 9/4	Gemini
5/12 to 6/27	Pisces	9/4 to 11/3	Cancer
6/27 to 12/31	Aries	11/3 to 12/31	Leo
2021			
1/1 to 1/6	Aries	*2025*	
1/6 to 3/3	Taurus	1/1 to 1/5	Leo
3/3 to 4/22	Gemini	1/5 to 4/17	Cancer
4/22 to 6/11	Cancer	4/17 to 6/16	Leo
6/11 to 7/29	Leo	6/16 to 8/6	Virgo
7/29 to 9/14	Virgo	8/6 to 9/21	Libra
9/14 to 10/30	Libra	9/21 to 11/4	Scorpio
10/30 to 12/12	Scorpio	11/4 to 12/14	Sagittarius
12/12 to 12/31	Sagittarius	12/14 to 12/31	Capricorn

JUPITER

Jupiter takes twelve years to travel once through the constellations of the zodiac, spending approximately eleven months in each sign. The following table will tell you which sign Jupiter was in when you were born.

For positions of Jupiter prior to 1936, go to "free Astrology Charts" on www.janspiller.com.

DATE	ZODIAC SIGN	DATE	ZODIAC SIGN
11/8/1935 to 12/1/1936	Sagittarius	1/17/1956 to 7/7/1956	Leo
12/1/1936 to 12/19/1937	Capricorn	7/7/1956 to 12/12/1956	Virgo
12/19/1937 to 5/13/1938	Aquarius	12/12/1956 to 2/19/1957	Libra
5/13/1938 to 7/29/1938	Pisces	2/19/1957 to 8/6/1957	Virgo
7/29/1938 to 12/29/1938	Aquarius	8/6/1957 to 1/13/1958	Libra
12/29/1938 to 5/11/1939	Pisces	1/13/1958 to 3/20/1958	Scorpio
5/11/1939 to 10/29/1939	Aries	3/20/1958 to 9/6/1958	Libra
10/29/1939 to 12/20/1939	Pisces	9/6/1958 to 2/10/1959	Scorpio
12/20/1939 to 5/15/1940	Aries	2/10/1959 to 4/24/1959	Sagittarius
5/15/1940 to 5/26/1941	Taurus	4/24/1959 to 10/5/1959	Scorpio
5/26/1941 to 6/9/1942	Gemini	10/5/1959 to 3/1/1960	Sagittarius
6/9/1942 to 6/30/1943	Cancer	3/1/1960 to 6/9/1960	Capricorn
6/30/1943 to 7/25/1944	Leo	6/9/1960 to 10/25/1960	Sagittarius
7/25/1944 to 8/24/1945	Virgo	10/25/1960 to 3/14/1961	Capricorn
8/24/1945 to 9/24/1946	Libra	3/14/1961 to 8/11/1961	Aquarius
9/24/1946 to 10/23/1947	Scorpio	8/11/1961 to 11/3/1961	Capricorn
10/23/1947 to 11/14/1948	Sagittarius	11/3/1961 to 3/25/1962	Aquarius
11/14/1948 to 4/12/1949	Capricorn	3/25/1962 to 4/3/1963	Pisces
4/12/1949 to 6/27/1949	Aquarius	4/3/1963 to 4/11/1964	Aries
6/27/1949 to 11/30/1949	Capricorn	4/11/1964 to 4/22/1965	Taurus
11/30/1949 to 4/14/1950	Aquarius	4/22/1965 to 9/20/1965	Gemini
4/14/1950 to 9/14/1950	Pisces	9/20/1965 to 11/16/1965	Cancer
9/14/1950 to 12/1/1950	Aquarius	11/16/1965 to 5/5/1966	Gemini
12/1/1950 to 4/21/1951	Pisces	5/5/1966 to 9/27/1966	Cancer
4/21/1951 to 4/28/1952	Aries	9/27/1966 to 1/15/1967	Leo
4/28/1952 to 5/9/1953	Taurus	1/15/1967 to 5/22/1967	Cancer
5/9/1953 to 5/23/1954	Gemini	5/22/1967 to 10/18/1967	Leo
5/23/1954 to 6/12/1955	Cancer	10/18/1967 to 2/26/1968	Virgo
6/12/1955 to 11/16/1955	Leo	2/26/1968 to 6/15/1968	Leo
11/16/1955 to 1/17/1956	Virgo	6/15/1968 to 11/15/1968	Virgo

DATE	ZODIAC SIGN	DATE	ZODIAC SIGN
11/15/1968 to 3/30/1969	Libra	8/17/1990 to 9/11/1991	Leo
3/30/1969 to 7/15/1969	Virgo	9/11/1991 to 10/10/1992	Virgo
7/15/1969 to 12/16/1969	Libra	10/10/1992 to 11/9/1993	Libra
12/16/1969 to 4/29/1970	Scorpio	11/9/1993 to 12/8/1994	Scorpio
4/29/1970 to 8/15/1970	Libra	12/8/1994 to 1/2/1996	Sagittarius
8/15/1970 to 1/13/1971	Scorpio	1/2/1996 to 1/21/1997	Capricorn
1/13/1971 to 6/4/1971	Sagittarius	1/21/1997 to 2/3/1998	Aquarius
6/4/1971 to 9/11/1971	Scorpio	2/3/1998 to 2/12/1999	Pisces
9/11/1971 to 2/6/1972	Sagittarius	2/12/1999 to 6/27/1999	Aries
2/6/1972 to 7/24/1972	Capricorn	6/27/1999 to 10/22/1999	Taurus
7/24/1972 to 9/25/1972	Sagittarius	10/22/1999 to 2/14/2000	Aries
9/25/1972 to 2/22/1973	Capricorn	2/14/2000 to 6/29/2000	Taurus
2/22/1973 to 3/7/1974	Aquarius	6/29/2000 to 7/12/2001	Gemini
3/7/1974 to 3/18/1975	Pisces	7/12/2001 to 8/1/2002	Cancer
3/18/1975 to 3/25/1976	Aries	8/1/2002 to 8/26/2003	Leo
3/25/1976 to 8/22/1976	Taurus	8/26/2003 to 9/24/2004	Virgo
8/22/1976 to 10/16/1976	Gemini	9/24/2004 to 10/25/2005	Libra
10/16/1976 to 4/3/1977	Taurus	10/25/2005 to 11/23/2006	Scorpio
4/3/1977 to 8/20/1977	Gemini	11/23/2006 to 12/18/2007	Sagittarius
8/20/1977 to 12/30/1977	Cancer	12/18/2007 to 1/5/2009	Capricorn
12/30/1977 to 4/11/1978	Gemini	1/5/2009 to 1/17/2010	Aquarius
4/11/1978 to 9/4/1978	Cancer	1/17/2010 to 6/5/2010	Pisces
9/4/1978 to 2/28/1979	Leo	6/5/2010 to 9/8/2010	Aries
2/28/1979 to 4/19/1979	Cancer	9/8/2010 to 1/22/2011	Pisces
4/19/1979 to 9/28/1979	Leo	1/22/2011 to 6/4/2011	Aries
9/28/1979 to 10/26/1980	Virgo	6/4/2011 to 6/11/2012	Taurus
10/26/1980 to 11/26/1981	Libra	6/11/2012 to 6/25/2013	Gemini
11/26/1981 to 12/25/1982	Scorpio	6/25/2013 to 7/15/2014	Cancer
12/25/1982 to 1/19/1984	Sagittarius	7/15/2014 to 8/10/2015	Leo
1/19/1984 to 2/6/1985	Capricorn	8/10/2015 to 9/8/2016	Virgo
2/6/1985 to 2/20/1986	Aquarius	9/8/2016 to 10/10/2017	Libra
2/20/1986 to 3/2/1987	Pisces	10/10/2017 to 11/8/2018	Scorpio
3/2/1987 to 3/8/1988	Aries	11/8/2018 to 12/2/2019	Sagittarius
3/8/1988 to 7/21/1988	Taurus	12/2/2019 to 12/19/2020	Capricorn
7/21/1988 to 11/30/1988	Gemini	12/19/2020 to 5/13/2021	Aquarius
11/30/1988 to 3/10/1989	Taurus	5/13/2021 to 7/28/2021	Pisces
3/10/1989 to 7/30/1989	Gemini	7/28/2021 to 12/28/2021	Aquarius
7/30/1989 to 8/17/1990	Cancer	12/28/2021 to 5/10/2022	Pisces

DATE	ZODIAC SIGN	DATE	ZODIAC SIGN
5/10/2022 to 10/27/2022	Aries	5/16/2023 to 5/25/2024	Taurus
10/27/2022 to 12/20/2022	Pisces	5/25/2024 to 6/9/2025	Gemini
12/20/2022 to 5/16/2023	Aries	6/9/2025 to 6/29/2026	Cancer

SATURN

Saturn, a slower moving planet, requires about twenty-nine years to circle the zodiac, spending approximately two and a half years in each of the signs. The following table will tell you which sign Saturn was in when you were born.

For positions of Saturn prior to 1935, go to "Free Astrology Charts" on www.janspiller.com.

DATE	ZODIAC SIGN	DATE	ZODIAC SIGN
2/14/1935 to 4/24/1937	Pisces	9/16/1964 to 12/15/1964	Aquarius
4/24/1937 to 10/17/1937	Aries	12/15/1964 to 3/3/1967	Pisces
10/17/1937 to 1/13/1938	Pisces	3/3/1967 to 4/29/1969	Aries
1/13/1938 to 7/5/1939	Aries	4/29/1969 to 6/18/1971	Taurus
7/5/1939 to 9/21/1939	Taurus	6/18/1971 to 1/9/1972	Gemini
9/21/1939 to 3/19/1940	Aries	1/9/1972 to 2/21/1972	Taurus
3/19/1940 to 5/8/1942	Taurus	2/21/1972 to 8/1/1973	Gemini
5/8/1942 to 6/19/1944	Gemini	8/1/1973 to 1/7/1974	Cancer
6/19/1944 to 8/2/1946	Cancer	1/7/1974 to 4/18/1974	Gemini
8/2/1946 to 9/18/1948	Leo	4/18/1974 to 9/16/1975	Cancer
9/18/1948 to 4/2/1949	Virgo	9/16/1975 to 1/14/1976	Leo
4/2/1949 to 5/29/1949	Leo	1/14/1976 to 6/4/1976	Cancer
5/29/1949 to 11/20/1950	Virgo	6/4/1976 to 11/16/1977	Leo
11/20/1950 to 3/7/1951	Libra	11/16/1977 to 1/4/1978	Virgo
3/7/1951 to 8/13/1951	Virgo	1/4/1978 to 7/26/1978	Leo
8/13/1951 to 10/22/1953	Libra	7/26/1978 to 9/20/1980	Virgo
10/22/1953 to 1/12/1956	Scorpio	9/20/1980 to 11/28/1982	Libra
1/12/1956 to 5/13/1956	Sagittarius	11/28/1982 to 5/6/1983	Scorpio
5/13/1956 to 10/10/1956	Scorpio	5/6/1983 to 8/24/1983	Libra
10/10/1956 to 1/5/1959	Sagittarius	8/24/1983 to 11/16/1985	Scorpio
1/5/1959 to 1/3/1962	Capricorn	11/16/1985 to 2/13/1988	Sagittarius
1/3/1962 to 3/23/1964	Aquarius	2/13/1988 to 6/9/1988	Capricorn
3/23/1964 to 9/16/1964	Pisces	6/9/1988 to 11/11/1988	Sagittarius

DATE	ZODIAC SIGN	DATE	ZODIAC SIGN
11/11/1988 to 2/6/1991	Capricorn	10/29/2009 to 4/7/2010	Libra
2/6/1991 to 5/20/1993	Aquarius	4/7/2010 to 7/21/2010	Virgo
5/20/1993 to 6/29/1993	Pisces	7/21/2010 to 10/5/2012	Libra
6/29/1993 to 1/28/1994	Aquarius	10/5/2012 to 12/23/2014	Scorpio
1/28/1994 to 4/6/1996	Pisces	12/23/2014 to 6/14/2015	Sagittarius
4/6/1996 to 6/8/1998	Aries	6/14/2015 to 9/17/2015	Scorpio
6/8/1998 to 10/25/1998	Taurus	9/17/2015 to 12/19/2017	Sagittarius
10/25/1998 to 2/28/1999	Aries	12/19/2017 to 3/21/2020	Capricorn
2/28/1999 to 8/9/2000	Taurus	3/21/2020 to 7/1/2020	Aquarius
8/9/2000 to 10/15/2000	Gemini	7/1/2020 to 12/16/2020	Capricorn
10/15/2000 to 4/20/2001	Taurus	12/16/2020 to 3/7/2023	Aquarius
4/20/2001 to 6/3/2003	Gemini	3/7/2023 to 5/24/2025	Pisces
6/3/2003 to 7/16/2005	Cancer	5/24/2025 to 8/31/2025	Aries
7/16/2005 to 9/2/2007	Leo	8/31/2025 to 2/13/2026	Pisces
9/2/2007 to 10/29/2009	Virgo		

URANUS

Uranus, one of the slower-moving planets, takes slightly more than eighty-four years to travel through all the constellations of the zodiac. Uranus spends approximately seven years in each sign. The following table will tell you in which sign Uranus was located at the time of your birth.

For positions of Uranus prior to 1936, go to "Free Astrology Charts" on www.janspiller.com.

DATE	ZODIAC SIGN	DATE	ZODIAC SIGN
3/27/1935 to 8/7/1941	Taurus	6/9/1956 to 11/1/1961	Leo
8/7/1941 to 10/4/1941	Gemini	11/1/1961 to 1/9/1962	Virgo
10/4/1941 to 5/14/1942	Taurus	1/9/1962 to 8/9/1962	Leo
5/14/1942 to 8/30/1948	Gemini	8/9/1962 to 9/28/1968	Virgo
8/30/1948 to 11/12/1948	Cancer	9/28/1968 to 5/20/1969	Libra
11/12/1948 to 6/9/1949	Gemini	5/20/1969 to 6/23/1969	Virgo
6/9/1949 to 8/24/1955	Cancer	6/23/1969 to 11/20/1974	Libra
8/24/1955 to 1/27/1956	Leo	11/20/1974 to 5/1/1975	Scorpio
1/27/1956 to 6/9/1956	Cancer	5/1/1975 to 9/7/1975	Libra

DATE	ZODIAC SIGN	DATE	ZODIAC SIGN
9/7/1975 to 2/16/1981	Scorpio	9/14/2003 to 12/29/2003	Aquarius
2/16/1981 to 3/20/1981	Sagittarius	12/29/2003 to 5/27/2010	Pisces
3/20/1981 to 11/16/1981	Scorpio	5/27/2010 to 8/13/2010	Aries
11/16/1981 to 2/14/1988	Sagittarius	8/13/2010 to 3/11/2011	Pisces
2/14/1988 to 5/26/1988	Capricorn	3/11/2011 to 5/15/2018	Aries
5/26/1988 to 12/2/1988	Sagittarius	5/15/2018 to 11/6/2018	Taurus
12/2/1988 to 4/1/1995	Capricorn	11/6/2018 to 3/5/2019	Aries
4/1/1995 to 6/8/1995	Aquarius	3/5/2019 to 7/6/2025	Taurus
6/8/1995 to 1/11/1996	Capricorn	7/6/2025 to 11/7/2025	Gemini
1/11/1996 to 3/10/2003	Aquarius	11/7/2025 to 4/25/2026	Taurus
3/10/2003 to 9/14/2003	Pisces		

NEPTUNE

Neptune, one of the slowest planets, takes nearly 165 years to travel once through the zodiac, or approximately fourteen and a half years in each astrological sign. The following table will tell you in which sign Neptune was located when you were born.

For the positions of Neptune prior to 1930, go to "Free Astrology Charts" on www. janspiller.com.

DATE	ZODIAC SIGN	DATE	ZODIAC SIGN
7/24/1929 to 10/3/1942	Virgo	6/22/1984 to 11/20/1984	Sagittarius
10/3/1942 to 4/16/1943	Libra	11/20/1984 to 1/28/1998	Capricorn
4/16/1943 to 8/2/1943	Virgo	1/28/1998 to 8/22/1998	Aquarius
8/2/1943 to 12/24/1955	Libra	8/22/1998 to 11/27/1998	Capricorn
12/24/1955 to 3/11/1956	Scorpio	11/27/1998 to 4/3/2011	Aquarius
3/11/1956 to 10/18/1956	Libra	4/3/2011 to 8/4/2011	Pisces
10/18/1956 to 6/15/1957	Scorpio	8/4/2011 to 2/3/2012	Aquarius
6/15/1957 to 8/5/1957	Libra	2/3/2012 to 3/29/2025	Pisces
8/5/1957 to 1/4/1970	Scorpio	3/29/2025 to 10/22/2025	Aries
1/4/1970 to 5/2/1970	Sagittarius	10/22/2025 to 1/25/2026	Pisces
5/2/1970 to 11/6/1970	Scorpio		
11/6/1970 to 1/18/1984	Sagittarius		
1/18/1984 to 6/22/1984	Capricorn		

PLUTO

Pluto, the slowest-moving of all the planets, spends 248 years in traveling just one time through all the constellations of the zodiac. Pluto stays an average of twenty years in each sign, although Pluto's orbit around the Sun is egg shaped and it moves through some of the signs much more rapidly than through others. Pluto's shortest time, in the sign of Scorpio, is twelve years, while it spends the longest time, thirty years, traveling through the constellation of Taurus. The following table will tell you which sign Pluto was in when you were born.

For the positions of Pluto prior to 1915 go to "Free Astrology Charts" on www.janspiller .com.

DATE	ZODIAC SIGN	DATE	ZODIAC SIGN
5/26/1914 to 10/7/1937	Cancer	11/5/1983 to 5/18/1984	Scorpio
10/7/1937 to 11/24/1937	Leo	5/18/1984 to 8/27/1984	Libra
11/24/1937 to 8/3/1938	Cancer	8/27/1984 to 1/16/1995	Scorpio
8/3/1938 to 2/7/1939	Leo	1/16/1995 to 4/20/1995	Sagittarius
2/7/1939 to 6/13/1939	Cancer	4/20/1995 to 11/10/1995	Scorpio
6/13/1939 to 10/19/1956	Leo	11/10/1995 to 1/25/2008	Sagittarius
10/19/1956 to 1/14/1957	Virgo	1/25/2008 to 6/13/2008	Capricorn
1/14/1957 to 8/18/1957	Leo	6/13/2008 to 11/26/2008	Sagittarius
8/18/1957 to 4/11/1958	Virgo	11/26/2008 to 3/23/2023	Capricorn
4/11/1958 to 6/10/1958	Leo	3/23/2023 to 6/10/2023	Aquarius
6/10/1958 to 10/4/1971	Virgo	6/10/2023 to 1/20/2024	Capricorn
10/4/1971 to 4/16/1972	Libra	1/20/2024 to 9/1/2024	Aquarius
4/16/1972 to 7/30/1972	Virgo	9/1/2024 to 11/19/2024	Capricorn
7/30/1972 to 11/5/1983	Libra	11/19/2024 to 3/8/2043	Aquarius

THE PRENATAL ECLIPSES: 1930–2050

SOLAR ECLIPSE

Find the date closest to your birth date to locate your prenatal solar eclipse. Be sure that the date is *before* your birth date because these eclipses are prenatal. To print out your entire free birth chart—including the houses containing your prenatal eclipses—go to www.janspiller.com and click on "Free Astrology Charts" on the home page.

For the positions of the solar eclipses prior to 1930, go to "Free Astrology Charts" on www. janspiller.com.

DATE	SIGN	DEGREE	DATE	SIGN	DEGREE
April 28, 1930	Taurus	07°45'	June 8, 1937	Gemini	17°36'
October 21, 1930	Libra	27°46'	December 2, 1937	Sagittarius	10°23'
April 18, 1931	Aries	27°03'	May 29, 1938	Gemini	07°32'
September 12, 1931	Virgo	18°27'	November 22, 1938	Scorpio	29°02'
March 7, 1932	Pisces	16°32'	April 19, 1939	Aries	28°43'
August 31, 1932	Virgo	08°10'	October 12, 1939	Libra	18°37'
February 24, 1933	Pisces	05°29'	April 7, 1940	Aries	17°52'
August 21, 1933	Leo	27°42'	October 1, 1940	Libra	08°11'
February 14, 1934	Aquarius	24°39'	March 27, 1941	Aries	06°46'
August 10, 1934	Leo	17°02'	September 21, 1941	Virgo	27°48'
January 5, 1934	Capricorn	13°57'	March 16, 1942	Pisces	25°46
February 3, 1935	Aquarius	13°56'	August 12, 1942	Leo	18°45'
June 30, 1935	Cancer	08°04'	September 10, 1942	Virgo	17°18'
July 30, 1935	Leo	06°18'	February 4, 1943	Aquarius	15°17'
December 25, 1935	Capricorn	03°01'	August 1, 1943	Leo	08°03'
June 19, 1936	Gemini	27°44'	January 25, 1944	Aquarius	04°33'
December 13, 1936	Sagittarius	21°49'	July 20, 1944	Cancer	27°22'

DATE	SIGN	DEGREE	DATE	SIGN	DEGREE
January 14, 1945	Capricorn	23°41'	July 31, 1962	Leo	07°49'
July 9, 1945	Cancer	16°57'	January 25, 1963	Aquarius	04°52'
January 3, 1946	Capricorn	12°33'	July 20, 1963	Cancer	27°24'
May 30, 1946	Gemini	08°49'	January 14, 1964	Capricorn	23°43'
June 29, 1946	Cancer	06°49'	June 10, 1964	Gemini	19°19'
November 23, 1946	Sagittarius	00°50'	July 9, 1964	Cancer	17°16'
May 20, 1947	Taurus	28°42'	December 4, 1964	Sagittarius	11°56'
November 12, 1947	Scorpio	19°36'	May 30, 1965	Gemini	09°13'
May 9, 1948	Taurus	18°22'	November 23, 1965	Sagittarius	00°40'
November 1, 1948	Scorpio	08°44'	May 20, 1966	Taurus	28°55'
April 28, 1949	Taurus	07°42'	November 12, 1966	Scorpio	19°45'
October 21, 1949	Libra	28°09'	May 9, 1967	Taurus	18°18'
March 18, 1950	Pisces	27°28'	November 2, 1967	Scorpio	09°07'
September 12, 1950	Virgo	18°48'	March 28, 1968	Aries	08°19'
March 7, 1951	Pisces	16°29'	September 22, 1968	Virgo	29°30'
September 1, 1951	Virgo	08°16'	March 18, 1969	Pisces	27°25'
February 25, 1952	Pisces	05°43'	September 11, 1969	Virgo	18°53'
August 20, 1952	Leo	27°31'	March 7, 1970	Pisces	16°44'
February 14, 1953	Aquarius	25°03'	August 31, 1970	Virgo	08°04'
July 11, 1953	Cancer	18°30'	February 25, 1971	Pisces	06°09'
August 9, 1953	Leo	16°45'	July 22, 1971	Cancer	28°56'
January 5, 1954	Capricorn	14°13'	August 20, 1971	Leo	27°15'
June 30, 1954	Cancer	08°10'	January 16, 1972	Capricorn	25°25'
December 25, 1954	Capricorn	02°59'	July 10, 1972	Cancer	18°37'
June 20, 1955	Gemini	28°05'	January 4, 1973	Capricorn	14°10'
December 14, 1955	Sagittarius	21°31'	June 30, 1973	Cancer	08°32'
June 8, 1956	Gemini	18°02'	December 24, 1973	Capricorn	02°40'
December 2, 1956	Sagittarius	10°09'	June 20, 1974	Gemini	28°30'
April 29, 1957	Taurus	09°23'	December 13, 1974	Sagittarius	21°17'
October 23, 1957	Libra	29°31'	May 11, 1975	Taurus	19°59'
April 19, 1958	Aries	28°34'	November 3, 1975	Scorpio	10°29'
October 12, 1958	Libra	19°01'	April 29, 1976	Taurus	09°13'
April 8, 1959	Aries	17°34'	October 23, 1976	Libra	29°55'
October 2, 1959	Libra	08°34'	April 18, 1977	Aries	28°17'
March 27, 1960	Aries	06°39'	October 12, 1977	Libra	19°24'
September 20, 1960	Virgo	27°58'	April 7, 1978	Aries	17°27'
February 15, 1961	Aquarius	26°25'	October 2, 1978	Libra	08°43'
August 11, 1961	Leo	18°31'	February 26, 1979	Pisces	07°29'
February 5, 1962	Aquarius	15°43'	August 22, 1979	Leo	29°01'

DATE	SIGN	DEGREE	DATE	SIGN	DEGREE
February 16, 1980	Aquarius	26°50'	February 26, 1998	Pisces	07°55'
August 10, 1980	Leo	18°17'	August 22, 1998	Leo	28°48'
February 4, 1981	Aquarius	16°02'	February 16, 1999	Aquarius	27°08'
July 31, 1981	Leo	07°51'	August 11, 1999	Leo	18°21'
January 25, 1982	Aquarius	04°54'	February 5, 2000	Aquarius	16°02'
June 21, 1982	Gemini	29°47'	July 31, 2000	Leo	08°12'
July 20, 1982	Cancer	27°43'	December 25, 2000	Capricorn	04°14'
December 15, 1982	Sagittarius	23°04'	June 21, 2001	Cancer	00°10'
June 11, 1983	Gemini	19°43'	December 14, 2001	Sagittarius	22°56'
December 4, 1983	Sagittarius	11°47'	June 10, 2002	Gemini	19°54'
May 30, 1984	Gemini	09°26'	December 4, 2002	Sagittarius	11°58'
November 22, 1984	Sagittarius	00°50'	May 31, 2003	Gemini	09°20'
May 19, 1985	Taurus	28°50'	November 23, 2003	Sagittarius	01°14'
November 12, 1985	Scorpio	20°09'	April 19, 2004	Aries	29°49'
April 9, 1986	Aries	19°06'	October 14, 2004	Libra	21°06'
October 3, 1986	Libra	10°16'	April 8, 2005	Aries	19°06'
March 29, 1987	Aries	08°18'	October 3, 2005	Libra	10°19'
September 23, 1987	Virgo	29°34'	March 29, 2006	Aries	08°35'
March 18, 1988	Pisces	27°42'	September 22, 2006	Virgo	29°20'
September 11, 1988	Virgo	18°40'	March 19, 2007	Pisces	28°07'
March 7, 1989	Pisces	17°10'	September 11, 2007	Virgo	18°25'
August 31, 1989	Virgo	07°48'	February 7, 2008	Aquarius	17°44'
January 26, 1990	Aquarius	06°35'	August 1, 2008	Leo	09°32'
July 22, 1990	Cancer	29°04'	January 26, 2009	Aquarius	06°30'
January 15, 1991	Capricorn	25°20'	July 22, 2009	Cancer	29°27'
July 11, 1991	Cancer	18°59'	January 15, 2010	Capricorn	25°01'
January 4, 1992	Capricorn	13°51'	July 11, 2010	Cancer	19°24'
June 30, 1992	Cancer	08°57'	January 4, 2011	Capricorn	13°39'
December 24, 1992	Capricorn	02°28'	June 1, 2011	Gemini	11°02'
May 21, 1993	Gemini	00°31'	July 1, 2011	Cancer	09°12'
November 13, 1993	Scorpio	21°32'	November 25, 2011	Sagittarius	02°37'
May 10, 1994	Taurus	19°48'	May 20, 2012	Gemini	00°21'
November 3, 1994	Scorpio	10°54'	November 13, 2012	Scorpio	21°57'
April 29, 1995	Taurus	08°56'	May 10, 2013	Taurus	19°31'
October 24, 1995	Scorpio	00°18'	November 3, 2013	Scorpio	11°16'
April 17, 1996	Aries	28°12'	April 29, 2014	Taurus	08°52'
October 12, 1996	Libra	19°32'	October 23, 2014	Scorpio	00°25'
March 9, 1997	Pisces	18°31'	March 20, 2015	Pisces	29°27'
September 1, 1997	Virgo	09°34'	September 13, 2015	Virgo	20°10'

DATE	SIGN	DEGREE	DATE	SIGN	DEGREE
March 9, 2016	Pisces	18°56'	September 23, 2033	Libra	00°51'
September 1, 2016	Virgo	09°21'	March 20, 2034	Pisces	29°52'
February 26, 2017	Pisces	08°12'	September 12, 2034	Virgo	19°59'
August 21, 2017	Leo	28°53'	March 9, 2035	Pisces	19°12'
February 15, 2018	Aquarius	27°08'	September 2, 2035	Virgo	09°28'
July 13, 2018	Cancer	20°41'	February 27, 2036	Pisces	08°10'
August 11, 2018	Leo	18°42'	July 23, 2036	Leo	01°09'
January 6, 2019	Capricorn	15°25'	August 21, 2036	Leo	29°14'
July 2, 2019	Cancer	10°38'	January 16, 2037	Capricorn	26°35'
December 26, 2019	Capricorn	04°07'	July 13, 2037	Cancer	21°04'
June 21, 2020	Cancer	00°21'	January 5, 2038	Capricorn	15°18'
December 14, 2020	Sagittarius	23°08'	July 2, 2038	Cancer	10°47'
June 10, 2021	Gemini	19°47'	December 26, 2038	Capricorn	04°20'
December 4, 2021	Sagittarius	12°22'	June 21, 2039	Cancer	00°13'
April 30, 2022	Taurus	10°28'	December 15, 2039	Sagittarius	23°33'
October 25, 2022	Scorpio	02°00'	May 11, 2040	Taurus	21°04'
April 20, 2023	Aries	29°50'	November 4, 2040	Scorpio	12°58'
October 14, 2023	Libra	21°08'	April 30, 2041	Taurus	10°30'
April 8, 2024	Aries	19°24'	October 25, 2041	Scorpio	02°01'
October 2, 2024	Libra	10°04'	April 20, 2042	Taurus	00°09'
March 29, 2025	Aries	09°00'	October 14, 2042	Libra	20°52'
September 21, 2025	Virgo	29°05'	April 9, 2043	Aries	19°50'
February 17, 2026	Aquarius	28°50'	October 3, 2043	Libra	09°49'
August 12, 2026	Leo	20°02'	February 28, 2044	Pisces	09°53'
February 6, 2027	Aquarius	17°38'	August 23, 2044	Virgo	00°34'
August 2, 2027	Leo	09°55'	February 16, 2045	Aquarius	28°43'
January 26, 2028	Aquarius	06°11'	August 12, 2045	Leo	20°25'
July 22, 2028	Cancer	29°51'	February 5, 2046	Aquarius	17°19'
January 14, 2029	Capricorn	24°50'	August 2, 2046	Leo	10°20'
June 12, 2029	Gemini	21°29'	January 26, 2047	Aquarius	06°00'
July 11, 2029	Cancer	19°38'	June 23, 2047	Cancer	01°56'
December 5, 2029	Sagittarius	13°45'	July 22, 2047	Leo	00°05'
June 1, 2030	Gemini	10°50'	December 16, 2047	Sagittarius	24°56'
November 25, 2030	Sagittarius	03°02'	June 11, 2048	Gemini	21°17'
May 21, 2031	Gemini	00°04'	December 5, 2048	Sagittarius	14°10'
November 14, 2031	Scorpio	22°18'	May 31, 2049	Gemini	10°34'
May 9, 2032	Taurus	19°29'	November 25, 2049	Sagittarius	03°23'
November 3, 2032	Scorpio	11°22'	May 20, 2050	Gemini	00°02'
March 30, 2033	Aries	10°21'	November 14, 2050	Scorpio	22°23'

LUNAR ECLIPSE

Find the date closest to your birth date to locate your prenatal lunar eclipse. Be sure that the date is *before* your birth date because these eclipses are prenatal. To print out your entire free birth chart—including the houses containing your prenatal eclipses—go to www.janspiller.com and click on "Free Astrology Charts" on the home page.

For the positions of the lunar eclipses prior to 1930, go to "Free Astrology Charts" on www.janspiller.com.

DATE	SIGN	DEGREE	DATE	SIGN	DEGREE
April 13, 1930	Libra	22°35'	March 3, 1942	Virgo	11°48'
October 7, 1930	Aries	13°47'	August 26, 1942	Pisces	02°17'
April 2, 1931	Libra	12°07'	February 20, 1943	Virgo	00°43'
September 26, 1931	Aries	02°45'	August 15, 1943	Aquarius	22°05'
March 22, 1932	Libra	01°41'	February 9, 1944	Leo	19°21'
September 14, 1932	Pisces	21°49'	July 6, 1944	Capricorn	13°58'
February 10, 1933	Leo	21°22'	August 4, 1944	Aquarius	11°59'
March 12, 1933	Virgo	21°05'	December 29, 1944	Cancer	07°47'
August 5, 1933	Aquarius	12°53'	June 25, 1945	Capricorn	03°40'
September 4, 1933	Pisces	11°12'	December 19, 1945	Gemini	26°50'
January 30, 1934	Leo	10°07'	June 14, 1946	Sagittarius	23°05'
July 26, 1934	Aquarius	02°48'	December 8, 1946	Gemini	16°03'
January 19, 1935	Cancer	28°39'	June 3, 1947	Sagittarius	12°22'
July 16, 1935	Capricorn	22°45'	November 28, 1947	Gemini	05°16'
January 8, 1936	Cancer	17°19'	April 23, 1948	Scorpio	03°18'
July 4, 1936	Capricorn	12°31'	October 18, 1948	Aries	24°37'
December 28, 1936	Cancer	06°16'	April 13, 1949	Libra	22°54'
May 25, 1937	Sagittarius	03°40'	October 7, 1949	Aries	13°30'
November 18, 1937	Taurus	25°35'	April 2, 1950	Libra	12°32'
May 14, 1938	Scorpio	22°54'	September 26, 1950	Aries	02°31'
November 7, 1938	Taurus	14°51'	February 21, 1951	Virgo	02°26'
May 3, 1939	Scorpio	12°18'	March 23, 1951	Libra	02°00'
October 28, 1939	Taurus	03°57'	August 17, 1951	Aquarius	23°25'
March 23, 1940	Libra	03°01'	September 15, 1951	Pisces	21°52'
April 22, 1940	Scorpio	01°54'	February 11, 1952	Leo	21°14'
October 16, 1940	Aries	22°49'	August 5, 1952	Aquarius	13°17'
March 13, 1941	Virgo	22°31'	January 29, 1953	Leo	09°48'
September 5, 1941	Pisces	12°45'	July 26, 1953	Aquarius	03°12'

DATE	SIGN	DEGREE	DATE	SIGN	DEGREE
January 19, 1954	Cancer	28°30'	September 15, 1970	Pisces	22°12'
July 16, 1954	Capricorn	22°57'	February 10, 1971	Leo	20°55'
January 8, 1955	Cancer	17°28'	August 6, 1971	Aquarius	13°41'
June 5, 1955	Sagittarius	14°08'	January 30, 1972	Leo	09°39'
November 29, 1955	Gemini	06°42'	July 26, 1972	Aquarius	03°24'
May 24, 1956	Sagittarius	03°25'	January 18, 1973	Cancer	28°40'
November 18, 1956	Taurus	25°55'	June 15, 1973	Sagittarius	24°35'
May 13, 1957	Scorpio	22°52'	July 15, 1973	Capricorn	22°51'
November 7, 1957	Taurus	14°55'	December 10, 1973	Gemini	17°51'
April 4, 1958	Libra	13°52'	June 4, 1974	Sagittarius	13°54'
May 3, 1958	Scorpio	12°34'	November 29, 1974	Gemini	07°01'
October 27, 1958	Taurus	03°43'	May 25, 1975	Sagittarius	03°25'
March 24, 1959	Libra	03°26'	November 18, 1975	Taurus	25°58'
September 17, 1959	Pisces	23°24'	May 13, 1976	Scorpio	23°10'
March 13, 1960	Virgo	22°47'	November 6, 1976	Taurus	14°41'
September 5, 1960	Pisces	12°53'	April 4, 1977	Libra	14°17'
March 2, 1961	Virgo	11°45'	September 27, 1977	Aries	04°07'
August 26, 1961	Pisces	02°39'	March 24, 1978	Libra	03°40'
February 19, 1962	Virgo	00°25'	September 16, 1978	Pisces	23°33'
July 17, 1962	Capricorn	24°25'	March 13, 1979	Virgo	22°42'
August 15, 1962	Aquarius	22°30'	September 6, 1979	Pisces	13°16'
January 9, 1963	Cancer	18°59'	March 1, 1980	Virgo	11°26'
July 6, 1963	Capricorn	14°06'	July 27, 1980	Aquarius	04°42'
December 30, 1963	Cancer	08°01'	August 26, 1980	Pisces	03°03'
June 25, 1964	Capricorn	03°30'	January 20, 1981	Leo	00°10'
December 19, 1964	Gemini	27°14'	July 17, 1981	Capricorn	24°31'
June 14, 1965	Sagittarius	22°48'	January 9, 1982	Cancer	19°14'
December 8, 1965	Gemini	16°25'	July 6, 1982	Capricorn	13°55'
May 4, 1966	Scorpio	13°56'	December 30, 1982	Cancer	08°27'
October 29, 1966	Taurus	05°32'	June 25, 1983	Capricorn	03°14'
April 24, 1967	Scorpio	03°37'	December 20, 1983	Gemini	27°36'
October 18, 1967	Aries	24°21'	May 15, 1984	Scorpio	24°32'
April 13, 1968	Libra	23°20'	June 13, 1984	Sagittarius	22°45'
October 6, 1968	Aries	13°17'	November 8, 1984	Taurus	16°30'
April 2, 1969	Libra	12°51'	May 4, 1985	Scorpio	14°17'
August 27, 1969	Pisces	03°58'	October 28, 1985	Taurus	05°15'
September 25, 1969	Aries	02°35'	April 24, 1986	Scorpio	04°03'
February 21, 1970	Virgo	02°18'	October 17, 1986	Aries	24°07'
August 17, 1970	Aquarius	23°49'	April 14, 1987	Libra	23°38'

DATE	SIGN	DEGREE	DATE	SIGN	DEGREE
October 7, 1987	Aries	13°22'	October 28, 2004	Taurus	05°02'
March 3, 1988	Virgo	13°18'	April 24, 2005	Scorpio	04°20'
August 27, 1988	Pisces	04°23'	October 17, 2005	Aries	24°13'
February 20, 1989	Virgo	01°59'	March 14, 2006	Virgo	24°15'
August 17, 1989	Aquarius	24°12'	September 7, 2006	Pisces	15°00'
February 9, 1990	Leo	20°47'	March 3, 2007	Virgo	13°00'
August 6, 1990	Aquarius	13°52'	August 28, 2007	Pisces	04°46'
January 30, 1991	Leo	09°51'	February 21, 2008	Virgo	01°53'
June 27, 1991	Capricorn	05°00'	August 16, 2008	Aquarius	24°21'
July 26, 1991	Aquarius	03°16'	February 9, 2009	Leo	20°60'
December 21, 1991	Gemini	29°03'	July 7, 2009	Capricorn	15°24'
June 14, 1992	Sagittarius	24°20'	August 6, 2009	Aquarius	13°43'
December 9, 1992	Gemini	18°10'	December 31, 2009	Cancer	10°15'
June 4, 1993	Sagittarius	13°55'	June 26, 2010	Capricorn	04°48'
November 29, 1993	Gemini	07°03'	December 21, 2010	Gemini	29°21'
May 25, 1994	Sagittarius	03°43'	June 15, 2011	Sagittarius	24°23'
November 18, 1994	Taurus	25°42'	December 10, 2011	Gemini	18°11'
April 15, 1995	Libra	25°04'	June 4, 2012	Sagittarius	14°14'
October 8, 1995	Aries	14°54'	November 28, 2012	Gemini	06°47'
April 4, 1995	Libra	14°31'	April 25, 2013	Scorpio	05°46'
September 27, 1996	Aries	04°17'	May 25, 2013	Sagittarius	04°08'
March 24, 1997	Libra	03°35'	October 18, 2013	Aries	25°45'
September 16, 1997	Pisces	23°56'	April 15, 2014	Libra	25°16'
March 13, 1998	Virgo	22°24'	October 8, 2014	Aries	15°05'
August 8, 1998	Aquarius	15°21'	April 4, 2015	Libra	14°24'
September 6, 1998	Pisces	13°40'	September 28, 2015	Aries	04°40'
January 31, 1999	Leo	11°20'	March 23, 2016	Libra	03°17'
July 28, 1999	Aquarius	04°58'	September 16, 2016	Pisces	24°20'
January 21, 2000	Leo	00°26'	February 11, 2017	Leo	22°28'
July 16, 2000	Capricorn	24°19'	August 7, 2017	Aquarius	15°25'
January 9, 2001	Cancer	19°39'	January 31, 2018	Leo	11°37'
July 5, 2001	Capricorn	13°39'	July 27, 2018	Aquarius	04°45'
December 30, 2001	Cancer	08°48'	January 21, 2019	Leo	00°52'
May 26, 2002	Sagittarius	05°04'	July 16, 2019	Capricorn	24°04'
June 24, 2002	Capricorn	03°11'	January 10, 2020	Cancer	20°00'
November 20, 2002	Taurus	27°33'	June 5, 2020	Sagittarius	15°34'
May 16, 2003	Scorpio	24°53'	July 5, 2020	Capricorn	13°38'
November 9, 2003	Taurus	16°13'	November 30, 2020	Gemini	08°38'
May 4, 2004	Scorpio	14°42'	May 26, 2021	Sagittarius	05°26'

DATE	SIGN	DEGREE	DATE	SIGN	DEGREE
November 19, 2021	Taurus	27°14'	August 7, 2036	Aquarius	15°12'
May 16, 2022	Scorpio	25°18'	January 31, 2037	Leo	12°02'
November 8, 2022	Taurus	16°01'	July 27, 2037	Aquarius	04°30'
May 5, 2023	Scorpio	14°58'	January 21, 2038	Leo	01°12'
October 28, 2023	Taurus	05°09'	June 17, 2038	Sagittarius	26°06'
March 25, 2024	Libra	05°07'	July 16, 2038	Capricorn	24°04'
September 18, 2024	Pisces	25°41'	December 11, 2038	Gemini	19°46'
March 14, 2025	Virgo	23°57'	June 6, 2039	Sagittarius	15°56'
September 7, 2025	Pisces	15°23'	November 30, 2039	Gemini	08°20'
March 3, 2026	Virgo	12°54'	May 26, 2040	Sagittarius	05°50'
August 28, 2026	Pisces	04°54'	November 18, 2040	Taurus	27°03'
February 20, 2027	Virgo	02°06'	May 16, 2041	Scorpio	25°33'
July 18, 2027	Capricorn	25°49'	November 8, 2041	Taurus	16°09'
August 17, 2027	Aquarius	24°12'	April 5, 2042	Libra	15°56'
January 12, 2028	Cancer	21°28'	September 29, 2042	Aries	06°26'
July 6, 2028	Capricorn	15°11'	March 25, 2043	Libra	04°50'
December 31, 2028	Cancer	10°33'	September 19, 2043	Pisces	26°02'
June 26, 2029	Capricorn	04°50'	March 13, 2044	Virgo	23°53'
December 20, 2029	Gemini	29°21'	September 7, 2044	Pisces	15°29'
June 15, 2030	Sagittarius	24°43'	March 3, 2045	Virgo	13°08'
December 9, 2030	Gemini	17°54'	August 27, 2045	Pisces	04°43'
May 7, 2031	Scorpio	16°25'	January 22, 2046	Leo	02°39'
June 5, 2031	Sagittarius	14°39'	July 18, 2046	Capricorn	25°37'
October 30, 2031	Taurus	06°41'	January 12, 2047	Cancer	21°44'
April 25, 2032	Scorpio	05°58'	July 7, 2047	Capricorn	15°17'
October 18, 2032	Aries	25°57'	January 1, 2048	Cancer	10°31'
April 14, 2033	Libra	25°09'	June 26, 2048	Capricorn	05°11'
October 8, 2033	Aries	15°29'	December 20, 2048	Gemini	29°03'
April 3, 2034	Libra	14°06'	May 17, 2049	Scorpio	27°00'
September 28, 2034	Aries	05°04'	June 15, 2049	Sagittarius	25°08'
February 22, 2035	Virgo	03°33'	November 9, 2049	Taurus	17°41'
August 19, 2035	Aquarius	25°55'	May 6, 2050	Scorpio	16°35'
February 11, 2036	Leo	22°45'	October 30, 2050	Taurus	06°54'

TO OBTAIN A FREE COPY OF
YOUR NATAL BIRTH CHART

FOR A FULL copy of your natal birth chart—including the sign and house locations of all your planets and aspects—go to www.janspiller.com and access this free information the following way:

On the home page, click on "Free Astrology Charts," then click on "Free Astrology Birth Chart & Mini-Interpretation." Enter your contact information and birth information (date of birth, place of birth, and time of birth if you know it) and your chart will be calculated for you free of charge. In addition to your astrology chart, the printout will include a written sheet of the position of all your planets and eclipses in their signs and houses as well as the aspects in your birth chart. One natal birth chart per day is free; unlimited charts are available to site members.

If you are uncertain about the exact time of your birth, the best sources for obtaining an accurate time are your birth certificate and written family records (baby book and so forth).

There are three copies of your birth certificate on file in the U.S. city in which you were born. Only *one* of these copies has your birth time on it. Therefore, in sending for your birth certificate, emphasize that you want them to send you the copy that states your *time* of birth.

TO OBTAIN A COPY OF YOUR U.S. BIRTH CERTIFICATE
WRITE TO:

County Clerk
Hall of Records
County Courthouse
(city and state in which you were born)

In requesting your birth certificate, include the following:

- your full name (as it was recorded on the birth certificate) and birth date and place
- your mother's maiden name
- your father's name
- a money order or check for five dollars (The fee for the service may be slightly more or less depending on the state. You can always call the hall of records in your birth city to find out the current fee for a birth certificate. A money order receives a faster response than a personal check does.)
- self-addressed, stamped envelope

ABOUT THE AUTHORS

MARNI ANGEL

Jan Spiller currently spends her time in New York City; Charleston, South Carolina; and Del Mar, California.

TRACY GRIFFIN, IMPRESSIVEPIX

Karen McCoy bi-locates between Sebring, Florida, and Long Beach, Mississippi, with her husband, Peter, and golden retriever Charlie.

www.janspiller.com
The official website of Jan Spiller

*A different kind of astrological website offering
an interactive and insightful experience every time*

Visit daily for all your Astrological needs

FREE:
- Full natal birth charts, including eclipses
- Daily horoscopes
- The Goddess Oracle—one free question a day
- Daily Moon positions: sign, phase, void of course times, plus the atmosphere of the day
- Tips for Mercury retrograde cycles
- Monthly New Moon and Full Moon tips
- Astrology 101
- The Jan Spiller Show—have a free reading on interactive web radio. Check site for details.

Personal Astrology Reports written by Jan Spiller: Honoring Past Life Contracts, Healing Destructive Relationship Habits, Current Window of Opportunity, Best Approach for Success in Career and Finance, and many more.

Empowering astrological products to inspire you in daily living: coffee mugs, T-shirts, and much, much more—visit JanSpillerProducts.com. Use the Power Wishing Fountain and check the website often to see when Jan will be available in the chat room.

www.karenmccoy.com
The official website of Karen McCoy

For Personal Astrological Readings with Karen McCoy, go to www .KarenMcCoy.com. Classes and retreats with Karen are also available.

www.astrograph.com

TimePassages astrological software, great for beginners and experts.